HEGEL'S LECTURES ON THE PHILOSOPHY OF WORLD HISTORY

A volume in the series

Agora Editions

General Editor: Thomas L. Pangle
Founding Editor: Allan Bloom

A list of titles in this series is available at
www.cornellpress.cornell.edu.

HEGEL'S LECTURES ON THE PHILOSOPHY OF WORLD HISTORY

THE ESSENTIALS

THOMAS L. PANGLE

CORNELL UNIVERSITY PRESS
Ithaca and London

Copyright © 2025 by Cornell University

All rights reserved. Except for brief quotations in a review, this book, or parts thereof, must not be reproduced in any form without permission in writing from the publisher. For information, address Cornell University Press, Sage House, 512 East State Street, Ithaca, New York 14850. Visit our website at cornellpress.cornell.edu.

First published 2025 by Cornell University Press

Library of Congress Cataloging-in-Publication Data

Names: Pangle, Thomas L. author | Hegel, Georg Wilhelm Friedrich, 1770–1831. Vorlesungen über die Philosophie der Geschichte. Selections. English
Title: Hegel's lectures on the philosophy of world history : the essentials / Thomas L. Pangle.
Description: Ithaca [New York] : Cornell University Press, 2025. | Series: Agora editions | Includes bibliographical references and index.
Identifiers: LCCN 2025008356 (print) | LCCN 2025008357 (ebook) | ISBN 9781501784576 hardcover | ISBN 9781501784583 paperback | ISBN 9781501784590 epub | ISBN 9781501784606 pdf
Subjects: LCSH: History—Philosophy
Classification: LCC D16.8 .P1545 2025 (print) | LCC D16.8 (ebook) | DDC 901—dc23/eng/20250806
LC record available at https://lccn.loc.gov/2025008356
LC ebook record available at https://lccn.loc.gov/2025008357

Contents

Translator's Preface	*vii*
1. Hegel's Introduction	1
2. The Oriental World, Part One: China	53
3. The Oriental World, Part Two: India	70
4. The Oriental World, Part Three: Persia	91
5. The Oriental World, Part Four: Egypt	114
6. The Greek World	130
7. The Roman World	178
8. The Germanic World	219
9. The Last Stage of World-History	259
Glossary	*271*
Index	*281*

Translator's Preface

Georg W. F. Hegel (1770–1831) is generally recognized as one of the giants of the tradition of philosophy and as the greatest of all philosophers of history. Hegel undertakes to teach that humanity's "world-history" has slowly and painfully, amid countless contingencies, revealed itself to be at its heart a necessitated progress by which reality as a rational whole has come to a complete, self-conscious wisdom that includes principles of liberal constitutionalism as the fully satisfactory, rational, political society. In Hegel's words: world history "is the necessary development" of "the spirit's self-consciousness and of its freedom—the interpretation and *actualization of the universal spirit*," in "its total encompassing, of innerness and externality." The "states, peoples, and individuals in this working of the world-spirit arise in their *specific determinate principles*, that have in their *constitutions* and in the total *range* of their *conditions* their interpretation and actuality—concerning which they are self-conscious, and into whose interests they are plunged"; but "at the same time, they are the unconscious tools and limbs of that inner working whereby these configurations pass away, while the spirit in and for itself, however, prepares and labors upon the transition to its next, higher stage": each of these stages "is a necessary, essential phase of" the total overall "Idea of the world-spirit, of which each is *its* present stage, its *absolute right*."[1]

World history so conceived is thus of massively crucial significance for Hegel's philosophy and political philosophy. Yet prior to his rather sudden death in 1831 at the age of sixty-one, Hegel did not execute a treatise setting forth his philosophy of world history. What we have instead are a number of meticulous student transcripts, along with some fragmented and truncated manuscript materials written by Hegel himself of his University of Berlin course of lectures on the philosophy

---

1. *Philosophy of Right*, secs. 341–42, 344, 345.

of world history, which he delivered five times—in 1822-23, 1824-25, 1826-27, 1828-29 (no considerable records of this year's version of the course are known), and 1830-31. And unlike in the case of his earlier lecture course on the philosophy of right or justice, Hegel unfortunately published no companion textbook volume for his lectures on the philosophy of history.[2] Not long after his death there was published (in 1837) *Georg Wilhelm Friedrich Hegel's Lectures on the Philosophy of History*, in which Hegel's close friend and follower Dr. Eduard Gans (1798-1839) interwove some of Hegel's manuscript remains with transcript material mainly from the last lecture course in 1830-31 as recorded by Hegel's son Karl, who had attended the course at the age of eighteen. In 1840 the son, now Dr. Karl Hegel, produced a considerably revised second edition of Gans's volume. In 1857 a translation into English (at some crucial places rather loose) of this second edition by John Sibree was published, and it has been ever since the principal vehicle for access in English to Hegel's philosophy of history as a whole.

In subsequent years there were published several successive German editions bringing together and critically addressing more of the records. In 1975 H. B. Nisbet published a translation of Johannes Hoffmeister's 1956 edition of some of the records of Hegel's introductory lectures.[3] In 1995, there was finally published, in the ongoing historical-critical edition of all Hegel's works, a volume edited by Walter Jaeschke containing ninety-five pages of Hegel's own manuscript remains pertaining to his introductory lectures on the philosophy of history, mainly from the last course-year, 1830-31 (see "GW 18" below). In 2011 there appeared an English translation of (1) the preceding, 1995 critical edition of Hegel's own manuscript remains, and (2) a 1996 German edition of the 1822-23 lectures, "intended as preliminary to the treatment of the lectures in the *Gesammelte Werke*" (the historical-critical edition that was then still in progress and unfinished).[4] This German "preliminary"

---

2. D. Georg Wilhelm Friedrich Hegel, *Naturrecht und Staatswissenschaft im Grundrisse: Zum Gebrauch für Seine Vorlesungen* [*Natural-right and Science of the State in Basic Outline: To Be Used for His Lectures*] (Berlin: Nicolaischen, 1821). This was reissued in the same year, by the same publisher, under the title *Grundlinien der Philosophie des Rechts* [*Basic Outlines of the Philosophy of Right*]. In English this is conventionally cited as *Philosophy of Right*.

3. G. W. F. Hegel, *Lectures on the Philosophy of World History, Introduction: Reason in History*, trans. H. B. Nisbet (Cambridge: Cambridge University Press, 1975); from G. W. F. Hegel, *Berliner Schriften 1818–31*, ed. Johannes Hoffmeister (Hamburg: Felix Meiner, 1956).

4. Quoting p. 8, n. 18 of G. W. F. Hegel, *Lectures on the Philosophy of World History*, vol. 1: *Manuscripts of the Introduction and the Lectures of 1822–23*, ed. and trans. Robert F. Brown and Peter C. Hodgson, with the assistance of William G. Geuss (Oxford: Clarendon Press, 2011); *Vorlesungen über die Philosophie der Weltgeschichte, Berlin 1822/1823*, ed. K. H. Ilting, K. Brehmer, and H. N. Seelmann (Hamburg: Felix Meiner, 1996).

included only a sparse apparatus criticus for the transcript, which does not allow the reader to learn of, and thus to form judgments as to the value of, alternative transcript renderings of key statements of Hegel's as he delivered the course in 1822-23.

But over the years 2015-20 there finally appeared the critical edition of all the known student transcripts—in four volumes, totaling some 1,600 pages or approximately 700,000 words. The editors chose to print, for each class year, the entirety of that one of the known transcripts that the editors judged to be the most accurate and complete, with a large apparatus criticus occupying the bottom third or so of each page, in which the editors printed what they judged to be all the significant variants and supplements found in the other known transcripts of the same class year's lectures.

I offer here a translation, as close to literal as is compatible with intelligible English, of selected passages from these critical editions, supplemented in some cases with my new translations of passages from the 1840 volume constructed by Karl Hegel, who probably had access to some materials that have subsequently disappeared. It is evident from all these records that, in each of the course-years, Hegel followed pretty much the same order of major divisions, an order that I have followed in the chapter divisions of this present volume. But from year to year Hegel's lectures manifestly varied considerably, not only in detail and emphasis and formulations but in the length and attention allotted to various parts. (This is true also of his introductory lectures, for which we can now compare and contrast his manuscript materials, mainly from 1830-31, with the transcripts of the very same 1830-31 lectures as actually heard and recorded by his son and by other students, as well as with the transcripts of his introductory lectures in other course-years.) From the historical-critical edition I have made a choice of passages, constituting about one seventh of the whole, and an ordered arrangement of the passages, which in my judgment provides the fullest and clearest expression of each principal part as well as the development overall of Hegel's integrated teaching on the philosophy of history as divine reason expressing itself dynamically in the whole of existence.

At the beginning of each selection, a footnote gives the source page numbers in the critical edition, or in the 1840 edition by Karl Hegel (I have sometimes affixed "t" or "b" to the page number, to indicate either the top or the bottom of the page); I have then added in parentheses, beginning with a tilde (~), the page numbers of parallel or similar passages in the other records of the lectures. Whenever I have translated or referred to a variant or supplement taken from the apparatus criticus on the cited page of the critical edition, I have done so in square brackets and named the alternate transcriber who is the source. Thus the reader who knows German can readily turn to the precise location of the original texts being translated, and can also readily inspect and compare parallel passages in other years' transcripts.

But the audience that I have in view is one that does not read German; it comprises primarily undergraduate and graduate students, as well as scholars across the disciplines, and a wider, nonacademic public—all having in common a desire for an introduction to Hegel's philosophy of history; and my ordered selection grows out of my own experiences with the texts as I have endeavored to teach American and Canadian students in college courses on Hegel's political philosophy. I have not been concerned to help the scholar who is interested in Hegel's intellectual biography and therefore seeks to follow and to study the sequence of the changes Hegel made in the presentation of his course of lectures from year to year: such a scholar will need to engage in a comparative study of the entirety of each year's records. My concern in the present volume is to present synoptically what Hegel might call the "essential phases" or "moments" in his philosophy of world history as an articulated, unfolding, organic whole.

The texts from which my selections have been made, with the abbreviations that I will use to designate them in the footnotes, are as follows:

GW = Hegel's *Gesammelte Werke*. 40 vols. projected. Hamburg: Felix Meiner, 1968–. The historical-critical edition of Hegel's works.

GW 18 = "Zur Philosophie der Weltgeschichte," in *Vorlesungsmanuskripte II (1816–31)*, ed. Walter Jaeschke; vol. 18 (published 1995) of the preceding *Gesammelte Werke*, 119–214, consisting of:

the remaining fragments of Hegel's own manuscripts related to the introductory portions of his lecture courses of 1822–28 (121–37), and

longer, nonfragmentary though incomplete manuscripts for the introductory portions of his lecture course in 1830–31 (138–207).

GW 27 = *Vorlesungen über die Philosophie der Weltgeschichte*, vol. 27 of the preceding *Gesammelte Werke*, in five separately bound parts (the fifth being an editorial appendix):

GW 27 [1] = The 1822–23 lectures, edited by Bernadette Collenberg-Plotnikov from the transcript by H. G. Hotho, with variants found in the transcripts of K. G. J. v. Griesheim, F. C. H. V. v. Kehler, and

K. R. Hagenbach. Published 2015. Accessible online at: https://archive.org/details/gesammeltewerkes0027hege/mode/2up.

GW 27 [2] = The 1824–25 lectures, edited by Walter Jaeschke and Rebecca Paimann from the transcript by F. C. H. V. v. Kehler, with enlargements and variants found in the transcripts of M. Pinder and H. W. Dove. Published 2019.

GW 27 [3] = The 1826–27 lectures, edited by Walter Jaeschke, Christoph Johannes Bauer, and Christiane Hackel from the transcripts by J. Hube, F. Walter, and S. Garzyński, with enlargements and variants found in the transcript of J. E. Erdmann. Published 2019.

GW 27 [4] = The 1830–31 lectures, edited by Walter Jaeschke and Christoph Johannes Bauer from the transcript by F. W. K. (Karl) Hegel, with variants found in the transcripts of J. Ackersdijck, A. Heimann, and J. H. Wichern. Published 2020.

1840 = *Georg Wilhelm Friedrich Hegel's Vorlesungen über die Philosophie der Geschichte*. Ed. Eduard Gans and Karl Hegel. Berlin: Duncker & Humbolt, 1840. Accessible online at: https://babel.hathitrust.org/cgi/pt?id=inu.30000005358753&view=1up&seq=22.

Chapter 1

Hegel's Introduction

¹The subject of these lectures is the philosophy of world-history. As for what sort of history world-history is, I need say nothing; the general notion of it is sufficient and also something that we can agree on. But that it is a philosophy of world-history that we are considering, that we want to *deal with*² history philosophically—that is what, even by the title of these lectures, can be striking, and certainly must seem to require an explanation or, even more, a justification.

"Reason Holds Sway Over the World"

³On the preliminary concept of what is philosophical about world-history I want to note this initially: that . . . one first makes the objection against philosophy that it approaches history with ideas and reflects on it according to these ideas. The single idea that it brings, however, is the simple idea of *reason*: that reason holds sway over the world, that therefore in world-history also, reason is underway. This conviction and insight is a *presupposition* from the point of view of history as such

---

1. GW 18.138 (~ GW 18.121; GW 27 [4] 1155 [Wichern]).
2. All italics will be from the original German editions.
3. GW 18.140–42, 144–45 (~ GW 27 [3] 796–800; GW 27 [4] 1156–59; 1840, 12–17).

overall. In philosophy itself, this is no presupposition: through speculative cognition it is *proved* that *reason* (we can stick with this expression here, without discussing more precisely its connection and relationship to God) is the *substance*, as the infinite[4] power, itself the *infinite matter* of all natural and spiritual life, as the *infinite form*, the activation of this its content: the *substance*, that through which and in which all actuality has its being and subsistence; the infinite *power*, in that reason is not so powerless as to bring only to the ideal, [141] to an ought, and only outside of actuality, who knows where—even merely as something particular that is present in the heads of a few humans; the infinite *content*, all essentiality and truth; and it is for itself its matter that it gives to its action to labor upon. Unlike finite action, it does not require the limiting factors of external materials, of given means, from which to derive sustenance and objects for its activity. It feeds upon itself and is itself the material that it labors on, even as it is itself its own presupposition, its goal, the absolute end-goal: so it is itself the activation and the bringing forth, out of the inner into appearance, not only of the natural universe, but also of the spiritual—into world-history. That only such an Idea[5] is the true, the eternal, the utterly powerful; that it reveals itself in the world, and that nothing is revealed in it except it, its mastery, and its honor—this is, as was said, proved in philosophy, and so it may here be *presupposed* as proven.

To those among you, my students, who are now not yet acquainted with philosophy, I could perhaps appeal to you to approach these lectures on world-history with a faith in reason, with the longing, with the thirst for knowledge of it. . . . In fact, however, I do not have to call for such a faith in advance. What I have said in a preliminary way and have still to say is not, in the perspective of our science, regarded as a simple presupposition, [142] but instead as an *overview* of the whole, as the

---

4. By his frequent use of the adjective "infinite" (unendlich) Hegel characterizes that which is bounded or limited only by itself, not by anything external to it—in contrast to the "finite" (endlich), which is limited or bounded by what is external to it.

5. For the meaning and connotation of Hegel's term "Idea" (which I will always capitalize), see GW 27 [1] 22: "God wills the most complete; and what he wills, can be only himself, his will. His will is not different from himself. This we call the Idea—and we have to abstract here from the religious expression, and grasp the concept in the form of thought." See also GW 12.236, *Science of Logic* [*Wissenschaft der Logik*] II, 2nd Part, 3rd section, "The Idea": "the absolute Idea alone is being, life that does not pass way, self-knowing truth, and is all truth. It is the sole subject matter and content of philosophy. . . . Nature and spirit are, overall, different ways of manifesting its concrete existence; art and religion are its different ways of grasping itself and giving itself an adequate concrete existence."

result of the inquiry that we have initiated—a result that is known to me because I already know the whole. So, what is primary, and will make itself evident from the consideration of world-history itself, is that it proceeds rationally, that it has been the rationally necessary course of the world-spirit.[6] The world-spirit is the spirit overall, the substance of history, the one spirit, whose nature is one and always the same, and in the concrete existence of the world explains this its one nature. . . .

[144] The Greek *Anaxagoras* first said that *nous*, understanding overall, or reason, rules the world—not an intelligence as self-conscious reason, not a spirit as such; these two we must certainly distinguish from one another: the movement of the solar system follows unalterable laws; these laws are its reason, but neither the sun nor the planets that revolve according to these laws have consciousness of them. It is the human being that raises these laws from existence and knows them. . . .

[145] One sees that what Socrates found unsatisfactory in the principle of Anaxagoras [Plato, *Phaedo* 97d–99d] concerned not the principle itself but the failure to apply it to concrete nature—that the latter is not understood, grasped, from this principle; that overall this principle remains *abstract*; more specifically, that nature is not grasped as a development of this very principle—not as an organization brought forth out of this principle, out of reason as cause.

"Knowledge of the Plan of Divine Providence"

[7]Reason's complete application has assumed another shape that is well known to us and concerning which we have conviction about it—namely, in the form of the religious truth that the world is not given over to chance and external, chance causes, but *a providence rules the world*. I made it clear earlier that I did not want to make a claim on your *faith* in the indicated principle. I might, however, have appealed to faith

---

6. For the meaning and connotation of Hegel's term "world-spirit," see also GW 27 [3] 812: "God and world-spirit border very near to one another in the representation. [Erdmann: This universal spirit, world-spirit, is not the same in meaning as God. The difference is that the world-spirit is the spirit in the world as it sets itself forth and explicates itself in human consciousness. The individual relates oneself as singular to this world-spirit, which is one's substance. The spirit as it exists in the world is spirit proceeding to make itself into what its concept is. This change is rational, meaning that the spirit as it explains itself to consciousness in the world is in accord with the eternal reason in itself. God is in the community, which is the human race essentially present and at hand. It is thus the appearing of God in human consciousness.]"

7. GW 18.146–49 (~ GW 27 [3] 800–802; GW 27 [4] 1160–61; 1840, 17–19).

in it in this religious form—were it not that it is the property of the science of philosophy that it does not allow presuppositions to count; or, to speak from a different side, because the science that we wish to treat ought itself to first furnish the proof, if not of the *truth*, then of *the correctness* of this foundational principle. Now the *truth*—that one, and indeed the divine, providence presides over the events of the world—corresponds with the indicated principle, in that the divine *providence* is the wisdom in accord with infinite power that actualizes its goals, that is, the absolute, rational, end-goal of the world. Reason is the totally free, self-determining *thinking*: nous.

But further, there is a disparity, nay an opposition, between this faith and our principle, precisely in the same way as between the fundamental statement of Anaxagoras and [147] the demand that Socrates makes of it: namely, this faith is likewise indeterminate—*faith* in *providence* overall—and does not advance to the determinate, to an application to the whole, to the embracing course of world events. The determinate in providence—that providence acts thus, or so—is called *the plan of providence*, the goal and the means, this destiny, this plan; but this plan is hidden from our eyes, indeed it is supposed to be presumption to want to know it.... In particular cases, it is allowed, here and there; [148] and heartfelt pious feelings discern in many individual occurrences, where others see only contingencies, not simply dispensations of God in general but also his providence, namely the goals that it has with such dispensations. But this is attended to only in singular instances.... In world-history, however, the individuals we have to do with are peoples, totalities that are states; we cannot, therefore, stay with what remains as this so to speak petty-business-view faith in providence—nor, similarly, with the universal, that there is a providence that rules the world, but that does not proceed to the specifics; instead we have to be much more *serious* about it. The concrete, the *ways* of providence, are the means, the phenomena in history, that lie open to us, and we have only to show their connection with that general principle.

But I have, in mentioning the knowledge of the plan of divine providence overall, recalled the importance of a peak question of our time: that of the possibility of knowing God; or much rather, belonging to the question, the doctrine, that has become a prejudice, that it is impossible to know God—which goes against what is commanded in holy Scripture as the highest duty, [149] that we should not merely love, but know God [John 8:32 and 1 Corinthians 8:3]. Denied is what is said there in Scripture, that the spirit is that which leads into the truth, that it knows all things, penetrating even into the depths of the Godhead [John 16:13 and 1 Corinthians 2:10].

[8]The true, overall, is a universal in itself, is essential, substantial—and such exists only in and for the thinking: the thinking spirit. The One that we call God is, however, the true, substantial, and in itself essential, individual, subjective truth. All else that we call the true is only a particular form of the eternal truth, having its content only in that, being only a ray of that. When one knows about the nothing, one knows about nothing true overall, and about nothing right, nothing ethically customary. As regards the relation of the Christian religion over and against this notion, what is distinctive about it is that the time has arrived that constitutes the absolute epoch in world-history—that Christendom has appeared, that humans know what is revealed, what God is. It has been revealed what the nature of God is.

[9]This is the mystery that the Christian religion has unveiled, that God is unity of the human and divine nature. This is the true Idea of what religion is. To the religion belongs also the ritual worship.[10] So this oneness of divine and human is the true Idea of religion. The understanding of modern times has made the divine Idea into an abstraction, into an essence that is beyond the human—has made it into a wall, its smoothness keeping out the human being who approaches, smashing his head. But now we see that unity, set forth as rational presupposition, allows itself to come forth in the religion. Its object is the truth itself.

---

8. GW 27 [2] 487.
9. GW 27 [1] 72–73.
10. Hagenbach's transcript reads here: "The ritual worship [Cultus] is the consciousness securing for itself that the divine spirit dwells in us." On the crucial importance of ritual worship (Cultus) in religion and not least in the final, absolute, Christian religion, see *Lectures on the Philosophy of Religion*, esp. 1827 version, GW 29 [2] 67–72 and 224, 226, as well as 324–46; see also GW 29 [2] 239–41 (1831 version) and GW 29 [1] 431–49 (1824 version); and above all Hegel's own 1821 manuscript, in *Vorlesungen über die Philosophie der Religion* (Hamburg: Felix Mainer, 1984), 3:85–97. There Hegel writes that in the *philosophic* or *theoretical* knowledge of the unity of divine and human, "I know nothing of myself. I am aware also of the finite from which I began, but from the negation of that, I have transitioned"—to "knowledge of God"; and "in this object I am absorbed." In contrast, ritual worship (Cultus) is the practical activity of "confession, penitence, anguish, dying, partaking of the sacrament, exaltation, glory"; and in "the sacrifice of the Mass, Christ daily being offered," there is a "mystical union," leading also to ethically customary practice; in this "I am for myself, over and against the object, and now have brought forward my singularity with the object," so as to "have *being* as filled with the object, but to *know* myself as filled with the object, to know this object as in me, and me as in the object, which is the truth." For Hegel's account of the ritual worship of Holy Communion in the final, rational religion, see also chap. 8 below.

In general, in religion two types are found: there is a religion of separation, in which God stands as an abstract essence on one side, in which thus the oneness of consciousness is not established. This has been the religion of Judaism, and it is still that of Mohammedanism; and it is also the religion of the present-day understanding. This religion of separation can have in turn a diversity of forms since a universal in the form of a natural essence can be portrayed in an elementary way, as air, fire, etc., or it can also be represented as thinking, as in Judaism, etc. In this universal, then, the human being recognizes oneself not as positive, but holds oneself as negative over and against that.

[73] The other way of religion is the unity of infinite and finite. This religion again has several forms. For example, the incarnations of the Indians, likewise Greek art, which portrays the divine in human shape; purer is this in the Christian, which allows the God to appear in his Son, and so brings the human being to a consciousness concerning the unity. It belongs to the true Idea of God that it is not a beyond over and against which stands the consciousness. So these are the forms of religion.

The existence of art is immediately dependent on this. The understanding can have no art, or at best only an art of sublimity, where shape is so dispersed that subjectivity seems to evaporate, inasmuch as shape becomes measureless. But art is essentially fine art and is the representing of the divine for the sensuous intuition—and to it belongs the form of subjectivity. Therefore the Christian religion too has art, because in it also the divine is apparent and does not remain something above and beyond.

Similarly, it depends on religion whether philosophy can find a place among a people; thus only among the Greeks and Christians could truly concrete philosophy have found a place. [Griesheim: As abstract, the Orientals have it too, but not present as unity of the finite and the infinite.] These are the chief points about religion.

[11]The beginning, the first, is what is immediately for itself. So it can appear, as if we have to begin history with the state of innocence. From this we have not started out: it is represented as unity of humanity

---

11. GW 27 [3] 834 (~ GW 27 [2] 732-33; GW 27 [3] 1080-81; GW 27 [4] 1175-77; 1840, 390-91). For other presentations by Hegel of this interpretation of the biblical account of Paradise and the Fall, see *Lectures on the Philosophy of Religion*, GW 29 [1] 97, 417-21; GW 29 [2] 77-82, 201-5, 255-56; *Encyclopedia of the Philosophical Sciences*, sec. 24, addn. 3 end, and sec. 405 addn.

with God and nature, and thereby as the state of lack of consciousness and of animality. Humanity God has made after his image—he is spirit; therefore the human must be that which the human ought to be, must fulfill his vocation as being rational; he ought as spirit not remain with the first. The spirit is only what it makes itself into; it is activity, self-production, self-comprehension. Therefore the condition, in which the human has not entered into division, is an animal condition, out of which one ought to bring oneself; it is not the condition of the spirit. *Paradisos*, animal garden; the animalistic is the immediate state. Only the animal, the child, is innocent; the human must have responsibility or guilt—which does not mean he ought to do something evil; he ought to do the good; but it must be his responsibility, inasmuch as he must have willed the action; his will must be there. Responsibility or guilt is not simply opposed to innocence—it is not simply crime, sin—rather, responsibility or guilt is, that to the individual is to be justly reckoned what he does; and judgment is only possible in the state of separation, of differentiation of the consciousness. The condition of wholeness, as existing, is the animalistic.

[12]I could have chosen not to mention (so as not to remind of that question about the possibility of the knowledge of God) that our contention—that reason rules and has ruled the world—is expressed in the religious form that providence holds sway over the world. But I did not wish to leave this out, partly in order to bring out some broader connections of these matters, partly also, however, not to indulge the suspicion that philosophy shies away from, and has to shy away from, recollecting the religious truths, and that it circumvents them, because it does not, so to speak, have a good conscience about them. Rather, things have come so far in more modern times that, in opposition to certain kinds of theology, philosophy has itself to take on the content of religion. I make only these general remarks: in the Christian religion God has revealed himself; that is, God has given it to humanity to know what he is, so that he is no longer something hidden, concealed; with this possibility, of knowing God, the duty to do so is laid upon us; and the development of the thinking spirit, which starts out from this foundation, the revelation of the divine essence, must eventually increase to the point that what initially was set before the feeling and representing spirit is also grasped by thought; the time must finally be when

---

12. GW 18.149–50 (~ GW 27 [2] 484–85, 487–88; GW 27 [3] 796–97; GW 27 [4] 1161–62).

this rich production of creative reason—which is what world-history is—will be comprehended; [150] whether it is the time for this cognition must depend on whether that, which is the end-goal of the world, has finally entered into actuality in a universal, conscious manner: this—the understanding of our time, our cognition—proceeds in gaining the insight that what is aimed at by eternal wisdom comes about on the ground of nature as well as on the ground of what is actual and active in the world. Our consideration is to this extent a *theodicy*, a justification of God, which Leibniz attempted metaphysically in his way, in still abstract and indeterminate categories; it ought to enable us to comprehend the bad in the world overall, including evil; the thinking spirit becomes reconciled with the negative; and it is in world-history that the whole mass of what is concretely bad is laid before our eyes.

[13]But when considering overall the destiny that virtue, ethical custom,[14] and religiosity have in history, we must not fall into the litany of lamentations to the effect that the good and the pious often or indeed most of the time fare badly in the world, while the wicked and the bad, on the contrary, do well. One commonly views doing well in many different ways, such as wealth, outward honor, and the like. But when the talk is about an end that exists in and for itself, the so-called doing well or ill of this or that single individual ought not to be made an element of the rational world order. But with more justice is it demanded of the goal of the world, not only happiness, a happy condition, of individuals, but that good, ethically customary, just goals should seek their fulfillment and guarantee under and in it. What

---

13. GW 18.168–69 (~ GW 27 [4] 1176–77; 1840, 43–46).
14. For the meaning of Hegel's crucial terms "Sitte," "Sittlichkeit," "sittlich," which I will translate "ethical custom," "customary ethics," "ethically customary," see GW 27 [4] 1188: Sittlichkeit "is to be distinguished from morality [Moralität]; morality is reflective Sittlichkeit, whereby there is a conviction; this is more the modern Sittlichkeit, not the ancient, the classical; it consists in the *individual* standing to his duty. —An Athenian citizen does as by instinct what he is supposed to do (defending his fatherland); in contrast I have by reflection the consciousness that my will is the beginning. Reflection—on whether this is *my* duty, on whether I will obey what is objective—that is morality. Sittlichkeit is solid worthiness, duty as substantial right, the unity of the individual with the substantial law. One says that habit is second nature, and one is correct; the first nature of the human being is one's unmediated being; the second is the creation of spirit, and this happens in the state." For the modern integration of ethical custom with morality in the fully rational society and state, see *Philosophy of Right*, esp. secs. 257–58, 270, and 141 Zusatz end: "The legally just and morality cannot exist for themselves, and they must have the ethically customary as support and foundation, for the legally just lacks the essential phase of subjectivity, which the moral, again, alone has, and so the pair of moments have for themselves no actuality.... The legally right exists only as a branch of a whole, as a climbing vine on a tree that stands fast in and for itself."

makes humans morally *dissatisfied*—a dissatisfaction, by which one does oneself some good—is that they do not find a correspondence between the present and what they hold to be right and good as the content of the universal goal, especially according to today's ideals of political institutions in particular; or they find no correspondence between the present and their taste for devising ideals—thoughts, foundational principles, insights—about which they give themselves a feeling of elevation. Over and against concrete existence they set what would be just in affairs. Here it is not particular interest, nor passion, that demands satisfaction but reason, justice, freedom. . . . [169] In no other age as in our own have universal propositions, thoughts, been advanced with greater pretension; whereas history has previously presented itself as the prominent appearance of a struggle of the passions, now, in our age—although the passions are not absent—it appears partly as a conflict of thoughts justifying themselves to one another, and partly as the struggle of passions and subjective interests essentially under the banner of such higher justifications. These rights—demanded in the name of what we have described as the definition of reason, as absolute given end, as their self-conscious freedom—are made to count as justice-demanding, even thereby absolute, ends, just like religion, the ethically customary, morality.

[15]Examples of the good of course elevate the feelings, and are often cited, because they bring the good into concrete representation. But the field of the destiny of peoples, of the overthrow of states, is on a different, higher, broader plane. One can refer statesmen to the experience given through history; [11] but the moralistic commandments provide little, and one needs a less grand field. In such complexities of affairs of the world one often finds that the simple moralistic commandments do not apply. History and experience teach that peoples overall have not learned from history, for each age lives in such an individual condition, upon which decision depends. This is in the character of the age, which is always different. The moralistic commandment applies itself to private relationships, and these I do not need to learn about from history. In the case of moralistic commandments, the core element in all such situations is produced by such a commandment. But under the pressure of world events, such a simple foundational contention does not apply, because the conditions are never the same, and what is taken

---

15. GW 27 [1] 10–12 (~ 1840, 9–10).

from recollection cannot prevail against the vitality of the moment. History is educational; study of the orators is necessary; but to direct more modern political relationships to look back to the activity and business of the Romans or Greeks always has something distorting about it. . . . [12] Montesquieu makes similarly foundational reflections.

[16]It is only the foundational, free, comprehensive view of situations, and the deep sense of the Idea (such as, e.g., in Montesquieu's *Spirit of the Laws*) that can give truth and interest to reflection.

[17]Only when one stands above can one have a correct overview of the subject and see each thing in its place—not when one looks up from below, contemplating through the lens of a *moralist bottle* or *other bit of wisdom*. In our time it is so much the more necessary to avoid the limited point of view of the classes that are more excluded from direct political actuality, from political reflection—from the life of the state: they bask in moralist foundational contentions, and trust to themselves as superior to the higher classes in knowing.

[18]It is rightly said that genius, talent, moral virtues and feelings, piety, can find a place in all regions, constitutions, and political circumstances—for which there is no lack of numerous favorite examples. . . .

[201] World-history moves itself on a higher ground than that on which morality has its proper place—which is that of private disposition, the conscience of individuals, and their own will and mode of action; these have their worth, imputation, reward or punishment for themselves; but what the end-goal of spirit, existing in and for itself, requires and brings fully forth—what providence does—lies above the duties and the liability to imputation, and expectation, that fall to individuality in regard to its ethical customs. Those who, in ethically customary determination, and hence with a nobler disposition, have resisted what the progress of the Idea of the spirit necessitated, stand higher in moral worth than those whose crimes, in a higher order, were transfigured into means of putting the will of this order to work. But by revaluations of this sort both parties stand, overall, only within the same sphere, of corruption; and it is therewith merely a formal kind of justice that the defenders of legal justification defend, already left behind by the living spirit and by God. The deeds of the *great* human beings—who are individuals of world-history—thus appear justified not

---

16. 1840, 10 (~ GW 27 [3] 809).
17. GW 18.129 (~ 1840, 6).
18. GW 18.199 and 201-2 (~ 1840, 81b-84).

only in their inner, unconscious significance, but also from the worldly standpoint. But from this latter, [202] demands deriving from moral spheres that do not belong must not be placed over and against world-historical deeds and those who bring them to completion; the litany of private virtues—modesty, humility, love of humanity, charity, etc.—must not be raised against them. World-history can disregard overall the sphere to which morality, and the much discussed and misunderstood dichotomy between the moral and politics, belong: not merely by refraining from judgments—though its principles and the necessary relationship of actions to these principles already are for itself the judgment—but also by leaving the individuals altogether out of account and unmentioned; for what world-history has to record are the deeds of the spirits of the peoples; and the individual configurations that these have assumed, on the external ground of actuality, could well be left to the proper scribblers about history.

"The Spirits of Peoples"

[19]The universal is thus the subject matter of world-history. This universal is to be more precisely defined. There are two sides of this to be considered. The spiritual principle is the totality of all particular points of view; and the principles themselves stand in a necessary sequence of stages, are the progeny of the spirit, which [15] in them completes itself to a totality in itself. [Hagenbach: The spirits of peoples are themselves only moments of the one spirit, which elevates itself through its spirits.] All sides that make themselves salient in a history—conditions of sciences, arts, etc.—stand in the closest interrelationship: this is often said, correctly. In speaking thus, one has spoken entirely correctly and has said something profound;[20] but one usually stops here, without developing and clarifying the unity of this soul itself. . . .

Now this spirit is something concrete; [16] we must become acquainted with it, for a spiritual principle can only through thinking be grasped. But this spirit itself has the drive to grasp *its own* thoughts; this has to do with the production of itself; the deepest aspect of spirit is the thinking; it is what it has to do, to think itself, to create itself for *its own* thought. But at first, it is aware only of the aims of what is finite;

---

19. GW 27 [1] 14–16 (~ GW 27 [2] 474–80, 490; GW 27 [3] 807–12).
20. GW 27 [2] 476: "this is a point of view that Montesquieu, especially, has grasped, and has sought in a spiritually rich way to put together and to present."

it knows nothing of itself, and does not possess its own innerness, but rather a defined actuality as its subject matter.

[21]An Englishman will say: "We are those who navigate the ocean, and have the commerce of the world; to whom the Indies belong and their riches; who have a parliament, juries, etc."—The relation of the individual to that [spirit of his people] is that he appropriates to himself this substantial being; that this becomes his way of feeling and capability, on the basis of which he is something. For he finds the being of the people to which he belongs an already established, firm world objectively present to him, with which he has to incorporate himself. In this its work, its world, the spirit of the people enjoys itself and finds its satisfaction.

The people is by custom ethical; it is virtuous; it is vigorous—in that it is bringing forth what it wills, and defending its work against external violence in the work of its objectifying. The conflict between what it is in itself, its subjectivity—its inner aim and essence—and what it actually is has been removed; it is by itself, it has itself objectively present.

But then this activity of the spirit is no longer needed; it has what it desired. The people can still do much in war and peace, at home and abroad; but the living, substantial soul itself is as no longer in activity. The foundational, highest interest has consequently vanished from its life, for interest is present only where there is opposition. The nation lives the same kind of life as the individual man when passing from maturity to old age—in the enjoyment of itself—in the satisfaction of being exactly what it desired and was able to attain. If its imagination did transcend that limit, it abandoned any such as goal, if the actuality was less than favorable—and restricted its aim by the conditions. This *habit* (the watch is wound up and goes on of itself) is [93] that which brings on natural death. Habit is activity without opposition, for which there can remain only a formal duration; in which the fullness and depth of the goal are out of the question as a merely external, sensuous existence that no longer plunges itself into the cause.... In order that a truly universal interest should arise, the spirit of a people must advance to will something new; but whence can this new come? It would be a higher, more universal conception of its own self, a transcending of its own principle; but thereby a principle of a wider determination, a new spirit, is at hand.

---

21. 1840, 92-93 (~ GW 27 [1] 39-40; see also GW 18.172, marginal note added by Hegel).

Such a new principle does in any case enter also into the spirit of a people that has arrived at its full development and actualization; it dies not a simply natural death, for it is not a mere single individual, but a spiritual, universal life; in its case natural death appears much more as its own death through its own self.

[22]The people must therefore have the thought of its life and circumstances, must be cognizant of its laws as known universalities; must know its religion—must progress to the doctrines of the religion, and not merely have a ritual worship. The spirit thus wills to know its universality, and only through this knowing does it make itself one with the side of its objectivity, which is the universal in it.

[23]This completion, however, is its decline; but from this emerges another epoch of world-history. [Griesheim: The particular spirit completes itself, the thought of itself, as it makes the transition to the principle of another people; and thus occurs a progress, an origination of high principles, a losing of the principles of peoples, an advance of the world to completion.]

[24]If we say initially that a people makes progress in itself, and oversteps itself, then the most proximate categories that strike us are those of cultural education overall: thus, development; cultural formation; over-refinement. The over-refinement is a source of its corruption. . . .

[39b] Spirit, inasmuch as it has achieved itself, no longer needs its activity. [40] The substantial soul is no longer in activity; now it is only oriented to individual aspects, having lost the highest interest of life, for only with antithesis is there interest. I only have an interest in something insofar as it is still concealed from me or insofar as it is my goal but is not yet fulfilled. Hence, its deeper interest disappears when a people has achieved itself and lives in the transition from adulthood to its old age, to the enjoyment of what it has achieved. It lives in the spirit of what it has become, in what it willed and has been able to attain. It has perhaps surrendered many aspects of its goal and has been satisfied within a narrow compass. So it now lives in the habitual routine of its being, and this habitual routine is what leads to natural death. . . . Natural death can show itself as political nullity, so that the people continues to vegetate, so that only the particular needs, particular interests

---

22. GW 27 [1] 42.
23. GW 27 [1] 16.
24. GW 27 [1] 36b and 39b–41 (~ GW 27 [3] 813–17).

of individuals predominate, and there is no longer the vitality of interest of a people's spirit. . . .

[41] [Griesheim: Peoples can drag on in a vegetative life and be spiritually dead in such a way that their negative that is within them does not come to light as division, as conflict—as we have seen in modernity with old imperial cities that have outwardly declined but inwardly remain naïve, without awareness of what happened to them. . . . Spirit as spirit prepares its own decline, which is, however, the coming forth of a new life.]

[25]Thus we see a people find satisfaction in the representation of and talk about the virtue that stands over against or in place of actual virtue, or that is taking its place. Thus grounds are given to self-consciousness to renounce the duties that once immediately fulfilled it; now the tendency is to demand grounds—that what has been acknowledged be connected firmly to something wholly universal; and so duty as such becomes something that does not count absolutely, but only insofar as the grounds for why it should count are known. Connected with this is the individuals separating themselves from the whole; for the ideality of consciousness is subjectivity, and it [44] tends to grasp itself as a particular subjectivity in the form of a this-here. This subjective inwardness, grasping itself in the form of singularity, is what brings forth vanity, selfishness, etc.—qualities that are contrary to faith, to immediacy. Thus the corruption of a people breaks out, the death of an ethically customary life. . . .

To the thinking subject, states appear to be a limitation. This is the path on which the spirit of a people, out of its depths, prepares its decline. This dissolution of the ethically customary world through thought is, however, necessarily the emergence of a new principle with new determinations. . . . In this dissolution brought about by the universal, however, the previous principle is maintained, but in such a way that its determinate mode or being is destroyed.

[26]Incidentally, it is to be remarked that in world-history, insofar as a principle of the spirit of a people has become a higher principle, this spirit of a people is now present as a different people, and world-history has made a transition from the people that previously was prominent to another people. For a people cannot traverse several such principles.

---

25. GW 27 [1] 43–44 (~ GW 27 [3] 814–16; 1840, 95).
26. GW 27 [1] 47.

[27]In world-history there have been several great periods of development that came to an end without apparently continuing themselves, but instead the whole tremendous accomplishment of cultural education was destroyed, which unfortunately must start over from the beginning in order to regain—with some help perhaps from salvaged fragments of those treasures and with a renewed and immeasurable expenditure of energy [185] and time, of crimes and suffering—one of the domains of past cultural-education that was achieved long ago. And there have been enduring developments, rich in every respect, expansive structures and systems of cultural education with their distinctive elements. The formal principle of development overall can neither assign superiority to one over another nor make intelligible the goal behind that decline of older periods of development, but it must consider such processes, or especially the retrogressions they include, as outwardly chance occurrences; and it can only judge their rank in accord with indeterminate viewpoints that are relative and not absolute ends, since the development is what finally matters.

"The End-Goal of World-History"

[28]Is there not to be thought out an end-goal for all this change? [Griesheim: In their particular aims we cannot find it created. The question confronts us, whether behind the din, the noisy surface phenomena, there is not an inner, silent, secret working, in which the strength of all phenomena becomes verified, and by which all comes to good?] ... The question concerns an innerness that is determinate in and for itself, the One whose eternal work it is to impel itself forth to the knowledge, to the enjoyment of itself. ...

[20] Should reason give us the final result, we would be in old age, which has only the recollection of what has been.

[29]When we reflect further about the determinations by which the spirit of a people dies, sometimes a natural death, sometimes through becoming altered by thought, this is a series of steps that appears to be nothing but a perfectibility that progresses infinitely, without ever coming to its goal. ... [48] But it appears to be only indeterminately posited progress, if no determinate configuration can withstand

---

27. GW 18.184-85 (~ 1840, 69-70).
28. GW 27 [1] 19-20 (~ GW 27 [2] 478-79; GW 27 [3] 794-96, 800; GW 27 [4] 1161-62).
29. GW 27 [1] 47-50 (~ GW 27 [3] 803-6).

critical thinking.... If only new principles constantly emerged, world-history would have no purpose, leading to a goal; no end would ever be in sight.... This brings us to the content of the absolute purpose that spirit sets for itself by means of world-history and that is therefore the work of world-history. We have thus far indicated the mode of the beginning, then secondly the moments of the progress. The latter must have a goal, a final end, and it is this final end that we now consider. This final goal lies in the given concept of spirit. [49] If we speak of it briefly, however, it remains abstract: if we speak of it as it is for the concept, we would be too expansive. Thus we can give here only a general representation.... To grasp this matter from the religious side, it is the exaltation as Lordship, and as honoring, of God.... The spirit we found to be this: what produces itself, making itself into and grasping itself as object.... [50] Its purpose, its absolute drive, is thus to give the consciousness of the essence such that it is known as the sole actual and true being, through which all has happened and brings itself about, that it thus is the power that has guided and guides the course of world-history.

[30]While we are thus concerned only with the Idea of spirit, and in world-history regard everything as only its manifestation, we have, in traversing the past—[98] however extended it may be—only to do with what is present; for philosophy, as occupying itself with the true, has to do with the eternally present. Nothing in the past is lost for it, for the Idea is present; spirit is immortal—meaning that for it nothing is gone and nothing is yet to be, but it essentially is. This is to say that the present form of spirit comprehends within it all earlier steps. These have indeed unfolded themselves in succession as independent; but what spirit is, it has always been in itself, essentially; distinctions are only the development of this in-itself. The life of the ever-present spirit is a circular run of stages, which looked at in one aspect still exist beside each other, and only as looked at from another point of view appear as past. The moments that spirit seems to have left behind it, it still possesses in the depth of its present.

[31]The Orientals are not yet conscious and do not yet know that spirit is free, and because they do not know it, they also are not it; for the spirit is only what it knows itself to be. The Orientals only know that *one* should be free, and such freedom is only willfulness.... The one, who

---

30. 1840, 97–98.
31. GW 27 [4] 1165–66 (~ 1840, 23–24).

should be free, is therefore only *despot*, and not free. Among the Greeks the consciousness of freedom first arose, and therefore they were free; but they and the Romans knew only that *a few* are free—not, however, the human being as such. Therefore among them slavery held sway, and freedom was contingent. The Germanic peoples first came to the consciousness that freedom expresses the proper nature of humans, and they came to this through the *Christian religion*. To bring this principle into actuality, and to execute this task—that became the slow and difficult labor of the human spirit, up until our time; with the Christian religion and its acceptance in the Roman state, [1166] slavery was not immediately sublated.[32] Still less did freedom come to hold sway. The application of the principle to actuality is the long process of history.

[33]Peoples with an *obscure* consciousness—or their *obscure* history—are not a subject matter, at least not of a philosophical, universal, world-history, whose goal is the knowledge of the *Idea* in history—the spirits of peoples, who have brought their principle to consciousness—to knowing, *what they are and what they are doing*.

[34]From such a history, sagas and folk songs are excluded, for these are primary but obscure means of establishing what has happened. . . . Also, poems do not belong here, in that they do not have historical truth, do not put forth determinate actuality. What belongs here primarily is a people that has a determinate consciousness, a personhood.

[35]When one wants to study substantial history, the spirit of nations, to live and to have lived in and with them, one must in studying *immerse oneself* in *certain writers*, and linger with them, and indeed one cannot linger long enough with them: here one has the history of a people, or regime, fresh, living, at first hand. . . . Such writers of history are: Herodotus, *the father*, that is, the originator, of history and indeed the greatest writer of history; and Thucydides—to be noted for naïveté worthy of wonder; *Xenophon's* Retreat of the ten thousand is an equally original book; and also *Polybius*; *Caesar's Commentaries* are likewise the masterpiece: a one-dimensional, simple work of a great spirit. To have

---

32. "To sublate, sublation" are English words invented by the early Hegel commentator J. H. Stirling in 1865, and since then regularly employed, to render the German terms "aufheben, Aufhebung"—which Hegel uses often—meaning, "a negating or superseding that preserves while overcoming and transforming, often in a new synthesis." I will follow this conventional translation.
33. GW 18.124.
34. GW 27 [1] 6.
35. GW 18.127–28 (~ GW 27 [1] 7–8).

such historians, it is necessary not *only that the cultural education* in *a people* [128] be present to a high *level*, but also that it not be limited to the *priesthood*, the *scholars*, etc., but rather be unified with the statesmen and generals.

[36]In such writers of history the *cultural education* of the *author* and of the *events* that he creates as his work—the spirit of the composer and the general spirit of the actions that he relates—are *one and the same*.

Thus, in the first place, he brings no reflection to bear—for he lives in the spirit of the materials and is not *over and above them*, as is reflection. In this unity also this is to be grasped: in an age, in which a greater differentiation between classes occurs, and in which the cultural-education and maxims of each individual belong, are connected to, his *class*, such a writer of *history* must have belonged to *the class of statesmen, generals*, etc., whose aims, intentions, and deeds are part of the same political sphere of the world that he describes. When the spirit of the material is itself *educationally cultivated*, it thus *knows* itself by itself; a major aspect of its life and activity is its *consciousness* about its purposes and interests and about its *foundational principles*. [126] One aspect of *its actions* is the way in which it *clarifies itself to others, acts* on *their imagination*, and manipulates their will. It is not then in terms of the *writer's own* reflections that he gives the explanation and *the portrayal of this consciousness*, but rather he allows the *persons* and *peoples themselves* to express what they will and how they know what they will. He does not put into their mouths alien words of his own devising; and when he elaborates upon them, then the content, and this cultural education, and this consciousness, are the same as the content and consciousness *of those whom he has speak in this fashion*. It is thus, for example, that we read in Thucydides the speeches of Pericles.

"Without Passion Nothing Great Has Been Accomplished"

[37]We have here the Idea as totality of ethically customary freedom. Two essential phases stand out: first, the Idea itself, as abstract; then second, the human passions. The two together form the woof and the warp in the fabric that history spreads before us. The Idea is the substantial power, but considered for itself it is only the universal. The arm, by which it actualizes itself, is the passions of the human beings. The

---

36. GW 18.125–26.
37. GW 27 [1] 23.

middle of these extremes, the reconciliation of both, in which they have their living unification, is ethically customary freedom.

[38]The question of the *means*, through which freedom brings itself forth into a world, leads us into the phenomena of history itself; whereas freedom as such is primarily the internal concept, the means that it employs are, in contrast, something external, the appearing, that sets itself immediately before our eyes in history. The initial *view of history*, however, shows us the business of human beings that proceeds from their needs, their passions, their interests, from the representations and goals that these produce, from their characters and talents; and indeed in such a way that in this spectacle of activity, only these needs, passions, interests, etc., appear as the *driving force*; the individuals certainly in part pursue more general purposes—something good—but in such a way that this good is itself of a limited kind: for example, noble love of fatherland, but of a land that stands in an insignificant relationship to the world and to the universal goals of the world; or a love for one's family, friends, rectitude overall: in short, all *virtues* fall here; only in such subjects, and in the sphere of their actualization, can we clearly see the determination of reason actualized; but these are singular individuals, who stand in a restricted relation to the mass of the human race, and so we must regard them as singular among normal individuals; and the reach of the concrete existence that their virtues [156] have, as effective, is correspondingly small. But in many cases passions, the goals of particular interests, the satisfaction of selfishness, are what is the most forceful; they have their power in that they do not heed any of the limitations that justice and morality want to impose on them; and the natural force of passion has a more immediate hold on human beings than the artificial and laboriously acquired discipline of order and measure, of justice and morality.

When we contemplate this spectacle of the passions, and the consequences of their force—the irrationality, not only for themselves, but especially for that which has good intentions and rightful goals; when there is set before our eyes in history the evil, the wickedness, the destruction of the noblest formations of peoples and states, the decline of the most flourishing empires that the human spirit has brought forth, we can—when we look with deep compassion upon the untold miseries of individual human beings—only end with sorrow at

---

38. GW 18.155-62, 164-65 (~ GW 27 [2] 472-73; GW 27 [3] 802-5; GW 27 [4] 1167-73; 1840, 25-40).

this transience overall; and especially since this decline is not a work of nature only, but of the will of human beings, we can all the more end up with moral sorrow, with the good spirit (if such is in us) repulsed by such a spectacle....

[157] But: even as we look upon history as this slaughter-bench upon which the happiness of peoples, the wisdom of states, and the virtues of individuals are brought as sacrifices, our thoughts are necessarily impelled to ask: *for whom, for what final purpose*, have these monstrous sacrifices been brought? ... From the beginning we have identified these same events, which offer this spectacle for gloomy feelings and brooding reflection, to be determined as the field in which we wish to see only the *means to* what we have claimed to be the substantial determination, the absolute, final end, or, what is the same thing, the true result of world-history....

[158] What we have called principle, end-goal, determination, or what is the spirit *in itself*, its nature, its concept, is only a *universal, abstract*. Principle, as well as foundational proposition, law, is a universal, something inner, that, as true as it may be in itself, is not completely actual. Goals, foundational propositions, and the like, are in our thoughts, first in our inner intention, or also in books, but not yet in actuality; or, what is first *in itself* is a possibility, a potency, but has not yet come out from its innerness into existence; it is one-sided (philosophy). There must come in another, second essential phase for its actualization, and this is the enactment, the actualization—and the principle of that is the will, the activity of human beings overall in the *world*. It is only through this activity that each concept, in itself a determination, becomes realized, actualized. The living law, the principle, does not count through itself without mediation; the activity that puts it to work and into concrete existence is from human need, drive, and further, its inclination and passion. That I bring something into action [159] and concrete existence must involve me; *I* must thereby be; I will to be satisfied through the accomplishment—it must be my *interest*; interest here means that by which there is being: a goal for which I ought to be active, that must somehow also be my goal.... This is the infinite right of the subject, the something phase of freedom—that the subject oneself must find satisfaction in an activity, labor; and if humans are to interest themselves for the sake of something, they must be able to be actively engaged in it; that is, they require an interest of their own, they will to have themselves in it and to find their own feeling-of-self in it. One must avoid a misunderstanding here: one finds fault, one says

in an evil sense, with right, that some individual is an interested party—that is, that he seeks only his private advantage, that is, this private advantage without feeling for the universal goal, partly even against it, curtailing, damaging, sacrificing it; but whoever is active on behalf of a cause is not merely interested overall but is interested *in it*. Language correctly expresses this distinction. Nothing happens or is brought to completion unless the individuals who are active thereby are also themselves satisfied—*themselves*, they who are particulars, that is, have needs, drives, and interests that are specific, are their own, although in common with others. . . . [160] Included among these needs are not only one's own needs and volitions but also one's own insight, conviction, or at least one's own estimation and opinion—assuming that the need for argument and understanding, reasoning, is otherwise already awakened; for when humans are active on behalf of a cause, they expect that the cause will appeal to them as such, that they should enter into it on the basis of their own opinion and conviction regarding the goodness of the cause, its justice, usefulness, advantage for them, etc. . . . And since interest can be described as passion, insofar as the whole of individuality applies itself to a single object with every fiber of the will, to the exclusion of many other interests and goals that one has and can have, and concentrates all its needs and resources on this end, we must say in general that *nothing great* has been accomplished in the world *without passion*. . . .

[161] From this elucidation of the second essential phase of historical actuality of a goal overall, it follows—if in light of what has been said we consider the state—that in this dimension a state will be in itself well-constituted and forceful if its universal goal coincides with the private interest of the citizen, each finding in the other its satisfaction and actualization: a proposition of the highest importance. But in the state, there needs to be numerous institutions, an invention of mechanisms gauged for the goal—involving a lengthy struggle of the understanding to bring awareness of what is gauged to the goal, as well as a struggle with the particular interest and passion, which must be subjected to a difficult and protracted discipline until this unity is achieved. The point in time at which the state attains such a unity marks the period in its history of its flourishing, of its virtue, its strength, and its fortune.

But *world-history* does not begin with some sort of *conscious goal*, as do the *specific* spheres of human beings. The simple drive to a common life itself surely has as its conscious purpose the securing of its life and property; and then, once such a common life has been established, such purposes are more widely defined—upholding the city, of Athens or of Rome, etc.; and with every new evil or exigency the task shows itself more precisely defined. World-history begins with its *universal goal*—that the *concept* of the spirit become satisfied—only *in itself*, that is, as *nature*—the inner, innermost, unconscious drive; [162] and the entire business of world-history is, as surely will be recalled, the work of bringing it to consciousness. . . . The immeasurable mass of volitions, interests, and activities constitutes the *instruments* and means by which the world-spirit accomplishes its goal, raising it to consciousness and making it actual; and this is only finding itself, coming to itself, and intuiting itself as actualization. But those expressions of the life of the individuals and of the peoples, in seeking and satisfying *their* ends, are at the same time the *means* and *instruments* of a *higher*, wider end, about which they know nothing, which they unconsciously carry out. It is this that can be open to question, and has been questioned, and what is frequently denied, decried and condemned, as dreaming, as philosophy. But I have from the very beginning made this clear, and our presupposition or faith (which, however, ought also only be postulated as result) makes no pretension here beyond *reason governing the world* and thus also having governed and continuing to govern world-history. . . .

[164] I want to adduce an example that will come later in its place. As itself historical, it contains, in a form that is properly relevant for us, that unification of the universal and the particular—of a determinacy necessary for itself with a goal that has the appearance of the accidental.

Caesar, threatened in the position to which he had ascended—a position in which he was not yet superior to the others who stood at the head of the state but was at least on a level near them—rose up in the interest of upholding his own position, honor, and security, in danger of succumbing to those who were becoming his enemies, [165] but who at the same time had the formal constitution of the state (and hence the power of apparent legal right) on the side of their own personal ends. The victory over them, since they held the might of sway over the provinces of the Roman Empire, gave him domination of the entire empire. Without changing the form of the constitution, he thereby became the individual holder of power in the state. By carrying out his originally negative end, he gained sole sway over Rome, which was at that time an intrinsically necessary determination in Roman and world-history.

[39]What happened was at first not his intention; by holding sway alone he wished to uphold himself—and thereby this holding sway became

---

39. GW 27 [4] 1173 (~ GW 27 [3] 804–5).

something lasting: the republican form disappeared and went over to being a despotism; this became a consequence that was necessary and according to reason, which reason has justified. The great human being in world-history is one who makes his goal such that it is also the goal of world-history, that it is *in the age*. In external history we have the particular, the drives and needs, immediately before our eyes: we see these engaged in mutual destruction, directed to ruin; but the Idea is the universal, and in the struggle it is unassailable and unscathed. This can be called the cunning of reason,[40] in that it employs these instruments while maintaining itself unscathed, or brings itself forth. The rational goal realizes itself through the needs, passions, and so forth of human beings; the particular is very insignificant over against the universal; the individuals are sacrificed and given up. World-history sets itself forth as the struggle of individuals; in the realm of particularity things proceed *naturally*, that is, force holds sway.

[41]Had Caesar kept himself with Cicero, he would have become nothing; but Caesar knew that the republic was a lie, that Cicero's speech was empty, and that another configuration, instead of this hollow one, must be established—that the configuration that he brought forth was the necessary one.

[42]Passion is the determination of the whole human being, what separates and distinguishes one from another. Every human being is specific, for a mere abstraction of humanity has no truth. "Passion" means here the determinacy of the human being; "character" is already too broad a term, because it encompasses all particularities. We are not concerned with the merely impotent interiority that lacks the strength to realize itself—and so we have nothing to do with merely putative intentions. In history we do not have to do with individuals who have certain intentions but then act like mice, maybe, or gnats. Rather, we have before us the colorful din of passions, and we contrast this din with the still simplicity of the Idea that has within itself the absolute end-goal, which it completes; and thus emerges the next question—about the connection of the two. World-history necessarily presents this connection, has

---

40. "Die List der Vernunft": this famous phrase appears also in the parallel passage GW 27 [3] 804-5 and on a loose sheet of notes that Hegel wrote while preparing his lectures of 1830-31: see GW 18.209. Hegel used the expression in *The Science of Logic*, in the chapter "Teleology," section C ("The Realized End"), GW 12.165-66: when reason's end directly makes an object its means, this "can be regarded as force [Gewalt]"; in contrast, when "*between* itself and the object" (that is to be used as a means), reason's end "*interposes* another object, this can be regarded as the *cunning* of reason."

41. GW 27 [2] 506 (~ GW 27 [1] 59; GW 27 [3] 1069).

42. GW 27 [1] 51-52, 56-60.

the unity of both, has this connection as its absolute foundation. This connection ought not to be something simply believed; activities ought not to be simply material, or external means, through which the Idea realizes itself—for the individuals are knowing and willing; they do not claim only to bring to completion what a higher sorcery wills; they have the just demand not to serve simply as means. We can also not say here that the connection is something incomprehensible, for we have before us philosophical world-history. . . . The connection takes on the well-known form of the unity of freedom and necessity. [52] Customarily one calls the particular will freedom, against which what is in and for itself is posited as necessity; in fact, however, only the relationship of the spirit to that which is in and for itself, as its own, is freedom. Willfulness is only a mixture of freedom and necessity, belonging only to what is opined to be freedom, the appearance, that stands under the determination of nature. . . .

[56] The question is, what form, what determination, does the universal have that brings the activity to appearance. The universal should become actual through activity. This is the standpoint of differentiation, of finitude. The agents acting from this standpoint will finite things, pursue purposes for themselves, will their particularity; the other side is that in these particular purposes at the same time there appears a universality of purposes, which we call good, etc. (If this universal does not appear, we find ourselves before the standpoint of abstract willfulness, which wills only the satisfaction of selfishness—but this standpoint lies behind us.) This universal, which appears from the viewpoint of finitude, is the particular good, which is present as ethically customary; it is a production of the universal, which already exists as the ethically customary; this can be called the maintaining of the ethically customary. This is no dead routine, but essentially a bringing forth—in the first instance of ethical custom, what counts as justice; not merely the abstraction of the good, but the determinacy of the good; the duty is to defend this fatherland, be it Rome or Sparta. The ethically customary is thus essentially something determinate. . . . [57] These are the duties that each individual knows, the objective aspect of one's class, of one's fatherland. There is no difficulty in knowing these; whoever starts discussing a lot about his duties is certainly a sick will, revealing itself. This determination thus has the universal as ethical custom, through which is the maintaining of the ethically customary sphere in place, brought about by each having to produce this

ethical custom by one's own activity. Against this universality of ethical custom there is a second universality that comes into prominence in the great figures of history; and herein enters the conflict. Within an ethically customary communal essence such conflict cannot come to the fore, since it is a necessary world of ethical custom, from which the single individual can only stray—without the universality of the ethical community suffering any damage, because the universal that menaces this universal is of a different sort; it has already been noted from where the danger comes. We remarked earlier in reference to the progress of the Idea that an ethically customary whole is limited and as such has a higher universal above it; and inasmuch as the latter comes to prominence, a doubling, an inner fragmentation occurs; the universal remains what it was inwardly, but the higher power within it rises to prominence and breaks in. This makes the transition, from one shape to another that is higher. . . .

It is the great historical individuals who grasp such a universal and turn it to their purposes. They can thus be called heroes, those who [58] from out of themselves create, will, and bring to completion something universal that is recognized. They become praised for having accomplished a universal that previously was only in itself. These historical individuals grasp such a universal, create it out of a source, whose content was not yet present in a known concrete existence and therefore seemed created from inside themselves. Thus they bring to completion, as accomplished deeds, new conditions of the world that appear initially to be only their own goals, their determination, their passion. Around the banner of such heroes everything gathers itself because it is they who articulate what the era is. This is what can be named the passions of the world-historical humans, where the universal appears here in the form of passion—but is the absolute. . . . This is in the age, the truth of the age; it is what is inwardly already prepared. Thus they have the absolute right on their side. Spirit makes itself count in this shape, and the humans are leaders of it. In this regard it is to be noted that the world-historical humans are the most insightful; what they will is the just, although it appears as their cause, because the others do not yet know. But the others must heed, because it is within them, it is theirs, and only now coming into concrete existence. Yet it appears, as was said, as the passion of the world-historical humans. . . .

[59] This is the true connection of passion and Idea. The necessity of the Idea, and what is called the passions of the historical individuals,

hang together; the goal of the Idea, the content of the passion, is thus one and the same. The passion appears, as it were, as something animal-like in the great [60] individuals; it appears that their being as spirit *and* natural are utterly one, and that this oneness constitutes their strength, in that they become driven unresistingly—and they satisfy themselves. Happy, they do not become; for it has become bitter to them, or they die at the moment they achieved their goal. Their personhood they sacrificed; their entire life was a sacrifice. And that they were not happy is a consolation for those who need such a consolation.

[43]In this regard it can be remarked that world-history is not a soil of happiness; for the periods of happiness are for history blank pages—since the object of history is, at the least, change. In world-history satisfaction cannot so much be called happiness because it is a question of the satisfaction of universal goals that stand over and above the sphere in which the ordinary inclinations [55] can satisfy themselves. The object of world-history is goals that are carried out with energy, by an abstract willing that is often directed against the happiness of the individual actors themselves *and* of other individuals. World-historical individuals have not sought happiness, yet they have satisfied themselves.

"Human Beings as Ends-in-Themselves"

[44]"Though we allow that the individualities, their purposes and the satisfaction of these, are sacrificed—their happiness overall surrendered to the empire of natural force and thereby to contingency as belonging to it—and we consider the individuals overall under the category of means, there still remains one side of them that we hesitate to view only in this light, even in the highest cases, for it is something utterly not subordinate, but rather in them it is in itself eternal and divine. This is morality, ethical custom, religiosity. Something already mentioned about the activation of rational goals by individuals overall is that their subjective side, their interest overall, their needs and drives, their opinions and insight, though a formal side, do, however, have an infinite right to have to be satisfied. . . . In fulfilling rational ends, humans not only simultaneously fulfill their own particular ends, whose content differs, but they also have a *part* in that rational end itself, and are thereby even *ends-in-themselves* . . . [167] in accord with the content of the goals. In this

---
43. GW 27 [1] 54–55.
44. GW 18.166–67 (~ GW 27 [4] 1174–76; 1840, 41–43).

determination falls everything that we would exempt from the category of a means: morality, ethical custom, religiosity. The human being is end-in-itself only through the divine that is in them—through that which from the start has been named reason, and as the active in itself is self-determining, comes to be called freedom; and we assert, without being able to go further here in elaboration, that even religiosity, ethical custom, and so forth, have herein their ground and source and thereby are elevated in themselves over outer necessity and contingency in itself. (But it is not to be forgotten that we only speak here of them insofar as they exist in individuals, that is, insofar as they are at home in individual freedom; in this determination, the *guilt* or *responsibility* falls on the individual self, for the religious and ethically customary weakness, corruption, and loss. This is the hallmark of the high, absolute determination of human beings, that one *knows* what good and evil is, and that even the *volition* is either the good or the wicked—in a word, that one can have guilt, responsibility not only for wickedness but also for goodness; and responsibility not for this and also that, and for all that is around one and for what one is and what is in one, but also for the good and wickedness that belong to one's individual freedom.)

[45]The religiosity, the ethical customs, of a limited life—a shepherd, a farmer—in their concentrated innerness, and their limitation to a few entirely simple relations of life, have infinite worth, and the same worth as the religiosity and ethical customs of an educated knowledge and of an existence that is richly ensconced in relations and affairs. This inner midpoint, this simple region of the right of subjective freedom, the seat of volition, decision, and action, the abstract content of conscience— that in which the responsibility and worth of individuals, their eternal judgment, are contained—remains untouched by the noisy clamor of world-history, untouched not only by external and temporal changes but also by the changes brought about by the absolute necessity of the concept of freedom itself.

[46]The unending drive of thinking is to establish in ourselves the real as something that is universal and ideal. In that the human being is such, knowing oneself as ideal, one ceases being simply natural, living simply in feelings and drives and in the simple productions of *one's own* drives. Because one knows this inwardly, the drives are restrained; representation, thought, [26] interposes between the urgency of the drive

---

45. GW 18.170 (~ 1840, 46).
46. GW 27 [1] 25–26.

and its satisfaction.... The human being does this, restrains one's drives and so deals with goals.... The determination can be the universal itself when one sets the entire universal as goal.... The most boundless universal is one's boundless freedom. The human being can posit this as goal. What is determining one is knowing oneself and one's own will. This makes the human being volitional.... This innerness is what makes the self-sufficiency of the human being.

[47]Freedom's consciousness contains this, that the individual grasps oneself as a person, that is, in one's singularity itself as in itself universal, the abstraction, the capacity of going away from everything particular, and therefore grasping itself as in itself infinite.... The moral itself, which is so closely connected with consciousness of freedom, can be quite pure while still deficient in such consciousness being present, insofar as it expresses only universal duties and rights as objective commandments, or also insofar as it expresses a simple negative, through the formal elevation of the going away from the sensuous and all sensuous motivation. Since Europeans have become acquainted with the *Chinese* morality (and the writings of *Confucius*), it has received the highest praise and most prestigious acknowledgment of its excellence from those who are familiar with the Christian morality; in the same way, the sublimity is acknowledged with which the *Indian* religion and poetry (regarding which, however, one must make the qualification: the higher sort), and in particular their philosophy, express and require the removal and sacrifice of sensuous things. Yet these two nations are deficient—one must say, completely—in the essential self-consciousness of the concept of freedom. For the Chinese, their moral rules are like natural laws, external positive commandments, compulsory rights and compulsory duties, or rules of mutual courtesy. [207] Freedom, through which the substantial determinations of reason can first become ethically customary disposition, is lacking; the moral is a matter of the state and is administered through ruling officials and the courts of law. Their works on the subject that are not books of state laws, and are in any case addressed to the subjective will and disposition, read like the moral writings of the Stoics: as a series of commandments necessary for the goal of happiness, so that willfulness appears to stand over and against them, to decide for itself whether they can follow such commandments or not. So then we have for the Chinese, as

---

47. GW 18.206–7 (~ 1840, 87–88).

for the Stoic moralists, the presentation of an abstract *subject*, the sage, as the culmination of such doctrines.

In the *Indian* doctrine of the renunciation of sensuality, desires, and earthly interests, affirmative ethically customary freedom is not the goal and end, but rather the annihilation of the consciousness—spiritual and even physical lifelessness.

[48]So long as it is only slumbering, the will is first overall a natural will that has not yet grasped the rational; and also justice and true law overall are not yet present for it. The individual's knowing of its goal is the unmoved mover, as Aristotle says: it is the true customary ethics; it must become conscious of the unmoved, and that the moving is in the individual. That it become moving in the individual requires that the subject be developed for itself to a condition of free ownership. It must thus come to consciousness of this eternally unmoved, and the individual subject must furthermore be free and independent for itself. What we have considered in *world-history* as the peoples making themselves independent, we must consider for the individuals in their peoples.

"The Nature of the State"

[49]Concerning the nature of the state overall, one must have concerning it the conception that in it, freedom becomes objective to itself; that in it, freedom is positively realized—in contrast to the representation that the state is a collection of human beings in which the freedom of all is limited, so that the state is the negation of freedom in such a way that for each person, only a small spot remains free, within which one could express one's freedom externally. The state is rather freedom in its objectivity, while the spot within which people have sought freedom is only willfulness, thus the opposite of freedom. Therefore the way in which philosophy [62] grasps the state is this, that the state is the actualization of freedom. This is its first determination; connected with this, it is that the human being only in the state has the standpoint where one is rational. Aristotle indeed says: "the human being outside the state is beast or god" [*Politics* 1253a29]. It was surely remarked earlier that the being of individuals, of lawful right, of art, of the sciences, are the acts of the peoples. Each is a child of *one's own* time, *and* of *one's own* people; what one truly is, is one's people, as in a state. Only this

---

48. GW 27 [2] 500.
49. GW 27 [1] 61–69.

deserves to be called one's being. Each is a better or worse representative of *one's own* age. This entity we earlier called the objective work of a people, and this constitutes the objectivity of each individual; this they are only; anything else is only their formal activity. All disciplined upbringing aims at this, that the individual should not remain subjective but be maintained in objectivity. The state can indeed be regarded as a means for the satisfaction of *one's own* goals; this view is, however, simply a one-sided error on the part of individuals; for the state is end, and the individuals have being only to the extent that they enact within themselves the substantiality of the people. The true will wills what matters, and this is the substantial. The true artist wills to depict what matters as it is for itself, and his own subjectivity must thereby disappear. So must the individual make what matters for one's people actual within oneself, and thus is one's subjective will, and what is universal in and for itself, also united in the subject. Everything that the individual is, is thanks to the state; the state is the ethically customary whole, not an abstraction that stands over against the individual. . . .

[63] It is not the case that individuals are the end and the state the means. [Griesheim: The relationship of end and means is not appropriate, for the state is not the abstract that stands over and against the citizens, but they are its moments, as in an organic life form, where no member is end and there is no means.] In the organism everything is end and means simultaneously. It is thus that the state is the Idea, as it is present on earth. Regarded more closely, the relationship of the state can appear as a family relationship: patriarchal. Such a relationship does constitute the transition from the family to the state. But the latter can also be constructed in a nonpatriarchal way. The definition of the state becomes clearer when we contrast it with the family. That is, the family is also an ethically customary whole, but in it love is that by which the unity is present. . . . The state, however, is unity not in the form of love, that is, oneness in the form of sentiment, but rather in the form of willing, of knowing the universal. This entails that members of the state have before them universality as force of nature, that ethical customs, habits, are present as the immediate mode of the ethically customary and in an immediate way [64] for the individual. [Griesheim: Also, in the state the self-sufficiency of individuals is present, for they are knowing—that is, they set their I over and against the universal.] In the second place, however, laws belong to a state, so that the universal is also in the form of the universal as known. . . . This is what elevates

the state to a spiritually existing community, whereas in the family, sentiment holds sway. In the state, the individual obeys the laws and in this obedience one has one's freedom, one's objectivity; for the laws are rational; thus in the laws the individual is related to one's own essence, one's own will. . . . Here, personhood enters. Personhood is not found in the family, but instead only a natural drive, heightened to spirituality and thus ethical custom. It is first in the state, where individuals are knowers of the universal, that they are reflected into themselves, that they have independence. What stands over against them is universal, the laws. Individuals are set apart from these laws; as singular they are over against the universal; the independence of individuals constitutes the division in the state, the antithesis, and this constitutes the state as a concrete whole. Thus what enters in the state is the essential phase of knowing and thinking. Connected with this is the fact that even all religion, art, science, thus cultural education overall, can emerge only in a state. For all have thinking as their principle. In religion, the absolute essence becomes represented; in the state, it is still limited as a specific people's spirit—thus the Athenians had Pallas Athena, and they worshiped their people's spirit as a divinity. Absolute knowing, however, is something distinct from this externality. . . .

[65] More closely considered the connection is this: [Hagenbach: already in the relationship of master and slave there is subjection of the will under another; the will remains, as one's will subjected—so not as one's own particular will;] this is surely present, that the subjective will obeys another. The subjection of the will means that the will as particular does not count; it is thus the working out of the particular will, from the natural appetites present, and on this depends the habit of directing oneself to and together with an other, and, in the state, knowing a universal and making it one's own goal. . . . And it is only when this happens that art, science, and religion culturally educate themselves. . . .

[66b] If one asks now what the concept of the state is, immediately the antithesis between the government—that is, the universal, the self-acting of the universal will against the subjective will—is, in the concept, [67] sublated and disappears. As long as this antithesis continues its struggle, the state is really not yet present and what is at stake is the existence of the state. . . . The rational concept of the state has thus already left this antithesis behind; and those who still posit this antithesis have not yet recognized the concept of the state. . . . The state as a living entity is to be thought of essentially as something developed,

as an organic system consisting in spheres that are independent for themselves, but so that the working of their independence is such as to produce this whole, that is, to sublate their independence. In the organism it is absolutely no longer a question of the opposition between universal and singular. . . .

The first form of the state is that the totality is still one that is enveloped; the spheres have not yet arrived at their independence; the second form is that these spheres and the individuality become free. The first form is compulsory; the second is a loosely tied unity of the liberated spheres where the unity is something new. The third is the one in which the spheres are independent only in finding the actualization of the production of the universal. [68] Recollecting concrete instances, we see that all states, all empires, run through these forms, and the whole of world-history can be divided according to these forms. . . .

[69] In the sciences it is otherwise: once something has been brought forth, it holds good for all times. It is a different matter with the constitution. As regards this, we can learn nothing from ancient history; for in ancient history there were principles that belong there, and were for themselves constantly final; the principle of the rational state is precisely that such principles are not final but on the whole decline. Moral principles can, to be sure, be extracted from history for the constitution, but not for the concept of freedom, which is what matters for the true constitution of the state.

[50]The life of the state in the individuals is what is called the *ethically customary*: the state, its laws, its institutions, are theirs—it is their right; also theirs is external possessions, in their nature—their soil, mountains, air, and waters, as their land, their fatherland; the history of this state, its deeds and the deeds of their forefathers, are theirs; it lives in their memory, having brought forth what now exists, what belongs to them. All is their possession, even as they are possessed by it; for it constitutes their substance, their being; their conception is thereby fulfilled, and their will is the willing of these laws and this fatherland. It is this spiritual collectivity, which is one essence, the *spirit* of one people: Athena. . . . This spirit of a people is a *determinate* spirit, and as has been said, is determined in accord with its development of the historical matter. . . . [173] It is a single individuality that in its essentiality is revered, and enjoyed as the essence, as the conceived divinity, in the *religion*; and

---

50. GW 18.172-73 (~ GW 27 [4] 1184-86; 1840, 65-66).

as image and intuition is portrayed in the *art*; and in thinking, is cognized and comprehended in the *philosophy*. Because these are the same in their original substance, their content and object, their shapes, exist in an inseparable unity with the spirit of the state. . . . This remark is especially important in light of the folly of our age, in wanting to devise and to implement state constitutions independently from religion. . . . If the state's legal principles and institutions are divorced from innerness, from the ultimate holy shrine of the conscience, from the silent sanctuary where the religion has its seat, they will not become actually central since they will remain in abstraction and indeterminacy.

[51]It has been correctly said that the state rests on religion. The principle of the state must be an absolute justification. The absolute justification is that the principle is known as an essential phase in the divine nature itself. This is closer to what it means to say that the state rests on religion. One has often heard the latter said in modern times, but one must not represent it as if the state is present and needs the religion, and as if religion were not there so that one must bring it into the state in bowls and buckets. One must therefore not believe that the state existed beforehand and had to introduce the religion into it; rather, the state comes out from the religion itself. The state comes eternally out of the religion; the principle of the state, the consciousness of the holy, is in the religion.

[52]Philosophy, too, must come to sight in the life of the state, inasmuch as that which culturally educates a content is, as already mentioned, the form proper to thought itself; but philosophy is simply the consciousness of this form itself, is the thinking of thinking, so that the proper material for its edifice is already prepared in the general cultural education; and in the development of the state itself, periods must occur through which the spirit of nobler natures is driven to flee from the present into ideal regions to find in them the reconciliation with itself that it can no longer enjoy in an actuality that is internally divided, partly inasmuch as the reflective understanding attacks everything sacred and profound that was naïvely in the religion, laws, and ethical customs of peoples, and debases and dilutes them into abstract, godless generalities—driving thought to become thinking reason, and in its own element to seek and to accomplish the reestablishment of the destroyed that it brought upon itself.

---

51. GW 27 [1] 74 (~ GW 27 [2] 492; GW 27 [3] 809-10; 1840, 63-64).
52. GW 18.204 (~ 1840, 85-86).

[53]The state itself is an abstraction, which itself has only universal reality in the citizens; but it is actual, and its only universal existence must determine itself through individual volition and activity. It involves the need for one rule and for state force overall—for singling out and selecting those who lead much of the affairs of state; for making decisions and determining how they are then to be executed; for giving orders to citizens who must put them into practice. If, for example, in democracy the people decides on war, a general must still be put at the top to command it. It is the constitution by which the state, as something abstract, first comes to life and actuality; but thereby the difference arises between ruler and ruled, command and obedience; [179] but obedience appears not to be in accord with freedom; and command appears to do the very opposite of what is required by the foundation of the state, by the concept of freedom. If sometimes the distinction between command and obedience is necessary because the matter could not proceed otherwise—and this indeed appears to be a necessity that is merely external to, indeed in conflict with, freedom abstractly defined—the arrangement at least must be such that the minimum possible of obedience is required of the citizens, and the minimum possible of willfulness is allowed to the command. The content of what it is necessary to command should be the main thing that is determined and decided by the people in accord with the will of many or of all individuals—and yet, again, the state as actuality, as individual unity, is to have might and strength.

The first of all determinations is overall the distinction between ruler and ruled, and constitutions have rightly been divided into monarchy, aristocracy, and democracy. It must only be noted that in monarchy itself a distinction must be made between despotism and monarchy as such.... Also possible are mixtures of several of these essential orderings—which are, however, thereby amorphous, in themselves unsustainable, and inconsistent configurations. The question, in this collision, is therefore, which is the *best* constitution: that is, by which institution, organization, or mechanism of state-force the purpose [180] of the state can be most securely attained. This purpose can of course be grasped in different ways, for example, the peaceful enjoyment of bourgeois civil life, general blessed happiness; such purposes have given rise to the so-called *ideal* of political regimes, especially the ideal of the upbringing of princes (Fenelon), or of rulers generally, of the aristocracy (Plato), in

---

53. GW 18.178–81 (~ GW 27 [4] 1192–97; 1840, 54–57).

which the chief concern is with the character of the subject who stands at the top, and no thought at all is given to the primary ideal, of the organic state institutions. The question about the best constitution is often posed in the sense that not only is the theory about it a matter of subjective, free deliberation, but also as if the actual introduction of the best or the better known constitution were a consequence of an entirely theoretically grasped decision—as though the type of constitution could be a matter of a wholly free, wide-ranging *choice*, not delimited by deliberation. In this thoroughly naïve sense, not indeed the Persian people but the Persian elite, having conspired to overthrow the pseudo-Smerdis and the Magi, after this successful undertaking and since no descendant of the Achaemenid family was still around, conferred on which constitution would be introduced into Persia; and Herodotus [3.76] reports thus naïvely this conference.

Nowadays, the constitution of a land or people is not presented as belonging so entirely to free choice. The foundational but abstractly formulated definition of freedom has led to the widespread theory that very generally the *republic* counts as the only just and true constitution; and there are even a number of men holding high positions of state power in a *monarchical* constitution, for example *Lafayette*, who have not contradicted such a view, or have subscribed to it. But they have seen that such a constitution, even if it were the best, in actuality cannot be introduced everywhere, and, because *humans are what they are*, one must make do with a lesser degree of freedom. As a consequence, under these circumstances, and in light of the moral condition of the people, the monarchical constitution may be the *most serviceable* one. [181] Also, from this perspective the necessity of a specific state constitution is made to depend on conditions that are merely externally contingent.

[54]In the theories of our time, manifold errors concerning the nature of the state are prevalent, [174] which count as established truths and have become prejudices. We want to go through only a few of them, stressing especially those that are related to the aim of our history.

The first that we encounter is the direct opposite of our concept (that the state is the actualization of freedom), the view, namely, that the human being by nature is free, but that in society and the state, which one enters by necessity, this natural freedom must be restricted. That the human being is free by nature is completely correct in the sense that one is this, by one's concept—but only in terms of determination,

---

54. GW 18.173-77 (~ GW 27 [4] 1189-91; 1840, 50-53).

that is, only *in itself*, the nature of an object means, in any case, its concept. But this proposition is also taken as referring to the human being in merely natural, immediate existence. In this sense a state-of-nature overall is assumed, in which the human being is presented as in possession of one's natural rights, in the unrestricted exercise and enjoyment of one's freedom. This assumption cannot count as something historical. If one did seriously want to make such a claim, it would be difficult to point to such a state that exists in the present time, or that has existed anytime in the past. One can of course point to states of wildness, but they are tied with raw passions and violent deeds; and no matter how uncultured they are, they are tied with social institutions that supposedly limit freedom. This assumption is one of those nebulous pictures that theory produces, a [175] representation that flows necessarily from it, and to which it then ascribes an existence without any sort of historical justification.

When we find such a state-of-nature in empirical existence, it conforms to its concept. Freedom as the ideality of the immediate and natural is not something immediate and natural, but must rather be acquired, first become attained, and through an endless mediation of discipline of knowing and of willing. Thus the state-of-nature is rather a state of injustice, of violence, of uncontrolled natural drives, of inhuman deeds and emotions. There is of course restriction imposed by the society and the state, but this is a restriction of these stupid emotions and raw drives, and of preferences based on reflection too, as well as of the needs, of willfulness, and of passion arising from cultural education. These restrictions are part of the mediation through which the consciousness and the will of freedom, in its true form—that is, rational, and in accord with its concept—are first brought forward. To freedom in accord with its concept belongs justice and ethical custom, and these are, in and for themselves, universal essentialities, objects, and aims that are discovered only by the activity of thinking that distinguishes itself from and develops over against sensuous willing....

[176] Second, there is another representation to be mentioned that generally inhibits the development of right into a legal form: namely, the *patriarchal*—a condition regarded as providing, either for the whole or at least for some of its individual branches, the relationships in which, along with the rightful and the ethically customary and heartfelt elements, members find their satisfaction; and only in conjunction with this is justice itself regarded as truly practiced in accord with its contents. The patriarchal condition is based on the family relationship, which is the earliest ethical customary life of all, after which that of the state as

the second develops, along with consciousness. The patriarchal relationship is the condition of a transition, in which the family has already grown into a clan or people, and in which the bond has already ceased to be one simply of love and trust and has become an association of *service*.

To give first the ethically customary life of the *family*: the family is only one person, the members of which have either (the parents) mutually surrendered to one another their personhood (and hence their legally just status along with their particular interests and selfish inclinations), or else they have not yet attained to it, as with the children (who begin in the state-of-nature previously described). Thus they are in a unity of feeling, in love, in trust, faith toward one another; in love, an individual has one's own consciousness in the consciousness of the other, and in this mutual divestment [177] each has attained not only the other but also oneself as in unity with the other. . . . The spirit of the family, the Penates, are thus a single substantial essence, even as the spirit of a people is in the state; and in both cases the ethically customary consists in the feeling, the consciousness, and the volition—not in the individual personhood and interests; but this unity is, in the family, essentially one of feeling and remains within the natural mode; the piety of the family is something to be most highly respected by the state, for through it, the state has in its members individuals who already are customarily ethical for themselves—which as persons they are not—and who bring to the state a genuine foundation in their feeling of being at one with a whole.

But the expansion of the family into a patriarchal whole transcends the ties of blood relationship, the natural side of its foundation, and beyond this the individuals must enter into the status of personhood.

To examine the patriarchal condition in its wider scope would lead especially to the consideration of the form of theocracy, for the head of the patriarchal clan is also its priest; when the family is overall not yet separated from the society and the state, then religion too is not yet set apart from society, and still less has religious piety itself become an inwardness of feeling.

"Geography in World-History"

[55]About this, it is first to be remarked that the climate is an abstract essential cause in relation to the shape taken by spirit. History indeed

---

55. GW 27 [1] 77 (~ GW 27 [2] 506-9; 1840, 98-99).

lives on the soil of the natural; but this is only one side, and the higher side is that of spirit, and the natural aspect, the climate, does not account for the individual. Thus it is tedious to hear about the mild Ionian sky and its influence on Homer; for the sky is still mild, and the Turks have no Homer.

[56]This geographical ground must not be taken to be an external occasion for history; rather it has a specific property, of a distinct type, to which the character of the peoples who emerge from it corresponds. [Hagenbach: Since they emerge from such a ground, the peoples have specific characteristics that are connected with the locality.] ... Such a connection appears initially to contradict the freedom of humans because humans have to raise themselves above natural determinacy. ... One must not think of the spiritual determinacy of peoples as dependent on the natural side, in such a way that one thinks of spirit as an abstraction to which the natural side gives its content, but rather the connection is: the peoples in history are particular spirits; and one must know from the nature of spirit that particularity does not obscure the universal, that rather the universal must particularize itself in order to become true. Inasmuch as the spirits of peoples are determined specifically, their determinacy on the one hand is spiritual, which then on the other hand [91] corresponds to a natural determinacy, so that the relationship is reciprocal.

[57]The temperate zone, and indeed the northern temperate zone, forms the stage of the world-theater. ... A necessary division is that into the new world vs. the old world; we do not make the division, but the world itself does it.

"The New World"

[58]What happens in America comes out from Europe, so all is still becoming, and accordingly America is the land of the future; the world-historical importance of this part of the world falls more in the future, therefore does not now concern us.

It can, even so, be called the land of yearning. Napoleon is supposed to have said:[59] "Cette vielle Europe m'ennuie" [this old Europe

---

56. GW 27 [1] 90–91 (~ GW 27 [2] 506–8).
57. GW 27 [1] 78 (~ GW 27 [2] 508–9, 513; GW 27 [4] 1203; 1840, 100).
58. GW 27 [4] 1207, 1209–14 (~ GW 27 [2] 512; GW 27 [3] 823–24; 1840, 104–7).
59. Mme. Germaine De Staël, *Considérations sur la Révolution française*, vol. 2, chap. 19, beg. (Paris: Charpentier, 1862 [orig. publ. 1818]), 133.

bores me]; this, many have said with him; and so America is seen as the longed-for land, as the land of hope. In fact, immigration seeks many advantages there, for the immigrants have left everything behind. . . .

[1209] In comparing South America (reckoning Mexico as part of it) with North America, we observe an astonishing contrast; if we dwell upon this contrast, it is to show also the contrast between North America and Europe. In North America we witness prosperity, an increase of industry and population, civil order and firm freedom; the whole federation constitutes but a single state, which has its political centers. In South America, on the contrary, we see that the republics rest only on military force; their whole history is only a continued upheaval; the federated states become disunited; others become united; and all these changes proceed through military revolutions. The more particular differences between the two parts of America show us two opposite directions, present in the state overall: the one in political respects, the other in regard to religion. [1210] South America, where the Spaniards asserted mastery, is Catholic; North America, Protestant. A further distinction is that South America was conquered; it had a government from the top firmly imposed; the Spaniards took over South America to master it, and to become rich through extortion, through political office. In this sense the Spaniards established themselves. They depended only on a distant motherland; by their power, conduct, and self-confidence they gained a great predominance over the Indians. In North America it is different; the North American free states were entirely populated by Europeans. The small populaces of the natives can scarcely be taken into account. Since in England, Puritans, Episcopalians, and Catholics were engaged in perpetual conflict, and now one party, now the other, had the upper hand, many emigrated to seek religious freedom in a foreign part of the world. These were industrious Europeans, who betook themselves to agriculture, tobacco and cotton planting, etc. Soon the whole attention of the inhabitants was given to working to fulfill needs: for peace, for bourgeois civil justice, security, freedom, and a community arising from the aggregation of individuals as atoms; so that the state was merely something external for the protection of property. . . . [1211] With the Protestant religion there is present a mutual confidence in the disposition of fellow citizens; this cannot find a place in the Catholic religion; here the religiosity is something for itself, becoming a mass of works directed to the health of the soul, and so these are sundered from the bourgeois civil life. In the Protestant church the religious works are the entire life, the activity of life overall. That is what makes the distinction that, among Catholics, no such mutual confidence can find a place; for in secular matters only force and voluntary subservience hold sway; the forms that are called constitutions are in this case only a resort of necessity, and are no protection against mistrust; there is no consciousness of a common disposition, but each is aware only of his own disposition in himself; there is an isolation of the individual that brings with it a need for the force of the state. To be sure, there are in South America enough forms set up; but they protect nothing; they are not rooted in the proper disposition: what is present are the passions of ambition that allow no stability, and the religion sets no limits against such, even though large donations are made to the church.

We have now to consider North America in comparison with Europe. North America is the perennial example of a republican constitution. [1212] A subjective unity stands at the top: a president, who, for the sake of security against ambition, is chosen only for four years. There is universal protection for property, and almost entire immunity from public burdens. This gives the predominant character of the North American state: the sense of the private man is aimed only at business and gain; the particular interest is absolutely overwhelming; the aim is not the universal but one's own enjoyment. This particularity is protected through a legal establishment; but this formal rule of just law and this directedness to particular goals are not what is higher; there can be a just lawfulness without justice, and so the American merchants are given the evil invitation to deceive under the protection of the law; there is lacking the inner disposition of justice. . . .

The Protestant principle brings with it that feeling counts, essentially, rather than an authority, or demands of faith. But one's own feeling can be the source of many forms of caprice. Everyone, it is said, may have one's own worldview, and so one may have also one's own religion. Through this splitting into infinite opinions arises a crowd of sects in North America, which cannot be hindered by any force; and so in North America the Protestant church does not exactly hold sway, since the church is not established as one, in and for itself. . . . [1213] This complete caprice is developed to such an extreme that the various congregations choose their own ministers and dismiss them according to their pleasure. . . . Lacking is that religious unity that has been maintained in European states, where deviations are limited to a few denominations.

We have now to consider further the political condition. In the North American free states the individual, with one's particular activity, is the fundamental determination. Accordingly, as regards the state, there is no solid unity present; the universal goal is not established as something fixed for itself, but activity is only directed at particular matters; there is no participation in the state's governing; the need for a firm combination does not yet exist—and in this regard there are two determinations to note: the need for an actual state and a firm government arise after there is a distinction of classes, when wealth and poverty become very great, and when such a relationship emerges that a large portion of the people can no longer satisfy its necessities in the way in which it has been accustomed so to do, and there is belief in claims that manifest a condition of inner tension. [1214] But this is not yet present in America. In England it has come to the highest level; there holds sway in England a tremendous wealth and a horrible poverty, with a pretension to something higher. North America will be comparable with Europe only after the space that that country presents to its inhabitants shall have been filled, . . . when the members of the bourgeois civil society shall be pressed back on each other.

[60]The new free states of North America are often cited as an example that even a large state can exist as free, that is, as a republic. . . . But North America is a still-forming state, a state in becoming, which does not yet have need of a monarchy because it has not yet developed to this point. It is a federation-state. These are the worst when it comes to foreign relations. Its peculiar location has prevented this condition from making things worse for it. If large states were closer, its precarious situation would essentially come to light, and this [81] was evident in the last war [the War of 1812] with England. . . . There was such tension between the southern and the northern states that, had the war continued longer, there would have come about a complete division of the state.

[61]There is a danger present: that the northern American and southern American states go to war, since the interests are in tension: the southern states rest on slavery, the aristocracy has the upper hand; in the north, industry, business, trade flourish. So it is a major consideration that a firm state force is not yet present, and therefore the comparison between the North American and European states must remain completely open.

---

60. GW 27 [1] 80–81.
61. GW 27 [4] 1215.

⁶²Since we want to determine the grounds of world-history, America is therefore also excluded from our consideration, and there can be only a few remarks made about it, in its relation to Europe.

The new world is always still a young world. America is the world of the future, but we have nothing to do with prophecy, as this in general is excluded from philosophy. America is still to be grasped in becoming.

⁶³We proceed now to the old world, for it is the one that concerns us more; and we have to consider its condition more closely. It is divided into three world-parts; and these divisions are necessary, because they correspond to the concept of thought. These three parts stand thus in an essential relationship and constitute a rational totality.

"Africa Proper"

⁶⁴The boundaries of Africa⁶⁵ proper are essentially the Gulf of Guinea; the eastern side (also not a straight line); and the third side forming the line in the Sudan from Niger on. To the north is principally the Sahara Desert. . . . These peoples have never emerged out of themselves, nor have they gained a foothold in history. . . . Africa remains in its own quiet: [85] sensuosity not driven out of itself, itself not driving, and having no further connection with history, except that in more modern times the inhabitants were brought into slavery. The general condition of slavery is such that it is said that slavery ought not to exist, that in and for itself it is unjust in terms of the matter's very concept. But this "ought" expresses a subjectivity; this "ought" is not historical; for what first *ought* to be, *is* not. What the ought lacks is substantial ethical custom, the rationality of a state in which it can have reality. In the rational state there is no slavery; that is found only where the spirit has not yet attained this point—where the Idea thus still has aspects according to

---

62. GW 27 [3] 821 (~ GW 27 [1] 81).
63. GW 27 [1] 81 (~ GW 27 [2] 513).
64. GW 27 [1] 84-85 (~ GW 27 [2] 518; GW 27 [4] 1229).
65. Some sources (other than Herodotus and Montesquieu) from which Hegel may have drawn for his understanding of sub-Saharan Africa: T. E. Bowditch, *Mission from Cape Coast Castle to Ashantee* (London: Murray, 1819); Hugh Clapperton, *Journal of a Second Expedition into the Interior of Africa, to which is added, Journal of Richard Lander from Kano to the Sea-coast* (London: Murray, 1829—see GW 27 [4] 1228). G. A. Cavazzi da Montecuccolo, *Istorica descrizione de'tre regni Congo, Matamba, et Angola* (Bologna: Monti, 1687); C. Ritter, *Die Erdkunde im Verhältnis zur Natur und zur Geschichte des Menschen, oder allgemeine, vergleichende Geographie, als sichere Grundlage des Studiums und Unterrichts in physicakalischen und historischen Wissenschaften*, 2 vols. (Berlin: Reimer, 1817-18—see GW 27 [1] 82; GW 27 [4] 1215); J. K. Tuckey, *Narrative of an Expedition to Explore the River Zaire, to which is added the Journal of Professor Smith* (New York: Kirk & Mercein, 1818).

which it is still only an ought to be. Slavery, therefore, is necessary at those stages where the state has not yet arrived at rationality. It is an essential phase in the transition to a higher stage.

[66]The negroes are led by Europeans into slavery and sold to America. In spite of that, their lot in their own land is even worse, since there a slavery quite as absolute exists; for it is the foundation of slavery overall that the human does not yet have a consciousness of one's freedom, and consequently sinks down to a thing, to an object of no value. ...

[122] The doctrine that we deduce from this condition of slavery among the negroes, and that constitutes the only side of the question that has an interest for our inquiry, is the doctrine that we know from the Idea: that the state-of-nature itself is the condition of absolute and thoroughgoing injustice. Every intermediate grade between it and the actualization of the rational state retains elements and aspects of injustice; therefore we find slavery even in the Greek and Roman states, as we do serfdom down to the most recent times. But being thus present, in a state, it is itself an essential phase of the advance from the merely isolated, sensual existence, an essential phase of disciplining, a mode of coming to participate in a higher ethical custom and the cultural education connected with it. Slavery is in and for itself injustice, for the essence of humanity is freedom; but for this, humanity must first become matured. The gradual abolition of slavery is therefore more measured and more just than its sudden sublation.

[67]We will see how this principle has lived only in religion at first, not yet in government and the state, and moreover, that there was a struggle in both the latter. The human being is free; but not from the beginning: there is no state-of-nature in which the human is happy, knowing, and aware of all.

[68]In the first distinguishing of human beings over and against nature, the human is still uncultured, not awakened to ethical custom, to consciousness of his rational freedom; but the human has at least this feeling: that he is on one side, and on the other side is nature; by him the natural must be subdued; it counts for nothing over against him. This he knows, and so do we; but we call the spiritual the divine; and in natural humans, the splitting off of the finite spirit in and for

---

66. 1840, 118, 122 (~ GW 27 [2] 521; GW 27 [3] 841–42; GW 27 [4] 1226).
67. GW 27 [4] 1166 [Heimann].
68. GW 27 [3] 838.

itself is not yet present. The human is what holds sway over nature, but we do not mean by that the human, the spiritual, in its immediacy.

[69]Overall the stage of culture at which the negro finds himself may be more nearly recognized in their religion. The primary thing that we ourselves mean by this conception is the consciousness on the part of humanity of a higher power (even when this is conceived only as a power of nature) over and against which the human being establishes oneself as a weaker, lower; religion begins with the consciousness that there is something higher than the human; but as regards the negroes as depicted by Herodotus, he says [2.32-33] that they are all *sorcerers*: now in sorcery[70] there is not the representation of a god, of an ethically customary faith that is present; rather, sorcery established that the human is the highest power, that the human alone commands; he holds himself as commander over against the power of nature; sorcery has therefore nothing to do with a spiritual reverence for divinity, nor with an empire of right. . . . [1224] And although people are necessarily conscious of dependence upon nature—for they need storms, the rain, cessation of the rainy period—yet this does not conduct them to the consciousness of something higher: it is they who command the elements, and this is the sorcery. Their kings have a class of ministers through whom they command the changes in nature, and so every place possesses in this way its sorcerers.

. . . They make their power also objective in their consciousness—but not as independent, as having being in and for itself: the worship is of *fetishes* (a Portuguese word). . . . They make offerings to them and requests, but there is always the consciousness that they themselves have made the fetish, which remains therefore always under their willfulness; . . . if any mischance occurs that the fetish has not averted, they destroy the fetish and so get rid of it, making another immediately.

What does point to something higher, however, is the *devotion to the dead,* in which their deceased ancestors [1225] and forefathers count

---

69. GW 27 [4], 1223-25, 1227 (~ GW 27 [2] 518-22; GW 27 [3] 833, 837-41; 1840, 115-17, 123).

70. On sorcery as "the whole first form of religion," see the 1824 *Lectures on the Philosophy of Religion* in GW 29 [1] 235-64, esp. 241: "in sorcery's self-conscious sense of power over nature a universal science begins to come into being . . . sorcery is present in all peoples and in every time, but in the higher religions a mediation enters with the objectivizing"; and the 1827 version, GW 29 [2] 83-91, esp. 84, "sorcery, which we cannot hold worthy of the name of religion," and 85, sorcery "is this, that the spiritual is the power over nature; but this spiritual is not yet as spirit, not yet in its universality, but is only the singular, contingent self-consciousness, the empirical self-consciousness of the human being, who knows that oneself in one's self-consciousness—even though it is only simple desire—is higher than nature, that it is a power over nature." See also the 1831 version, GW 29 [2] 245-46.

as a power over against the living. Their conception in the matter is that these ancestors exercise vengeance and inflict upon humans various injuries, in the sense in which this was believed of witches in the Middle Ages. Yet the power of the dead is not held superior to that of the living, for the negroes command their dead and lay spells upon them; in this way what is substantial remains always in the power of the subject. The negroes have the further belief that the human being does *not naturally* die, and they ascribe the causes, as well as the causes of the process of illness, not to natural causes: even as in the Middle Ages everything bad was ascribed to witches, so the negroes see everything as sorcery that comes from enemies or the dead, and they turn themselves to their own sorcery in order to get revenge on their living enemies or to punish the dead. In this is the elevation of humanity over nature, but so that the chance will of humans stands higher than nature, which one looks upon as a means, to which one does not pay the respect of treating it in a way conditioned by itself, but which one commands; the will of humans is accordingly posited as the highest; there is present no respect for a truly higher; and it follows from this that humans have no respect for themselves—since it is first with the consciousness of a higher essence that the human being attains value, and thereby arrives at a true respect. Among the negroes there is present this *lack of respect for humanity* in relation to one another, and this lack of respect is the foundational determination in respect to their justice and their customary ethics....

[1227] There are also among the negroes *states*—if one want to call them such: a master stands at the top, for sensual savagery can be held together only by despotic force.

[71]At this point we leave Africa, not to make any mention of it again. For it is no historical part of the world; it has no movement and development to exhibit. Historical movements in it—that is, in its northern part—belong to the Asiatic and European world. ... What we understand by Africa proper is the unhistorical, undeveloped spirit, still encased in the natural, and that had to be presented here only as on the threshold of world-history.

Now we find ourselves, after we have pushed this away from ourselves, for the first time at the real theater of world-history. It now only remains for us to give a prefatory sketch of the geographical basis of Asia and of Europe.

---

71. 1840, 123.

"Asia, the World of Dawning"

[72]Thus far we have viewed natural conditions as being more negative for world-history. In Asia they become positive. World-history is spirit in the element of worldliness; thus we must also recognize the natural and the corporeal in it.... In Asia dawns the light of self-consciousness as the state; so, first, the physical localities are to be considered.... [Griesheim: Asia is the land of antithesis.]

[87] The chief antitheses here in Asia are a highland vs. wide, tremendous plains. These two localities are necessary as a source for wholly antithetical human dispositions. What is distinctive is the essential interaction between them, the mountain dwellers with their inner restlessness, the valley dwellers with their rootedness....

[88] The second part is mid-Asia, where the mountain peoples predominate, and where we must also reckon with the Arabs. It has the character of the highland, but in plains. This is the sphere of antithesis at its greatest freedom, as light and darkness, where there occurs overall the abstraction of spiritual intuition, of this One—above all the Mohammedan. Persia also belongs here.

[73]The rearing of cattle is the business of the uplands, agriculture and the culture of trade is the work of the valley dwellers, while commerce and the art of sailing constitute the third and last principle. Patriarchal independence is closely bound up with the first principle, property and the relation of master and slave with the second, and civil freedom with the third principle. In the uplands, the various kinds of cattle breeding, the rearing of horses, camels, and sheep (not so much of oxen), and the calm nomad life go with the very different, roving and restless character of their conquests.... More interesting of course are the peoples of the plains. In agriculture alone, surely, lies the cessation of roving; it demands foresight and solicitude for the future. Reflection on a universal is thereby awakened; and herein, surely, lies the principle of property and of trade. In cultured lands of this kind, China, India, and Babylonia have risen. But since these peoples that have dwelled in these lands have shut themselves up, and have not appropriated the principle of the sea, or did so only at the period when their cultural education was coming into being, and as their navigation remained without influence on their culture, a relation to the rest of history could

---

72. GW 27 [1] 86–88 (~ GW 27 [4] 86).
73. 1840, 125–26 (~ GW 27 [2] 528).

only exist in their case through their being sought out and investigated by others. . . . [126] What is most remarkable in this land, it has not kept for itself, but sent over to Europe. It lays down the origination of all religious and of all political principles, but in Europe their development has first taken place.

"The Nature of Europe"

[74]In the European nature no single type of nature stands out; here, rather, one form of nature is offset by the others. The soil here is such as to bring with it freedom from the forces of nature, so that here, universal humanity can emerge. . . .

For Asia the sea has no significance; the Asian peoples have shut themselves off from it. China proper has no ships, and in India, religion positively prohibits the art of ships. The Egyptians, too, at the time of their highest flourishing, [94] had no navigation on the sea, although river navigation was very lively. . . .

A European state can only in connection with the sea be great. The sea indeed separates land; but it connects humans. The sea is the distinctive feature lacking in Asian life. This is the going forth of life beyond itself. . . . This commerce becomes something courageous, noble. From it arises a distinct consciousness of individual independence, of freedom in antithesis to the constraint of the commerce. Courage stands at the heart of the goal itself; a courage is essentially bound up with the understanding, bound up with the greatest cunning. . . . [95] The ship, this swan, so easy in its movement, is an instrument that pays highest honor to the understanding. This audacity of the understanding is what is missing from the splendid edifice of Asian ethically customary life.

[75]The Mediterranean Sea sunders the old world, but in such a way as to facilitate communication. . . . [82] The Mediterranean Sea is characterized by its many gulfs; therefore it is not an ocean that offers an empty and endless journey out into the undetermined, to which human beings can only relate negatively. A great difference among peoples is between those who let themselves go to sea and those who avoid it. The Mediterranean Sea of itself calls human beings to take to it because on the whole it is a border, and thus has such a positive relation to them. . . . [90t] This sea is very characteristic; this midpoint is what

---
74. GW 27 [1] 93–95 (~ GW 27 [2] 529–30; GW 27 [3] 828–29; GW 27 [4] 1219–20).
75. GW 27 [1] 81–82, 90t (~ GW 27 [2] 530; GW 27 [3] 821, 828–29).

invigorates, leading all together; without it, world history could not exist....

[Griesheim: The character of Greek life comes forth from the soil, a coastline that leads to individual isolation. Thus the land of Greece is a reflection of the splintering within Greek life. The Roman Empire could also not have been established in the middle of the continent; Roman world-dominion could rather exist only on the sea, and indeed on the Mediterranean Sea, the center of the ancient world.]

"The Picture of the Whole"

[76]The preceding discussion has now brought us closer to the principles that underlie world-history. We want to proceed to these principles of world-history themselves. Now, therefore, the picture of the whole lies before us.

[77]World-history is the disciplining of the unlimitedness of the natural will to the universal, to subjective freedom. The East knew and knows only that one is free; the Greek and Roman world, that some are free; the Germanic world knows that all are free. The first form that we observe in history is despotism, but not with complete willfulness; the [1231] second is democracy and aristocracy; the third is monarchy.

In regard to the understanding of this division it is to be remarked that *substantial freedom* is to be distinguished from *subjective freedom*: substantial freedom is the reason of the will; this reason expands insofar as it develops into the state; this is the determinacy of reason, and is thereby not the insight, the will, that is subjective freedom simply as present—not the will that determines itself in the individual self, the reflectiveness of the individual in one's conscience; instead, the laws, the commandments, stand fast in and for themselves, while over and against these the subject maintains oneself in total service. Now insofar as these laws do not correspond to their own principle, the subject is like a child who without his own will and his own insight obeys the parents; but as subjective freedom emerges and the human rises up in spirit from external actuality, the opposition of reflectiveness enters in, containing the negation of the actuality; this is a distancing from the immediate present; this pulling back contains an antithesis that builds itself up within itself; from this antithesis is built God, the divine that

---

76. GW 27 [1] 95 (~ GW 27 [2] 530).
77. GW 27 [4] 1230-32 (~ GW 27 [2] 530-31; 1840, 128-29).

is in thought, and that stands over and against the subject as a beyond: this God is a substantiality, but as one that is spiritual.

In that immediate consciousness belonging to the East, these two—the substantial and the immediate being—[1232] are not yet distinguished. The substantial does also distinguish itself over and against the individual, but the antithesis is not yet in the spirit.

This is prefatory, to make understandable the division.

The East is that with which we have to begin. In its political life we find realized here rational freedom, developing itself but without advancing to subjective freedom in itself. This is the *childhood of history*. Magnificent edifices structure the oriental empires, in which we find all rational ordinances and arrangements, but in such a way that individuals are mere accidents. These revolve around a center, around the master, who, first as patriarch, stands at the head—not as despot in the sense of the Roman Caesarean empire, but as enforcing the ethically customary and substantial.

[78]This first dimension is the state as based on the family relationship. We have here to consider an organization based on paternal providential care maintaining the whole by punishment, admonition, and discipline. It is a prosaic realm, an enduring realm, an unhistorical history, without having antithesis within itself, so that such a condition does not change itself internally, but from without; and the true change lies only within, when this condition changes itself only when something external breaks in.... [97] States that stand on the same given principle are restless and so are continuously falling, with the new that replaces also sinking into the same falling, and in this restless change there is no true advance, but it remains eternally one and the same.

But inasmuch as the state is outwardly directed, a premonition of the individual principle enters. Conflict and struggle entail a self-concentrating into individuality. This premonition first appears, however, as powerless individuals, as universal, unconscious principle, as something natural, as light, which is not yet the light of the personal soul. This second shape, that of restless alteration that produces nothing, the shape of time, occurs in the Middle East, and is called the boyhood, in which the states are at odds with one another. This expands itself into the age of youth, the *Greek* realm.

---

78. GW 27 [1] 96–98 (~ GW 27 [2] 531–34; GW 27 [3] 818–19; GW 27 [4] 1232–36).

Realm and state are distinct here, for the essence of Greece was at the beginning not a state but a multitude of states: that is here the characteristic. This is the realm of beautiful freedom. The principle of this configuration is that of naïve, ethically customary unity; but as individual personality, the single person feels himself to be free as an individual unity with universal substance. This is the realm of beauty, the most cheerful, most charming realm, but also the utterly ephemeral one, the quickly wilting bloom, the inwardly most restless shape—since through reflection it itself must pervert its soundness. For beauty unites the antithetical principles, and the principle of individual freedom is precisely the opposite of naïve ethical custom. Thus constant unrest is here. [98] Personhood's reflection can be sustained in unity with immediate ethical custom for only a moment; reflection tears it apart; ... and through the power that subjectivity exercises against the naïve universality, immediacy must be elevated to abstract thought of universality. The Greeks intuited their unity; the Romans reflected upon it.

And so we step into the Roman world, into the adulthood of hard work that hearkens to duty, serving a universal purpose, a state, in universal principles, the laws: and this is operative neither in the willfulness of the master nor in its own beautiful willfulness. Here is the sacrifice of individuality to universality, a universality in which the individual goes under and attains one's own purpose only in the universal. Such an empire seems to be made for eternity, especially when it conducts itself also in accord with the subjective principle of satisfaction as religion—when it becomes the Holy Roman Empire. But we saw this empire fall two decades ago. As abstract universality, it is the work of the Roman world to incorporate the individual peoples, to subjugate them in its abstract universality.

The transition to the next principle is to be seen as the internal struggle of abstract universality against the principle of particular subjectivity.

[79]The development of this empire proceeds in two dimensions. On one side, as based on reflection, on abstract universality, it has the express, explicit antithesis in itself: it thus establishes essentially in itself the struggle that that antithesis supposes, with the necessary result that willful individuality—the purely contingent and thoroughly worldly power of one master—gets the better of that abstract universality. ...

---

79. 1840, 133–35 (~ GW 27 [2] 535–36).

For when in the course of history personhood gains the ascendant, and the breaking up into atoms can only be externally restrained, then the subjective might of mastery comes forward as if summoned to this task.... The individual seeks in the developing private law the consolation for the lost freedom: this is the purely *worldly* reconciliation of the antithesis. But now the pain inflicted by despotism comes to be felt, and spirit, driven back into its utmost depths, leaves the godless world, seeks for a reconciliation in itself, and begins now the life of innerness, of a consummate concrete innerness, that possesses at the same time a substantiality that is not grounded only in external existence. There thus arises the spiritual reconciliation within, where the individual personality is purified and elevated into universality—into a subjectivity that is universal for itself, into a divine personality. To the merely worldly empire, this spiritual one is in opposition, as the empire of a subjectivity that has attained to the knowledge of itself—and indeed in its essence: the empire of the actualized spirit.

With this, the Germanic realm enters, the fourth [134] essential phase of world-history. This phase would answer, in the comparison with the periods of human life, to *old age*. The old age of nature is weakness; the old age of spirit is its perfect maturity and strength—in which it returns to unity, but as spirit.

This realm begins with the reconciliation that occurs in Christianity; but it is only *in itself*, and it therefore begins with the tremendous opposition between the spiritual, religious principle, and the barbarian actuality. For spirit as the consciousness of an inner world is, at the commencement, itself still abstract. Worldliness is consequently given over to brutality and willfulness. This brutality and willfulness encounter first the *Mohammedan* principle—the enlightenment of the oriental world. We find it developing itself later, and more rapidly, than Christianity; for the latter needed eight centuries to grow up into its worldly configuration. But the principle of the Germanic world attained concrete actuality only through the Germanic nations. The opposition between the spiritual principle in the ecclesiastical state, with the brutal and wild barbarism in the secular state, is here present. The secular ought to be in harmony with the spiritual principle, but that is only an ought. The secular power forsaken by the spirit must first vanish in opposition to the ecclesiastical; but, in that this latter degrades itself to mere secularity, it loses its determinacy and power. From this corruption of the ecclesiastical—that is, of the church—results the higher form of rational thought; spirit once more driven back upon itself produces its work in an intellectual shape and becomes capable of realizing the rational out of the secular principle alone. Thus it happens that . . . the empire of thought is actually brought into being. The antithesis of church and state vanishes; the spirit finds itself in actuality and [135] develops this latter as an organic existence in itself. The state no longer follows the church, and is no longer subordinate to it. The latter asserts no prerogative, and the spiritual is no longer estranged from the state. Freedom has found the means of realizing its concept, with its truth. This is the goal of world-history, and we have to traverse the long way that has been thus cursorily traced out. Length of time is something thoroughly relative, and spirit belongs to eternity. A specified length of time means nothing to it.

[80]So freedom finds its concept in actualization, having built itself into an objective system of an intrinsically organized existence. This is the goal: that the spirit builds itself into a nature, a world, that is in accord with it, so that the subject of its concept of spirit finds actualization in this second nature, in this actuality achieved through the concept of the spirit.

[81]These are, therefore, the moments to be considered. The first was the substantial immediacy of ethical custom; the second the antithesis of subjectivity and abstract universality; the third the unity of the subjective with universality.

---

80. GW 27 [2] 537.
81. GW 27 [1] 102.

CHAPTER 2

The Oriental World, Part One
China

¹The oriental world has as its character the substantiality of the ethically customary, and substantial power displays itself in it: the ethically customary determinations are expressed as laws, but in such a way that the subjective will is governed by these laws as by an external power, so that formal freedom, disposition, conscience, is not present; the laws are administered in an external way, and there is a compulsory right. Our civil right indeed also contains compulsory duties, because this right rests on the abstract personhood—in that I have property, I can therein be compelled; but this compulsion for us pertains only to what is external; the properly customary ethics is something else. Now when the ethically customary feelings in the family are commanded in an external way, this is entirely correct as regards the content, but in such a way that innerness is itself made external; there is a lack of [1237] disposition, feeling, will.

²There is no want of a will to command it, but of a will to perform as commanded, from within. Because spirit has not yet attained innerness, it manifests itself overall as natural spirituality. The external and the internal, law and insight within, still form an undivided unity, as do

---

1. GW 27 [4] 1236–37 (~ GW 27 [2] 538–39; GW 27 [3] 846–47; 1840, 136).
2. 1840, 137–40 (~ GW 27 [2] 538–42; GW 27 [3] 846–50; GW 27 [4] 1236–38).

the religion and the state. The constitution is on the whole a theocracy, and the realm of divinity is also a secular realm, as the secular realm is no less divine. What we call God is not yet in the oriental consciousness, for our God emerges first in an elevation to the supersensual; and we obey because what we do, we do from ourselves—whereas there, the law is what counts in itself, without a need for this subjective confirmation. The human does not have therein the intuition of one's own self, but of a will that is thoroughly alien to one. . . .

With *China* and the *Mongols* (the realm of theocratic mastery), history begins. Both have the patriarchal for their principle, and in the sense that in China it is developed into an organized system of secular statehood—[138] while among the Mongols, it limits itself to the simplicity of a spiritual, religious, encompassing realm. In China the monarch is chief as patriarch: the laws of the state are in part legally just, in part moral, so that the internal law—the knowledge on the part of the individual of the content of one's will, as one's own innerness—even this is present as an external commandment. The sphere of innerness does not then attain to maturity here, since the moral laws are treated as state laws, and the legally just for its part contains the mere appearance of the moral. All that we call subjectivity is concentrated in the head of state, who, in what he determines, acts for what is best—the health and piety of the whole.

In contrast to this secular realm stands, as spiritual, the Mongol realm, over which is the Lama, who is honored as God. In this latter realm of the spiritual there is no secular life of the state.

In the second configuration, the *Indian* realm, we see first the breaking up of the unity of the state-organism—of the perfect machinery as exists in China: the several powers appear as dissevered and free over and against each other. The different castes are of course fixed; but through the religion that established them, they become natural distinctions. Thereby the individuals are still further stripped of selfhood—although it could appear as if they won the distinctions by becoming free, in that the organism of the state no longer is, as in China, determined and arranged by a substantial subject, but the distinctions that exist come from nature, and become differences of caste. The unity, in which these divisions must finally come together, is religious; and thus originates theocratic aristocracy and its despotism.[3] Here indeed begins, therefore,

---

3. "In China is theocratic despotism; here, *theocratic aristocracy*"—GW 27 [3] 848.

the distinction of the spiritual consciousness over and against secular conditions; but as differentiation is the main consideration, so also there is [139] in the religion the principle of the isolation of the essential phases of the Idea—which entails what is most extreme, namely the representation of an abstract One and simple God, vs. the universal sensual power of nature. The connection of the two is only a constant exchange, a restless hurrying from one extreme to the other, a wild giddiness without consequence, which must appear as madness to a regulated, intelligent consciousness.

The third great configuration—presenting a contrast to the immovable unity of China and to the wild and sweeping, unbound unrest of India—is the *Persian* realm. China is entirely and exactly oriental; India we might compare with Greece, Persia on the other hand with Rome. In Persia, namely, the theocratic power appears as a monarchy. Now monarchy is that kind of constitution that does indeed unite the members under the top, over all—but regards this neither as the absolute, universally determining, nor as the willful mastery sitting on the throne, but as a will whose legality is shared by its subjects. So we have a general principle, a law, lying at the basis of all, but which, as still natural, is burdened by the antithesis. The representation, therefore, that spirit makes of itself at this stage is of a wholly natural kind: light. This universal principle is as much a determination for the monarch as for each of the subjects, and the Persian spirit is accordingly clear, illuminated—the Idea of a people in pure ethical custom, as in a holy community. But this has, on the side of its being a natural community, the antithesis in it still not overcome; and its holiness contains the determination of an ought. On the other hand, this antithesis manifests itself in Persia as the empire over hostile peoples, and the union of differentiated nations. The Persian unity is not that abstract one of the Chinese realm, [140] but it is determined as mastery over many and various peoples, which it unites under the mild force of universality as a blessing sun shining over all, awakening and warming. This universal, as only the root, leaves all the several members free for what may be expansion and ramification. In the system of these several peoples, all the various principles also confront one another and exist together. We find, in this multitude of nations, roving nomads; then we see in Babylonia and Syria commerce and business developing, with the wildest sensuality, the most released turbulence. By way of the coasts, there is connection outside. In the midst of this confusion the spiritual God of the Jews encounters us—like Brahm, existing only for thought, yet jealous and excluding from his being, and sublating, all distinctly particular manifestations such as are freely allowed in other religions.

This Persian empire, then, since it can tolerate these several principles, exhibits within itself the living antithesis, and is not abstract and calm, as China and India, and makes an actual transition in world-history.[4]

If Persia forms the external transition to Greek life, the inner transition is mediated through *Egypt*. Here the abstract antitheses become broken through: a breaking through that effects their solution. This reconciliation, only in itself, exhibits much more the struggle of the most contradictory determinations, which are not yet capable of unifying themselves, but, setting up this birth as the problem to be solved, make themselves a riddle for themselves and for others, the solution of which is first the *Greek* world.

[5]We begin then with the Asiatic principle. The valley plains are the terrain of life here, not the mountains and ravines. . . . First we go to the Chinese river valleys, and from there to India, to the river valley of the Ganges and of the Indus; to this we link mention of the Tibetans and Mongols. The second is the mid-Asiatic life in the river valley of the Tigris and Euphrates, where the state comes into conflict with the mountains.

"The Empire of China"

[6]We begin with this empire, as with the oldest;[7] its principle, however, is of such substantiality that the oldest is also the newest—since history shows us China very early containing the seed from which it then developed itself, and very early developing to the organization and to the condition in which we now see it: so that in China the newest is also the oldest. The opposition between objective, rational will, and subjective freedom, insight proper, does not come forth—[1239] and this opposition is that which is the principle of all movement and thereby all change; China maintains itself in the unity of objective and subjective willing and has become this fixity, so that the present condition has become also that of the most ancient times.

---

4. "The third configuration is the Persian monarchy. . . . We had in China theocratic despotism and in India theocratic aristocracy; we have here the rule of this principle, *theocratic monarchy*"—GW 27 [3] 849.

5. GW 27 [1] 102 (~ GW 27 [4] 1237).

6. GW 27 [4] 1238-39 (~ GW 27 [2] 542-43; GW 27 [3] 851; 1840, 141-42).

7. For some major sources (in addition to Montesquieu's *Spirit of the Laws*) upon which Hegel seems to have drawn for his understanding of China, see the bibliography at the end of this chapter.

[8]Subjective movement is still wanting, so every change is excluded, and the fixedness of a character that recurs eternally takes the place of what we would call the historical. China and India lie, as it were, still outside world-history, as the presupposition of essential phases [142] whose combination will be their first living progress.

[9]The tremendous population of China proper, from which Chinese Tartary is excluded (although these are under the immediate mastery of China), stands under a most highly ordered government that is most just, most mild, most wise. The laws are developed, and agriculture, commerce, industry, and sciences flourish. There are cities with more than a million inhabitants.

What is even more astonishing is that this people has a continuous, well-ordered, entirely believable history that stretches over five thousand years with great exactitude—and, unlike the Greek and Roman history, more believable. No land in the world has such [104] a continuous, credible, ancient history. This realm remains always independent for itself, remaining always what it has been, although it was conquered, in the thirteenth century, by Genghis Khan, and later, after the time of our Thirty Years War, by the Manchu Tatars—without being changed. And so it is an unhistorical empire, for it has developed itself in itself undisturbed, not destroyed from without. No alien principle came to establish itself in place of the ancient one. In that we are speaking about the most ancient history of this empire, we are not speaking of something past but instead of a shape that it has today. (The same is the case in India.) The principle of this empire is given in universal terms, and the wonder is that it is simply the natural concept of the state, and brings with it a developed culture that has not changed the first childish principle. . . .

[105] Every people has original books that contain its myths, the ancient elements of its intuition, set down in a sensory mode, giving the development of established relationships. Such an original book is for us the Bible, for the Greeks Homer.

[10]Among the Chinese these books are called "kings," and constitute the foundation of all their studies. The *Shu-king* contains the history, treats of the government of the ancient kings, and gives the statutes enacted by this or that monarch. The *Y-king* consists of figures, which

---

8. 1840, 141–42.
9. GW 27 [1] 103–5 (~ GW 27 [3] 851–53; GW 27 [4] 1239).
10. 1840, 143–44 (~ GW 27 [1] 105–9; GW 27 [2] 544–45; GW 27 [3] 853–54; GW 27 [4] 1240–42).

have been regarded as the bases of the Chinese writing, and this book is also considered the groundwork of the Chinese meditation. For it begins with the abstractions of unity and duality, and then treats of the concrete existence of such abstract forms of thought. Lastly, the *Shi-king* is the book of the oldest poems of various sorts. . . . Besides these three books of archives that are specially honored and studied, there are two others, less important: the *Li-li* (or *Li-ling*) that records the customs and ceremonial observances pertaining to the imperial dignity, and that of the state functionaries—with an appendix, *Yo-king*, treating of music; and the *Tshun-tsin*, the chronicle of the kingdom Lu, where Confucius appeared. These books are the groundwork of the history, the ethical custom, and the laws of China. . . .

[144] We can of course not go further into the details of this history, which itself does not develop, and would hinder our development.

"The Patriarchal Relation is Predominant"

[11]To consider the *spirit* of the constitution, which has always remained the same: it follows from the general principle. This is, namely, the unmediated unity of the substantial spirit and the individual; this, however, is the spirit of the family, which is here extended over the most populous land. The essential phase of subjectivity—that is to say, the reflection upon itself of the individual will, in antithesis to the substantial, as the power in which it is absorbed, or, the recognition of this power as its own essentiality, in which it knows itself free—is here not yet present. The universal will displays its activity immediately through that of the individual: the latter has no self-cognizance at all in antithesis to the substance, which it does not yet regard as a power standing over against it—as, for example, in Judaism, the jealous God is known as the negation of the individual. Here in China the universal will immediately says what the individual is to do, and the latter complies and obeys with proportionate renunciation of reflection and self. If one does not obey, if one thus virtually separates oneself from the substance, inasmuch as this separation is not mediated by a retreat within, the punishment one undergoes does not affect one internally, but simply one's outward existence. The essential phase of subjectivity is therefore as much missing from this state totality as the state totality is, on its side,

---

11. 1840, 147-48 (~ GW 27 [1] 113; GW 27 [2] 548; GW 27 [3] 871-73; GW 27 [4] 1244).

altogether without a foundation in the dispositions. For the substance is an unmediated individual, the emperor, whose law constitutes the disposition. Nevertheless, this absence of disposition is not willfulness, which itself would indicate disposition of will that is subjectivity and mobility; instead, here the universal is what counts—the substance, which, still inflexible, resembles nothing but itself.

Now this relation, expressed more closely and more conformably with its conception, is the *family*. On this form of ethically customary binding alone rests the Chinese state, and it is objective family piety that characterizes it. The Chinese know themselves as belonging to their family, and at the same time as children of the state. In the family itself there are no personhoods, [148] for the substantial unity in which they exist as members of it is the unity of consanguinity and the natural. In the state they have as little personhood; for there the patriarchal relation is predominant, and the government rests on the paternal foresight of the emperor, who keeps all in order.

[12]No duty is so strictly commanded as that of children to elders. Children have no property, are perpetual minors, must serve their elders, care for them, be deferential to them, and must mourn them for three years, during which period they may not hold any office, marry, or attend public gatherings. During this period of mourning even the emperor does not rule and may not marry. [114] The mother is also honored, even as is the father. . . . The father is responsible for the wrongs of the children. The harshest punishments are decreed for wrongs committed by family members against one another or for those of children against the parents. If a son speaks disparagingly of his elders he is strangled; if he raises his hand against them he is strangled; if he injures them, he is grabbed with pincers and torn to pieces. [Griesheim: Younger brothers are subject to older brothers in the same way. If they justly accuse of wrongdoing some person who outranks them, then they themselves are unjustly exiled, beheaded.] . . . [115] A father has an interest in having children to take care of his burial after his death, to honor and to adorn the grave. At distinguished graves the relatives mourn for months. . . . In addition to maintaining and adorning the grave there is a third high duty, to honor the ancestors.

---

12. GW 27 [1] 113–15 (~ GW 27 [2] 549–50, 557–59; GW 27 [3] 873–75; GW 27 [4] 1244–46; 1840, 148–50).

[13][Griesheim: The empire is not a theocracy like that of the Turks, where the Quran is the book of divine and human law; and the rule is not unlimited like that of the Hebrews or Jews, whose ruler only expresses the will of God; likewise it is no aristocracy of birth, no feudal establishment; also there is no dependence on wealth as in England; rather, the monarch alone wields the highest, all pervasive force. The laws are not laws that conflict with the will of the monarch, but instead the kind of laws by which all things are maintained in accord with his will. The government has a wholly paternal outlook. The emperor has all matters reported to him, and sharpens or softens judgments by giving a rightful account of his reasons. He frequently makes to his people very wide-ranging declarations about his actions that are published in the court newspaper of Beijing.] . . .

The emperor necessarily must have subordinates, for he cannot govern by himself. These officials are of two kinds, both called mandarins, and number fifteen thousand scholars and twenty thousand military personnel. To become a mandarin scholar requires great studies. . . . [117] By these officials is the empire governed. . . . The officials are honored like the emperor by the people. . . . [118] In office, the mandarin is responsible for everything. He does not escape responsibility for anything, as if no blame at all should rest on him. Failings incur the harshest punishment. The most trifling matter can lead to the greatest punishment. [Griesheim: The mandarin has a sword hanging over his head.] . . .

As for the rights of the citizen, it is noteworthy that there are no castes and no birthrights other than that regarding inheritance. Whoever wants to be admitted to the class of mandarins [119] must distinguish himself by his aptitude. Only the foremost mandarins have the right to insist that their sons occupy a post. But these are very minor. So there is no class of officials to which only certain families belong. Thus there is no preference based on birth. As regards private property, this was introduced in China, and for its protection there are laws and well-ordered courts. . . . A third factor pertaining to rights of citizens is that slavery is still practiced. Any father can even sell a son. Also, the government can have committed into slavery the women, children, and concubines. But then the women take their own lives. . . .

---

13. GW 27 [1] 116-22, 126-27 (~ GW 27 [2] 550-57; GW 27 [3] 859-69; GW 27 [4] 1246-48, 1253-55; 1840, 150-60).

The whole rests upon the person of a monarch, on his officials, whose [120] activity derives from him, and on oversight of these officials that goes from top down to bottom. This hierarchy constitutes the cohesiveness, and its main feature is that the reins are tightly held. Every inferior is overseen by his superior. What matters, then, is the moral personality of the emperor; for there are no spheres that, acting independently on their own, take care of their own domain as do social classes and the like; rather, everything derives solely from the emperor. At the apex is an individual person with unlimited power. In the long series of these emperors, over four to five millennia, China has had a great number of good rulers. The oriental worthiness emerges as moral excellence....

[121] Such a constitution of the emperor's individuality is in any case contingent, although the upbringing of royal princes is very much directed to inculcating this morality into the character, for all depends upon it. [Griesheim: They live, on the one hand, in strict orderliness, but on the other hand they live being treated with distinct, full deference; so it is always contingent whether they will become moral in character.] If the tension from the center allows it, when the emperor does not watch over the state, then the whole comes apart, for there is present no lawful power, no conscience, formed for itself, of the officials. Instead, what ought to be law is something determined from the top down; the laws thus depend on the individuality of the emperor. And this loosening of the reins can readily occur even without the throne being occupied by a tyrant who has wild desires (as indeed French tragedies portray tyrants). There only need be a certain indolence, a faith or confidence of the monarch in his associates, his spouse, etc., and so the slackening sets in. And such confidence is quite possible with a moral upbringing.... [122] So the empire can fall into a condition of injustice, of willfulness, of domination through force by the officials. This happens often in the Orient, even under the government of well-intentioned, noble princes....

[126] Among the Chinese the being-for-oneself is not respected, and so honor has no place there, and neither does the product that comes forth from inner freedom.... To consider this abstract principle in concrete detail: ... to begin with, what was already brought forward, that in China slavery is still found. One can sell oneself, and parents can sell their children. A second point is punishment overall. When a crime is committed, the entire family—wife, children, parents, brothers, friends—share the punishments; and this is wholly contrary to the

recognition of moral freedom, contrary to the imputation of wrongdoing, to moral self-determination as such. . . . [127] A further punishment is corporal disciplining, to which even the highest mandarin is subject. Such disciplining is incompatible with our sense of honor. . . . Corporal punishment can in one sense count for little, since the human being is only injured in his lowest aspect, merely outwardly, as a mere living existence. But corporal punishment is the most humiliating because the human being so afflicted is thought of as being coerced with regard to his inner being. This presumes the *absolute* connection between inner and outer aspects, yet the human being knows oneself as morally independent of this connection.

"The State Has the Sciences under Its Control"

[14]The lack of proper innerness extends itself also to the sciences. . . . [131] They pursue the sciences but not in the free interest of science. Science and cultural education, compiling of information, is mainly empirical in nature: not theoretical, not a free interest of thought as thought, but instead the sciences stand in service to the state, to needs. The state has the sciences under its control, as means; and so a simply scholarly life, or simple interest in science as science, is not called for by the state. . . . [133] Now as for the science itself, there is a lot of praise for it, especially for Confucius. His educating is mainly moralistic. He was a moralist overall, not actually a philosopher; for theory that engages itself in thinking as such is not found in him. For a couple of years he was a government official, and his teachings are expressed like the proverbs of Solomon. For science, something more is required. With Plato, Aristotle, Socrates, he is not to be compared. He was about what Solon was, if we understand by this that he was a lawgiver of *his own* people.

"Ideal Art Cannot Flourish among Them"

[15]In regard to the fine arts the consequence of all this is that ideal art cannot flourish among them. In the mechanics of art, the Chinese are, to be sure, skilled; [136] but they lack the creative power of the spirit, the free innerness; creativity is not to be expected here. They have

---

14. GW 27 [1] 130–31, 133 (~ GW 27 [2] 559–60; GW 27 [3] 875–78; GW 27 [4] 1248–50; 1840, 163–67).
15. GW 27 [1] 135–36 (~ GW 27 [2] 561; GW 27 [3] 878–80; GW 27 [4] 1251; 1840, 168).

beautiful landscape painting, they have portraits, but they never attain the brilliance that is produced in ours by means of shadows and light. Their floral painting is good as regards precision. In all these they have the highest precision, but the ideal is to the highest degree alien to them. Only in cultivating gardens do they excel; theirs are not rigid and formal.

"The State Religion" vs. "the Private Religion"

[16]Finally, with regard to religion, knowledge is difficult to come by because the Europeans could only obtain it insofar as they had missionaries, but as missionaries they could not get at it. The state religion must in China first be distinguished from the private religion. The main thing is that the state religion here is in one aspect patriarchal religion, although it has still other aspects distinguishing it from that. We can express this patriarchal religion briefly thus: the human beings pray to God as the lord of the earth and of the heaven, as good, as rewarding virtue, as punishing evil and crime. This simple religion is essentially the state religion of the Chinese. It is pure and simple on account of its abstraction. The profundity of nature and of spirit is, however, not present in such a religion. . . . [137] Their highest being they call Tien or Chancti (the first means heaven, the second the highest master). . . . [138] The Chinese who are learned in the state religion, whom the missionaries call atheists, take this abstract being as the primordial of the [139] understanding, with the significance that can be given to fate. From this primordial, all comes forth. The Chinese have in general the representation of a just lord of nature and of human dealings. This entails that the emperor alone is called son of Tien, and he alone brings the sacrificial offering on behalf of his *entire* people. . . . [140] A second essential phase of this religion is that, while Tien is indeed the one Lord, he is not polemical so that he alone ought to be honored, but many others have a place under this One. . . .

Now for reason, it is essential that the absolute not be this One, but instead particularize itself, and that the particular also be posited in the absolute and in it be recognized and appear. . . . The initial exaltation, which does not yet grasp the universal itself in its determinacy, is one of bestowing universal status on the souls of particular things, as we find

---

16. GW 27 [1] 136–41 (~ GW 27 [2] 561–70; GW 27 [3] 880–84; GW 27 [4] 1254–57; 1840, 160–63).

with the Genies of the Chinese. [141] These Genies are all things—sun, moon and stars, time, the year, the hour—each has its own "Shen." The Shen love human beings and are arrayed over and under one another as are the mandarins. . . . The Shen have their temples everywhere. People turn to them in the conviction that all natural events depend on them. . . . The Shen are not exactly honored as deities, but instead as subordinates to Tien. The Chinese have idols, graven images of these Shen. . . . The temples of the Shen have priests. Of these bonzes there are a great many monasteries.

[17]In the Chinese religion there lies still that essential phase of sorcery, [162] as the giving to humans the absolute determining. If the emperor behaves well, things can only go well; heaven must allow good to happen. A second side of this religion is that, as the general aspect of the relation to heaven lies with the emperor, he has also its more particular bearings in his hands; this is the particular well-being of individuals and provinces—which have each a Genie, which is subject to the emperor, who pays adoration only to the general power of heaven, while the several spirits of the natural realm follow his laws.[18] He is thus made the proper legislator for heaven as well as for earth. To these Genies, each of which enjoys an honoring peculiar to itself, certain sculptured forms are assigned. These are disgusting idols, which are not yet objects of art, because nothing spiritual is represented in them. They are therefore only awful, frightful, negative, and watching—as among the Greeks do the River Gods, the Nymphs, and Dryads—over single elements and natural objects. . . . But not less does every province and town, every mountain and river possess a specific Genie. All

---

17. 1840, 161–63 (~ GW 27 [3] 884–86).

18. In his 1827 *Lectures on the Philosophy of Religion* (GW 29 [2] 91–92) Hegel designates the Chinese state religion as "a developed sorcery-religion" (eine ausgebildete Zauberreligion). He explains as follows (see also GW 29 [2] 360 and GW 29 [1] [1824] 241–43, 253–55): "by this Tien or heaven, which is first a physical power, we seem, insofar as it also determines itself morally, to have gotten beyond this sphere of nature religion and of the sorcerer. But when we consider it more closely, we are still standing entirely within that sphere, where the single human being, the will, the empirical consciousness of the single human, is the highest. . . . The emperor is ruler of the earth; heaven is not; the latter has not given laws nor gives them, for humans to respect—divine laws, laws of religion, of ethical custom. Tien or heaven does not rule nature, but the emperor rules all, and *only he* is in connection with this Tien; he alone brings sacrifices to Tien." But in Hegel's 1831 version, as somewhat loosely preserved by David Strauss, Hegel is reported to have said (GW 29 [2] 249): "The Chinese state religion is in its foundation a pantheism such as the *Lama-Buddhistic religion*. . . . Everything in the Chinese religion reduces itself to a moralistic life; one can therefore call it a moralistic atheism. The duties and standards of determination, while they are of older origin, are contained especially in the writings of Confucius."

these spirits are subordinate to the emperor.... If a mischance occurs in any part, the Genie is deposed, as a mandarin would be.... [163] The bonzes are soothsayers and exorcists: for the Chinese are given to infinite superstition; the latter rests on the want of subjective independence of the inner and presupposes the very opposite of freedom of spirit. In every undertaking—for example, if the site of a house, or of a grave, etc., is to be determined—the advice of the soothsayers is asked.

"The Religion of the Lamas"

[19]The religion of the Lamas is different; in comparison to that of the Chinese emperor, it is not developed into a state religion, but one can call it a higher, disinterested religion, as more inner, more spiritual. The state religion is not inner, in accord with subjectivity.

[20]Insofar as this religion essentially grounds itself in the substance, the power, of the natural, it is in any case the consciousness of this absolute power as a spirituality that is present.... This spirituality can, however, be defined in varying ways. Even as the Africans had a sensuous definition—that it is the human being, the empirical individual—so the Chinese have indeed the consciousness of a spirituality, but as a living, mortal, human being....

The religion has at its peak partly the Dalai Lama, and partly the religion of Fo or Buddha. Each of these two religions has its own seats or bases in peoples, among whom these are the chief or only religions. These religions are, among the Chinese, more sectarian, in part bound together with the state religion. As regards the religion of Fo, this is principally at home in India beyond the Ganges, among the Burmese, in Ceylon, in Siam, and in many parts of India proper. The religion of the Dalai Lama has its seat in the Mongolian peoples in Tibet....

Among the Chinese who adhere to the religion of Fo there is found abstract speculation that one can look upon as the Chinese philosophy.... [887] From Laozi, a philosopher of the epoch of Confucius, extracts have been taken: ... there is a connection with the Buddhist religion. On another side, there is the sect of Dao or Tao (Reason), in which much that is very abstract has come to sight. Reason has brought forth the One; the One, the Two; the Two, the Three; this Three, the totality. Platonic determinations have been detected in this.... The

---

19. GW 27 [2] 550.
20. GW 27 [3] 886–89 (~ GW 27 [1] 142–43; GW 27 [2] 566–69).

Chinese occupy themselves with abstract speculation, with thinking about this ultimate, pure abstractness. So this is not any philosophy in the strict sense. In philosophy one must go from the abstract to the concrete; but here abstraction is the most unripe, incomplete that can be envisaged. This thinking begins as totally abstract, and this abstraction and the toiling over it does not lead to innerness, to the principle of freedom, of law, of a constitution that fosters freedom. It can be tied to or produce a constitution that contains a universal lack of freedom. . . .

[888] Buddha, standing at the peak, is considered as a mortal in whom God incarnates himself from time to time; and the followers of the teaching themselves stand in, and make themselves worthy through this identification with the absolute. The highest point to which this identification with God comes is the nullification of all conception, thought—complete indifference over and against everything, inactivity: this is called Nirvana. This complete emptiness, objectively expressed by them, is the Nothing, the Absolute, the Ground of all; . . . to this nothingness the human ought to elevate oneself.

[889] The other sect or religion is the religion of the Dalai Lama—a human being who is looked upon and revered as God. He is mortal as human; but the God incarnates himself and when he leaves the life of one, he is in the life of another, who is sought out by the priesthood. This Dalai Lama is not in China itself; there are three chief Lamas outside China—but they stand in connection with China. . . . The emperor of China himself worships also the Dalai Lama. . . .

As for the Indians overall, so for the Buddhists in China, a major doctrine is that of the transmigration of souls. . . . The transmigration is not absolute: the highest that the human being can attain is to come to this Nirvana, this pure emptiness; and whoever achieves the latter is one with God, remains unaltered, no longer has to go over into the beastly or human forms and exist in these subordinate particular ways. With this is bound up a host of superstitions.

[21]We have earlier remarked that there are particular sects. One is that of Laozi. With this begins a completely different ordering. They propose to themselves that through withdrawal into self, through study and the like, one becomes master over the Shen—and in addition, that the more profound devotees become Shen themselves. So here is a beginning of the elevation of human beings to the divine, of the absolute identification with the divine absolute.

---

21. GW 27 [1] 142.

Appendix: Daoism and Its Significance

In his 1827 *Lectures on the Philosophy of Religion* (GW 29 [2] 91, 95–98, 101–2) Hegel treats Daoism or Taoism and Laozi in greater detail and somewhat differently, as "the ancient Chinese religion—the religion of the Tao, a distinct God, *Reason*" (91). The "*next step* out of this first configuration of the natural religion" is "the turning back of the consciousness into itself, the requirement that the consciousness meditate within itself—and this is the sect of the Tao." In it, "these humans who turn themselves to thinking, to going back inside to the abstraction of thought, have thereby the aim of becoming immortal, pure essence for themselves" (95).

There was "in later time a renewal, an improvement, of the teaching of the Tao," which "became ascribed preeminently to Laozi, a sage who was somewhat older than, but in the same era as, Confucius and Pythagoras." Whereas "Confucius is thoroughly a moralist, no speculative philosopher," in "the sect of the Tao is the beginning of the transition into thinking, the pure element—but on that, no higher spiritual religion grounded itself." The "determinations of the Tao remained complete abstractions, and the vitality, the consciousness, the spiritual, was lacking, so to speak, in the Tao itself, and was entirely in the unmediated humans: so Laozi is also a Shen, or appears as Buddha." Just "as Tien, this One, is the mastery, but as this abstract foundation, while it is the emperor that is the actuality of this foundation—the factual lord"—so "the same is the case for this concept of Reason"; this is "even the abstract foundation that first has its actuality in existing human beings"—who, however, "have no immanent, fulfilled innerness" (96).

This means, Hegel contends, that the practical "relationship is to the state constitution, the being ruled from outside." With "this religion there is bound up no real morality, no immanent rationality, through which the human has value, worth in oneself." From this "there follows" the "highest, most contingent superstition. The Chinese are the most superstitious people in the world" (97).

Then there is "the *second* form that is linked with this going-within-self," and "has many determinations, configurations"; and among them is the "religion of Fo in China, or of Buddha"; "with this is linked the religion of the *Lamas*," who are "the substance, as living, as present here." In "the character of the peoples" who believe in these religions "lies the elevation of this substantiality over unmediated, singular consciousness, as is put forward in sorcery," and "over desire, over the singular will," with "the aim for humans as highest being" the "attaining of pure stillness in oneself" or of "the nothing, the being-nothing" (97–98).

While "God is grasped overall as nothingness," he is also "known as this immediate human, as Fo, Buddha, Dalai Lama." Here Hegel digresses to observe that "to us, this unity can appear as the most repugnant, scandalous, unbelievable—that a human being with all sensuous needs can be viewed by humans as God, as he who eternally creates, maintains, brings forth the world." But "we are to learn to understand this representation, and by understanding it, to justify it"—to "show how it has ground, its rationality, its place in reason." To be sure, "it belongs to this that we have insight into what is defective therein." What is "difficult is to understand the necessity of such a form of religion, its truth, how it is connected with reason: that is harder than showing how something is senseless." And "to clarify this, here is the place to recollect the activity of nature, the spirit of nature, the soul of nature—by which we do not mean that the spirit of nature is a conscious spirit; we do not think of this in terms of consciousness." For example, "the human being is spirit, and one's spirit determines itself as soul, as this oneness of the living—this is its vitality, which in the elaboration of the organization is only one, pervading and maintaining all"; and "this actuality is present in the human being so long as one lives, without one knowing about or willing this"; and yet "one's soul is the underlying cause—that is, the originating thing that does the actuating." This "unconsciously working rationality or unconsciously rational activating, the activating of nature, is what the ancients called *nous*. Anaxagoras said, *nous* rules the world. This is not conscious rationality" (101–2).

Bibliography

Abel-Rémusat, J.-P. *Iu-Kiao-Li, ou Les Deux cousines, Roman Chinois*. 3 vols. Paris: Moutardier, 1826. See GW 31 [1] 950–51; GW 31 [2] 1871.

Abel-Rémusat, J.-P. *Mémoire sur la vie et les opinions des Lao-Tseu*. Paris: Imprimerie Royale, 1823. See GW 27 [2] 568.

Abel-Rémusat, J.-P. *Observations sur quelque points de la doctrine Samanéenne, et en particulier sur les noms de la triade suprême chez les différens peuples Bouddhistes*. Paris: Imprimerie Royale, 1831. See GW 31 [1] 641; GW 31 [2] 1871.

Barrow, J. *Voyage en Chine, formant le complément du voyage de Lord Macartney*. Paris: Buisson, 1805.

THE ORIENTAL WORLD: CHINA

Couplet, P. *The Morals of Confucius, a Chinese Philosopher*. London: Taylor, 1691.
Gaubil, Fr. A., and M. J. de Guignes, trans. *Le Chou-King, un des livres sacrés des Chinois*. Paris: Tilliard, 1770.
Grossier, Abbé J.-B. A. *De la Chine*. 7 vols. 3rd ed. Paris: Pillet, 1818–20. See GW 27 [3] 855.
Halhed, N. B., ed. *A Code of Gentoo Law*. N.p., 1781.
Harnisch, W., comp. *Die wichtigsten neuern Land-und Seereisen*. Vol. 5. Leipzig: Fleischer, 1825.
Mailla, J. A. M. de M. de. *Histoire générale de la Chine*. 13 vols. Paris: Pierres, 1777–85.
Marshman, J. *The Works of Confucius*. Vol. 1. Serampore: Mission Press, 1809. See GW 27 [1] 133; GW 27 [2] 560; GW 27 [4] 1249.
Mémoires concernant l'histoire, les sciences, les arts, les moeurs, les usages, etc. des Chinois, par les missionaires de Pekin. 16 vols. Paris: Nyon, 1776–91 and 1814. See GW 27 [1] 105–6; GW 27 [2] 544.
Pauw, C. de. *Recherches philosophiques sur les Egyptiens et les Chinois*. 2 vols. Berlin: Decker, 1773.
Schwabe, J. J., ed. *Allgemeine Historie der Reisen zu Wasser und zu Lande*. Vol. 6. Leipzig: Arksee and Mirkus, 1748–74.
Staunton, G. T. *An Authentic Account of an Embassy from the King of Great Britain to the Emperor of China*. 2 vols. London: Nicol, 1797. See GW 27 [2] 560; GW 27 [3] 863.
Turner, S. *An Account of an Embassy to the Court of the Teshoo Lama*. London: Bulmer, 1800. See GW 27 [1] 201–2; GW 27 [2] 569; GW 27 [3] 892; GW 27 [4] 1266.

CHAPTER 3

The Oriental World, Part Two
India

[1]We transition to the second great world-historical configuration, the Indian.[2] Like China, it is on the whole still present. In the sequence of historical configurations it is a very early configuration, so it is old, but has remained stationary and fixed, and has consummated itself in the most complete cultural development—even though in foreign affairs India is no longer independent.

[3]India has been open in relation the rest of the world, and thus it appears as an effective link in the chain of world-history, while the Chinese empire lies outside this—as a first that, however, still has not gotten under way or moved outside itself. India also presents itself as a world-historical people. From India is derived wisdom, culture, as well as treasures of nature; and so all peoples have turned their eyes to India, to access its treasures. . . . There is no great nation [144] that has not acquired a foothold in India.

---

1. GW 27 [2] 570 (~ GW 27 [3] 898; 1840, 169).
2. For some major sources, in addition to classical Greek texts (Arrian, Pliny, Ptolemy, and Strabo), upon which Hegel seems to have drawn for his understanding of India, see the bibliography at the end of this chapter.
3. GW 27 [1] 143-44 (~ GW 27 [2] 571-72; GW 27 [3] 894; GW 27 [4] 1265-66; 1840, 173-74).

⁴In India we come to a higher stage for the concept. We see first of all the relation to substantial singularity, and this activated through particularity, which is what rules over the individuals. . . . The defect is that . . . subjective freedom is not present in this relationship. . . . The essential phase of particularity begins here; but this particularity does not advance to the independent freedom of the individual, not to ethical custom, morality; feeling, freedom, conscience, are higher categories that cannot yet find place in this particularity, which comes forth as a determination of nature.

⁵In recent times the discovery has been made that the Sanskrit language lies at the foundation of all further developments of European languages: for example, the Greek, Latin, and German. India, moreover, was the center of emigration for all the western world; but this external world-historical relation is more a natural diffusion of peoples from this point. Although even in India the elements of further developments might be found, and although we could find traces of their being transmitted to the West, this transmission has been nevertheless so abstract that what among later peoples can have interest for us is not anything derived from India, but much rather something concrete, which the later peoples themselves have cultivated, and in regard to which they have done their best to forget the Indian elements. The spread of the Indian is prehistorical, for history is only that which makes an essential epoch in the development of spirit. Overall, the diffusion of the Indian is only a dumb, deedless expansion: that is, without political action. The Indians have made no foreign domination, but have been always themselves dominated.

"The State, the Antithesis to That of the Chinese"

⁶With regard to the political and religious life, first to be considered therein is the advance and distinction over and against the Chinese—where there is the equality of all individuals, but tied together with regimentation from the center, so that the individuality, the particular, attained to no independence, to no subjective freedom. The next step from this is that, against this sameness, differentiation comes to

---

4. GW 27 [3] 893.
5. 1840, 173 (~ GW 27 [1] 194–97; GW 27 [2] 570–71; GW 27 [3] 918–19; GW 27 [4] 1264–65).
6. GW 27 [2] 573–74 (~ GW 27 [4] 1274; 1840, 175–76).

the fore, and difference becomes determined independently over and against this externally all-overmastering unity that we see in China—[574] that the independence of the particular prevails. To an organic life belongs the unity of the organism, the one soul, but inasmuch as it is an organic life, it belongs to it that it is constituted from differentiated special parts, properly members, that in their particularity develop themselves to a whole system—but so that their activity reconstitutes the oneness. This freedom, the independence of particularity, is wanting in China.

[7]China is the patriarchal whole, and wholeness, oneness, is the [192] fundamental determination. The Indian is the second essential phase of the Idea, namely, that of differentiation—of determined, firm differentiation. This differentiation, as human differentiation (which ought to be subordinate to the spirit of unity) remains simply natural, a setting in stone of the classes, under one another. Because the distinction is so ossified, there is present inequality, differentiation, multiplicity, while there is no place here for rationality, freedom, a political condition. This natural differentiation thus becomes fixed, and this is the principle of the Indians. This is, in the world-historical context, the other principle, although it stands in no connection, either backward with China or forward with the rest. The world-historical advance is therefore only present in itself—as in the case of animals and flowers that form a system, albeit one in which, as individuals, they emerge from the soil for themselves, without one species appearing in connection with the others. The connection is not explicit, but instead exists only for the reflecting spirit. This is the most nonrational way, of nature, and the Indian principle in this naturalness partakes of this connectedness only conceptually, not in the phenomena.

[8]So differentiation is the great determination that is necessary through the concept, and that is the characteristic of the Indian configuration. It emerges from this unity of despotism and the individuality of the independent members; yet these differentiations fall back into nature, so that instead of activating an organic life free for itself and from it freely bringing forth the unity, they petrify and become rigid, and this rigidity of the differentiations has condemned and degraded the Indian people, the Indian culture, to the most abandoned serfdom in every spiritual respect. These distinctions are known under the name

---

7. GW 27 [1] 191–92 (~ GW 27 [2] 573–74; GW 27 [3] 899).
8. GW 27 [2] 574 (~ GW 27 [4] 1274; 1840, 176).

of the *castes*. In every state there are distinctions of occupations that must manifest themselves: *classes*; but the individuals, the whole, must be maintained in subjective freedom, in morality, in the inner ethical customs of the individuals. Here, the differentiations are differentiations of the *occupations*, the *classes*.

[9]Here emerges a most noteworthy determination, of absolute importance for the concept of the state, the antithesis to that of the Chinese. In China there is lacking the essential phase according to which the Idea of the state ought to be concrete, in subdivisions internally in-itself determined and organically articulated, not something abstract but an establishment for itself of differences in such a way that they exist by means of the whole, and the whole by means of them. These distinctions are universal—universal particularities: the whole of the state is something substantial, but, particularizing itself, it partitions itself into distinct occupations. This is the differentiation that we see coming to the fore in India. . . . [153] China does not reach the point at which these distinct elements develop themselves into branches, into communities within the whole. In India these universal particularities emerge, and in the characteristic determinacy of castes. The first occupation in the state involves intelligent, spiritual, religious, and scientific life. The second is the practical occupation of force, the defense external and internal, the military occupation. The third occupation is that of the skilled trades and has the goal of freeing from needs.[10] The fourth, attaching itself to the others, is that of the servants, which, insofar as it is a private serving, cannot have a standing of its own. The distinction of these occupations is, in accord with the concept, determined through reason. [Griesheim: Here is now the question, which form do these distinctions take in India? Distinction and classification of the individuals into general occupations is necessary in every state. In India it emerges in a specific way. The feature distinctive to the Indians is that these determinations of the concept become natural distinctions, based on birth. For us, this occurs by subjective freedom, in that everyone can determine upon any of these specific roles for themselves, commensurate with their own views, intentions, circumstances.

---

9. GW 27 [1] 152-54 (~ GW 27 [2] 574-78; GW 27 [3] 898-902; GW 27 [4] 1274-77; 1840, 179-80).

10. Contrast GW 27 [1] 156, Griesheim: "the third caste is called Waischja. It is on the whole the landowners and householders. The fourth are the laborers, handcraftsmen, peasants; in addition a fifth, the ignoble caste of the disdained Nischa, Parria. Beyond this general division there are many subdivisions."

But for the Indians these differences are thoroughly bound to a natural determination.]

Plato's state-constitution recognizes these distinctions too, but since the personal will of the individual is ruled out, the supervisors assign the individuals to the classes, according to an educated, ethically customary will. In this case the subjective freedom of individuals is not respected even though the determining factor is not based on nature as for the Indians.

For us, [154] social class is overall subordinate, and the spiritual, religious, ethically customary, and legal sphere is something higher, in which everyone has, or can have, equal, *universal* rights. The social classes belong to the particularity of bourgeois civil life, from which the universality of the will is independent for itself, as a sphere in which each one can be at home. For the Indians, however, the distinctions are, as we said, natural, and they encapsulate the entire institution of Indian life; upon them depend all the religious and legal commandments.

[11]The foundation of the Indian life of the state, when we examine it more closely, is the following. Whereas the state ought to be overall the unity of the particular will and the universal, and thus the actualizing of the universal will (the state presupposes consciousness of free will), in China the objective will is law, but standing outside the individual; we saw that among the Chinese the moralistic is made into the content of civil law, so that innerness is handled as external. For the Indians, there is in the first place an innerness of [151] the external, but a unity in which neither does nature constitute an understandable whole, nor does what is spiritual stand as free will over against this naturalness; instead, there is still unmediated unity. Thus, lacking is spirit's withdrawal, for itself, whereby the law of freedom is recognized as being for it. Thus, lacking is freedom as will being for itself, and also as in the form of subjective will. Thus there is lacking everything necessary for a state. Therefore in India there can thus be no state. It is a people but no state. [Griesheim: Now there is a social life together, and indeed, as will be shown, a life that is very cultivated, but in such a way that there is no foundation present for determining what in this life is ethically customary, just, and moral—no religiosity as conscience, etc.]—for all these have as their principle the spirit as freedom. Thus insofar as there is a ruling regime here, it is a despotism totally without foundation.

---

11. GW 27 [1] 150–51 (~ GW 27 [2] 572–73, 591–93).

[12]For concrete relationships, thus nothing is left but contingency of willing, of willfulness that cannot arrive at a constitution. . . . The condition as the Europeans found it was a host of greater and smaller principalities dominated by Muslim and Indian dynasties. . . . These lands indeed had ruling families, ancient and new, mostly from the warrior caste but also occasionally from the Brahman caste, as is the Peshwa of the Maratha kingdom. We see at once [182] that the succession within these families is utterly uncertain. . . . What belongs to security of the succession is overall an ethically customary, legal condition; not merely the law of succession. . . . Hence their history is a ceaseless series of conspiracies, uprisings, brutalities, of princely family members against one another, as well as a series of conspiracies of generals and state servants overall.

"The Civil Legislation"

[13]The civil legislation is contained in the legislation of Manu, found in collections and compilations [Griesheim: that have been translated by the English]. This legislation is very incomplete and confused.

A first, very important point is whether or not those farming the land are its owners, or not—whether they are propertied, or are day-laborers. This is a very difficult question to answer. When the English came into possession of Bengal with its twenty million inhabitants (now directly or indirectly they hold sway over all India, one hundred million inhabitants, the majority of whom are direct subjects of the English), it was of the greatest importance to determine whether the farmers are landowners. The question is so difficult on account of the great encumbrances and levies on the land. . . .

[163] The second point to be considered is regarding testimony before a court. The king cannot give testimony, nor the cook, nor dancers, nor women. A man with sons can; one who only has daughters cannot. In the laws of Manu, false testimony is permitted when the life of a man is at stake, who otherwise must die. . . . Insofar as the severity of the kings is recognized, untruth is preferred to truth—and in many other [164] cases: for example, when it is advantageous to a Brahman.

---

12. GW 27 [1] 181-82 (~ GW 27 [2] 594; GW 27 [3] 905-9; GW 27 [4] 1271-72).
13. GW 27 [1] 161, 163-66 (~ GW 27 [2] 578-80; GW 27 [3] 904-5; GW 27 [4] 1285-87).

Yet another determination concerns debts. Notable in this regard is the amount of interest: the very amount itself, then and thereafter too, is a function of caste distinctions. . . .

[165] As for what concerns justice and personal freedom, there is not a shadow of it present.

As regards right of inheritance, the female sex is wholly excluded, and must even not make a will. . . . What is to be stated overall about the condition of wives is that they are incapable of testifying in court, may not even make a will, and are in general subordinate and in a state of degradation: they may not even eat in the presence of the husband. It is further the case that wives are more or less purchased by the bridegroom. . . . The young woman has no choice regarding a husband, but the parents make the choice. . . . If the parents do not find a spouse, then the young woman can be provided for in another way since polygamy is allowed. (A wife first possesses her right in monogamy, where she is established as the equal of *the* husband. Without this, her right as a wife is absent.) There are regions in [166] India where there is also polyandry, where the female sex is treated even more contemptibly. By means of this Indian polygamous relationship, a father can readily provide for his daughter, by giving her as wife to a reputable Brahman; the result is that many a Brahman has thirty to forty wives, only a very few of whom he knows. All these relationships exhibit the lowly condition of the wife in India.

[14]The lower castes are punished more harshly than are the higher castes for the same crimes, except for theft, where the punishment intensifies as the caste position becomes higher. In general, the principle governing punishments is that of abstract reprisal. For instance, whoever slanders someone will be punished on his tongue, and so forth. Manu has stipulated ten places for physical punishment of the under-castes. But a Brahman who commits a crime, which in the case of another caste makes one subject to exile and corporeal punishment, is supposed to be exiled but not punished physically. In contrast a Shudra who, by hand or foot, injures a Brahman or a person from another higher caste, will have his [160] foot or hand cut off. . . . Caste status can be lost if one is neglectful of the duties of one's caste. Such a person is an outcast and beyond all protection of the laws and is then shunned by everyone. But caste status can be reacquired, and indeed in various ways.

---

14. GW 27 [1] 159–60 (~ GW 27 [2] 578–79; GW 27 [3] 902–3; GW 27 [4] 1283–84).

[15]Each caste has its own rules concerning the minutest things of daily life. One must have bathed before eating. [158] If one has not bathed, then one does not eat. The different castes do not eat together—a practice that is lost in the circumstances of war. An Indian may not touch a dead bird nor possess its feathers, nor wear leather made from cowhide. Hence one must see to one's own provisions. Each caste has its own determinate occupation, and particular rules to follow; there is overall the most differentiated civil right. At the apex stand the Brahmans, elevated above the others, as for us human beings are over animals. Only Brahmans may pursue science, and read the holy books, the Vedas. A Shudra (from the fourth class) is not allowed to memorize passages of these books or to learn any prayers. A Shudra who knows such things will be punished by death. According to the laws of Manu, Brahmans cannot advise, or teach prayers to, a Shudra. If a Shudra troubles a Brahman, he can be condemned to death. The Brahman counts, overall, as a god. Any Hindu can fall down before a Brahman and declare him to be his god. Brahmans wear a four-part cord about the neck. Upon seeing it the ordinary Hindu falls down and prays to it. A Brahman may receive something only from a Brahman. [159] The Brahman is called twice-born and occupies a position so exalted that a king can in no way attain it no matter how high he ascends.

[16]The Brahmans stand under a yoke of the most external practices, which are repeated daily in the course of the most insignificant occupations. [167] (The ethically customary for the human being is such as to regard indifferent matters as indifferent.) For the Indians, all the dealings that pertain to needs are carried out subject to a host of laws that for themselves are entirely senseless, so that the Indian conducts his life in a senseless bondage. The Brahman has to keep in mind the most complex matters in this regard. Throughout the entire day he has to complete specific ceremonies; upon arising, he must subject himself to certain rules: get up this way, wash oneself this way, pray this way, speak thus, do that, all the while reciting special formulas. . . . There is host of things whereby he can contaminate himself. For instance, he must be wearing not one garment, but two. He must not be naked while bathing. In urinating he has a lot to watch out for: he may not urinate in the direction of wood—that is forbidden, out; nor in rivers,

---

15. GW 27 [1] 157-59 (~ GW 27 [2] 580-82; GW 27 [3] 903; GW 27 [4] 1278; 1840, 184-85).
16. GW 27 [1] 166b-168 (~ GW 27 [2] 589; GW 27 [4] 1281-83; 1840, 184-85).

nor turned toward the sun; instead, toward the south in the evening, toward the north in daytime. He who disregards one of these must perform a purification. To all castes is it forbidden to walk upon ashes, hair, flax seeds, or potsherds. There are similar prescriptions of this kind. By a few hours after sunrise a Brahman can have committed thirty to forty transgressions. . . .

[168] Thus dependent on external matters lives the Indian. Inner freedom, morality, one's own sense, can find no place here. In this bondage to externals is the Indian, so that he can have no indwelling ethical custom.

"Dreaming Spirit, as the Generic Principle of the Indian Nature"

[17]Here the difficulty is encountered, as to which presentation one should take up, since the Indian theology is extremely vast, and the representations of it are extremely diverse. One sees that what stands in the lawbook of Manu about God and the creation diverges widely from any other portrayal to be found in the Vedas, etc. The portrayals are therefore extremely dissimilar, and one can escape their confusion only by culling out the universal spirit of this religion. . . . To the Indians the One manifests itself as absolute substance, but as existing soul of the world, as one existing matter (Materie) in which both spiritual and material (Matrielles) are subordinated. This one substantiality constitutes the foundation, and everything determinate is only something [171] dreamed, nothing secure. The One and All is the foundational idea; everything is just a modification or vanishing form of the One. So pantheism constitutes the foundation. These configurations into which this One passes over are something indeterminate, self-dissolving. . . . For the Indian there is nothing miraculous, because he has no secure natural law; all is miracle overall.[18]

---

17. GW 27 [1] 170–71.

18. In his 1827 *Lectures on the Philosophy of Religion* Hegel clarifies key differences between the Hindu and the biblical conceptions of the ultimate ground (GW 29 [2] 150, 152, 153, 155): "God's *creating* [Schaffen] is very different from *going forth* [Hervorgehen]"; "from Brama the gods go forth; . . . what has gone forth is the existing, actual, so that the ground out of which it has gone forth is as sublated." In the Jewish Bible, "God is over against the world, . . . as the Subject, which remains absolutely first. Here is the ground-determining God, Subjectivity determining itself out of itself," and "is not the substance, but the subjective Oneness, the *absolute power*," while "the natural is only something posited, ideal, not self-standing." As a consequence, "the world is now prosaic"; "here, now, is what we call natural or necessary

[19]We want to seek to grasp the Indian principle, in contrast to the Chinese. As opposed to China, India appears to be fantasy land, a land of wonders. In China everything was understanding devoid of fantasy [Hagenbach: a prosaic life, where even disposition is legally regulated, from outside]. In India, in contrast, there is no object that stands fast against poetry and fantasy, that is not transformed by imagination, that is not made poetic and wondrous. In China, there is moralistic content of the law; in India, we of course find a multitude of stipulations regarding conduct, but these determinations do not have the moralistic as their content, and instead they have superstitions as their content, without spirit and feeling. . . . Their entire condition is to be grasped as one of dreaming. Rationality, morality, subjectivity are negated, thrown away, and there is, on one side, a wild strength of imagination along with sensuous enjoyment, [145] and, on the other side, a dead abstraction of inwardness. Between them the Indian vacillates to and fro. . . .

The Chinese are without filled inwardness; the content of self-determination is for them given in an external regime that determines it. This is abstract innerness. The necessary advance from this is the filling, becoming, of an inner world. For the Chinese the world of the spirit is only in relation to state and utility. [146] The next step forward is for the determinacy, previously posited externally, to become inward, such that what is inward not be merely abstract—such that the spirit instead construct from itself its own world, that the world be configured into an idealism. This advance we see in the Indians [Hagenbach: although here the idealism is one of the imagination devoid of reason and of freedom, a mere dreaming in which there is only a simulation of truth and in which the preponderance of the content is abstract imagination]. . . . In dreams, furthermore, the profoundest depths of spirit do express themselves too—as supreme nonsense; and so with the Indians we do see the consciousness of the highest Idea, the most sublime determinations, intermingled with the most willful cloud-configurations.

[20]Now inasmuch, however, as in this dreaming, abstract and absolute thought itself enters as content, one can say: it is God, in the frenzy of his dreaming, that we see here represented. For it is not simply the

---

connection; here it is, also, that the category of 'miracle' ['Wunder'] can first emerge, over and against the natural connection of things. In the earlier religions there is no miracle. In the Indian, everything is already crazy from the start [In der Indischen ist Alles schon verrückt von Haus aus]."

19. GW 27 [1] 144–46 (~ GW 27 [3] 912–15; GW 27 [4] 1267–68; 1840, 169–71).
20. 1840, 170.

dreaming of an empirical individual, who possesses his distinct personality, and really unfetters this, but it is the dreaming of the unlimited spirit itself.

[21]The character of *dreaming* spirit, as the generic principle of the Indian nature, is to be more closely defined. In a dream, the individual ceases to know oneself as *this*, in contradistinction from objects. When awake, I exist for myself, and the rest is an objectivity over and against me, and I over and against it. As external, the rest of existence expands itself to an understandably connected whole and a system of relations, in which my individual being is itself a member—an individual being connected with that. This is the sphere of understanding. In dreaming, on the contrary, this separation is suspended. Spirit has ceased to exist for itself over and against the rest, and thus overall the separation of the external and individual dissolves before its universality and its essence. The dreaming Indian is therefore all that we call finite and individual and, at the same time, infinitely universal and unlimited—a something in itself divine. The Indian view of things is a totally universal pantheism, and indeed a pantheism [172] of the force of imagination, not of thought. There is one substance, and all individualizations are directly enlivened and animated into particular powers.

[22]The way things *are* in their interconnection is that they *are*, first, singular—but have laws for their deeper interconnection, a universal truth, that is distinct from their singularity. The most universal expression of this essential character is the abstract God of the Chinese. The Indians do not distinguish the singularities of things from their interconnection, their essence. That is how we have the pantheism of the Indians. It is no polytheism, [148] for their intuition is one of universal pantheism—not, however, that of [rational] thought, as in Spinozism, but pantheism of depiction. Spinozism thinks only the universal as substance. For the Indians, the universal is not that of thought, [Griesheim: but instead, collected stuff is immediately and crudely imported into the universal; it is not idealized through the strength of spirit, not elevated to free beauty; the sensed stuff is only expanded limitlessly, and thereby the divine is bizarrely transmogrified and itself made to be ridiculous]. . . . Accordingly, our representation, of God's becoming a human being, is for them not impressive, for it is not a

---

21. 1840, 171–72.
22. GW 27 [1] 147–49 (~ GW 27 [3] 912–13).

particularly important thought, inasmuch as everything is the incarnation—the ape, the parrot, as well as the cow, and so forth. . . . Thus the particular is posited in unity with the universal, [149] as the sensed. Abstractly taken, this unity is the true; but here, taken in singularity, this unity becomes absurd and unworthy. In this sensualizing of God two versions are to be distinguished: in the pantheism, it is thoroughly universal; or, in the depiction, [Hagenbach: there is a thorough dependence on the sensed, which appears as divinized, or else is concentrated on a few highpoints or on one point].

[23]On the other side, over against this dreaming, there is the actuality of a helpless servitude in the way human beings are classified, and on that the whole cultural education depends.

"The Principle of the Indian Religion is the Coming Forth of Diversity"

[24]The presentation of the caste relationship leads directly to the consideration of the religion. For the bonds of caste are, as already remarked, not merely secular, but essentially religious, and the Brahmans in their highness are themselves the gods, in living presence. In the laws of Manu it is said: "Let the king, even in highest need, not arouse the Brahmans against him; for they can destroy him with their power—they who bring about the fire, sun, moon, etc." They are servants neither of God nor of his community, but are God himself to the other castes—a relationship that constitutes the perverseness of the Indian spirit. The dreaming unity of spirit and nature, which involves a monstrous bewilderment in regard to all configurations and relations, we have already recognized as the principle [190] of the Indian spirit. The Indian mythology is therefore only a wild extravagance of fancy, in which nothing is stable, which transitions abruptly from the commonest to the highest, from the most sublime to the most disgusting and trivial. Thus it is also difficult to discover what the Indians understand by "Brahm." . . . The English have taken a good deal of trouble to find out what Brahm properly is. Wilford has asserted that . . . when they are asked, "What are you

---

23. GW 27 [1] 197.
24. 1840, 189–91 (~ 1840, 181; GW 27 [2] 583–84, 590–91; GW 27 [3] 913–14; GW 27 [4] 1278–81).

doing, what is the meaning of that silent meditation that some of your learned men speak of doing?" the answer is:

> When I pray to the honor of one of the Gods, I sit down—the foot of either leg on the thigh of the other—look toward heaven, and calmly elevate my thoughts with my hands folded in silence; then I say, 'I am Brahm the highest essence.' Of being Brahm, we are not conscious to ourselves, by reason of the Maya (the worldly delusion). It is forbidden to pray to him, and to offer sacrifices to him; for this would be to adore ourselves. It can always only be emanations of Brahm that we address.

[191] Translating these ideas into our own process of thought, Brahm is therefore the pure unity of thought in itself, God as simple in himself. . . . Vishnu says, "I am Brahm"; and the Sun, the Air, the Seas are called Brahm. Brahm would then be substance in its simplicity, which essentially explodes itself into the wild diversity. For this abstraction, this pure unity, is that which lies at the foundation of all—the root of all determinacy. In knowing this unity, all objectivity falls away; for the purely abstract is knowing in itself in its most extended vacuity. To attain this death of life during life itself, to achieve this abstraction, requires the disappearance of all ethically customary activity and volition, and of all knowing too, as in the religion of Fo; and that is why the penances already spoken of are undertaken.

The complement to the abstraction Brahm would be the concrete contents, for the principle of the Indian religion is the coming forth of diversity. These fall outside that abstract thought, and are as that which emanates from it, as sensuously distinct, or the thought-diversity in an unmediated sensuous form. In this way the concrete content is without spirit and wildly scattered, except as reabsorbed in the pure ideality of Brahm. So the other deities are things of sense: Mountains, Streams, Beasts, the Sun, the Moon, the Ganges.

[25]Furthermore, particular animals are revered: bulls, cows, elephants, and monkeys. There is a city inhabited by monkeys, for whom fakirs serve. These monkeys are highly vicious. The living thing overall is respected by the Indian to the extent that it may not be killed. This respect for animals is connected to the conception of the transmigration of souls. Whereas we consider [173] soul as a consciousness, the consciousness of oneself as this person—our soul thus has consciousness

---

25. GW 27 [1] 172-75, 178 (~ GW 27 [2] 591; GW 27 [3] 915-16).

of its own self-identity-as-this—the Indians represent transmigration as the soul going forth into a different body. For the Indian there is no personal continuation of the soul. There is a becoming one with the universal soul. There is a contradiction in holding at one time to maintenance of the individual in a different body, then to merging into the universal, the One. Here again is confusion. They regard their blind or crippled persons as though they are afflicted by these natural incapacities as punishment for crimes from a prior life. . . . To the objects of nature belong universal natural essence, and so productive strength that is worshiped in the most disgraceful fashion: the male and female genitals are worshiped. There are pervasive symbols for these. Mount Mehruh from which all streams flow, is also just the male organ. Masts of ships are symbols for it too.

[174] The Indian self-consciousness, as lacking freedom, lacks the innerness to stand before God; instead it can only relate itself to him as negating oneself in him. This absolute negating of oneself is the highest point of Indian self-consciousness. . . . In this abstraction self-consciousness does of course comport itself as thinking, and in this proximity to the highest point the speculative echoes of representation emerge; but they are only fathomable by someone who knows the speculative overall. . . . [175] The representations that the Indians have of the One are worthy. They say that this One is eternal, omnipotent, omnipresent. This One has no temple, no worshipful honoring. The human being has no positive relation to it. . . .

[178] The other side, now, is the relationship of the individual to the god in ritual observance. This is a vulgar idolatry. What's interesting is only to ask what appears to them as highest, in the relation to God. This highest is the slaying of naturalness through abstraction, the going forth to the point of self-destruction. Hence we find sacrifice, and human sacrifice. Sacrifice is in part recognition of the nothingness of the earthly, such that recognition of the worthlessness of the earthly is evidenced by divesting oneself of this worthlessness. Such sacrifice is something external. (The truer sacrifice is for a human being's willfulness and subjective particularity to be overcome through the universal.)

[26]If we ask further, how far their religion allows the *ethically customary* of the Indians to appear, the answer is that the former is as distinct from the latter, as Brahm from his concrete content. . . . On the one side, their virtue consists in the abstraction from all activity, in being-Brahm;

---

26. 1840, 193.

on the other side, every action with them is a prescribed external usage, not a free activity, mediated through inner selfhood.

[27]One can in one's judgment of the morality of the Indian easily be misled by writings about the mildness, the tenderness, the beauty, of their imagination full of sentiment; but in nations utterly corrupt, there are aspects that may be called tender and noble. We have Chinese poems in which [1289] the tenderest relations of love are depicted; in which delineations of deep feeling, humility, shame, propriety are found, and that one may compare with all that European literature contains. The same is found in many Indian poems; but ethical custom, morality, freedom of spirit, willed ethical custom, consciousness of individual right, are entirely distinct from these; only duties of caste are found in India, and not duties of humanity, and thereby it follows that the Indians are a most completely degraded people: their elevation consists in abstraction, in abstract existence, in consciousness of Brahm, in the annihilation of spiritual and physical existence. This elevation has nothing concrete, and the sinking into the abstract universal has no connection with the actual. . . . Cunning and deceit is the fundamental character of the Indian; cheating, stealing, robbery, murder are entirely included in his ethical customs, which include humble crouching and abjectness before a victor and lord, complete and reckless cruelty to the vanquished and subjected.

[28]The Brahmans are by birth already in possession of the divine. The caste differentiation involves, therefore, a distinction between deities—those who are present vs. mere finite mortals. The other castes may likewise become partakers in rebirth; but they must subject themselves to infinite self-denial, torture, and penance. Contempt of life, and of living humanity, is the foundation for this. A large number of the non-Brahmanical population strive to attain rebirth. [182] They are called the yogis. . . . However cowardly and weak the Indians may be in other respects, so little do they hesitate to sacrifice themselves to the highest—to annihilation; and an ethical custom that comes from this is the wives burning themselves after the death of their husbands. [183] Should a wife contravene this traditional usage, she would be severed from all society and live in solitude. An Englishman relates that he also saw a woman burn herself because she had lost her child; he did all that he could to divert her away from her purpose; at last he applied to her

---

27. GW 27 [4] 1288–89 (~ GW 27 [2] 591–92; GW 27 [3] 910–12; 1840, 193–96).
28. 1840, 181–83 (~ GW 27 [3] 911–12; GW 27 [4] 1280–83).

husband who was standing by, but who showed himself perfectly indifferent, opining that he had more wives at home. Sometimes twenty women are seen throwing themselves at the same time into the Ganges, and on the Himalaya range an Englishman found three women seeking the source of the Ganges, in order to put an end to their life in this holy river. At a worship of the gods in the famous temple of Juggernaut in Orissa, on the Bay of Bengal, where millions of Indians gather together, the image of the god Vishnu is drawn in procession on a wagon: about five hundred men set it in motion, and many fling themselves down before its wheels to be crushed to pieces. The whole seashore is already strewed with the body parts of persons who have thus sacrificed themselves. Infanticide is also very common in India. Mothers throw their children into the Ganges, or let them die slowly under the rays of the sun. The morality that is involved in respect for human life is not present among the Indians.

"Buddhist Religion, Linked to Lamaism"

[29]We now have remaining for our brief consideration something yet related to the Indian world, namely, the range of peoples that belong to the Buddhist religion, linked to Lamaism.

We saw the Indian spirit as one of dreaming.... Its foundation is the One and All, which casts itself about in a great many natural and spiritual shapes, and the manifestation is on the one side crudely sensory, on the other side the most profound thinking absorbed in itself.... Over and against this dream life (this whirl that is actually without truth) stands first a naïve dream life, which is cruder and not so widespread as the Indian, but therefore also has not entered into the servitude; instead, it grasps itself more simply in actuality, also more simply in its configuration of representation. The spirit is more concentrated in itself and hence brings its representation more to oneness and comports itself more freely in actuality; it is not amenable to caste distinctions. This is the character of the world that is related to the Indian; to it [198] belong a number of diverse peoples and lands; their history is only partly confined to India; partly it is a vast spilling over that is like a flood.... Buddha, of whom it is believed that he is the same as Fo, and whom in Ceylon is called Gautama, constitutes the Other,

---

29. GW 27 [1] 197–202.

over and against Brahma: he was in India, and he is indigenous there. There is great controversy as to which of the two religions is the more ancient.... According to the Brahmans, Buddha himself emerged as the ninth incarnation of God and is also [199] the founder of the first lunar dynasty; for there is also a tradition drawing the distinction between solar and lunar kings. Buddha is represented as king, as teacher, as God; so he appears even in Brahmanic settings, just as the Buddhists also in turn allow the Indian representation of deities to count for them....

There are, to be sure, also Indian reformers. Many peoples have freed themselves from the caste divisions—preeminently the Sikhs, who inhabit a northern region of the Indus. Two hundred years ago the Mohammedan pressure increased and there arose a reformer who, together with his people, sought to gain independence from the superstitions of both sides through viewpoints alone, not through force. When a follower of this man had been put to death by the Mohammedans his friends rose up against Mohammedans and Indians. Nowadays, this people lives as a kind of republic. So here we have *one* people that, by reformation, established their religion.[30]

According to all the historical evidence, however, the Buddhists seem to be a much more ancient people. The second thing is to indicate the character of this religion, and the third, its historical path. [200] This religion is in every respect more humane, and this is so much the case with regard to the representation of God that in one aspect their highest God was a human being, and in another their God is to them still living as a human being; so they revere a living human being as God. The first is the case with the Buddha. They have extravagant stories about his earthly life equivalent to those we see with the rest of the Indians. He attained Nirvana, a condition of the highest abstraction, in which spirit is immersed within itself, in which he was freed from everything, a condition we can to that extent call bliss. They attain this condition after death. Whoever attains Nirvana has become Buddha. So this one, Gautama, is the honored god. He was not some sort of natural being, not heaven or the sun, but instead was essentially a human being. They say that he was at the same time eternal, immortal. They ascribe to him all the attributes that we assign to the supreme being. He is revered; his image is set up in temples.... Linked with this, however, is also the revering of a living human being, who is the highest Lama—in whom the God is present for them. Such a living incarnation is found also [201] in

---

30. See similarly GW 27 [3] 906.

India itself, in the neighborhood of Bombay, where this incarnation is seen in a single family. . . . In a grander style there is something similar in Tibet proper, in the land that extends beyond the Himalayas. Three such Lamas are revered. . . . These are human beings who are revered as the God being present; service to them is in the Buddhist religion linked to the representation that this is Buddha present and living. This entails here the great confusion (albeit one not as bad as the Indian) that the mastery of a One over all the many gods is the foundation. . . .

[202] So the Lama is then he through whom the God of the people is present, and the relationship is of a kind that overall stands very close to pantheism. Nevertheless, it is not the Indian pantheism, where every mountain, every stream, every Brahman is divine, such that Brahm is immediately present. In the worship of the Lamas the sweeping pantheism has coalesced into the One. These peoples distinguish themselves from the Indians generally through their higher rank in freedom. They know themselves in their Lama and have a friendlier intuition of their God.

[31]These good-hearted peoples, who are a freer sort than the Indians with their lovable, delicate weakness, can, to be sure, expand outward, and then like wild rivers they inundate everything; as an entire people [205]—not in warrior tribes—they sweep through the world in unsettled fermentation, and in restless expansion; by laying waste, they subject all to themselves. But such rain showers abate as they have started. Under Genghis Khan, most prominently, such surges took place especially, pressing all the way to Silesia. After him Timur, the Mongol prince (or actually a Turk) was also such a one who stormed through the world.

So, as a whole, this world belongs to the Indian. But whereas the Indians are one whole, whose differentiations are rigid, these latter peoples have not arrived at this internal culture, and instead are more disparate, although they are thereby freer.

Appendix: The Paradoxical Relation of Indian Religion to Philosophy

In his *Lectures on the History of Philosophy*, 1825–26 (GW 30 [3] 857–60), Hegel begins by saying that "what we call oriental philosophy is much more the Oriental's religious way of representing overall, a religious representation, a worldview, that is very close to what comes to be called philosophy." Although "we have distinguished the configurations in

---

31. GW 27 [1] 204–5.

which the true takes the form of religion from the form that it takes through thinking in philosophy," the "oriental philosophy is religious philosophy"—"and the grounds must be given why" the oriental religious thinking is to be "considered also as philosophy." In the "Roman, Greek, and Christian religion, our thinking turns less to philosophy"; we "are less unified with it." The "Greek and Roman gods are configurations for themselves, as is Christ and the God of the Jews." And "we let them remain standing, on the whole; we do not hold them to be objects for philosophizing"; and "it would be quite the task, to interpret, to transform, such mythological or Christian configurations into philosophic objects." In contrast, "with the oriental religions we are much more immediately reminded of the philosophic way of thinking; it lies closer." The "difference is grounded in this": "the principle of freedom of the individual enters into the elements of the Greek, and much more into the Christian." In contrast, "where the essential phase of subjectivity is not in the foreground, as in the Orient, the religious representations are not individualized"; "they have the character of universal representations, which therefore appear as philosophic representations, as philosophic thoughts." They do, "to be sure, also have individual configurations, such as Brahma, Vishnu, Shiva; but the individuality is only superficial"; the "individuality, because freedom is lacking, is not stable." In "the oriental religion the chief relationship is this: that the one substance as such is the only truth, and the individual has no worth in itself and can gain none insofar as it holds itself over and against the in-and-for-itself-being; it can only have true worth through inserting itself into this substance, whereby it ceases to be subject, vanishing into unconsciousness." In the "Greek and Christian religion, in contrast, the individual knows oneself to be free and maintains oneself as such"; and "then it is in any case much more difficult for thought to free itself from this individuality and to constitute itself." The "in-itself higher standpoint of the Greek freedom of individuality" makes "more difficult the work for thinking," for "giving value to the universal."

Hegel further observes (872–73) that oriental religion discovered "the great thought" that "in thinking is contained the negation of the object; and the negative relationship is necessary, in order to grasp it"; this "is much more profound than talk about immediate consciousness." And "when it is said that, on the contrary, the Orientals have lived in unity with nature, this is a very superficial and one-dimensional expression." They discovered the "true unity" that "contains essentially the phase of the negation of nature as it is in immediacy."

Bibliography

Bentley, J. "On the Hindu Systems of Astronomy, etc." *Asiatic Researches*[32] 8 (1808): 193–244. See GW 27 [1] 190; GW 27 [3] 852, 896, 908; GW 27 [4] 1271.

Bohlen, P. von. *Das alte Indien mit besonderer Rücksicht auf Aegypten.* 2 vols. Königsberg: Bornträger, 1830. See GW 31 [1] 657–58; GW 31 [2] 1881; GW 31 [4] 1289.

Buchanan, F. "On the Religion and Literature of the Burmas." *Asiatic Researches* 6 (1801): 163–308.

Buchanan, F. "Particulars of the Jains." *Asiatic Researches* 9 (1809): 299. See GW 27 [4] 1289.

Carey, W., and J. Marshman, eds. and trans. *The Ramayuna [sic] of Valmeeki.* 3 vols. Serampore: Mission Press, 1806–10.

Colebrooke, H. T. *A Digest of Hindu Law; on Contracts and Successions: With a Commentary by Jagannatka Tarkapanchanana.* 3 vols. Calcutta: Debrett, 1801. See GW 27 [4] 1273.

Colebrooke, H. T. "Enumeration of Indian Classes." *Asiatic Researches* 5 (1799): 53–67. See GW 27 [2] 595; GW 27 [3] 896.

Colebrooke, H. T. "Observations on the Sects of Jains." *Asiatic Researches* 9 (1809): 287–322.

Colebrooke, H. T. "On the Duties of a Faithful Hindu Widow." *Asiatic Researches* 4 (1799): 205–15.

Colebrooke, H. T. "On the Philosophy of the Hindus." *Transactions of the Royal Asiatic Society* 1 (1824): 19–43, 92–118, 439–66, 549–79. See GW 27 [4] 1270.

Colebrooke, H. T. "On the Religious Ceremonies of the Hindus, and of the Bra'hmens Especially, Essay I." *Asiatic Researches* 5 (1799): 345–68; "Essays II and III." *Asiatic Researches* 7 (1803): 232–87, 288–311.

Colebrooke, H. T. "On the Vēdas, or Sacred Writings of the Hindus." *Asiatic Researches* 8 (1808): 377–497.

Colebrooke, H. T. *Two Treatises of the Hindu Law of Inheritance.* Calcutta: Hubbard, 1810.

Creuzer, F. *Symbolik und Mythologie der alten Völker.* 4 vols. Leipzig: Leske, 1819–21. See GW 27 [2] 665, 671.

Creuzer, F., and J. D. Guigniaut. *Religions de l'antiquité, considérés principalement dans leurs formes symboliques et mythologiques.* Paris: Treuttel et Würtz, 1825. See GW 31 [1] 696–703; GW 31 [2] 1909.

Dow, A. *Die Geschichte von Hindostan.* 3 vols. Leipzig: Junius, 1772–74.

Dubois, J. A. *Description of the Character, Manners and Customs of the People of India, and of Their Institutions, Religious and Civil.* 2 vols. London: Longman, 1817. See GW 27 [1] 168; GW 27 [4] 1289.

Elphinstone, M. *An Account of the Kingdom of Caubul and Dependencies in Persia, Tartary, and India.* London: Longman, 1815. See GW 27 [1] 206; GW 27 [3] 919.

---

32. This journal was originally published in Calcutta starting in 1788, and republished, verbatim, in London, starting a decade later: bibliographic listings here give the year of the London publications to which Hegel is more likely to have had access.

Halhed, N. B., ed. *A Code of Gentoo Law*. N.p., 1781.
Harnisch, W., compiler. *Die wichtigsten neuern Land-und Seereisen*. Vols. 5 and 7. Leipzig: Fleischer, 1825.
Humboldt, W. von. *Über die unter den Namen Bhagavad-Gítá bekannte Episode des Maha-Bharata*. Berlin: Royal Academy of Sciences, 1826. Hegel's review essay is available in English in H. Herring, *G. W. F. Hegel's On the Episode of the Mahabharat Known by the Name Bhagavad-Gita by Wilhelm Von Humboldt*. New Delhi: Indian Council of Philosophical Research, 1995.
Jones, W., trans. *Institutes of Hindu Law; or, The Ordinances of Menu [sic], According to the Gloss of Cullúca*. London: Sewell, 1796. See GW 27 [4] 1271, 1273.
Jones, W. "On Asiatic History, Civil and Natural." *Asiatic Researches* 4 (1799) 1–17.
Jones, W. "On the Gods of Greece, Italy, and India." *Asiatic Researches* 1 (1799): 221–75.
Jones, W. "On the Philosophy of the Asiatics." *Asiatic Researches* 4 (1799) 164–80.
Jones, W. *The Works of Sir William Jones*. 6 vols. London: Robinson and Evans, 1799. See GW 27 [1] 168, 185; GW 27 [2] 572; GW 27 [3] 924; GW 27 [4] 1271.
Malcolm, Brigadier General. "Sketch of the Sikhs." *Asiatic Researches* 11 (1810): 197–292.
Mill, James. *The History of British India*. 3 vols. London: Baldwin, Cradock, and Joy, 1817.
Moor, E. "Account of an Hereditary Living Deity, to Whom Devotion Is Paid by Bramins of Poona and Its Neighbourhood." *Asiatic Researches* 7 (1803): 381–95.
Paterson, J. D. "Of the Origin of the Hindu Religion." *Asiatic Researches* 8 (1808): 44–87.
Ritter, Carl. *Die Vorhalle europäischer Völkergeschichten vor Herodotus, um den Kaukasus und an den Gesatden des Pontus*. Berlin: Reimer, 1820. See GW 27 [1] 82, 195–96; GW 27 [2] 515, 570; GW 27 [3] 856, 1092; GW 27 [4] 1312.
Roy, Remmohin. *Rāmamohana Rāya*. Jena: Schmid, 1817. See GW 31 [1] 854–55.
Schlegel, A. W. von, ed., with commentary and Latin trans. *Bhagavad-Gita*. Bonn: Weber, 1823.
Schlegel, A. W. von, ed. with a Latin trans. *Ramayana*. Bonn: Weber, 1829. See GW 27 [4] 1273.
Shore, J. "On Some Extraordinary Facts, Customs, and Practices of the Hindus." *Asiatic Researches* 4 (1799): 331–50.
Turner, S. *An Account of an Embassy to the Court of the Teshoo Lama*. London: Bulmer, 1800. See GW 27 [1] 201–2; GW 27 [2] 569; GW 27 [3] 892; GW 27 [4] 1266.
Vishnu Sharma (attrib.). *The Heetopades of Veeshnoo-Sarma*. Trans. C. Wilkins. Bath: Cruttwell, 1787.
Wilford, F. "An Essay on the Sacred Isles in the West." *Asiatic Researches* 8 (1808): 245–368 and 9 (1809): 32–243. See GW 27 [1] 189.
Wilford, F. "On Mount Caucasus." *Asiatic Researches* 6 (1801): 455–536. See GW 27 [1] 209; GW 27 [2] 584; GW 27 [4] 1271.
Wilkins, C., trans. *Bhagavad-Gita*. London: Nourse, 1785.
Wilson, H. H. *The Mackenzie Collection: A Descriptive Catalogue of the Oriental Manuscripts and Other Articles etc. of the South of India, collected by the late C. Mackenzie*. Calcutta: Asiatic Press, 1828. See GW 27 [1] 162.

CHAPTER 4

The Oriental World, Part Three
Persia

[1]With the empire of Persia we enter for the first time into world-history.[2] China lies outside connection with world-history, although it is an essential phase, even as India, which has only a mute connection without effect. With Persia, however, there is a specific, clear connectedness. . . . [206] When we come to the Persian we find an empire outwardly [207] directed, and so for the first time one that moves world-history.

[3]The interconnectedness of the previous configurations is an interconnectedness of the concept, a more inner necessity, that is, however, not an interconnectedness that is manifest. The connectedness of the concept is in and for itself the innerness of spirit, which brings forth these configurations, but not to outer connectedness. The outer connectedness is connectedness with outer history. In India the connectedness of the concept does not come to consciousness. The transition to manifestation constitutes itself through force, through empirical,

---

1. GW 27 [1] 205–7 (~ GW 27 [2] 596; GW 27 [4] 1291; 1840, 211–12).
2. For some major sources, in addition to classical Greek texts (especially Herodotus, Xenophon, Plutarch, and Diodorus Siculus), upon which Hegel seems to have drawn for his understanding of Persia, see the bibliography at the end of this chapter.
3. GW 27 [3] 919 (~ GW 27 [4] 1291–92).

91

concrete interest, not quietly through the concept. The inner connectedness of the concept is secret, or is present only for the thinking spirit. With the Persian Empire we enter, one can say, for the first time into history, into being-in-process.

"Geographical Position"

[4]First as to *geographical position*, we see China and India as dull brooding of spirit, in fruitful plains—distinct from which is the high girdle of mountains with their wandering hordes. The peoples of the heights, in their conquest, did not change the spirit of the plains, but imbibed it themselves. But in Persia these principles are united in their distinctiveness, and the mountain peoples, with their principle, became predominant.

[5]In India we saw the spreading of life in sweltering valleys separated from the highland. In Persia both principles are united in their relationship—in conflict. The one part of the whole is the highland that bears the general name of Persia; to it belong the mountain ranges and the valleys that attach to them. The other part is the river valleys of the Tigris, Euphrates, Oxus (Amu), and Jaxartes.

To characterize the highland: it is not such an elevated land as that of Chinese Tartary; instead it is somewhat lower relative to the valley plains, and therefore has singular features of fertility. . . . [208] Another chain of mountains extends to the Persian Gulf and alongside the gulf. Along this chain the ancient land of Persia lies; it extends to the Indian Ocean and along the Indus, and terminates at the Suleiman Mountains. This elevated plain is Iran as such, in its nonspecific designation, and makes the focal point for our examination. To the north is Bactria, to the east India, to the west Babylon and Assyria, with Syria and Armenia farther west, and farthest is Asia Minor. Persia plays its role on this terrain.

"For the First Time There Comes to Sight an Empire"

[6]When we examine the Persian Empire more closely, here for the first time there comes to sight an empire: that is, a totality of mastery holding together in itself elements that are entirely heterogeneous (of course

---

4. 1840, 214 (~ GW 27 [1] 207; GW 27 [2] 598–99).
5. GW 27 [1] 207–8 (~ 1840, 214).
6. GW 27 [1] 206–7 (~ GW 27 [3] 922–23).

only relatively). The peoples who were combined into one here were to the highest degree diverse in language, ethical customs, and religion. This empire had a very long and splendid continuance, and the way it was held together is to be considered something nearer to the Idea of the state than the preceding essential phases. This empire is neither patriarchal, as in China, nor so rigid as the Indian, nor so evanescent a configuration as that of the Mongols, nor oppressive as that of the Turks, but instead one sees here a series of peoples persisting in standing on their own and yet dependent on a point of unity that could hold them content....

[207] In this empire, we see, as regards its principle, the unification of the previous principles: In China there was the unification of the whole under the mastery of an external, moralistic will that determined a person's innermost will. Against this was the principle of the Indians, that of absolute differentiation set in stone by nature. In the Persian Empire we see the differentiation of the individualizations of the nations, and indeed such that the differentiations are left free, while yet overcome in a point of unity, and held together.

[7]It is not so much a configuration as it is a tying of so many peoples together into one knot. It is a unique entity, a kind of free union of peoples, with a single focal point of the shining glory of all of them. [230] It is no political whole of shared ethical customs and laws, but the many peoples stick to their own individualities. Cyrus allows the Jews to reconstitute their own folkways, and this allowance for individuality is a greatness of Cyrus. Princes remain apart in their own tribal mastery; surely the generosity of Cyrus broadened their domain. We can take a brief look at the unique characteristics of these peoples. From the Jews and the other peoples we then see, however, that they are constricted in inflexible individuality, incapable of uniting themselves under universal thoughts and laws, but all have their own determinate natures, yet in such a way that they do not stand in isolation but instead come into the most manifold relationships that lead to hostility, so that only the iron force of the Persians can hold them together and by compulsion prevent them from carrying on in an outwardly hostile way. We read in the prophets the lamentations about the quarrels between the two realms of Judah and Israel, and against the Egyptians, etc.; so we can easily conceive how the prophets could have arrived at such hatred of

---

7. GW 27 [1] 229–31 (~ GW 27 [2] 598, 606; GW 27 [3] 936–38; GW 27 [4] 1292–93; 1840, 229–30).

foreign peoples, and we learn how beneficial for the Near East was the consolidation that came about through Cyrus. Later on, in place of this iron rule, we see entering on the scene the fanaticism of the Mohammedan religion. Romans and Greeks held sway as foreign powers over these peoples, but Mohammedan fanaticism emerged from the Near East itself, destroying every individuality of these peoples, wiping out all differentiation, by a principle [Griesheim: in which all are the same but] that is evidently incapable of building a political relationship. The only rational relationship of the Near East therefore was one in which through an iron force [231] these peoples were coerced into not bringing themselves to ruin.

[8]Cyrus, a Persian from the house of the Achaemenids, from Persia, was related to the Median royal house. The first thing that Cyrus did was to become master of the Median Empire. According to Herodotus, the Median king was his grandfather, over whom Cyrus was victorious. The Medes were, like the Persians, a mountain people, with little cultural education. In the history of [the grandfather] Astyages we find very great harshness [Herodotus 1.107-30]. . . . The second conquest by Cyrus was the victory over Croesus. . . . [229] Cyrus conquered Sardis, and from then on the Persians were rich, in possession of superfluity [Herodotus 1.75-92, 130]. The coasts of Asia Minor Cyrus similarly subdued to himself, conquering a multitude of Greek colonial cities. . . . Through this conquest the Persians came into touch with the Greeks [Herodotus 1.141]. The third war of Cyrus was the conquest of Babylon, and of the Syrians, up to the Mediterranean Sea [Herodotus 1.188-91]. Cyrus's final fight was against the Massagetae, a Scythian people beyond the Oxus, which in the Persian language is called Turan. Here Cyrus died, says Herodotus. . . . Cyrus died in battle [Herodotus 1.201-14]. His deed was the unifying of the Near Eastern peoples through arms. The unification had no further political and religious meaning.

[9]The death of heroes who have formed an epoch in world-history characterizes itself in accord with their mission. Cyrus thus died in his mission, which was the union of the Near East under one mastery, without a further object.

---

8. GW 27 [1] 228-29 (~ GW 27 [2] 605-6; GW 27 [3] 935-36; GW 27 [4] 1302-4; 1840, 227-28).

9. 1840, 228 (~ GW 27 [2] 606; GW 27 [3] 936).

[10]Through his deeds Cyrus became then that great world-historical figure. [Wichern: Cyrus is now the first great world-historical figure, who established himself on the peak of Asia.]

[11]As for the more specific features of Persian mastery, we thus see the Persians as an uncultured mountain people who hold sway over peoples who are other than they, in such a way that the Persians do not mingle themselves with them. Going down into the valleys, the Persians still stand with only one foot in the valleys and the other foot on their mountains, just as the Manchus remain this warrior people, and the emperor annually lives for a time outside the wall in tents with his horsemen, engaged in the hunt for wild animals. Even so do the English hold sway in India, without descending to the principle of the subject people. Thus the Persians endeavored for a long time to maintain themselves in this distinctiveness, although they did not sustain it. With the Persians we see independence, courage, freedom of disposition as ethical custom, which can only exist together with a wildness that gives way when particular factors in life intervene, and it then becomes ethically customary weakness. . . . [1840, 230: It was not given to the Asiatics to unite self-dependence, freedom, and substantial force of spirit, with culture, that is, an interest for diverse pursuits and an acquaintance with the conveniences of life; for them, free valor consists only in wildness of ethical customs; it is not the calm valor of order; and when their spirit opens itself to diversity of interests, it immediately passes into weakness, lets itself sink, and makes human beings the slaves of an ethical custom of feebleness.]

[233] The Persian prince counted as lord over all property. Wherever he came, gifts were brought to him as signs that everything belongs to him and that each and every people have everything only by his favor. Within Persia itself, however, the king distributed gifts. It is evident that under this mastery many individuals had tremendous riches. Each people had to bestow a specific thing on the king and on the satraps. . . .

So we observe the Persian Empire as this union of many peoples engaging in wars against the Greeks, its host not divided into regiments but instead made up of peoples, distinct in their weapons, attire, military discipline. Their march was a kind of movement of peoples, [234] and Herodotus even says about it that the warriors with whom they dwelt at home were those they also wished to be with in battle. . . .

---

10. GW 27 [4] 1302.
11. GW 27 [1] 231, 233–34 (~ GW 27 [2] 606–8; GW 27 [3] 938–41; 1840, 230–33).

The Persian, the worshiper of the light, of purity, hovers tolerantly over the whole. The Persians also became conscious of this tolerance. Herodotus reports [3.38] that Darius son of Hystaspes had brought the Indians and the Greeks together and asked the Greeks whether they didn't wish to eat their deceased parents, upon which they recoiled in horror. He then turned to the Indians, asking whether they wished to burn their dead. When these people then recoiled, he declared that each must stick with their own ethical customs.

[12]Thus the mastery of the Persians was by no means oppressive, either in secular or religious respects. The Persians, says Herodotus [1.131], had indeed no idols, even ridiculed anthropomorphic representations of the gods; but they tolerated every religion—although there may be found outbreaks of wrath against idolatry: Greek temples were destroyed, and the images of the gods were broken in pieces.

"That Light Which Shines and Illuminates the Other"

[13]The elements of this empire are first the Zend people and, on the other side, the Assyrian and Babylonian, with the third the Median, the Persian proper, and fourth the Syrian, extending to the Mediterranean Sea.

The Zend people has its name from the Zend language. In this language are written the books that a Frenchman discovered in the 1750s. These books contain the teachings of the Religion of Light, which doubtless was the religion of ancient Persia, although not [209] in the specific form of the Zend books. The name of the teacher is Zoroaster, as the ancients called him. This Zend people is doubtless connected with the ancient Persians, although it is certainly just as uncontestable that the ancient Persians who came to the fore under Cyrus were not made up exclusively of this Zend people. . . . These Zend books are not without gaps, although the most important part of them is known. . . . These scriptures are a self-contained whole, connected to the religion of ancient Persia, but nevertheless a whole on their own. . . .

[211] From the Zend books it appears that the people had simple ethical customs, although we find chieftains and class distinctions. The main thing that we must consider first is the doctrine of the Zend, the

---

12. 1840, 233 (~ GW 27 [3] 941–42).
13. GW 27 [1] 208–9, 211–12 (~ 1840, 214–17).

doctrine of the Magi, which is present even today, although in a more elaborated configuration.

This religion of the Magi involves the higher, spiritual element of Persia overall. In the Persian religion we see a worship of nature but no idolatry—a higher atmosphere greets us. Singular natural things such as sun and moon do not constitute the foundation of the configurations that are revered. . . . We saw Brahman as indeterminate unity, not the actual concreteness of spirit. With the Persians there is [212] worship of nature as the light, the simple, physical essence that is pure like thought. . . . Free thought is not yet the free foundation, but instead, something sensible is intuited—yet something sensible as wholly universal, thus in the form of thought; and insofar as this sensible is known as something inward, the meaning is a thought, a cognition, a knowing, something good. This is the higher standpoint of the Persians overall. Thus their soul has raised itself up to this higher purity, to something sensible in the universal form of thought.

[14]Where the Zend people, mentioned in the religious books of Zoroaster, lived is difficult to determine. In Media and Persia the religion of Zoroaster prevailed, and Xenophon mentions that Cyrus adopted it:[15] but none of these countries was the proper habitat of the Zend people. Zoroaster himself calls it the pure Aryan. . . .

[226] All the data suggest that a close connection is to be sought between the Magi and the Zend religion, but that, although the Magi preserved and extended it, it experienced great modifications in the transmission to the various peoples. Xenophon says [*Education of Cyrus* 8.1.43] that Cyrus was the first to sacrifice to God according to the fashion of the Magi. The Medes therefore acted as a medium for propagating the Zend religion.

[16]The Persians are the first historical people; the Persian is the first empire that has passed away. While [212] China and India remain stationary and perpetuate a natural, vegetative concrete-existence even to the present, this land has undergone those developments and revolutions that alone manifest a historical condition. The Chinese and Indian empires can only on their own account and for us come into the connectedness of history. Here, however, in Persia, first arises that

---

14. 1840, 216, 226.
15. *Education of Cyrus* 4.5.14, 51; 4.6.11; 7.3.1; 7.5.35, 57; 8.3.11, 24.
16. 1840, 211–14 (~ GW 27 [2] 596–97, 600; GW 27 [3] 921–22, 927–28; GW 27 [4] 1291–92).

light that shines and illuminates the other; for *Zoroaster's* light is the first that belongs to the world of consciousness—to spirit as relation to what is other. We see in the Persian Empire a pure elevated unity, as the substance that leaves the particular free; as the light, which only manifests what the bodies are for themselves; a unity that holds sway over individuals only to excite them to become strong for themselves, to develop their particularity and make it count.... The principle of development begins with the Persian history, and thereby makes this the beginning in the proper sense of world-history; for the universal interest of spirit in history is to attain infinite being-in-itself of subjectivity—by the absolute antithesis, to come to reconciliation.

The transition that we have to make is thus only in the concept, not in the external historical connectedness. The principle itself is this: that the universal, which we have seen in Brahm, now comes to consciousness—becomes an object, and acquires a positive import for humanity.... [213] But inasmuch as this universal becomes objective, it acquires an affirmative nature: the human being becomes free and confronts the highest, which is made objective for the human being. This universality we see exhibited in Persia—and therewith a differentiation from the universal that is, at the same time, an identification of the individual with the universal. In the Chinese and Indian principle, this differentiation is not present, but only unity of spirituality and naturalness is present. But spirit that is still in the natural condition has the problem of freeing itself from the latter. Rights and duties in India are bound up with classes, and are thereby only something particular belonging to humans by nature; in China this unity is present in the form of paternalism.... In the Persian principle, unity first elevates itself to the differentiation from the merely natural; it is the negating of the relation that is only unmediated, that is not mediated by the will. The unity comes in the Persian principle to manifestation as Light, which here is not simply light as such, the most universal physical element, but is at the same time also the purity of spirit, that is, the good. Thereby however is the particular—the being-bound with *limited* nature—abolished. Light, in a physical and spiritual sense, counts, therefore, as the elevation, the freedom, from the natural; the human being relates oneself to light, to the good, as to something objective, which by one's will is acknowledged, reverenced, and activated.

Now, when we look back once more—and we cannot do so too frequently—on the configurations that we have traversed in arriving at this point, we see in China the totality of an ethically customary whole, but without subjectivity; this totality divided into members, but without independence. [214] We found only an external ordering of this unity. In India, on the contrary, differentiation came to the fore; but as unspiritual, as incipient being-in-itself, but with the condition that the differentiation is insurmountable; and spirit remains bound in the limitations of nature, thus as distortion of itself. Now in Persia there stands, above this separation of castes, that purity of light, of the good, which all are equally able to approach, and in which all equally may be hallowed. . . . The fact that each has a share in that principle secures to each a value for oneself.

[17]This One, Universal, is of course not yet recognized as the free unity of thought; not yet worshipped in spirit and in truth; it is still clothed, with the configuration of light. But the light is not Lama, not Brahman, not mountain, not brute, not this or that particular existence—it is sensuous universality itself; simple manifestation. The Persian religion is therefore no idol-worship; it does not adore individual natural things, but the universal itself. Light has the signification of the spiritual; it is the configuration of the good and true—the substantiality of knowledge and volition [218] as well as of all natural things. Light puts the human being in a position to be able to exercise choice; and one can only make a choice when one has emerged from that which had absorbed one. But light has immediately within itself an opposite, namely, darkness—just as evil is the antithesis of good. Even as good would not be present for the human being, if evil were not there; and even as one can be truly good only when one knows the evil, so light does not exist without darkness. Among the Persians, Ormuzd and Ahriman present this antithesis. Ormuzd is the Lord of the realm of light, of good; Ahriman that of darkness, of evil. But there is a still higher being from whom both proceeded, a universal without antithesis, called *Zeruane-Akerene*—the unlimited All. The All is something very abstract; it does not exist for itself, and Ormuzd and Ahriman have arisen from it. This dualism is commonly brought as a reproach against oriental thought; and, insofar as the contradiction is taken to remain absolute, it is in any case the irreligious understanding that sticks with it. But spirit must have the antithesis; the principle of the dualism belongs therefore to the concept of spirit, which, as concrete, has the differentiation in its essence. Among the Persians, the pure has

---

17. 1840, 217–20 (~ GW 27 [1] 211–19; GW 27 [2] 597, 601–2; GW 27 [3] 922, 928; GW 27 [4] 1294–97).

come to consciousness, as has the impure; and spirit, in that it grasps itself, must essentially place the universal positive over and against the particular negative: it is by the overcoming of this antithesis that spirit is born again. The deficiency in the Persian principle is only that the unity of the antithesis is not known in complete configuration; for in that indeterminate representation of the uncreated All, whence Ormuzd and Ahriman proceeded, the unity is only the absolutely first, and does not bring the antithesis back to itself. Ormuzd creates in self-determination—but also according to the decree of Zeruane-Akerene (so the representation is wavering); and the reconciliation [219] of the antithesis consists only in the contest that Ormuzd carries on with Ahriman, and in which he will at last conquer.

Ormuzd is the Lord of Light, and he creates all that is beautiful and masterful in the world, which is a realm of the Sun. He is the excellent, the good, the positive in all natural and spiritual concrete-existence. Light is the body of Ormuzd; thence the worship of fire, because Ormuzd is present in all light; but he is not the Sun or the Moon itself; rather, in these the Persians venerate only the Light, which is Ormuzd. Zoroaster asks Ormuzd who he is. He answers: "My name is ground and center of all essence, highest wisdom and science, destroyer of the world's badness, and maintainer of the all, fullness of blessedness, pure will," etc. That which comes from Ormuzd is living, independent, and lasting; the word is a testimony to this; prayers are his productions. Darkness is, on the contrary, the body of Ahriman; but an eternal fire banishes him from the temples.

The goal of everyone is to keep oneself pure, and to spread this purity around one. The precepts that have the latter in view are very diffuse; but the moral determinations are mild. It is said: if someone loads you with reviling and insults, but subsequently humbles himself, call him friend. We read in the *Vendidad* that sacrifices consist chiefly of the flesh of clean animals, of flowers and fruits, milk and perfumes. It is said there:

> As man was created pure and worthy of heaven, he becomes pure again through the law of the servants of Ormuzd, which is purity itself—if he purifies himself by sanctity of thought, of word, and of deed. What is pure thought?—That which ascends to the beginning of things. What is pure word?—The word of Ormuzd (the word is thus personified and imports the living spirit of the whole revelation of Ormuzd). What is pure deed?—The humble adoration of the heavenly hosts, created at the beginning.

[220] In this it is demanded that the human being should be good: one's own will, subjective freedom, is presupposed.

Ormuzd is not limited to singularity. Sun, Moon, and five other stars, which remind us of planets—those illuminating and illuminated bodies—are the primary images of Ormuzd; the *Amshaspand*, his first sons. Among these, Mithra is also named. . . . Later on, great importance is assigned to Mithra as the mediator between Ormuzd and humans. . . . Besides those noticed there are other protecting spirits, under the Amshaspand, who stand as their superiors and are the governors and preservers of the world.[18]

[19][Griesheim: There is yet another, concrete antithesis to note. [216] There is, namely, in the Zend books, talk of the two pure worlds of Ormuzd, one of which is the earthly realm, the immediately living concrete existence of the human being, from which is distinguished the second, of the individual Feroers, or the "Feruer," as it is written. They are present everywhere and are at home in the realm of soul, and every body has such a Feroer—every plant and tree; wherever there is activity, life are the "Ferver."]

"Ritual Observance"

[20]The religion of Ormuzd as *ritual observance* is that humans should conduct themselves in harmony with the Realm of Light. The universal commandment is therefore, as already said, spiritual and corporeal purity, which consists in many prayers to Ormuzd. It was made specially obligatory upon the Persians to maintain life—to plant trees, to dig wells, to fertilize deserts—in order that, overall, life, the positive, the pure, might further itself, and the realm of Ormuzd might be universally extended. External purity is contravened by touching a dead animal, and there are many provisions for becoming purified from such.

---

18. In his 1827 *Lectures on the Philosophy of Religion* (GW 29 [2] 123–24) Hegel adds: "Everything that is living—sun, star, tree—is revered as good; but only the good, the Light in it, not its particular configuration, its finite, transitory mode. . . . So also is the state conceived: the prince of the Parsees—and so ought it also to have been among the Persians—as representative of the highest Light, not the pure Ormuzd himself; his officials as representatives of the planets and stars seen as ministers, helpers of Ormuzd. One among these is *Mithra*, whom Herodotus certainly knows as the *mesitēs*, Mediator." (In fact, it is not Herodotus, but Plutarch who speaks of Mithra in this way, in his *About Isis and Osiris* 369e.)

19. GW 27 [1] 215b–16 (~ GW 27 [3] 928–29; 1840, 220).

20. 1840, 221 (~ GW 27 [1] 216; GW 27 [3] 929–30).

Herodotus relates [1.189–90] of Cyrus that when he went against Babylon, and the River Gyndes [modern Diala] engulfed one of the horses of the Chariot of the Sun, he was occupied for a year in punishing it, by diverting its stream into small canals, to deprive it of its force. Thus Xerxes, when the sea broke in pieces his bridges, had chains laid upon it [Herodotus 7.35–36] as the wicked and pernicious being—Ahriman.

[21]Sacrificial offerings do not have the meaning they have for other peoples—namely, that an individual [218] relinquishes something of his own property, characterizing it as nonessential as opposed to the deity, and so gives a portion of that property, or entirely his own self, needlessly, without having to, to the deity. For the Indians this sacrifice extends to the surrendering of one's life to the deity, so that in this *absolute* negativity an Indian is only seeking to gain some worth. The Zend people themselves do make sacrificial offerings; animal offerings are commanded and are forthcoming—but are not needlessly thrown away; the sacrifice consists only in that the priest recites certain prayers while slaughtering the animal. So what takes place is only a dedication of the beast. Explicit prayers are commanded only for daily consecrations; but these are not regarded as sacrificial offerings. There is no doing what is negative against oneself to prove one's respect for Ormuzd.

A religious celebration is that of the consecrated bread and chalice in remembrance and honor of Hom, as founder of the old revelation (as Zoroaster is the reviver). To honor Hom there is a special celebration that consists of the consecration and partaking of unleavened bread, as well as the presentation and partaking of a chalice containing a beverage from Hom juice. "Hom" is thus the revealer and "Hom" is also a plant, the juice of which is then drunk. So this is something mirroring our Christian sacrament of the Lord's supper; and the church fathers even found this observance in the Mithra worship of Roman times, even into the Christian era too, and they say that through it the evil demons want to make fun of what is good. Zoroaster has Hom say: "Whoever [219] consumes me with thankful prayer is sacrificing to me, and receives from me the goods of the world." This ceremony in remembrance of Hom was also celebrated in the slaughter of a beast as a sacrificial offering.

This is the ancient religion of the Zend people, a foundation that made its way over to the Persians and the Medes. It is the purest nature religion, in that Light is the object of reverence, and the entire

---

21. GW 27 [1] 217b–19 (~ GW 27 [3] 929–30).

relationship of the ritual observance is upheld just as purely as the object itself. It is nature religion as pure as there can be.

"The Civil Laws"

[22]There are three kinds of laws. [217] The first pertains to personal security. Whoever draws the blood of another or moves to strike, undergoes punishment—predominantly lashes. There is no capital punishment. Punishment for many things occurs in the afterlife. It is remarkable that there is no mention at all of the crimes of murder, although the series of books containing the laws seems to be complete. Later on, of course, in more developed conditions, such punishments were legislated—although there is no punishment for murder of one's parents, because these crimes are too horrible to have possibly been committed.

The second kind of law is more concerned with religious precepts, the first of which is that punishments befall anyone who speaks contemptuously of a holy man and deliberately lives contrary to the laws of Ormuzd.

The third kind contains the "Mithra-sins," and preeminently moral laws. Mithra comes to the fore as the one who presides over the inner, the ethically customary in the human being. The punishment for a moral transgression is much harsher. The precepts of justice are found here. For breaking one's word the punishment is three hundred lashes or three hundred years of punishment in hell. Whoever steals money receives in the other world three hundred years of punishment in hell. These then are the Mithra-laws. The civil laws thus indicate the extreme simplicity of the culture, and many of them are for the most part moral commandments.

Syria

[23]Syria contains in itself the greatest contrasts, of very diverse peoples arising from antithetical spirits. The first point, the first special aspect, is (1) Phoenician commerce [Handel]; then (2) the Syrian condition overall; then (3) the Israelite people. In these there lies the elements through which nature travels to a higher condition, what we call "human" as such, and with which we can sympathize more.

---

22. GW 27 [1] 216b-17.
23. GW 27 [3] 943.

"Phoenician Commerce": "An Entirely New Principle"

[24]Phoenician commerce had its locus on a narrow strip often only two hours' travel time in width, bordered on the east by Lebanon, which protected it from the continent. Along this strip arose a series of cities—Tyre etc. We see here the emergence of commerce as isolated in its distinctiveness. It is not here an essential phase of the whole, of the state; instead it is abstract for itself.[25] We see here this commerce in part reaching into the interior of the land, but the main directedness is to the Mediterranean Sea. The Phoenicians showed themselves to be productive and resourceful, but what is most particularly noteworthy about them is their wide-ranging and bold seafaring even on the Atlantic Ocean. . . .

[236] Thus we see a people that, by simply pursuing commerce, in its own fashion, is in these times a world-discovering people; and so we see a progression as was previously not in Asia: the human being, self-reliant over and against nature, becoming master of nature. Whereas in Central Asia humans worshiped nature as a power over them, here they deliver themselves from nature, seek to guard against it, overcome it. Herewith emerges an element incompatible with nature-worship—an emancipation from this power and its many petty rituals of worship. The spiritual life, the awakening self-confidence of human beings, turns them away from this dependence, and from petty ceremonies.

[26]In this way there emerges an entirely new principle. Inactivity ceases, as also mere rude courage; in their place enters the activity of industry (Industrie), and that circumspect boldness that, while it dares the perils of the deep, is also prudently thoughtful about the means. Here everything depends on humanity's activity, its valor, its understanding—while the goals are also for its sake. Human will and activity here have priority, not nature and its bounty. . . . The principle of industry contains the antithesis of what is received from nature; for natural objects are worked up for use and ornament, but in industry, humanity is itself the goal, and treats nature as something subjected to it, on which humans impress the seal of their activity. Understanding is courage here, and ingenuity is better than mere natural boldness. Here we see the peoples liberated from the fear of nature and its slavish worship.

---

24. GW 27 [1] 235–36 (~ GW 27 [2] 611–12; GW 27 [3] 943–44; GW 27 [4] 1306–7).
25. "not connected to other principles"—GW 27 [3] 943.
26. 1840, 234–36 (~ GW 27 [2] 609–10, 612–13; GW 27 [3] 943–45).

Comparing herewith the *religious* conceptions: [235] we see in *Babylon*, in the *Syrian* tribes, and in *Phrygia*, first a rude, vulgar, sensual idolatry.... The [biblical] Prophets give the most terrible pictures of the latter (though their repulsive character must be partly ascribed to the hatred of Jews against neighboring peoples). In the Book of Wisdom such depictions are especially ample. Not only was there a worship of natural things, but also of the universal power of nature—as Astarte, Cybele, the Diana of Ephesus. The religious observance was a sensuous confusion, with frenzy and revelry: sensuality and cruelty are its two characteristic traits. "When they hold a festival, they act as if insane," says the Book of Wisdom (14:28). With the sensual life, since it is a consciousness that does not reach the universal, cruelty is connected; because nature as such is the highest, the human being has no value, or only the most trifling....

[236] We find on the other hand something different among the *Phoenicians*, that bold seafaring people. Herodotus tells us [2.44] that at Tyre Hercules was worshiped.... This worship is particularly indicative of the character of the people; for it is Hercules of whom the Greeks say that he raised himself to Olympus by dint of human courage and daring.

"The Death of God"

[27]Along this coast nature as a universal was worshiped, under the names of Astarte, Cybele, etc. This divine worship was in one sense still very sensual and dissolute, though celebrated with spirited enthusiasm, while the Indians' worship is dead and cold; the latter are elevated to the higher state only when they achieve a loss of consciousness through the death of spirit—humans have worth only by the death of consciousness or of the natural. Here in this religion, however, we see emerging the element of spiritual infusion—though, to be sure, it goes so far as dissoluteness. But there was in it an elevation to a higher state, one beyond finitude, coupled with feeling of self.

[237] Here is the place to touch upon the worship of Adonis at Byblos,[28] with which that of Cybele and Attis harmonized. The worship of Adonis consisted in two parts: one essential phase is the festival of the death of Adonis, the second is his rediscovery. The first is a festival

---

27. GW 27 [1] 236–37 (~ GW 27 [2] 612–14; GW 27 [3] 945–46; GW 27 [4] 1307–8).
28. "Other Near-Eastern cities also had something connected with this"—GW 27 [2] 613–14.

of grief, in which the women grieve for the dead god, and give themselves over to the most extravagant laments. This is a proceeding that is alien to the oriental spirit. In India, ... elevation consists in the heroism of impassivity.... [Griesheim: Among the Phoenicians, sorrow achieves the respect due to it; the human being thereby senses oneself, and this sensing allows one to know oneself as being here and now.] In sorrow, the human being senses one's subjectivity, one's particularity, one's thisness, one's actuality, and by this sensing one may know oneself as this objectivity. Sorrow is the sensing of the negative, in which is at the same time the infinite affirmation—not the sheerly abstract negative, but instead at the same time the feeling of self, the positive, that relates itself to this negative. So here we see human feeling come on the scene.

[29]In regard to the worship of Adonis we find a notable passage in the Book of Wisdom (14:13, etc.), in which it says: "The idols were not from the beginning—but were thought up through the vain honoring of humans, who are short-lived. For a father, afflicted with pain and sorrow for his *son* (Adonis) all-too-early taken away from him, when he had made an image of him, held him to be a god, who was a dead human, and founded for his people worship and sacrifices." [237] ... A universality of sorrow is established: for death becomes immanent in the divine, and the god dies. Among the Persians we saw Light and Darkness struggling with each other, but here both principles are united in one, the Absolute. Here also the negative is only the natural; but, as the death of God, it is not only the determination of something limited, but is pure negativity itself. This point is important, because the divine overall ought to be grasped as spirit, which involves its being concrete, and having in itself the essential phase of negativity.... The negative itself is an essential phase of the god: the natural, death, the religious observance appropriate to which is sorrow. So it is in the festival of the death of Adonis, and of his resurrection, that the concrete comes to consciousness. Adonis is a youth, who is torn from his parents and dies too early.... When [238] a youth is snatched away by death, the occurrence is regarded as not making sense, ... for youth, death is a contradiction. And this is the deeper element: that in the god, the negative, the contradiction, is manifested, and that the religious observance rendered to him involves both elements—the sorrow felt for the being snatched away, and the joy over the god's being found again.[30]

---

29. 1840, 236–38 (~ GW 27 [2] 613–14; GW 27 [3] 945–46).
30. In his 1827 *Lectures on the Philosophy of Religion* (GW 29 [2] 127) Hegel adds: "the Dalai Lama dies; likewise Indra the god of the natural, and others also: they die, and come again.

"The Jewish People"

³¹Among the many petty Syrian peoples, the *Jewish people* is for us especially important, on account of the Mosaic religion. This is the religion of the Persians, with the differentiation that the physical aspect is stripped away from the pure Light; the highest—what is in *and* for itself—becomes known as the good, as subject, as God; the principle of pure knowing, of pure thinking, which is only for thinking, certainly originated very early in the Jewish people.

³²Here the Persian unity, the Persian Light, pure, natural, spiritual unity, is purified from the essential phase, from the element of naturalness; and here there becomes consciously recognized the highest, ultimate, true, as the One that is no longer identical with the natural, but has thrown this off. This highpoint, a peak that on one side still stands in the Orient, on the other side is determined as transcending, to thought, to knowing, as the highest—that is, thinking that is for the sake of thinking. When belief is made the principle, what matters is *how* one believes; when one believes in the one God, not in the God as Light, but in the God purified of the natural, then the belief is absolutely thinking; what one believes, that one also knows . . . and that is the belief held by the Israelite people—only in thinking. When this religion is called a religion of feeling, what the feeling contains, the One, is the thinking. Thinking becomes also feeling. . . . But feeling is subjective form, the lowest; the beast itself also feels.

³³Its original and fundamental book is the Old Testament. There we have the determinate intuition of its spirit. The Jewish principle stands over and against the Phoenician, where we see something spiritual revered, but still in very confined human shape; the Jewish is over and against, in that the spiritual element is entirely purified, and the content of thinking, the thinking of itself, the One God, comes to consciousness, as the Pure, the One. Here the spiritual is in such an extreme determination—known as purer absolute thought. This principle is

---

But this dying is different from the negativity that is being discussed here, which is death insofar as it belongs to the subject. . . . The thousand-times dying of Indra is of a different kind: the substance remains one and the same; it only leaves behind this individual body of one Lama but has immediately chosen another; the substance is not concerned in this dying, this negation, . . . it does not have the sorrow of death.—The dying of god that we have here is in himself: the negation is immanent in his essence, in himself, and thereby this god is characterized essentially as subject. The subject is this: that it, in itself, gives to itself being-other, and through negation brings about itself this return into self."

31. GW 27 [4] 1308.
32. GW 27 [3] 947.
33. GW 27 [2] 614–15 (~ GW 27 [1] 238–39; GW 27 [3] 946–47; 1840, 238–39).

over and against the Asiatic unity of nature with spirit, where the spirit does not become free because it is still sunk in nature. True, the pure Brahm is the same content as the God of the Jews; it does not become object, however, but [615] only a background of the subject. Among the Persians, Light is the physical, external unity. It is here that the break occurs between the West and the East, where spirit goes down into itself, grasps itself in its depth, and gains the abstract spiritual foundation of the truth.

[34]Here begins the essential phase of the overturning of the Eastern principle, the essential phase of the changeover from nature to spirit. Eastern people say that nature is the foundation, is what is first and eternal, and they proceed from nature to anything further. But now, with the Jews, we see the spiritual as the foundation for the first time.

[35]Nature, which in the East is the primary and fundamental, is now depressed to the status of the created; and spirit now is first. Of God it becomes known that he is the creator of all humans, as he is of all nature, and is absolute activity overall. But this great principle, in its wider determination, [239] is *exclusive* oneness. This religion must necessarily possess the element of exclusiveness, which consists essentially in this—that only the one people recognizes the One, and is recognized by him. The God of the Jewish People is only the God of Abraham and of his seed; national individuality and a particular, local worship are involved in such a conception of deity.[36] Over and against this God, all other gods are false:[37] and indeed the distinction between true and false is completely abstract; for as regards the false gods, it is not recognized that a manifestation of the divine shines into them. Now every spiritual actuality—and all the more every religion—is so constituted that whatever it may be, an affirmative essential phase is contained in it. However erroneous a religion may be, it nevertheless possesses the truth, although in a mutilated way. In every religion there is divine presence, a divine relationship; and a philosophy of history has to seek out the essential phase of the spiritual even in the most imperfect shapes. But a religion is not as such good just because it is a religion; one must not fall into that laxity of saying that it is not a matter of the substance

---

34. GW 27 [1] 238.

35. 1840, 238-42 (~ GW 27 [1] 238-39; GW 27 [2] 615-19; GW 27 [3] 946-47).

36. "So that the actuality of his love restricts itself to the Jewish nationality, to a natural family"—GW 27 [2] 615.

37. "And rightly so, as in Christianity . . . with the religion of the One is tied the notable exclusivity"—GW 27 [2] 615.

but only of the form.³⁸ This lax easygoingness the Jewish religion does not have, inasmuch as it is absolutely exclusive.

The spiritual speaks of itself here as immediately free of the sensuous, and nature is reduced to what is external and ungodly. This is the exact truth about nature, for only later can the Idea attain a reconciliation in this its externalization; its first expression will be in opposition to nature; for spirit, which had been hitherto devalued, here first attains its value, while nature resumes its proper position. Nature is itself external, it is posited, it is created; and this conception, that God is lord and creator of nature, brings God to being the exalted, with the whole of nature God's adornment, and to be expended in his service. In contrast with this exaltation, [240] the Indian's is only that of the indefinite. Through the spirituality overall, the sensuous and unethical custom are no longer privileged, but disparaged as ungodliness. Only the One, the spirit, the nonsensuous is the truth; thought is free for itself, and true morality and righteousness can now emerge, for God is honored by righteousness, and right doing is walking in the way of the Lord. With this is conjoined happiness, life, and temporal prosperity, as reward; for it is said: "that thou mayest live long on the earth" [Deut. 4:40]. Also, the possibility of a *historical* view is here present; for here is the prosaic understanding, putting the limited and circumscribed in its place, and comprehending it as the configuration proper to finitude: humans are regarded as individuals, not as incarnations of God; sun as sun, mountains as mountains—not as possessing spirit and will.

We see among this people a severe worship, as relationship to pure thought. The subject as concrete does not become free, because the absolute itself is not comprehended as the *concrete* spirit; because spirit appears grasped still as nonspirit. Innerness we indeed have before us—the pure heart, repentance, devotion; but the particular concrete individuality has not become objective to itself in the absolute, and it therefore remains closely bound to the observance of ceremonies and of the law, whose ground is the pure freedom as abstract.³⁹ The Jews possess that which they are, through the One: consequently the subject has no freedom for itself. Spinoza regards the law book of Moses as having been given by God to the Jews as

---

38. "A laxity belonging to our times, in making these pieties the same"—GW 27 [2] 615.
39. Cf. GW 27 [3] 948–49: "But later the Law developed itself in terms of the heart and its feeling; innerness of the will, and directedness of this will to the One, God, is established as the highest matter."

a punishment—a rod of correction. The subject never comes to the consciousness of one's independence; on that account we do not find among the Jews any belief in the immortality of the soul; for the subject does not exist in and for itself. But though in Judaism the subject is without worth, the family is, on the contrary, independent, [241] for the worship of Jehovah is bound up with the family, which is thereby substantial. The state, however, is not consonant with the Judaic principle and is alien to the legislation of Moses. . . . On the whole, the Jewish history has grand features of character; but it is contaminated by a sanctified exclusivity toward the spirits of other nations (the destruction of the inhabitants of Canaan being even commanded), and by a defect of culture overall, and by the superstition that is brought in through the conception of the higher worth attached only to this nation. Miracles, too, form a disturbing feature in this history as history—for insofar as the concrete consciousness is not free, the concrete insight is also not free; nature is de-divinized, but understanding of it is not yet there.

The family grew, through the dominating of Canaan, into a people, taking a whole land into possession, and erecting in Jerusalem a temple for the generality. A real state union was not, however, present. In case of danger, heroes arose, who placed themselves at the head of the armies; but the people was for the most part in subjection. Later on, kings were chosen, and it was they who first rendered the Jews independent. David even made conquests. Originally the legislation is adapted to the family only; yet in the books of Moses the wish for a king is anticipated. The priests ought to choose him: he ought not to be a foreigner, not to have horsemen in large numbers, and to have few wives.[40] After a short period of glory the realm suffered internal disruption and divided itself. As there was only one tribe of Levites, and only one temple in Jerusalem, by the division of the realm [242] idolatry had to enter immediately. The One God could not be honored in different temples, and there could not be two realms of one religion. However spiritual may be the thought of God as objective, the subjective side—the worship rendered to him—is still very limited and unspiritual.

---

40. "Difficult demands for a state that transitions to a kingship from never having once had a republican constitution"—GW 27 [2] 619.

Appendix: Note on Judaism in Hegel's *Lectures on the Philosophy of Religion*

In his 1827 *Lectures on the Philosophy of Religion*[41]—perhaps under the influence of his disciple Eduard Gans, a Jew who was a leading founder of the "Wissenschaft des Judentums"—Hegel discusses the Jewish religion with more respect, in greater depth, and as historically more significant: he presents it as the "religion of sublimity," and not as a development of Persia, nor as *preceding* Phoenician and Egyptian and Greek religion, but instead as paired with, and as a higher stage than (and therefore *after*), Greek religion or "the religion of beauty."

As "pure thinking," the God of the Jews "is withdrawn from the natural, and so" from "sensible representation"; and "for us this is what first merits the name of God." Moreover, in this God "the ethically customary rationality of freedom, and the unity of this rationality existing for itself, is the true subjectivity, is itself-in-itself determining subjectivity." This "is the wisdom and the holiness." The "contents of the Greek gods, the ethically customary powers, are not holy, because they are still particular, limited" (GW 29 [2] 149-50). The "finite subject in its self-containment one cannot call sublime"; but "the subject here," in Jewish religion, "is the absolute, in and for itself; it is the Holy." And "sublimity is in the first place the appearing, the relation, of this Subject to the world" (154). The "purpose of God" is "to be known by consciousness, to become known"; this "can first be said to be the *theoretical* purpose—the more determinate is the *practical*"; this latter is "the ethically customary purpose, the *ethically customary*—that humans, in what they do, have before their eyes the lawful, the just" (155).

Hegel proceeds (160-61) to present the Roman religion as "the unity of the [Greek] religion of beauty and [the Jewish religion] of sublimity." In Roman religion, on the one hand "the religion of beauty loses the concrete individuality of its gods, and also the content—the ethically customary, independent content: the gods become put down as mere means"; on the other hand, "the religion of sublimity loses the directedness to the One, eternal, above the earth"; "the two become combined, in one goal, which is comprehensive, universally external, at first universally empirical." The "goal in the religion of sublimity, insofar as it is also a limited one, is also an essential goal, but not yet developed. Thus

---

41. GW 29 [2] 149-59; contrast the versions of 1821, 1824, and 1831 (GW 29 [1] 51-52, 335-52; GW 29 [2] 254-57).

its innerness is the family, the natural customary ethics as such"; in Roman religion, "this goal is the extended one: the embracing, essential goal is the state overall."

Eventually Hegel characterizes Christianity, "the completed religion" (169), as the "reconciliation" of the "antithesis" between Judaism and Roman Stoicism or skepticism—explaining as follows: the biblical account of the Fall expresses that "the human being should recognize the infinity of the antithesis between good and evil in oneself, and that one—one is something natural—should know oneself to be evil as naturalness." Now "this antithesis has overall two forms: *on one side*" is "the *antithesis over and against God*"; "*on the other side* is the unhappiness" that is "the *antithesis over and against the world,* that one is in rupture with the world" (204).

In "the relationship of rupture from the one extreme, from God, the human being who has in oneself this consciousness—that, deepest within oneself, one is this contradiction (between good and evil)—has thereby the infinite agony concerning oneself" (205). And "the result, the determinate manner of this agony, is *my humiliation,* remorse: the agony over myself is that I, as natural, am not in proportion to that which I simultaneously know that I should be in my knowing and willing" (206).

In "the relationship to the other extreme," the human being finds that one's "satisfaction as naturally needy has no right, no claim," while "the higher, ethically customary demands are demands, determinations, of freedom"; and "insofar as these do not find their satisfaction in concrete existence in the external world, one is in unhappiness"—which "is what drives the human being back into oneself, and since in one is the fixed demand for rationality of the world, one gives up the world and seeks happiness, satisfaction, in the collecting of oneself in oneself" (206).

So "we have these two forms": "that agony that comes from the universal, from on high, we saw in the Jewish people." The "other, the being driven back into oneself from the unhappiness, is the standpoint in which the Roman world ended—the universal unhappiness of the world," thus "Stoicism or skepticism" (206-7).

"The concept of the preceding religions has purified itself into this antithesis," and "that this antithesis showed itself and set itself forth as existing need, is expressed thus: 'When the time had fully come . . .' [Galatians 4:4]—that is, the Spirit, the need for the Spirit, is at hand, that points to the reconciliation" (208).

Bibliography

Creuzer, F. *Symbolik und Mythologie der alten Völker.* 4 vols. Leipzig: Leske, 1819–21. See GW 27 [2] 665, 671.
Creuzer, F., and J. D. Guigniaut. *Religions de l'antiquité, considérés principalement dans leurs formes symboliques et mythologiques.* Paris: Treuttel et Würtz, 1825. See GW 31 [1] 696–703; GW 31 [2] 1909.
Elphinstone, M. *An Account of the Kingdom of Caubul and Dependencies in Persia, Tartary, and India.* London: Longman, 1815. See GW 27 [1] 206; GW 27 [3] 919.
Görres, J. J. *Das Heldenbuch von Iran aus dem Schah Namah des Firdussi* [sic]. 2 vols. Heidelberg: Reimer, 1820. See GW 31 [1] 720–21; GW 31 [2] 1907; GW 31 [3] 925; GW 31 [4] 1298.
Görres, J. J. *Mythengeschichte der asiatischen Welt.* 2 vols. Mohr and Zimmer, 1810.
Hafis, Mohammed Schemsed-Din. *Der Diwan.* 2 vols. Trans. Joseph v. Hammer [-Purgstall] et al. Stuttgart: Cotta, 1812. See GW 31 [1] 726–28.
Hammer-Purgstall, J. von. *Geschichte der schönen Redeskünste Persiens.* Vienna: Heubner and Wolfe, 1818.
Heeren, A. H. L. *Ideen über die Politik, den Verkehr und den Handel der vornehmsten Völker der alten Welt.* 2 vols. Göttingen: Vandenhoeck und Ruprecht, 1804–5. The chapter on India is 1:291–704.
Niebuhr, C. *Reisebeschreibung nach Arabien und den angrenzenden Ländern.* 2 vols. Copenhagen: Möller, 1774 and 1778.
Niebuhr, C. *Reise und Beobachtungen durch Egypten und Arabien aus den grossern Werken verschneidener gelehrten Reisenden.* 2 vols. Bern: Steiner, 1779 and 1781. See GW 31 [1] 824–29; GW 31 [2] 1943.
Rhode, J. G. *Die heilige Sage und das gesammte Religionsystem der alten Baktrer, Meder, und Perser oder des Zendvolks.* Frankfurt am Main: Hermann, 1820.
Rhode, J. G. *Ueber Alter und Werth einiger morgenländischen Urkunden, in Beziehuyng auf Religion, Geschichte und Alterthumskunde überhaupt.* Breslau: Holäufer, 1817. See GW 31 [1] 857; GW 31 [2] 1954.
Ritter, Carl. *Die Erdkunde im Verhältnis zur Natur und zur Geschichte des Menschen, oder allgemeine, vergleichende Geographie, als sichere Grundlage des Studiums und Unterrichts in physicakalischen und historischen Wissenschaften.* 2 vols. Berlin: Reimer, 1817–18. See GW 27 [4] 1312.
Ritter, Carl. *Die Vorhalle europäischer Völkergeschichten vor Herodotus, um den Kaukasus und an den Gesatden des Pontus.* Berlin: Reimer, 1820. See GW 27 [1] 82, 195–96; GW 27 [2] 515, 570; GW 27 [3] 856, 1092; GW 27 [4] 1312.
Shahnama: see above, Görres, *Das Heldenbuch.*
Wilford, F. "On Mount Caucasus." *Asiatic Researches* 6 (1801): 455–536. See GW 27 [1] 209; GW 27 [2] 584.
Zoroaster, *Zend-Avesta, Zoroasters lebendiges Wort.* Trans. and ed. J. F. Kleuker from the French edition of A. du Perron. 5 vols. Riga: Hartknoch, 1776–83. See GW 27 [1] 208–9; GW 27 [4] 1293.

CHAPTER 5

The Oriental World, Part Four
Egypt

[1]In Egypt we see put together the essential phases that in the Persian monarchy emerged singly. We found among the Persians the adoration of Light as the universal essence of nature. This principle then develops itself in essential phases that relate to each other indifferently; the one essential phase is the being-immersed in the sensuous, among the Babylonians and Syrians; the other is the spiritual, in twofold [243] form: on the one hand the incipient consciousness of the concrete spirit in the worship of Adonis; and then as pure and abstract thought among the Jews; in the former the unity of the concrete is lacking, in the latter the concrete itself is lacking. To unite these contradictory elements is the problem or task; and this problem or task is present in Egypt.[2]

[3]What we see in these essential phases is the elevation of the human being above nature, above the employment of the elements of nature for their own sake; then, that pure thought as the absolute is recognized;

---

1. 1840, 242–43.
2. For some major sources, in addition to classical Greek texts (above all Herodotus, esp. bk. 2, and Diodorus Siculus, esp. 1.42 ff., and Plutarch, esp. *About Isis and Osiris*) upon which Hegel seems to have drawn for his understanding of Egypt, see the bibliography at the end of this chapter.
3. GW 27 [1] 239 (~ GW 27 [2] 619).

and that sorrow contains its element that makes it count. These are elements of a new self-consciousness, in which is the challenge, that human beings pose for themselves an entirely new problem or task that they have to solve. The land of Egypt has this problem or task to solve.[4]

[5]The executing of this task, however, appears much rather to be this: that in the individuality of this people, the riddle appears posed—and not solved. Placing ourselves before Egypt, it can be that the recollection of the Sphinx presents itself. . . . The Sphinx, moreover, is the symbol of the Egyptians—this twofold figure, human and animal, symbolizes the spirit that tears itself away from the animal, but has not yet completely grasped itself, does not yet stand on its own feet.

[6]It has certainly been remarked that Egypt is the land of the riddle, the land that has presented itself symbolically in the Sphinx—and the seeing through, the solution of this riddle belonged to the Greek spirit; only the Greek spirit could bring clarity to it: Oedipus, it is said, solved the riddle, and the content of it was, the freedom of spirit, which was still dark in the Egyptian principle, even though certainly contained in it.

Egypt contains the Asiatic and the African element but also the determinate transition from Asiatic to European.

[7]As Persia constitutes the outer, Egypt constitutes the inner transition to the next principle, of the free Greek life.

"The Model of an Ethically Customary, Regulated Condition"

[8]The Egyptians were also, like the Indians, divided into castes, and the children took over the trades and businesses of their elders, and as a consequence, they developed the arts so much that this hereditary system—in the way and manner of the Egyptians—did not produce the same disadvantages as in India. . . . In the caste divisions there was not that fixity and rigidity as in India, but we see the castes in unrest and struggle with one another.

---

4. See also GW 27 [3] 951: "Egypt is the transition point from the oriental principle to the western, Greek."
5. GW 27 [1] 239 (~ GW 27 [2] 619; GW 27 [4] 1309, 1318).
6. GW 27 [4] 1311; see also 1330-32 (~ [3] 977).
7. GW 27 [3] 850; see also 951 and 976.
8. GW 27 [4] 1313.

⁹Of the mode of life of the Egyptians, Herodotus gives us a very detailed report [2.35–98]. He tells of everything that appears to him to deviate especially from Greek ethical customs, including the most minute details: that the Egyptians had specialist physicians devoted to particular diseases; that the women were engaged in occupations outside the house, but the men remained in the house to weave—and so forth. In one part of Egypt polygamy held sway; in the other, monogamy was the universal ethical custom. As to the institutions of the police, it was required that every Egyptian should present himself, at a certain time, before his superintendent, and must state from what resources he obtained his livelihood; if he could not do this, he would be punished with death.... The greatest care, moreover, was observed in the division of the arable land, by the planning of canals and dikes.... The *courts of justice* were administered with very great care.... About the priesthood [1317] it is reported that they had a very well-ordered mode of life.¹⁰ ... Even the king led a very regulated life.

The understanding displayed in their legislative institutions appears characteristic of the Egyptians; this understanding, which manifests itself in the practical, we also recognize in the productions of art and science.... We have been amazed at the understanding of the Egyptians especially in mechanics—their powerful edifices, such as no other people has to exhibit, and that excel all others in greatness and solidity, sufficiently prove their artful skill. This understanding in civility, in science, the Egyptians gave to themselves, and all the more remarkably in that the people had nothing to do with the politics. Diodorus Siculus says [1.74.6] that the Egyptians are the only people whose citizens have nothing to do with public affairs—to a Greek and a Roman this must be striking.

---

9. GW 27 [4] 1316–17 (~ GW 27 [1] 246–47; GW 27 [2] 622–23; GW 27 [3] 957–58; 1840, 249–50).

10. Contrast, from the versions first published (in 1832 and 1840) of Hegel's *Lectures on the Philosophy of Religion*—based in part on records we no longer have, maybe of the 1831 lectures—the following (GW 29 [2] 392): "Also in the *political* condition of Egypt, ... history speaks often of the struggles of the kings with the priestly caste, and Herodotus [2.124, 128] mentions this as also from the earliest times—that the king Cheops allowed the temple of the priests to be closed, while other kings totally subjected the priestly caste and excluded them. This antithesis is no longer oriental; we see here the human free will raising itself to revolt against the religion. This emergence from dependence is a trait that it is essential to bring to the fore."

[11]On account of the understanding in its arrangements, Egypt was regarded by the ancients as the model of an ethically customary, regulated condition—as an ideal such as Pythagoras realized in a limited, select society, and such as Plato set forth on a larger scale. But such ideals take no account of passion. A condition that is to be adopted and acted upon as absolutely complete, in which everything has been considered, and especially the upbringing and habituation to it, with its becoming a second nature, is altogether opposed to the nature of spirit, which makes the present life the object on which it acts; and the infinite drive of activity is to change the present life. This drive expressed itself also in Egypt, in a peculiar way.

Egyptian Religion: "The Field of the Symbolic"

[12]Now it seems that, with these conditions, there must have come forth a comparably tranquil religion. But when we pass over to this subject, we are bowled over when we behold and examine the most opposite and marvelous phenomena—and see that the political condition is only one aspect, and that we are dealing with an ardent, active, laboring condition, with an African people that, in its enclosure, is inwardly aroused, aglow, and afire; it has nothing to do with what is outside, but the tremendous labor actively operates within its own horizon by means of the most extraordinary productions. . . .

[250] When we consider the character of the Egyptian religion more closely, we must hold fast to the fact that we are still within the bounds of a nature-religion. When we say God, we set before ourselves an essence of thought, and go from this to further determinations. But here in Egypt we have to hold fast to the natural intuition, to forgo our habitual thought of an essence beyond the earth and the heaven, and simply keep our sensuous eyes and power of imagination open.

As regards the nature-intuition of the Egyptian, we do not have before us the universal Chinese heaven, nor the universal natural foundation of the Indian, nor the pure Light of the Persian; we have no incarnation to [251] think about, and no heroes to recollect, for whom human nature constitutes the foundation. We have to do here with a particular nature: it is a closed world overall in which the Egyptian lives, and this world is also the foundational intuition in the religion

---

11. 1840, 251.
12. GW 27 [1] 249–51 (~ GW 27 [2] 625; GW 27 [4] 1317–18; 1840, 252–53).

CHAPTER 5

of the Egyptian—what they are, as their substantial being, as their essence. This particular world as religious is not the sensuous, but is grasped together in a representation that is its essence—but such that, on account of the enclosure of the Egyptian, the inside of this intuition simultaneously is determined as a symbol, inasmuch as a wider meaning is recollected therein. And so we find ourselves, in the Egyptian religion, through and through on the field of the symbolic.

[13]Herodotus looked all around in Egypt, made himself acquainted with the priests, and yet said nothing about its profound religious character; to him the enigma remained enigmatic. Diodorus likewise sought out Egypt, during the time of Augustus, and gives us manifold data.... Yet something is always lacking [241] for going deeper in discovery, and this is: an Egyptian written work.... The writers of history mention no Egyptian Homer, no dramatists. Although Herodotus and Diodorus were in Egypt, they impart nothing about books.... So this spirit expresses itself only from written works not in its own language, and on the other hand from the mute works of their architecture.

[14]The Egyptian knows how to express himself in building, in hieroglyph, not in the manner of speaking: the Muse of speech did not dwell with them; instead, the Muse of stone and sculpture.

[15]The fundamental intuition, of that which counts for the Egyptians as the essence, rests on the character of the natural world in which they live, and more specifically on the character of the physical cycle of nature that the Nile with the sun determines. These two—the condition of the sun with the condition of the Nile—are an interconnection; this is to the Egyptian all in all. The Nile is the fundamental determinant of the land overall; beyond the Nile valley begins the desert; on the north, it is shut in by the sea and on the south by torrid heat.... [254] The existence of the Egyptian does not depend on the brightness of the sun, or the rain, but for him there is only these entirely simple conditions, which form the foundation of his mode of life and life-activities. There is a definite physical cycle, which the Nile pursues and which is tied with the course of the sun: the latter advances, reaches its height, and then retrogrades. So also the Nile.

This foundation of the life of the Egyptians makes, moreover, the determinate content of their religion.

---

13. GW 27 [1] 240–41 (~ GW 27 [2] 620; GW 27 [3] 952; 1840, 243–44).
14. GW 27 [3] 953.
15. 1840, 253–54 (~ GW 27 [1] 251–52; GW 27 [2] 625; GW 27 [4] 1319–20).

[16]The *Nile* and the *Sun* are the divinities set forth as humanoid divinities; the divine cycle, the divine history, are identical. In the winter solstice the strength of the Sun has reached its minimum, but it is to be born again; thus also *Osiris* is born, having been killed by *Typhon*, by the enemy—the burning wind of the desert. *Isis*, the Earth, from whom the strength of the Sun and of the Nile has been withdrawn, yearns after him: she gathers the scattered bones of Osiris, and laments over him, and all Egypt bewails with her the death of Osiris, in a song that Herodotus [2.79] calls Linus or Maneros. . . . Here again sorrow is regarded as something divine, and the same honor is assigned to it here as among the Phoenicians, as we have seen. Then, Hermes embalms Osiris; and his grave is shown in various places. Osiris is now judge over the dead and is lord of the realm of the unseen ones. These are the foundational representations of the Egyptian religious observance: Osiris, the Sun, the Nile; this triplicity is united in one knot; the Sun is the symbol, in which Osiris and the history of that god are known, and the Nile is likewise this symbol. It is not only the natural representations that are to be understood therein, but also the spiritual: Osiris is also regarded as the inventor of the means of using the natural; to him is ascribed the invention of the plow, the hoe, etc.; he also gives to humans laws, and a civil order, and the religious ritual; he thus places in humans' hands the means of labor, and secures their labor through laws. Osiris is also the image of the seed that is placed in the earth, as also the image of the course of life. [1322] This heterogeneity—the phenomena of nature and the spiritual—is woven together into one knot, and the natural is to be taken as not only the natural, while the spiritual is not only the spiritual.

The parallelism of the course of human life with the Nile, the Sun, and Osiris is not to be regarded as a mere likeness—as if the becoming-born, the increase in strength, the height of vigor and fertility, the decline and weakness, exhibited themselves in these different phenomena, in an equal or similar way. This is not so much a likeness, an external setting together of similarities, but imagination has conceived in this variety *one subject*, one vital happening; the *substantial* unity is even the oriental principle; . . . in the substantial the heterogeneous shows itself therein as pressing and driving, and in an unclarity of consciousness that is very different from Greek clarity.

---

16. GW 27 [4] 1321–22 (~ GW 27 [1] 252–54; GW 27 [2] 626–27; GW 27 [3] 966–68; 1840, 255–56).

CHAPTER 5

[17]Osiris represents the Nile and the Sun: Sun and Nile are, on the other hand, symbols of humanoid life—each is signification, each is symbol; the symbol changes itself into signification, and this is symbol of the symbol, becoming signification. No determination is picture without at the same time being signification; each is both; the one is clarified by the other. Thus there arises one rich conception, which is tied together from many conceptions, in which the individuality remains foundational and is not resolved into the universal.

[18]This self-contained whole was the essence, the chief divinity of the Egyptian: Isis and Osiris and this duality—Osiris the Nile and the Sun, Isis the Earth and the Moon. This is the foundational divinity of the Egyptian, what belongs to and is distinctive in their religion. This Isis and Osiris are themselves produced—for overall, where the religion comes from nature, the god comes to sight not as the absolute first, as in a religion of thought. . . . Yet this nature-intuition is, further, a history, a process.

[19]When *we* speak of symbol, we have the conception that a universal conception is expressed through an image: Mars as image, for example, of the abstract conception war. But in Isis and Osiris, we do not have this duality (image, of universal, abstract conception). Instead, we have a convoluted bundle of symbols, each of which is of another symbol, not of an abstract conception.

This Egyptian ground of representations is characteristic of them.

[20]Besides this fundamental conception, we find now several special divinities. . . . A great divinity is *Ammon*, in whom lies the determination of the equinox; he is also the giver of oracles. But even so, Osiris again is brought forth as the grounder of the oracles. Similarly the power of production, coming from Osiris, is set forth as a special divinity. But even so, Osiris himself is this power of production. Isis is the Earth, the Moon, the fertility of nature. As an important essential phase of Osiris, *Anubis* (*Thoth*) is raised up—the Egyptian Hermes. [257] . . . This is the spiritual, not as one infinite, free mastery of nature, but as a particular next to the powers of nature and a particular according to its content. Thus the Egyptians had also divinities as spiritual activities and actualities; but these themselves are partly limited by their content—partly appearing as natural symbols. . . . Anubis is called friend and

---

17. 1840, 256 (~ GW 27 [1] 251).
18. GW 27 [1] 252 (~ GW 27 [3] 967).
19. GW 27 [1] 255 (~ GW 27 [4] 1317–18).
20. 1840, 256–57 (~ GW 27 [1] 255–56, 264–66; GW 27 [3] 965–66).

companion of Osiris. To him is ascribed the invention of writing, then of science generally—he is credited with grammar, astronomy, mensuration, music, and medicine. He first divided the day into twelve hours: he was moreover the first lawgiver, the first instructor in religious observances and holy objects, and in gymnastics and dance; he discovered the olive. But, notwithstanding all these spiritual attributes, this divinity is something quite other than the God of thought; only particular human arts and inventions are associated with him; moreover this god is entirely bound back up with natural existence, and is degraded in natural symbols: he is represented with a dog's head, as an animalized god; and besides this mask, a natural existence is bound up with the thought of this divinity; for he is at the same time Sirius, the Dog Star. He is thus limited in respect of content, as he is sensuous in concrete existence.

[21]We have seen the union between the spiritual and the lifeless: the wider and higher side is the fact that the Egyptians, while they observed the spiritual as manifested in the Nile, in the Sun, in the sowing of seed, so also saw it in *animal life*. The animal is something living; there belongs to it subjective life—and for this reason it is in no way the case that the peoples who have worshiped the sun and the stars, etc., are to be respected more highly than those who have worshiped brutes: but contrariwise. The Egyptians revered animal life; they contemplated therein the inner and incomprehensible.

[22]We also, when we contemplate the life and action of brutes, wonder at their instinct, their activity adapted to goals, their restlessness, excitability, and liveliness; for they are highly agile and very effective in pursuing their life goals, yet at the same time silent and enclosed. One does not know what is going on in these beasts and cannot rely on them. . . . The animals are in fact the incomprehensible. A human cannot [259] by imagination or conception enter into the nature of a dog, whatever resemblance he himself might have to it; it remains something altogether alien to him. It is in two departments that the so-called incomprehensible meets humans: in living nature, and in spirit. But it is truly only in nature that the human has to encounter the incomprehensible; for spirit is even this, the being revealed to itself: spirit understands and comprehends spirit. The dumb self-consciousness of the Egyptians, therefore, to which the thought of human freedom is not yet revealed, venerates the soul as still shut up within and made

---

21. GW 27 [4] 1323 (~ GW 27 [1] 256; GW 27 [2] 629; GW 27 [3] 955, 961–65; 1840, 258).
22. 1840, 258–62 (~ GW 27 [4] 1323–25).

dumb by life, and sympathizes with brute life. We find a veneration of mere vitality among other nations also. . . . But among the Egyptians this veneration of beasts was in any case carried to a most stupid and inhuman superstition. . . . If someone killed another [260] designedly, he was punished with death; but even the undesigned killing of some animals might entail death. . . . They would let human beings perish by famine, rather than allow the sacred animals to be killed, or the provision made for them diminished. . . .

The brute form is also again turned into a symbol. . . . The hidden, the spiritual, emerges as a human face from the brute essence. The multiform sphinxes, with lions' bodies [261] and virgins' heads, or as male sphinxes (*androsphinxes*) with beards, are evidence supporting the view that the meaning of the spiritual is the problem to be solved, as the riddle overall is not the utterance of something unknown, but is the challenge to bring it forth—the willing, that it ought to reveal itself.

But conversely, the human form is also disfigured by a brute face, with the view of giving it a specific and particular expression. The beautiful art of Greece knows how to attain a specific expression through the spiritual character given to an image in the form of beauty, and does not need to deform the human face in order to be understood. The Egyptians appended a clarification to the human forms of the gods, by means of heads and masks of brutes. . . . The priests, also, in performing their functions, are masked as falcons, jackals, bulls, etc.; . . . so also the embalmers, and the scribes. . . .

[262] Spirit that stands in the intuition of particular natural forms, and is therein a striving and picturing spirit, changes for itself the immediate natural intuition, *for example*, of the Nile, the sun, etc., into images, in which spirit has a share. It is, as we have seen, symbolizing spirit; and as such, it strives to master these symbolizations, and to bring them before itself. The more enigmatic and dark it is to itself, so much the more does it feel the drive in itself to labor to free itself from its confinement, and to gain an objective view.

Art as "a Necessary Need for the Egyptians"

[23]This leads us to mention *Egyptian art*. This was a necessary need for the Egyptians, proceeding from them necessarily. . . . In order that *art* be able to come forth, to belong, to come about, the spiritual must

---

23. GW 27 [2] 633–34.

become self-conscious. But where the spirit is known as the *One*, art does not belong; the One is grasped only with abstract thought, and the consciousness of the same can find a place only within; the Judaic and Muhammadan religions allow for no artwork: at least, as among the Protestants, they have nothing serious to do with religious art, the highest art, where the consciousness depicts itself spiritually. Art falls in the middle, as consciousness of the spiritual, but this has not yet reached the form of the spiritual itself, only the representation of it in an initial external way; the external must show itself as spiritual, and through [634] spirit be changed, worked upon, brought forward by labor. . . . When the spiritual has achieved its higher form in consciousness, when it is freer, higher spirit, then art becomes something superfluous; but insofar as the spiritual has not finished with the natural determinacy, it is still consciousness, and needs the natural way of intuiting—an external picture that is expression of the spirit. . . .

Among the Egyptians art is a necessary need, but it cannot yet be purely beautiful, classical art, because the spiritual is not yet grasped as true spirituality in its principle, because the spiritual still strives in competition with the natural to become free. The fermentation in the content is also in the subjective consciousness, and even thus in the content; this is what Egyptian art has produced. What we know from the Egyptians themselves, wherein they give their own manifestations, is architecture and sculpture. The Egyptian spirit has become the tremendous taskmaster that has within itself the drive to bring itself forth, but cannot free itself from the immediately sensed, the Sun, Moon.[24]

[25]It is the distinguishing feature of the Egyptian spirit that it stands before us as this tremendous taskmaster. It is not splendor, nor play, nor enjoyment, or the like, that it seeks, but instead, the drive that urges it is the impulse to understand itself; and it has no other material or ground to work on, in order to teach itself what it is, and to actualize itself for itself, than this working in stone; and what it engraves on the stone are its riddles: these hieroglyphs. The hieroglyphs are twofold—the hieroglyphs proper, designed rather to express language, and having reference to subjective conception; and the other hieroglyphs, those

---

24. See also the 1827 *Lectures on the Philosophy of Religion* (GW 29 [2] 132): "This work of an entire people is still not in and for itself pure, fine art, but the drive to fine art. Fine art entails this determination: spirit must become free from desire, from the natural overall, from being subjugated through inner and outer nature; it must become free in itself; it must have the need to know itself as free, so as to be the object of its own consciousness."

25. 1840, 262–63 (~ GW 27 [3] 969).

tremendous masses of architecture and sculpture, with which Egypt is covered.

[263] Of these works I will mention no others than those devoted to the dead, and that especially draw our attention. . . .

It is essential to see what meaning this realm of the dead had for the Egyptian: one may from this recognize what representation he made for himself of humanity.

"The Realm of the Dead"

[26]For us the conception of immortality is essentially the determination that the human being is destined for eternity, that the spirit has an eternal purpose distinct from temporality. Where this depth of the soul goes unmentioned, what can appear to be a continuation is weak and lacking in interest. This higher destiny that is conferred upon human life by faith constitutes faith's high interest. For the Egyptians, however, the consciousness of such a higher purpose has not yet arisen. . . . Immortality was for them in the sense of abstract oneness, to be taken as atom, which does not yet suffice for the determination of spirit. They thought of this oneness as immortal, yet in such a way that this atom had no content of an eternal, universal kind but instead only as a particularized existence, so that the soul passes over into the body of an animal. . . .

[273] Furthermore, by embalming of the dead the Egyptians gave a continuation. . . . But precisely in this quest to give the body continuation, we see that they had no genuine sense of immortality; for in the latter, the bodily is precisely the more insignificant, and only an outward respect ought to be shown it. This embalming instead testifies far more to their high esteem for the finite, corporeal, particular that the soul has as body.[27]

---

26. GW 27 [1] 272-73 (~ GW 27 [2] 632-33; GW 27 [3] 970-71; GW 27 [4] 1326-28).

27. Contrast the version of the *Lectures on the Philosophy of Religion* that was first published in 1832 and 1840, based in part on records we no longer possess (GW 29 [2] 390): "One can wonder that, although the Egyptians believed in the immortality of the soul, they nonetheless devoted so much care to their dead: one can believe that the human being, when one holds that the soul is immortal, should no longer be so concerned with one's body; but it is precisely the peoples who do not believe in the immortality of the soul who have little respect for the body after its death and do not take care for its preservation. The respect that the dead are given is thoroughly dependent on the thought of immortality. When the body that is no longer united with the soul has fallen under the force of nature, the human at least wants nature *as such* not to exert its force and its physical necessity on the soulless body, this noble

²⁸The Egyptians made their dead into mummies, with that, then they were done with the dead, and no further veneration was paid them. Herodotus relates [2.85] of the Egyptians that when any person died, the women went about loudly lamenting; but the notion of an immortality, as among us, did not provide a consolation.

. . . One sees that the Egyptians, but especially their kings, made it the business of their life to build their graves, and to give their bodies a permanent abode. It is remarkable that what had been needed for the business of life was buried with the dead.

²⁹Prior to the burial of a private person and that of a king, there was a public tribunal held and a funeral oration was held, with a narration of the person's life, and extolling of the virtues. If the bystanders did not concur, they could make accusations against the deceased. Hence the tribunal for the dead is not represented as held in the underworld. In general, we have no justification for being reminded here of our Last Judgment, [274] because the judging of the dead here is done by the living, not by a judge in the beyond.³⁰

---

container of the soul, but it must be the human who brings this about, more or less; so they seek, on the contrary, to protect the body, or else to give it, as if of its own free will, back to the earth, or to destroy it through fire."

28. 1840, 265 (~ GW 27 [2] 631; GW 27 [3] 971-72).

29. GW 27 [1] 273-74 (~ GW 27 [2] 632-33; GW 27 [3] 971-72; GW 27 [4] 1329-30).

30. Contrast the 1827 *Lectures on the Philosophy of Religion* (GW 29 [2] 128-30): "As he is represented, Osiris is defined as lord in the realm of the Amendes; even as he is the lord of the living, so is he also lord of what no longer continues to exist sensuously—of the soul, continuing to exist as separated from the body, from the sensuous, from the transitory. [1831 version: In this lies the higher determination of humanity.] Typhon, the evil one, is overcome, as is sorrow, and Osiris is the judge, in accord with right and rightfulness. The evil one is overcome, condemned; thereby for the first time, just judgment enters, in the sense that the judging is decisive, that is, that the good has the force to make itself count, and to negate the negator, the evil one. When we say: Osiris is a lord of the dead, this means that the dead are those who are not established in the sensuous, natural realm, but endure for themselves above the sensuous, natural. Linked with this, that the singular subject is known as enduring, withdrawn from the transitory, secure for itself, different from the sensuous. It is therefore a word of the highest import that Herodotus says [2.123] about immortality—that the Egyptians were the first to say that the soul of the human is immortal. . . . The soul knows itself as subject, as totality, as true independence, and thereby as immortal. [1831 version: The higher determination of humanity thereby comes into consciousness.] This is the universal. Around this universal plays an infinite crowd of representations, of divinities. Osiris is only one of these, . . . but he has elevated himself above all the deities distinctively as lord of the dead, as Serapis, as that in which one finds the greatest interest. . . . Osiris became the central point not of the immediate but of the spiritual, intellectual world. . . . But it is not an immediate human that is revered by the Egyptians—its existence is . . . in the realm of representation. . . . Thus the Idea is established in this soil of representation, and therein is this defect, that it is only the representation of subjectivity, that subjectivity is only abstractly there on its foundation."

Another circumstance, recounted by Herodotus [2.78], is that images of deceased relatives were set up at banquets, with the admonition: "Eat and drink, for you will become such a one as this." So the reminder of death was no occasion for reminding the living that death involved knowledge of a higher destiny; instead, the images of the dead were used to encourage taking advantage of the present by seizing upon life's sensual pleasures.

[31]Since death thus haunted the minds of the Egyptians during life, it might be supposed that their disposition was melancholy. But the thought of death by no means occasioned depression among them.... Death was thus to them rather a call to enjoy life.

"The Peculiarities of the Egyptian Spirit"

[32]The orientation is to vitality in the present, in which we see the Egyptians, on one hand, engaging themselves with a powerful understanding of their own strength that is self-confident and is wondrous in the operations of the state, as it is in the mechanical and technical operations in their edifices; on the other hand, we see the strength in transforming the particular and the finite. We have observed this characteristic of transforming natural particularity through symbolization, of representing one representation in another, in such a way that the one becomes symbol for the other.... yet going forth not into thought, but instead only into another particularity that transforms the one intelligible representation into a different one, such that what is universal always remains something other, inside. Herein lies the subjection to what is particular and special, and the strength [275] to will to break through it.

[33]If, in conclusion, we combine what has been said here of the peculiarities of the Egyptian spirit in all its aspects, the foundational intuition is that the two elements of actuality—spirit sunk in nature, and the drive to its liberation—are here held together in mutually antagonistic struggle. We behold the antithesis of nature and spirit, not the unmediated unity, also not the concrete—where nature is posited only as soil for the manifestation of spirit; against the first and second of these unities [nature and spirit] stands the Egyptian in the middle, as contradictory. The sides of this unity are in abstract independence,

---

31. 1840, 266 (~ GW 27 [4] 1330).
32. GW 27 [1] 274–75 (~ GW 27 [3] 973–75).
33. 1840, 267–68 (~ GW 27 [3] 972–76; GW 27 [4] 1317–18).

and their unity presented only as a problem. We have, therefore, on the *one* side, a prodigious confinement and limitation to particularity, wild sensuality with African hardness, animal worship, enjoyment of life. . . . The *other* side is the struggle of spirit for its liberation—the fantasy of images next to the abstract understanding of the mechanical labors connected [268] with the production of these images. The same understanding, the strength to alter the particulars, and that steadfast circumspection that stands above immediate appearance, shows itself in the state policing and the state mechanism, in the use of the land, etc.; and the contrast to this is the severe binding by ethical custom and superstition to which humanity among them is inexorably subject.

[34]When we compare this individual character of the Egyptians with their religion and their civic life, we see that there is in this a uniform determinacy: this abstract immortality, this steadfastness, this atom—not yet concrete individuality; steadfast understanding at work in a particularity of goals and intuitions, but even so with endless striving, a circumspection and straining full of character that, for private purposes, risks everything, transforms everything. . . . The Egyptian understanding stands on the one hand in particularity and does not raise itself up to the point of grasping itself as universal, but in this confinement this spirit shows itself [278] to be at the same time free, bold, and brave. It renders its natural intuition symbolically and positions itself as the means to something universal that, however, does not make its appearance. It involves a confinement and a struggle against it, a mastery over particularity, but not yet as ideal particularity. In itself it is indeed ideal, but not yet for itself, because the Egyptian spirit sublates the self-enclosed state, utilizing it for the sake of another self-enclosed state, and does not yet have as its explicit purpose the positive result or the universal itself. That this particularity is also for itself ideal is what must now come forward as the free, cheerful spirit of Greece.

"The Determinate Transition"

[35]An Egyptian priest has said that the Greeks remain eternally only children;[36] on the contrary, we can say that the Egyptians are vigorous

---

34. GW 27 [1] 277–78 (~ 1840, 268–69)
35. 1840, 269 (~ GW 27 [1] 278).
36. Plato's *Timaeaus* 22b (Critias is speaking, reporting what Solon said about his trip to Egypt): "And he said that one of the priests, a very old one, said 'Oh Solon, Solon! You Greeks

boys, driven toward selfhood, who want nothing but clarity about themselves, in an ideal form, in order to become *young men*. In the oriental spirit there remains as foundation the massive substantiality of spirit immersed in nature; to the Egyptian spirit it has become impossible—though it is still involved in infinite confinement—to remain contented with that. . . .

But as evidence that to the consciousness of the Egyptians their spirit is itself in the form of a *problem or task*, we can appeal to the famous inscription in the all-holy sanctuary of the Goddess Neith at Sais: "*I am what is, what was, and what will be; no one has lifted (sublated) my tunic.*"[37] Herein is expressed what the Egyptian spirit is—although one often has the opinion that this pronouncement counts for all times.

[38] Here is expressed this unknown—the presentiment and intimation of something higher—and its not-being-unveiled. Proclus in his *Timaeus Commentary* presents this inscription with the addition: "What I have borne, is Helios." Helios is the Sun of Spirit. The famous festival of Light was celebrated at Sais of Neith (Pallas), equivalent to our light festival and to the lantern festival of the Chinese. . . . This sun, Helios, to which this shrouded goddess has given birth, is the Greek spirit, Helios, the Phoebus Apollo. . . . From the Greek Apollo we learn that the inscription on his temple was: "Human, know thyself." And Apollo was the [280] knowing God. Self-knowledge is here not the commonplace, psychic being of human recognition; instead, here is expressed the highest, the absolute command—that spirit should know itself in its essence. This is that for which is the labor of the world, the striving of all religion; and a more sublime inscription, as well as a more defining expression of the Greek spirit, does not exist. In these meaningful phrases is the determinate transition expressed.

[39] It is not the particular human being who should become acquainted with what makes one special, but humanity *overall* ought to know itself.

---

are ever children; there is not an old Greek!' Upon hearing this, he said that he said, 'How do you mean this?'—'You are young,' he replied, "all, in your souls. For you do not have in them, through ancient hearing, any archaic opinion, nor learning hoary with time.'"

37. Plutarch (*About Isis and Osiris* 354c): "the philosophy of the Egyptian priests is mostly veiled in myths and speeches containing cloudy expressions and intimations of the truth, as they themselves unhesitatingly show by appropriately stationing, before their sanctuaries, sphinxes—as having enigmatic wisdom about theology. And in Sais there is the statue of Athena (whom they conventionally believe to be Isis)—having such an inscription: 'I am all, what has come into being, and being, and what will be; and my tunic no mortal has yet lifted.'"

38. GW 27 [1] 279-80 (~ GW 27 [3] 976; GW 27 [4] 1331).

39. 1840, 269-70 (~ GW 27 [1] 280; GW 27 [3] 976; GW 27 [4] 1331).

This commandment was given for the Greeks, and in the Greek spirit humanity establishes itself in its clarity and in the culturally developed condition itself. Wonderfully, then, must the Greek legend astonish us, which relates that the Sphinx [270]—the Egyptian image—appeared in Thebes, and indeed with the words: "What is that, which in the morning goes on four legs, at midday on two, and in the evening on three?" Oedipus, with the solution—that this is the human being—precipitated the Sphinx from the rock. The solution and liberation of the oriental spirit, which in Egypt had advanced so far as the problem, is by all means this: that the inner of nature is thought, which has its existence only in the human consciousness.

Bibliography

Belzoni, G. B. *Narrative of the Operations and Recent Discoveries in Egypt and Nubia.* London: Murray, 1820. See GW 27 [1] 259, 269-70; GW 27 [2] 629, 631; GW 27 [3] 954, 962, 970; GW 27 [4] 1324, 1328.

Bohlen, P. von. *Das alte Indien mit besonderer Rücksicht auf Aegypten.* 2 vols. Königsberg: Bornträger, 1830. See GW 31 [1] 657-58; GW 31 [2] 1881; GW 31 [4] 1289.

Champollion, J.-F. *L'Egypte sous les Pharaons.* 2 vols. Paris: De Bure, 1814. See GW 31 [1] 833; GW 31 [2] 1887; GW 27 [4] 1311, 1312.

Elphinstone, M. *An Account of the Kingdom of Caubul and Dependencies in Persia, Tartary, and India.* London: Longman, 1815. See GW 27 [1] 206; GW 27 [3] 919.

Guigniaut, J. D. *Le Dieu Sérapis et son origine, ses rapports, ses attributs et son histoire.* Paris: Hachette, 1828. See GW 31 [1] 723-24; GW 31 [2] 1909.

Hirt, A. *Ueber die Bildung der aegyptischen Gottheiten.* Berlin: Royal Academy of Sciences, 1821.

Niebuhr, C. *Reise und Beobachtungen durch Egypten und Arabien aus den grossern Werken verschneidener gelehrten Reisenden.* 2 vols. Bern: Steiner, 1779-81. See GW 31 [1] 824-29; GW 31 [2] 1943.

Passalacqua, J. *Catalogue raisonné et historique des antiquités découvertes en Egypte.* Paris: Galerie d'Antiquités égyptiennes, 1826. See GW 31 [1] 833-34; GW 31 [2] 1946.

Pauw, C. de. *Recherches philosophiques sur les Egyptiens et les Chinois.* 2 vols. Berlin: Decker, 1773.

Quatremère, E. *Mémoires géographiques et historiques sur l'Egypte.* 2 vols. Paris: Schoell, 1811. See GW 31 [1] 843-46; GW 31 [2] 1950.

Chapter 6

The Greek World

¹The *inner* transition to Greece, according to the concept, constitutes itself out of the Egyptian spirit; Egypt, however, became a province of the great Persian Empire, and the *historical* transition takes place by the encounter between the Persian and the Greek world. We find here for the first time a historical transition, that is, by way of an empire declining. China and India, as we have already stressed, have remained; Persia has not. The transition to Greece is, indeed, internal; but here also external, as a transition of mastery—a state of affairs that from this time forward is always again repeated. For the Greeks turn over to the Romans the mastery and the culture, and the Romans are subdued by the Germans.

... [271b] It was not the weakness of the Persians (although Babylon was certainly enervating) that allowed them to sink, but the unwieldiness of the weaponry, the unorganized character, of their host, against the Greek organization—that is, the higher principle overcame the inferior. The abstract principle of the Persians displayed its [272] defectiveness as an unorganized, nonconcrete unity of disparate contradictories, in which the Persian intuition of Light stood side by side with Syrian

---

1. 1840, 270-72 (~ GW 27 [2] 639-40).

voluptuous enjoyment of life, with the activity and courage of the commercial, sea-danger-braving Phoenicians, with the abstraction of pure thought of the Jewish religion, and the inner drive of Egypt—an aggregate of elements that awaited their idealization, and could receive it only in *free individuality*. The Greeks are to be seen as the people in whom these elements obtained their interpenetration, as spirit deepened itself in itself, triumphed over particularity, and thereby emancipated itself.

[2]Here we see throughout regard only for the Persian people, not for the wide range of so many nations. The administration had in view the Persians as such, who held themselves apart, having no community of justice shared with other peoples. Tribute and service in war were the chief connecting elements. The Persian mastery thus gained no inner legitimacy, no common measure of justice and [283] common measure of law with the subjects. Defining themselves in this way as separate, the Persians were only the abstract masters, and such a relationship necessarily brings with it a lack of justice and a lack of law. And this relationship brought about the internal weakness of the Persian Empire.

[3]Against this aggregate, the Greek unity, cultural education, and discipline carried the victory. . . . In that we now transition to the Greek world we enter the classical world, and the principle that we now have before us is this: that self-conscious freedom enters—the light, the individuality, that possesses itself for itself: this One, this I-ness, that appeared among the Egyptians as abstract and, therewith, struggling. Now, the spirit becomes liberated in its concrete existence and in actuality. Unity of the spirit with nature one supposes to be something high—yes, even the highest—but it is as such superficial, abstract, and indeterminate; the sunken consciousness must sublate itself out of the particular, in order to bring about a harmony in which the spirit comes to sight as predominant; there ought to prevail not a neutrality between spirit and nature (one as good as the other), but a harmony, a unity, in which the spirit is mastering. This first, fresh, vital unity we see among the Greeks, the limit of which is their being-unconstrained; by progressing the spirit must leave behind this being-unconstrained, in order to elevate itself to abstract universality, as in the Roman and Germanic Empire, where there enters the principle of unity through the suppression of individuality. Among the Greeks [1333] what holds sway is the fresh vitality of the freedom of the spirit—which is to be compared with

---

2. GW 27 [1] 282–83 (~ GW 27 [2] 640–41; GW 27 [4] 1331–32).
3. GW 27 [4] 1332–33 (~ GW 27 [2] 641–42).

adolescence and thus can be named the *adolescence of the spirit*, even as we conceive for ourselves youth as having a first serious determinateness before itself, inasmuch as it becomes conscious of preparing itself so as to make itself capable of the work that stands before it.

⁴In regard to Greek life, there is this to say: that herein there is not yet an effort on behalf of abstract understanding as a goal, setting for itself a universal goal and working for it. What is present here is the concrete, still sensuous, ground of life that has a sensuous presence, which is, however, born of the spiritual. . . . [Hagenbach: The sensuous-spiritual oriental intuition forms the basis—but produced from the individual spirit. The Greek world has the oriental world as presupposition; it starts out from the divinity of nature but reconstructs it, and gives it the spiritual as essence, as inner principle, as soul.]

⁵Greece presents to us the cheerful aspect of youthful freshness, of spiritual vitality. It is here first that advancing spirit makes itself the content of its will and of its knowledge; but [274] in such a way that state, family, law, religion are at the same time goals of individuality, and this is individuality only through those aims.

In contrast, the mature man lives in work, for an objective goal, which he pursues consistently, even against his individuality.

The highest figuration that the Greek imagination had was Achilles, the son of the poet, the Homeric youth of the Trojan War. Homer is the element in which the Greek world lives, as humanity does in the air.

The Greek life is a truly youthful condition. Achilles, the ideal youth of *poetry*, commenced it: Alexander the Great, the ideal youth of *reality*, led it to its end. Both appear in struggle with Asia. Achilles, as the principal figure in the national expedition of the Greeks against Troy, does not stand at its head, but is subordinate to the king of kings; he cannot be made leader without becoming a fantastic. On the contrary, the second youth, Alexander—the freest and most beautiful individuality that reality has ever produced—advances to the peak of this youthful life that is now perfected in itself, and accomplishes the revenge against Asia.

⁶Between the two occur the political configurations, the configurations of the Greek essence of the state, of the life of the state: democracy,

---

4. GW 27 [1] 284.
5. 1840, 273-74 (~ GW 27 [1] 283-84; GW 27 [2] 641-42; GW 27 [3] 981-82; GW 27 [4] 1332-33).
6. GW 27 [3] 982.

which in its true mode has been, and *only* can be, present in Greece. It is the state in its most beautiful youthfulness.

"Three Periods"

[7]Now in the Greek world we find three periods, and it is to be noted that for what follows this remains a general division, and comes forth for every subsequent people.... The first period is the commencement; the second the contact with the world-historical people backwards—that of the Greek with the Persian; the third period is the contact with the later world-historical empire, for the Greeks the contact with the Romans.

In the first epoch, the first period begins and goes to the point of completion in itself, that makes a single people possible, proceeding from the earlier world-historical people.... For a second or third people, which has a precondition, an alien culture is involved in its beginning, and so the people has, from the beginning, a doubling within itself—so that, on the one hand, it proceeds from itself, and on the other hand, from an alien people; and its maturation proceeds by bringing this doubling into a unity. For the people has to digest this alien element and to expel from itself what must remain alien. This first period ends, therefore, with the bringing together of [286] a people's inner, real strength, which is applied against its precondition in the earlier people.

The second period is that of a people's happiness.... Reaching its peak within, and victorious in relation to the outside, the tension turns inward and brings about a split within, a split into a real and an ideal existence, in the mode of thinking of itself as having become objective to itself [Griesheim: as it conceives itself through art and science]. Thereby begins the period of its decline, which is the third, and constitutes the contact with the following world-historical people, which builds the higher stage of world-history.

"The Land of the Greeks"

[8][Griesheim: First we have to consider the land of the Greeks. It consists in] a crowd of islands of the Aegean Sea and a mainland that is also

---

7. GW 27 [1] 285-86 (~ GW 27 [2] 642-43; GW 27 [3] 982-83; GW 27 [4] 1333b-1334; 1840, 274-75).
8. GW 27 [1] 286-87 (~ GW 27 [2] 643-44, 647-48; GW 27 [3] 983; GW 27 [4] 1334, 1336-38; 1840, 275-76).

134 CHAPTER 6

island-like—partly peninsula, partly a crowd of spits of land, and frequently bisected by bays. The interior has alternating hilly areas or even mountains with narrow plains and valleys intersected by small streams: no large rivers whose alluvial soil nourishes a uniform race to whom the entire heaven offers merely a type of [287] dependence. Here in Greece this much-divided land is lightly connected [1840, 275: in easy relation and interconnection by the sea]. This is the elementary character of the locality, and of the Greek spirit: self-subsistent individuality, which is not unified from the start by a patriarchal bond, but standing for itself, and having to find its own unity in a higher medium, of law and spiritual customary ethics.

"Intermingling of Peoples"

[9]Only superficial foolishness posits for itself that a beautiful whole of ethical custom could come about through a single development of a homogeneity—a race that remains tied by family relations. . . . These conceptions are contrary to the concept. Experiences of history demonstrate the opposite.

[288] The beginning of Greek life shows us a mixture and intersection and migration of tribes and peoples, of some of whom we do not know the extent of their Greek nature, and of tribes whose entirely non-Greek nature we do know. . . . In Europe, all the nations have arisen through an intermingling. Thus the element of heterogeneity is essential to a world-historical people. Greeks, Romans, Germanic peoples first made themselves one out of heterogeneity.

[10][Griesheim: There was no place for the vengeful war between clans, because the Greeks originated not from clans but from intermingling. . . . So there was no patriarchal family structure present that might have spared a person from first making oneself respectable.]

"Famous Royal Dynasties"

[11]What we refer to as the Greek people is a conglomeration of tribes that came together from elsewhere. From this race of aliens [Griesheim:

---

9. GW 27 [1] 287–88 (~ GW 27 [2] 644–46, 648–49; GW 27 [3] 983–86; GW 27 [4] 1334–38; 1840, 276–77).
10. GW 27 [1] 301.
11. GW 27 [1] 291, 293–95 (~ GW 27 [2] 649–50; GW 27 [3] 987–88; GW 27 [4] 1338–42; 1840, 280–81).

were founded the many famous royal dynasties, and thereby more enduring centers, distinct configurations, centers for mastery, for given personalities, heroic lords for a previously disunited crowd. Thereby also originated more permanent centers, which emerged as cities or developed into them.] The building of citadels was a major element through which the restless wanderers established themselves. . . . [293 Hagenbach and Griesheim: Here we find heroes who have the mastery over the people, whose subordination to them is not by caste relationship, nor is there here patriarchal relationship; instead, the heroes are aliens, and there is no oppression such as we see later. There is no need for a fixed law; rather it was an entirely loose, open, and personal relationship.] . . . On the one hand, the royal power belonged to a family, but on the other hand it rested on their personal qualities of courage, of understanding of divine and human things. . . . [294] Depictions of this are best delineated in the Homeric poems. Agamemnon stands as first over all the other kings; without them he undertakes nothing essential: each gives his advice and there is no mere voting but each speaks according to his opinion, and the prince decides what can happen in accord with this will. The people go with their princes into this war more or less out of trust and respect for them. . . . The people in this war do, in general, little; rather it is the princes themselves who must fight the battles. [Griesheim: The people are not simply driven along like an apathetic herd, such as a caste in India. Nor are they fighting for a cause of their own, but as witnesses to the deeds and glory of their princes, who elevate both by their own strength.] In this way of conducting a war there is something entirely characteristic. . . . [295] And the relationship in which Agamemnon stands to the other princes is the same in which Zeus stands to the other gods—who also wrangle with Zeus, but not to the point of breaking the bonds.

[12]The kingship must certainly not be equated with monarchy—the need for which first becomes necessary in a mature society. Unity under one overall, without real law, where spiritedness and courage give preeminence, show the immaturity of development: contingency, willfulness count in the eyes of those who obey—the passion of Achilles establishes itself; and also the passion of the princes, over and against their subordinates, makes itself count.

[13]In considering his story more closely, we find in Oedipus spiritual clarity bound with the greatest ignorance about himself. Here we have

---

12. GW 27 [2] 650.
13. GW 27 [1] 280.

the first lordship, the patriarchal lordship. It is apart from knowledge, and full of atrocity, for knowledge is a principle heterogeneous to the patriarchal, and the oriental must give way. It is through political freedom that this ancient knowledge first attains clarity.

[14][Griesheim: From this royal dignity, the people obtained little; and when the consensus of the people once became the practice, then the king was of little importance.] For [296] a court of justice could be presided over by someone with experience, from the community; in war, the most courageous could lead; and as regards human and divine things, the shrewdest; the princely dignity and its perpetuation resting on birth was not yet necessary in such conditions. (It is important to recognize the conditions under which monarchy is absolutely necessary.) Social conditions at the beginning of Greece were such that the royal dignity became superfluous once it had fulfilled what it had to do. It is singular that the kings were not driven out, but instead the royal families stepped down without hatred and strife, dying out naturally.... Thus the kings were not driven out as they were by the Romans, but they simply dissolved, and their memory was always esteemed and loved. Within these dynasties, we see conspicuously a lot of atrocities. Most kings fell through dreadful overthrows.... Passion of will breaks out destructively. Internalized conscience, law, do not yet have power over the heart's feelings. The people remain entirely outside all interests in such [297] atrocities; they are not involved in them. The people are represented in the tragic chorus.... The people is only an inactive spectator, appealing to the gods, but there is no judging power over such individuals, neither externally, nor internally in their own conscience. Hence, their passions play out destructively for them, but without bringing harm to the people. So the royal dynasties are superfluous to the social order, and they declined as a result of their own actions.

[15]Such heroic individualities as those of the princes are so remarkably suited for subjects of dramatic art [284] on this very account that they form their resolutions independently and individually and not through universal laws binding on every citizen; their action and their downfall are individual. The people appears separated from the royal houses, and the latter count as something alien, as something higher, that fights out and suffers its fate for itself.

---

14. GW 27 [1] 295–97 (~ GW 27 [2] 649–50; GW 27 [3] 988–91; GW 27 [4] 1340–41; 1840, 281–82).

15. 1840, 283–84 (~ GW 27 [3] 990–91).

"After the Trojan War"

[16]After the Trojan War, the royal houses thus fell; and many changes thereby entered.... The history now recedes again more into darkness, and though the Trojan War and its several occurrences are very precisely known to us, we are uncertain respecting the important transactions of the time following, [1342] for a period of several centuries; no common undertaking is manifest, unless we consider such affairs as Thucydides reports [1.1-19].... The great prosperity of the Greek cities in that time is shown, as Thucydides says, in the sending out of colonies in all directions.... This sending out of colonies, especially during the time period between the Trojan War and Cyrus, is a characteristic manifestation. In the several cities the people had the governmental power in their hands, since they gave the decision in higher affairs; in consequence of the long peace, population and development advanced; the immediate result was the amassing of great riches, with which the appearance of great want and poverty were bound up.... A large part of the poorer class would not submit to the life of neediness, for everyone felt himself a free citizen; the only expedient that remained, therefore, was colonization; ... [1343] but even this helped very little, in that immediately the inequality in means of life reemerged in the state.... The passions were rekindled with renewed force among the citizens, and riches were soon made use of for securing mastery: thus *tyrants* arose in the cities of Greece.

[17]These tyrants in the cities occur in the time when Cyrus founded the Persian monarchy, so that the Greeks in Asia Minor were subordinated to the Persian Empire. In this period, during which darkness reigns completely in the historical record because little worthy history happened, occurs the seedling, growth, and self-definition of the Greek spirit, which emerges as developed, having achieved a firm configuration.[18]

---

16. GW 27 [4] 1341-43 (~ GW 27 [2] 650-51; GW 27 [3] 990-92; 1840, 284-86).
17. GW 27 [2] 651 (~ GW 27 [4] 1343; 1840, 285-86).
18. See also Hegel's 1825-26 *Lectures on the History of Philosophy* (GW 30 [3] 898-99): the time of Cyrus is "the epoch of the decline of the Ionian cities, of Greek freedom in Asia Minor—a beautiful world that had taken shape for itself, and stood on a higher plane of cultural education; and at that point philosophy arose.... Croesus and the Lydians had posed the first threat to Ionian freedom; only later on was it utterly destroyed by Persian lordship.... Simultaneously with this decline of the Ionian cities, in the rest of Greece legal institutions arose, ... lawful unions of citizens. It was in these circumstances that the sages

[19]No despotic force unites the multitude, as it does in Asia. The individual is here not without rights, and should no longer disappear into the whole; there is also not yet here any abstract goal, any principle of universality, to which individuals could be subordinated. . . . Later, and only against the Persians, do we see Greece united—and for the first time, as the states disintegrated, did the second youth, Alexander, bring them together in a whole. . . . [298] The stronger unification was by the oracles and national games and festivals. What counted as politically unifying was the notion that a developing Greek state counted as something sacred and revered. . . . But the Lacedaemonians perpetrated the unholiness of subjugating and enslaving the Messenians [Griesheim: a free people; and it was not until centuries later that Epaminondas sublated this unholiness].

[20]The special peculiarity through which the Greek states distinguished themselves from one another was a difference like that of the beautiful divinities, each of whom had its special character and special concrete existence, yet so that this special character maintained the influence of their common divinity.

"Greek Cultural Education"

[21]That in regard to which we have to study the Greeks as one, as a world-historical people, is their Greek cultural education. . . . In the realm of this cultural education each of us feels at home; it is [299] an eternal present that can culturally educate us and that each has to acquire for oneself: an enjoyment of the beautiful. [Griesheim: Here begins the conscious connection of the chain of the Tradition.] We by the Romans, they by the Greeks, are culturally educated. . . . In regard to the Greek cultural education there are two systems, depending on whether the Greeks received their art and science from outside or from themselves. Historically it appears as if the Greeks took from themselves their cultural education and produced all its subsequent stages. We see an uninterrupted succession of stages of cultural education without needing to go to external sources, and the specifically Greek we find only in

---

emerged. . . . Seven were known, but their names were listed variously; Diogenes Laertius names only Thales, Bias, Pittacus, and Solon."
    19. GW 27 [1] 297–98.
    20. 1840, 336.
    21. GW 27 [1] 298–300, 302–4 (~ GW 27 [3] 997–98; 1840, 294–95).

Greece. But it is equally historical that the Greeks started with what was alien, and this is necessary.... A presupposition of foreign origin is just as necessary as is a reworking of the same that passes through its own independent stages. A closer [300] look at Greek cultural education can reveal only the exceptional, and this preeminently in fine art....

[302] In this serene condition we see now the drive of the individual to display oneself, to make seen what each has made of oneself, so as to make oneself count with others and to take pleasure in this making oneself count.

Sensual pleasure was not the basis of Greek life, and neither was dullness and superstition. Among other barbarians we see the drive to allow oneself to be seen by adornment: the body ought to be judged by externals, and these externals ought not to represent something for oneself, but ought to serve another. We see the Greek individuals achieving a strength that can remain standing. They came early to honor their feeling of self for itself. But what the individuals are at first only for themselves, [303] they must prove, by display to others. And this shows itself early among the Greeks as a peaceful competitive struggle. We see the Greeks dominated neither by superstition nor by vanity—which first enters later.

This drive of joyful self-feeling, opposed to the simply sensuous, [Griesheim: opposing itself to raw self-feeling,] constitutes the chief determining character of the Greeks, and this drive developed itself among them into fine art. [Hagenbach: It begins with an unneedy work that must be grasped as subjective in such a way that it enables one to make oneself into something and thereby to show to others that the character of the universal is expressed in oneself.] ... The first subjective beginning consists in the development of the body, in the building of the body into a work of art.... [304] Hence the games are so ancient: wrestling, javelin, and discus throwing.

[22]If we consider now the inner nature of these games, first to be observed is that the game is opposed to seriousness, to dependence and need. With such wrestling, running, contending, there was nothing serious; in it there was no need of self-defense, no necessity of combat. Serious is work that has reference to need: I or nature must succumb; if the one is to continue, the other must fall. Against this seriousness, however, the game contains the higher seriousness; for in it nature is

---

22. 1840, 296–97 (~ GW 27 [2] 661–62; GW 27 [4] 1350–51).

constructed into spirit, and although [297] in these contests the subject has not advanced to the highest seriousness, of thinking, the human being thus shows in this activity of corporeality one's freedom: that the body, namely, has been transformed into an organ of the spirit.

[23]With these activities song and dance link themselves, dance being the dominant form, whereby song is subordinate—the outer expression of a raw gaiety. On the shield of Achilles are such dances mentioned; they are themselves works of art. This dancing, like that which was on the shield of Daedalus, has only the goal of joyfulness, without connection to a festival of worship of divinity. The goal is thus only to display oneself, to allow admiration of one's skill. Later the singing became independent, attained accompanying instruments, and demanded a content out of mental representation. And as an image of the mental representation became free for itself in song, so the mental representation became externally, overall, a beautiful, free configuration by which the humans displayed themselves in their beautiful skill.... This organ, the voice, is not merely a sensory articulation, nor merely an immediate manifesting of beings; it is also a manifesting of mental representation.... This content can be highly diverse in kind; but, to the extent that it is formed by spirit, it is sensory content that is elevated to a universality, or a sensed concrete existence of spirit is maintained as something universal. This universal we want [305] to designate in its highest content as the religious content.

[24]When we go back to the start of Greek cultural education, we first observe how the Greeks hearken to the manifestations of nature that are present around them in such a great manifoldness; the physical condition of their land does not have such a characteristic unity as to exercise a coercive power over the inhabitants; rather, nature is on the whole diversified, and therefore does not gain so great an influence. We behold the Greeks on the one hand animated in all directions, unsettled, scattered, dependent on the chance of the outer world; and on the other hand, spiritually perceiving the manifestations of nature, and taking up an appropriating and strong relation over and against it. When we turn to the beginning of their religion, to the foundations of their mythic representations, similar is their relation to the natural conditions, but in a unification. The Diana of Ephesus, that is, Nature as the universal Mother, the Cybele and [1344] Astarte of Syria—such

---

23. GW 27 [1] 304–5.
24. GW 27 [4] 1343–44 (~ GW 27 [3] 993–94; 1840, 286).

universal conceptions remain Asiatic, and do not get transmitted to Greece. What appears to us as the Greeks' relationship with the most manifold natural conditions is that we see them hearkening to the natural manifestations, as forming presentiments, with inner questioning about their meaning. This relationship full of presentiment, of hearkening, of hunger for the meaning, is depicted for us in the collected image of *Pan*: Pan, the *All*—which, when it further developed itself, became that universal Mother Nature; but Pan is not the objective whole—instead, the indefinite, which is bound together with the essential phase of the subjective; he is the universal thrill in the silence of the forests; therefore he is especially revered in sylvan Arcadia: (a Panic terror is a common expression for groundless terror). Pan, this thrill-exciter, became then represented as a flute player: he is thus not the objective that is only surmised; rather, he lets himself be heard, on the seven-reeded pipe (which adumbrates the harmony of the seven spheres). Even so the Greeks hearkened to the murmur of the springs and asked, "what meaning does it have?" And the interpretation, the clarification, of these natural changes, of the sensed—the meaning of the spiritual: that is the activity of the subjective spirit to which the Greeks gave the name *manteia*. Most of the Greek divinities were spiritual individuals, but their beginning was an essential natural phase: thus also the underlying ground of the *Muses* is the springs, then the Naiads as the Nymphs of the springs.

[25]As Aristotle says [*Metaphysics* 982b11-12] that philosophy emerges from wonder, [287] so the Greek intuition of nature emerges from this wonder. This does not mean that spirit meets something extraordinary, which it compares with the usual; for the understanding's view of a regular course of nature, and the reflective reference to that, is not yet present; but the aroused Greek spirit wonders much more at the *natural* in nature; it does not stop stupidly before it as before a given, but as before something primarily alien to the spirit, in relation to which, however, the Greek spirit has a presentiment of confidence, and the faith that nature bears something within it that is friendly, with which the spirit may sustain a positive relation. This *wondering*, and this *presentiment*, are here the fundamental categories; but the Hellenes did not stay with these modes, but posited the inner, about which the presentiment questioned, into a distinct conception, as object of consciousness. The natural counts not as immediate but as going through the spirit,

---

25. 1840, 286-88 (~ GW 27 [2] 652-55; GW 27 [3] 994-95, 1002-3).

which mediates it; the human being has the natural only as arousing, and the natural can count for the human being only as that which the human has made spiritual out of it. This spiritual start is then also not to be taken merely as an explanation that *we* only make; rather, it is present in a multitude of conceptions of the Greeks themselves. . . .

In this given we have, on the one hand, the indefinite, which, however, lets itself be heard; and on the other hand there is that which [288] becomes heard—a certain subjective imagining and clarifying of what is heard. . . . The Naiads or springs are the external beginning of the Muses. Yet the immortal songs of the Muses are not that which one hears when one hears the murmuring of the springs; rather, they are the productions of the sensitive listening spirit that in itself is productive, in its hearkening. . . . To *manteia* belongs the matter and the clarifier, who brings out the meaning. Plato speaks of it in reference to dreams, and to that delirium into which humans fall during sickness; an interpreter, *mantis*, is needed to clarify these dreams and this delirium. Nature answered the Greek's questions: this is true in the sense that the human being has answered the questioning of nature from his own spirit. The intuition becomes thereby purely poetical, for the spirit makes therein the sense, which the natural image expresses. Overall the Greeks sought an interpretation and meaning of the natural.

[26]Homer tells, in the last book of the *Odyssey*, that while the Greeks were holding a great funeral in honor of Achilles, and were sunk deep in mourning, a great tossing and storm came over the sea: the Greeks had the notion of dispersing in terror, when Nestor stood up and *clarified* this manifestation for them: Thetis, he said, comes with her Nymphs, to lament for the death of her son. When a pestilence broke out in the camp of the Greeks, the priest Calchas gave the interpretation to them: Apollo was incensed at their not having restored the daughter of his priest Chryses when a ransom had been offered. The *oracle* originally had also entirely this form of interpretation: only in the dream, the inspiration, did the human being have the gift of prophecy—but then it belonged to someone singular, to know how to interpret its word, and this is the *mantis*. The oldest oracle was at Dodona in Aetolia (in the district of today's Janina). Herodotus says [2.56-58] that the first priestesses of the temple there were from Egypt; and yet this temple was taken to be a totally ancient Greek one. The rustling of the leaves of the

---

26. GW 27 [4] 1345-46 (~ GW 27 [3] 995-96; 1840, 289).

sacred oaks was the form of prognostication there (*phullomanteia*). . . . The poet was then especially this *mantis* among the Greeks: at the commencement of the *Iliad*, [1346] Achilles is angry against Agamemnon, and has in mind to draw his sword; but on a sudden he checks the movement of his arm; the poet explains this, by saying: it was Pallas-Athene (Wisdom, Consideration) that restrained him. This explanation is thus the inner, the sense, the truth, which becomes known; and the poets became in this way the teachers of the Greeks—but above all, it was *Homer*: all art and science were linked to him and created from him, and especially painting and the plastic arts take rich content from his poetry. Herodotus said: *"Homer and Hesiod have made for the Greeks their gods"*—a great pronouncement; . . .[27] But even so, Herodotus says: Greece has its gods from Egypt,[28] and that the Greeks asked in Dodona whether they ought to accept these gods.[29] This seems self-contradictory, but is entirely consistent. The natural, as that from which the human becomes clarified—the inner, essential, itself is the origin of the divinities overall, but such that in the art of the Greeks, historical skills especially also could have come from Egypt, and so the beginning of the religion can be from outside, but through its independent spirit it has transformed the one from the other.

[30]The *manteia* overall is poetry—not willful imagining, but an imagination that introduces the spiritual into the natural and is meaningful knowing. The Greek spirit is therefore on the whole without superstition, in that it changes the sensuous into the meaningful, so that the determinations come from spirit—although superstition comes in again from another quarter, as will be observed when determinations

---

27. Herodotus 2.53.1–2: "From where each of the gods came, or if all existed always, and what are the shapes [eidē] belonging to them, was not known until the day before yesterday so to speak. For I opine [dokeō] the epoch of Hesiod and Homer to be not more than four hundred years ago. And these are the ones who poetized [made] a theogony for the Greeks, giving to the gods their names and honors, and distributing among them the arts, and signaling their shapes."

28. Herodotus 2.50.1–2: "The names of just about all of the gods came from Egypt into Greece. For I discovered by undertaking inquiries that they came from the barbarians; and I am of the opinion [dokeō] that they came especially from Egypt. For except Poseidon and the Dioscuri (as I said before), and also Ares and Hestia and Themis and the Graces and Nereids, the names of the other gods have always existed among the Egyptians and in that land. And I am saying what the Egyptians themselves say."

29. Herodotus 2.52.2–3: "And when, after a time had passed, they made inquiry of the oracle in Dodona concerning the names, . . . if they should adopt the names that came from the barbarians, the oracle bade the use of them."

30. 1840, 290.

for what is held to be so and for activity are created from another source than the spiritual.

The stimuli of the Greek spirit are not, however, to be limited simply to the above outer and inner; the traditional element—derived from the alien, the already delivered cultural education, divinities, and worship of divinities—must also be reckoned with.

[31]To the alien element belong notably the Greek mystery-rites, which have engaged curiosity over the centuries.... They were an ancient form of worship of gods deriving in part from alien sources. If we ask about their content, the history indicates that these mysteries contained ancient nature religion—that they necessarily contained this, and nothing further.

[32]Spiritual subjectivity is primary with the Greeks. The nature-god is, however, maintained on one side, but determined only as the beginning, the starting point that is sublated in the spiritual progress. The Greeks have Selene, Kronos, etc. But they call these Titans and they are of a different [312] race from that of Zeus. This distinction between the old and the new gods is an essential phase in the concept of the Greek intuition.[33] The Titans in part are preserved, in part dispensed with by the self-conscious spirit.... They are in part preserved as nature gods, in part maintained as the resonance of the natural power in the new gods—but as resonance, as essential phase. Thus Apollo is the knowing one, and this has the resonance of being the god of light. Poseidon still has the resonance of elemental natural power.... In this regard it is to be said that the Greeks on the side of the foundation in nature are inclined to the oriental mode, and the natural foundation comes to them from the Orient in such a way that springs, trees, waves, rivers are also represented in the form of divinities.... And of course this imagining is more beautiful than that of the Orientals, and this comes from the Greeks honoring the human—because it alone is capable of

---

31. GW 27 [1] 313 (~ GW 27 [2] 668–71; GW 27 [3] 1003–4; GW 27 [4] 1347; 1840, 302–3).
32. GW 27 [1] 311–12 (~ GW 27 [2] 663–66; GW 27 [3] 1000–1002; 1840, 298–99).
33. In his *Lectures on the Philosophy of Religion*, Hegel emphasizes this distinction within the Greek gods still more (1824 version, GW 29 [1] 356–59; 1827 version, GW 29 [2] 138–41; 1831 version, GW 29 [2] 263–64); see esp. 1827, GW 29 [2] 138: "A chief determination in the mythology is that the gods under Zeus, through a war, through violent force, achieved for themselves the mastery—that the spiritual principle dethroned the Giants, the Titans; the simple natural power was defeated by the spirit. [Huhe: This is not empty fable, this is the essence of the Greek religion.] ... In the war of the gods is the entire history of the Greek gods expressed.... The natural gods are banished to the edge of the world, beyond the self-conscious world—but they also have maintained their right ... so that they constitute *one* determination of the spiritual, of the spiritual gods; in the spiritual gods themselves this natural phase is contained, but only as resonance of the natural, only as one side of themselves."

being the sensuous appearance of the spiritual. Honoring the finite in human mode, they have made human the configurations of knowledge, etc.—not distorted, as with the Orientals.

"Where Superstition Still Holds Sway"

[34]But while detaching itself from nature, it has a side where superstition still holds sway, . . . as shows itself in the oracles. . . . We see that the Greeks questioned the oracles about particular concerns. . . . [317] It was not about the ethically customary, or matters of justice, that advice was given here. We note that inasmuch as we contrast the relationship in the Christian religion, we find the God of the Christian defined as this-here, the actual human being, having become *this-here*. Thus in the nature of God is this determination established, and so [Griesheim: the familiar trust of Christians in God is because God has the human experience of such a suffering]. With this confidence, the individual can decide and resolve things for oneself. . . . Infinite subjectivity, the *I* will: inasmuch as the determination of *this* willing is not yet invested in God, the abstract willing of the subject still has no right. . . . The deciding the human being has not yet grasped as one's own; and if that were to be the deciding, it would be without justification. For the human being is absolutely justified only insofar as he knows the nature of the *this-here* and the divine nature. Thus the Greeks [318] have not in themselves the counsel about the decision-making about their particular concerns. . . . This is a very important circumstance explaining why we have among the Greeks that superstition of the oracles. When we see, for example, the noble Pausanias prior to the Battle of Plataea fretting over the sacrificial animals, it is necessary to ask how this is congruent with the free Greek spirit. This apparently bizarre circumstance is thus connected with the concept of the Greek spirit—and talk about priestly betrayal is superficial. Precisely this circumstance is what reveals the difference between the Greek and the Christian religions.

"Fate"

[35]Closely connected with the oracles is another Greek notion, namely, that of Fate. . . . For Christians, Providence, faith, stands opposed to what we call Fate for the Greeks. But for Christians as well as for Greeks,

---

34. GW 27 [1] 316–18 (~ GW 27 [4] 1357).
35. GW 27 [1] 318–19 (~ GW 27 [3] 1004–6, 1011–12).

in regard to the particular there is something incomprehensible, not understood—for destiny unfolds itself on a soil that appears to us as contingency in that it deals with particularities that are not justified, as opposed to what exists freely in and for itself. The particularities of [319] circumstances, the life journey of the individual, are something incomprehensible for Greeks and Christians; but the Christian has the notion that all this contingency God guides and leads to his best. Thus the Christian assumes that his own best is a divine object. The Greeks lacked this notion, because what is particular, the goal of individuals, was not taken up into God. The Greeks accepted single events as they found them, and they did not have the thought that what is best for them would be an ultimate goal. So they were left with only the thought that, "so it is." They remained standing with simple being. Me—that I would be goal, this did not enter their thinking. "So it is, and the human being must submit oneself": this was their ultimate. About this we must at the same time say that in this Fate, in this "so it is," it is to be remembered that in this notion no superstition is present, as there is in the oracle, where the human being is unfree. In the notion of Fate is freedom—though only formal; for the human accepts that which is, and lets it happen; for there is no discord between him and what exists. The human is only unfree when the outer does not conform to the goal. In the human being making no goal for oneself, and sinking all in the onefold notion—"so it is"—there is a unity between a person and that which is. So there a person is single, in serenity. Inasmuch as one has no particular goal, however, what is other is surely sublated in one: serenity and freedom are present. But this is no solace, for solace assumes that I do have a goal, and the notion that it is to be satisfied. This solace is not present, for the subjection does not need the solace, since the individual in one's particularity does not view oneself as goal. The deeper demands of subjectivity are not satisfied here; but the relationship is not an unreasonable one. If one were to want to view destiny as a blind power over right and ethical custom, that would be spiritless, but that was not Fate for the Greeks. Divine justice is something other than the cycle of destiny.

"To Sum Up What the Greek Spirit Is"

[36]If we wish now to sum up what the *Greek spirit* is, this makes the fundamental determination: that the freedom of the spirit is conditioned

---

36. 1840, 291-93 (~ GW 27 [2] 658-59; GW 27 [3] 996-97; GW 27 [4] 1350).

by and in essential relation to a natural stimulus. The Greek freedom is excited through something other; and it is therein free, in that, out of itself it transforms and produces the stimulus. This determination is the midpoint between the loss of self on the part of humans (such as we observe in the Asiatic principle, where the spiritual and divine exist only in a natural way), and the infinite subjectivity as pure certainty of itself—the thought, that the I is the soil [292] for all that ought to count.... Spirituality is therefore not yet absolutely free and not yet completed *out of* itself, its own stimulus....

In the human being, the natural side is the heart, the inclination, the passion, the temperament: this becomes now spiritually developed, to free individuality—so that the character is not placed in relation to universal ethically customary powers, as duties, but the ethically customary is as particular being, and willing of the sense, and of the particular subjectivity. This makes the Greek character *beautiful individuality* that is brought forth through the spirit, in that it transforms the natural into its own expression. The activity of the spirit does not yet here possess in itself the material and organ of expression, but it needs the natural stimulus and the natural matter: it is not free, self-determining spirituality, but naturalness built on spirituality—spiritual individuality. The Greek spirit is the plastic artist, who forms the stone into a work of art. By this forming the stone does not remain mere stone, with the form only brought to it from without; but it is made, against its nature, into an expression of the spiritual, and so transformed. Conversely, the artist *needs*, for his spiritual conceptions, the stone, the colors, the sensuous forms, to express his idea; without such an element he can no more become conscious of the idea himself, than make it objective for the others—since it cannot in thought become an object to him. The Egyptian spirit also was this worker in matter, but the natural had not yet been subjected to the spiritual; it remained in contest and struggle with it; the natural remained [293] ever for itself, and one side of the image—as in the body of the Sphinx. In Greek beauty the sensuous is only a sign, expression, hull, in which the spirit manifests itself.

It must still be added that, while the Greek spirit is this transforming-forming, it knows itself free in its forms; for it is their creator, and they are the so-called "human works." They are, however, not merely this, but the eternal truth and the power of spirit in and for itself, and quite as really uncreated as created by man. He has respect and veneration for these intuitions and images, for this Zeus in Olympia and this Pallas on the Acropolis, even as for the laws of the state and the ethical customs; but he, the human being, is the mother's womb that conceived them, he the breast that suckled them, he the spiritual to which their grandeur and purity are owing. So he is cheerful in them, and not only free in himself, but with the consciousness of his freedom; thus the honor of the human is entwined in the worship of the divine. Humans honor the divine in and for itself, but at the same time as *their* deed, their production, and their concrete existence: thus the divine receives its honor mediated through the honor paid to the human, and the human mediates the honor of the divine.

So defined is the *beautiful individuality* that constitutes the center of the Greek character. Now the several radiations, in which this concept realizes itself, are to be considered more closely. All form works of art; we may grasp them in a threefold form: as the *subjective* work of art, that is, the cultural education of the human oneself; as the *objective* work of art, *that is*, the configuring of the world of divinities; lastly, as the *political* work of art, the manner of the constitution, and of the individual in it.

[37]Freedom is, however, with the Greeks not yet itself the object but is still united with the humanly natural. Now the determination of this, what it is that forms the basis of the Greek intuition of the universal, becomes manifest when we consider two sides: first, why is it that the Greeks do not yet think the absolute [Hagenbach: worship the absolute in spirit and in truth,] why spirit does not yet appear to spirit in the spirit; and on the other side, why God does not at the same time appear to the Greeks in the flesh, although they had the in-and-for-itself-being in unity with the human.

Thus for the Greeks the spirit is not yet the invisible, spiritual, non-sensuous; for the Greeks are the closest principle to the Orientals, whose basic intuition was of the substantial unity of spirit and nature....

[307] As regards this side we must say that the Greek principle is not yet elevated to a world of thought....

Now the other aspect is that the Greeks certainly elevated spirit to subjectivity and the natural overall they relegated to the side of appearance. This natural serves as expression of the appearance of subjective spirituality, and this natural can be only the humanly natural, for only in the human shape can the spirit as such appear. Inasmuch as the Greek [308] set forth its essence as human, one can ask why God does not appear to the Greek as human, and they fashion God for themselves only in marble or in pictures of the imagination. This characteristic is

---

37. GW 27 [1] 306–11 (~ GW 27 [2] 672–74; GW 27 [3] 998–1000; 1840, 304–5).

connected with our earlier collective considerations, that the human being only had worth as such insofar as one had made oneself into the appearance of the beautiful. [Griesheim: It was only the Greeks who developed themselves in this way; all the others were barbarians, and even among the Greeks there were real Greeks and slaves.] Whoever was born a Greek still had to first make oneself into a Greek—and this is indeed an essential quality of spirit, to make oneself into what one is. But the spirit must also be essentially and intrinsically what is originally free, and this is the concept of spirit that the Greeks did not yet grasp, because they were not yet thinking. . . . [309] They did not yet have the notion that the human being is created in the image of God and is intrinsically free. For this reason they could not yet have the conception of the unity of divine and human nature, for human nature as such did not yet count for them as capable of receiving the divine, but only the human being who had brought oneself forth as idealized. . . . The spirit that has matured inwardly to a totality is the first that no longer needs to imaginatively build the natural into spiritual form. When thought is free for itself, it thinks the external; and, by thinking it, can leave this externality in its immediate existence, as it is. . . . If thought is free for itself, reflective, then there is no need for the natural to be given form. . . . The totality of the Idea requires that the Idea should have consummated both sides—thought, and the sensuous on the other side—so that it should ramify itself into singularization. Only this infinite antithesis attains the profundity of the Idea, which has the strength to hold the antithesis together in this profundity. One can indeed reproach the Greek religion for being anthropomorphic; but its defect is that it is not anthropomorphic enough; it did not know God in immediate existence. The Greeks have heroes, but in Homer they are not yet revered as divine. . . .

[310] The god of the Greeks is the human idealized into beauty. As the human being is exalted in outer aspect, so also must the human be in the spiritual aspect, to which belong knowledge, justice, goodness. When these attributes are exalted to their essentiality, we refer to them as the highest good, etc. But this is only a quantitative exaltation. The true exaltation would be [311] the sublation of the spirit out of its finitude. The exalted spirit is the spirit that at the same time has power over nature.

[38]The Greeks became conscious of the power of the spirit, and indeed in the way of image: it is *ideal*, classical ideal (the Idea is something

---

38. GW 27 [4] 1349–50.

spiritual, something essential, explicit for the sensuous depiction); this ideal is not thus something beyond, however, but the force of the same power of the spirit—Athena is, on the one side, the city of Athens, this existence of the city, belonging to the citizens even as they belong to it; [Wichern: and at the same time the genius, the spirit of the Athenian citizen, and thus objective, independent]. Even so is Eros, Aphrodite: Eros is on the one side something objective, but also the very power, the very feeling—thus something thoroughly human—because the spiritual essentials are depicted in their specificity; [1350] what is known as human is not the absolute spirit but the particularized spirit. . . . This is the freedom of the Greeks, this freedom that stops itself at a power in which the spirit finds itself; the Greeks became free in their religion in that they thus built up for themselves, by imagination, the spiritual powers; to that the classical art belongs, in that it has as foundation a substantial content; even so does the human being for the Greeks have a beautiful individuality: the existing individual has built oneself into a beautiful configuration and corporeality; the gods are works of art, and even so have the individuals built themselves into works of art and as such display themselves, . . . even as with the gods, corporeality is no hindrance to the spirit being their goal.

[39]The true defect of the Greek religion, as contrasted with the Christian, is now that in it the *appearance* is the highest mode by which the whole of the divine overall is constituted, while in the Christian religion the appearance is regarded only as an *essential phase* of the divine. Here the appearing God dies and is grasped as sublating itself; it is as having died that Christ is first depicted as sitting at the right hand of God. The Greek god, on the contrary, exists for the Hellenes perennially as appearing—only in marble, in metal or wood, or conceived as figured by the imagination.

"The Life of the State"

[40][Griesheim: Immediately connected with the Greek religion is the constitution of Greece.] The beginnings have already been discussed, and how that royal force that had been brought in from foreign lineages finally fell away as superfluous. The positive by which the Greek constitution distinguishes itself is [Griesheim: the democracy, which

---

39. 1840, 304 (~ GW 27 [2] 675).
40. GW 27 [1] 320 (~ GW 27 [3] 1006–7).

only here could attain this development, and only here be so admired.] The oriental world brilliantly developed despotism. The Roman world is that of aristocracy, and the Germanic world that of monarchy.

[41]The Greek spirit is the spirit of the first harmonizing of the following two sides: the substantial, universal, eternal spirit; and the personal, subjective, individual spirit. In this harmony the ethically customary, and substantiality, become known as one's own will as essence of the individual; it is one's own reason, one's own will, right, ethical custom. In this unity the will of the subject is virtue—his goal [, his interest (Erdmann),] is even this content, the substantial, the rational. This appears essentially as the state. It is not simply something common, cultivated, but rather it is existing, actually universal—or universal actuality. That is life of the state, in which the universal, the law, in developing lawful measure, stands over the individual, but where the highest goal [Garzyński: highest interest] of the individual is this actual universality: the fatherland—the natural state.... It is self-conscious freedom.... This is not present as law that is external and iron, but it is the will of the individual, through which he is determined and upheld.

[981] This self-conscious freedom is the spirit of the West, the spirit that goes back into itself, itself turns back to itself, seeks what it wills, what counts, not as something beyond, but it has it in itself! The Greek spirit can be known as the spirit of humanity, of the humane. It is the first spirit that is the humane spirit only, as such. That is what forms its limitation—from which limitation, later, there is relation to the higher. It is the spirit of humanity. The Easterners were indeed also humans; by the humane, we mean that the ethically customary, the in and for itself objective, independent from willfulness, recognizes the human, belongs to it, activates it, insofar as it knows and wills it as its own.

[42]On the other hand, however, the subjectivity was not yet infinite reflection within itself, not yet the wholly free ideality of thought, to which the conscience belongs—the absolute determination regarding the particularity; conscience thus did not have here a place; humans did not feel the requirement that everything should be justified before human inwardness. There had not yet occurred this breach in which independent inwardness forms itself, seeking to determine for itself in thought, what is right and ethically customary, and recognizing only this to be justified. Since this breach has not yet occurred, this world

---

41. GW 27 [3] 980–81.
42. GW 27 [1] 320–24 (~ GW 27 [2] 676–78; GW 27 [3] 1008–9; 1840, 306–9).

is not yet erected; the particular will is not yet free; the particularity of conviction does not yet make itself count, the passions are not yet in what holds the state together.

Over and against such particular powers of the spirit and the will, which inwardly want to make themselves free, the [modern] state appears as external, and since it is determined as external, to which the subjective free will is not subjectively bound, the state must have [321] its own distinctive bond, because the spirit, the conscience, is something established. So the state must provide itself another mainstay. When such a set of circumstances demands it, then is the time for monarchy. This external order that is then necessary has to give itself a central point, which can only be a secure knot if it has been tied naturally and is present. Thus the essential phase of naturalness is called for and taken up into the ethically customary order. Then this established order can take up the element of naturalness and can support the state apart from and, yes, even contrary to the convictions of the individual.... All these determinations we do not yet find with the Greeks. However, in order to be able to do justice to their constitution, one must have mastered these propositions; it is only when one has its concept that one is permitted to discuss conceptions of the constitution. Inwardness is close to the Greek spirit and will soon surface in it, where the subjective spirit and, together with it, opinions appear. This appearing, however, can enter only as destructive, because the constitution has not yet developed to this point, and so that principle is manifest as only destructive in it. In the Greek constitution, therefore, we start from the unity of subjective and objective will, whereas the oriental world starts out from the patriarchal principle, and the modern world from subjective freedom. Since these latter two principles are not present in the Greek world, the central thing here is beauty, which in terms of the political leads to the constitution that sets Greece apart. This is beautiful, but truth is always higher. This beautiful center is where the ethically customary and the just is grasped by the free individual—but not yet in the determination of morality, [322] and instead as ethical custom, as the objective aspect of willing, the willing that has not yet deepened a being for itself in ideality.... The will is no longer bound from the outset since it is no longer in unity with the natural, as in the oriental. Thus the content is the free, rational. As to the form, it is that of immediacy. The law of the ethically customary is valid here simply because it is. The fatherland requires it, and therefore it must happen. This is here the simple reflection, the simple customary ethic by which we live. Here there is no higher ground for obedience. In beauty the Idea is in sensuous presentation and expressed for sensuous representation. And ethical custom here, which does not yet have in it morality, is here as ethical custom and habit, still a way of nature, necessity. Thus the law has here the form of immediacy; the particularity of will is not yet present. Hence the common essence can reside in the decision of the citizen, and this will of the citizen must be the foundation of the constitution—for there is no principle that could hinder the present ethical custom in its working. Thus here the democratic constitution is the absolutely necessary form. The will here is still the objective will; Athena, the goddess, is still Athens, still the spirit of the people, still the spirit of the citizens. . . .

[323] When we speak of such a constitution, it can frequently be represented in our time in particular to be the best. One can say that state interests, decisions, and ordinances of the state should be the concern of all; this is entirely correct. A second tenet one adduces is that individuals, as singular, have the right to deliberate and to decide about their matters, which are public, because these are their most essential concerns. The citizens will choose what is best for themselves, and they will best understand what that is, and thus should have the right to do so.

However, a more essential consideration is the question as to who these single persons are who are to have this choice. They are single, individuals, citizens; and of them it must be said that they only have this justification to the extent that their will is still the objective will, not split between the interiority of subjectivity and what is universally objective—only to the extent, therefore, that their will is still the simple unity of substantial volition. And this is indeed the standpoint of the Greeks, but no longer in the modern world, where Christ says, "My empire is not of this world" [John 18:36]—where, then, the split exists and the inwardness and eternity of spirit within itself are found. The objective will should not be called the good will, for the good will is distinguished from the objective; the good will is the moral will that judges in accord with an inner rational determination, in accord with a knowledge of duty, judging in accord with the inner determination of what should happen to the individual and the state. [324] This good will is no longer the substantial, objective will. It can appear to be a remarkable destiny of the human race that, as soon as it arrives at subjective inwardness, at this religion of freedom, of spirituality, that humanity then can no longer have what one often in various ways calls freedom, namely, democracy. These determinations one must know, in order to avoid idle chatter about a constitution.

CHAPTER 6

⁴³This democratic constitution, which in its beauty, but also its evanescence, existed in Greece, can only find a place in small states. The larger the state is, the less vital becomes the whole state business for the individuals. The interests of the individuals, their particularity, their diverse ways of earning a living, diverge from the communal general affairs. The individual self as such becomes alienated from itself. . . . What belongs to democracy is the unmediated being-present of the citizen, whereby the faith in the community, the close acquaintance, the trust, become fixedly grounded and determined in the disposition of each in daily life. When in great empires voices are assembled, these paper voices are something totally different from when the forum assembles the citizens in the communal meeting place. In the latter is the presence, here and now, of the utterances, of the hearing of the utterances, of the lighting of the fire of enthusiasm in consciousness and trust—all of which is essentially irreplaceable for a common law.

⁴⁴Only in such cities can the interests be the same for the whole; in large empires, on the contrary, diverse interests that conflict are to be found. The living together in one city, the circumstance that one sees another daily, make a common cultural education and a living democracy possible. In democracy, the main point is that the character of the citizen be from one mold. One must be present at the critical stages of business; in decision, one must take part not simply with one's single vote but in the drive of moving and being moved with the passion and interest of the whole man absorbed in the affair, and the warmth with which a resolve was made being equally present during its execution. The insight, to which all must be brought, must be produced in individual members through the mediating warmth of *oratory*. If this were attempted by *writing*, in an abstract, lifeless way, the individuals would not be set universally ablaze; and the greater the crowd, the less weight would each individual vote have. In a large empire one could certainly make an inquiry, votes might be gathered in all the communities, and the results reckoned up—as was done by the French Convention. But this is a dead essence, and there the world is broken into fragments and dissipated into a mere paper-world.

⁴⁵Another circumstance that is prominent here is *slavery*. This was a necessary condition of a beautiful democracy, where it was the right

---

43. GW 27 [3] 1010 (~ GW 27 [1] 326; GW 27 [2] 677; GW 27 [4] 1357; 1840, 311-12).
44. 1840, 311 (~ GW 27 [1] 326; GW 27 [2] 677; GW 27 [4] 1357).
45. 1840, 310-11 (~ GW 27 [1] 325-26; GW 27 [2] 639; GW 27 [3] 1010-11; GW 27 [4] 1356-57).

and duty of every citizen to deliver or to listen to orations respecting the management of the state in the place of public assembly, to exercise oneself in the gymnasia, and to join in the celebration of festivals. It was a necessary condition of such occupations that the citizen should be removed from handicraft work, and consequently, that what among us falls to free citizens—the work of daily life—should be done by slaves. The equality of the citizen brought with it the exclusion of the slave. Slavery first ends when the will is infinitely reflected into itself, when right is conceived as pertaining to the freeman, but the human being is free according to his universal nature, as endowed with reason. Here, however, we still occupy the standpoint of customary ethics, which is [311] only habit and ethical custom, and thereby still a particularity, in concrete existence.

[46]*Virtue* is the foundation of democracy, says Montesquieu [*Spirit of the Laws*, esp. parts 1 and 2]; this expression is as important as it is true, [307] in reference to the notion that one usually makes for oneself of democracy. Here, what is essential for the individual is the substance of justice, the matters of the state, the general interest—but it is so as ethical custom, in the manner of the objective will, so that morality in the precise sense, the innerness of conviction and intention, is not yet present.... [308] Of the Greeks in the first and true configuration of their freedom, we may declare that they had no conscience; what held sway in them was the habit of living for the fatherland without further reflection. The state in the abstract—which to our understanding is the essential—was unknown to them, but for them the end was their living fatherland: this Athens, this Sparta, these temples, these altars, this way of living together, this circle of fellow-citizens, these ethical customs and habits. To the Greek the fatherland was a necessity, without which one could not live.

"The Most Brilliant Period of Greece"

[47]We come now to the *second period* of Greek history. The first period saw the Greek spirit attain its strength and maturity—that it is so. The second contains how it *displays* itself, appearing in its brilliance, bringing itself forward to a work for the world, and justifying its principle in struggle, and achieving victory against attack.

---

46. 1840, 306b–308 (~ GW 27 [2] 678; GW 27 [3] 1006–9; GW 27 [4] 1352–54).
47. 1840, 312 (~ GW 27 [1] 326).

156　CHAPTER 6

The period of contact with the preceding world-historical people is overall to be regarded as the *second* in the history of each nation. The world-historical contact of the Greeks was that with the Persians; Greece therein exhibited itself at its most masterful.

[48]The first point, therefore, is the contact of the Greeks with the Persians, the events that Herodotus calls the Median War. [327] This history, as brilliant as it is, is not here to be considered further, as it is well known. Here it is only to be recalled that not all Greeks took part in it, that a great part allied with the Persians and fought against the Greeks. Only once do we see the Greeks united. Their disunion is a necessary phase, and particularity had to gain the upper hand over the communal Hellenism. Athens and Sparta especially distinguished themselves. . . .

To be further noted is the favor of destiny. . . . There is no people that does not have heroic deeds; all fatherlands are courageously defended; but these countless battles and heroes [328] do not live in immortal brilliance as do those of the Greeks. One can speak of simple luck, but one must thereby consider how fame allots its crowns. It rewards, not according to the subjective side of deserving, but in accord with the nature of the case. The Western and Eastern stood here so opposed that the interests of world-history and of the electoral state lay in the balance. All other, especially defensive, interests of a fatherland that one can mention are dwarfed in comparison. . . . On the one side there was the oriental despotism, the entire Eastern world united under a single master, mighty in numbers and with the advantage of being under a single mastery. And these Persians, these Orientals, are not to be derided. Herodotus speaks quite otherwise of them; and while some of the peoples were soft, most were belligerent and strong, with a wild, raw courage. Over against this tremendous mass of warrior peoples under one [329] leader stood a pair of peoples of limited means in free individuality, so that indeed never has the superiority of the noble strength of spirituality over the mass displayed itself in such splendor.

[49]The images of the gods were an abomination to the Persians, who worshiped what is shapeless, the formless. In spite of the disunion of the Greeks, the Persian fleet was beaten at Salamis. . . . Bigger battles, unquestionably, have been fought; but it is these that live immortally, not in the historical records of peoples only, but also of science [314]

---

48. GW 27 [1] 326–29 (~ GW 27 [2] 681–82; GW 27 [3] 1012–13; GW 27 [4] 1357–59; 1840, 313–14).
49. 1840, 313–14.

and of art, of the noble and of the ethically customary overall. For this was world-historical victory; it saved cultural education and spiritual power, and took all strength from the Asiatic principle.... This war, and then the development after this victory of the states that stood at the top after this war, is the most brilliant period of Greece: everything that the Greek principle involved completely developed itself and brought itself to sight.

"The Greatest Opposition Was between Athens and Sparta"

[50]The people, having been aroused, and no longer having an outside object of its activity, must seek it inwardly, in inner dissension and struggle. Thus we see here struggles of the Greek states with one another, partly of individual states against one another and partly among individual parties in the individual states. Athens and Sparta constituted the greatest opposition. Around this swirled the interests of the rest.

[51]The Athenians continued their wars of domination for a long time, and thereby attained a high degree of prosperity, while the Lacedaemonians, who had no sea power, remained quiet.

[52]One must give recognition to both, for each of these two developments of spirit and character and constitution is a very worthy configuration. One cannot refrain from judging between them; but to judging belongs a standard, which depends on the idea that one brings; the judgment has many categories: strict ethical custom, morality, courage; but the standard is: ethically customary virtue, that is, here, civic virtue—the disposition that is in unity with the state. That is common to both, Athens and Sparta. But there is further to be considered the free development of what belongs to the individual: whether individuality has equally developed itself into spiritual individuality, spiritual works of art; whether the individual has attained right, as has the whole, and whether this freedom of the individual has standing, remains standing, in this substantial unity of the whole. When one thus brings judging to the ancients, we must not turn to Xenophon, Plato, the Socratics, but to those who apply themselves to understanding the state as it is present and who have led it—to practicing statesmen, who have the conscious image of what the inner nature of the state itself is. Pericles

---

50. GW 27 [1] 329.
51. 1840, 314.
52. GW 27 [2] 682–83 (~ GW 27 [3] 1013–14).

is such a one, who in the divine circle of Greek individuality is by the Greeks called Zeus himself [Aristophanes, *Acharnians* 530-31]. One has grounds to say that we, removed by the distance of time, [683] may modestly want to know better than Pericles: he was in any case a partisan Athenian patriot. But he had a fundamental consciousness about the substantial character of his fatherland, and the greatness of his spirit consisted in this consciousness; and when we make comparisons, when we are capable of making a different fundamental judgment about who has Idea and historical knowledge, we come to see the [funeral] oration of Pericles (which is perhaps enlarged by the deep spirit of Thucydides [2.35-46]—both were culturally educated spirits): this must serve as commentary on the constitution.

Both states became democratic. Now an entirely abstract democracy is something that overall cannot stand: affairs are always particular affairs, having a long duration that cannot be cared for by the crowd as such, that requires a single person at the top, or a plurality that forms a council that brings affairs along in such a way that they can be laid before the crowd. Democratic conducting of war would be absurd. So in every state there was a select group that discussed affairs until they could be brought before the crowd.

[53]In Athens, the various branches of human industry—agriculture, handicraft, trade (especially by sea)—united themselves, but gave rise to much dissension. An antagonism of ancient and wealthy families vs. such as were poorer had earlier brought itself into being.... The political condition wavered between aristocracy and democracy. Solon effected, by his division into four property-classes, a temperament between these opposites; they all together formed the assembly of the people for deliberation and for decision on public affairs; but the offices of government were reserved for the three upper classes.

[54]If one says that an essential aspect of democracy is that in it the people determine the laws, it can appear striking, how here one individual gave the constitutional law. [Hagenbach: The law that Solon gave was not only constitutional but also the law of private right.] It is a very superficial expression to say that in democracy lawgiving is in the people's hands. For democracy is already a constitution; it is already the development of a lawful condition where the laws are already firm

---

53. 1840, 315 (~ GW 27 [1] 330-31; GW 27 [2] 683-84; GW 27 [3] 1014-15; GW 27 [4] 1352-53, 1359).
54. GW 27 [1] 331-32.

THE GREEK WORLD   159

so that a further elaboration is only something inessential. The real laws, on which [332] things depend, are already established in every constitution insofar as it is one. Solon gave the Athenians a democratic constitution, in such a fashion that the aristocratic was an essential phase thereof—the wealthy in regard to the state administration still had an advantage.[55]

[56]Immediately after the Solonic lawgiving, during the lifetime of Solon, a tyrant arose in Athens. Pisistratus empowered himself with the mastery, after Solon had in vain asked his fellow citizens to maintain their freedom. One sees how weakly the constitution was inscribed in the consciousness, in the spirit of the individuals. . . . In general, Pisistratus maintained the entire legislation of Solon. . . . [1016] One sees that the mastery of Pisistratus was necessary: on the one side, to hold together the powerful families;[57] on the other side, to habituate the Athenians to this Solonic law, to make living in accord with it habit and ethical custom. So when the Athenians became habituated to it,

---

55. See also Hegel's 1825-26 *Lectures on the History of Philosophy* (GW 30 [3] 900): "Solon and Lycurgus count as lawgivers, but they did nothing more than to cast lawgiving that was Ionic (Solon) or Doric (Lycurgus) into another form and to bring an end to current disorder, alleviating this evil condition by effective laws." And see the 1823-24 version, GW 30 [2] 523-24, interpreting the famous report by Herodotus (1.29-32) of Solon's dialogue with Croesus—"from which," Hegel avers, "we see the standpoint of Greek reflection of this epoch": "Solon says, 'no one is to be deemed happy prior to his death.' Blessed happiness is thus here the highest goal, as in Kant it counts as the ultimate determination. In the response of Solon there lies on one side an elevation above the sensuous, over that which is for appetite. Blessed happiness rests on inner and outer enjoyment; but it entails the further totality of the establishment of enjoyment—a universal, a rule for single enjoyments, a rule dictating that one not allow oneself to give in to the momentaneous, that one check the appetite, and have before one's eyes a universal standard. So here reflection stands between what is for mere sensuality and what is for justice and duty as such. The universal for itself is not the principle, but Solon stands in the midpoint of reflection."

56. GW 27 [3] 1015-16 (~ GW 27 [2] 684; GW 27 [4] 1359-60; 1840, 315-16).

57. See also 1840, 316: "The mastery by Pisistratus and his sons appears to have been necessary in order to put down the power of families and factions, in order to habituate them to order and peace, and the citizens to the Solonic legislation"; and the first published version of Hegel's *Lectures on the History of Philosophy—Vorlesungen über die Geschichte der Philosophie*, ed. C. L. Michelet, 3 vols. (Berlin: Duncker and Humbolt, 1840—based in part on materials we no longer have), 1:177-79: "Most of the lawgivers and administrators of the states themselves undertook to apply force on the people and to be their tyrants. Where they did not undertake it themselves, in such states it had to be done by other individuals, for it was necessary. . . . What was separated in Solon and Pisistratus, we find united in *Periander* in Corinth, and in *Pittacus* in Mitilene." Discussing in the *Encyclopedia* (sec. 435, Zusatz) the necessity that "all humans," and "all peoples, therefore," must undergo the master-slave dialectical relationship, Hegel says: "Thus it was necessary, for example, that after Solon had given to the Athenians democratic, free laws, *Pisistratus* forged for himself a rule by force through which he disciplined the Athenians into obeying those laws."

the mastery of the Pisistratae was superfluous—and they were easily murdered and banished. It belongs to a constitution that is lawful that it become ethically customary habit so that it will also be transformed into spiritual substance.

The attempt has been made in modern times to give to a people a constitution that is alien to the people's own spirit, that has neither an inner nor an external root in the people's spirit. Such an a priori constitution is certainly for itself powerless.

[58]After the Pisistratae were expelled, . . . parties reemerged again: the Alcmaeonidae, who took the lead in the insurrection, favored the democracy; on the other hand, the Spartans aided the adverse party of Isagoras, which followed an aristocratic direction. The Alcmaeonidae, with Cleisthenes at their head, kept the upper hand. He made the constitution still more democratic than it had been. . . . Finally, Pericles rendered the constitution yet more democratic by diminishing the essential dignity of the Areopagus, and bringing cases that had hitherto belonged to it before the people and the tribunals.

Pericles was a statesman of formative ancient character: when he devoted himself to the life of the state, he renounced private life, withdrew from all feasts and banquets, and pursued without intermission his aim, of being useful to the state—by which he attained such an exalted position, that Aristophanes [*Acharnians* 530-31] calls him the Zeus of Athens. We cannot but admire him in the highest degree: he stood at the head of a lightheaded but highly refined and thoroughly cultivated people; the only means by which he could obtain power and authority over them [317] were his personality and the conviction he produced of his being a man thoroughly noble, exclusively intent upon the welfare of the state, and above the norm in spirit and knowledge. On the side of the power of individuality we can find no statesman that is like him.

In the democratic constitution generally there is the widest scope for the development of great political characters; for it stands out in not only allowing but summoning the individuals to make their talents count. . . .

In Athens a vital freedom was present, and a vital equality of ethical custom and of spiritual culture; and if inequality of property could not be avoided, it did not reach an extreme. Together with this equality,

---

58. 1840, 316-18 (~ GW 27 [2] 685; GW 27 [3] 1016-18; GW 27 [4] 1355, 1360-62).

and within this freedom, all diversities of character and of talent, all variety of individuality, could in the freest manner make themselves count, and find from the environment the most abundant stimulus to development; for on the whole the essential phases of the Athenian essence were the independence of the individual, and a cultural education animated by the spirit of the beautiful.[59] It was Pericles who brought about the production of those eternal monuments of sculpture whose scanty remains astonish posterity; it was before this people that the dramas of Aeschylus and Sophocles were performed; and later on those of Euripides ... in which the principle of corruption is for sure more recognizable.... From this people sprang a circle of men who have become classic natures for all centuries; for to this number belong, besides those already named, Thucydides, Socrates, Plato, and further Aristophanes, [318] who preserved entire the political seriousness of his people at the time of its inner corruption, and who in this seriousness wrote and dramatized for the good of the fatherland.

The blame that attaches itself to the Athenians in Xenophon and Plato goes more to that later time, when misfortune and the corruption of the democracy were certainly present.

[60]The great political characters shaped themselves out of the distinctive democratic constitution, where each individual is challenged and required to make count his talent, when one knows how to satisfy the

---

59. See also Hegel's 1825–26 *Lectures on the History of Philosophy* (GW 30 [3] 970): "Each individual had his substantial consciousness in unity with the laws, with the state; but at the same time the individuality, the spirit, the thought, of the individual was left free to validate, to express, to develop itself, and so we see in this principle of freedom individuality emerge in its greatness. The principle of subjective freedom appears at first still bound in unity with the universal foundation of the Greek customary ethics, legality, even mythology—and so in this unity, the principle of subjective freedom brought forth in its development those great works of the beautiful plastic arts and the immortal works of poetry and history. Thus the principle of subjective freedom had not yet taken the form in which the content is also supposed to be something subjectively special, or at least in distinction from the universal foundation, the universal customary ethics, the universal religion, the universal laws.... We will later see the form of subjectivity become free for itself and emerge in antithesis to the substantial, to the ethically customary, to the religion, to the laws. The foundation for this principle of subjectivity, but the still entirely general foundation, we see in Anaxagoras, who lived a bit before Socrates although they still knew of one another." And also GW 30 [3] 1084: "The principle of subjective freedom is something later, is the principle of the modern constructed age; this principle is in the Greek age also known—but as the principle of the corruption of the Greek state, of the Greek way of life. It was the corruption because the Greek spirit, constitutions, laws were not constituted and could not be constituted so that within them this principle could emerge; the two are not homogeneous and so Greek customary ethics and habit must fall."

60. GW 27 [1] 333–34.

lightheartedness and demands of a very cultured people. The religion gave to talent the highest stimulus for art, because the god is the beautiful individuality elevated to ideality, the principle of the spiritual Idea in sensuous element, so that this element served the god. Thus was the god also honored in the festival—externally, not inwardly in the heart, not so that the innerness was filled with the thought of god and with this conception. Athens thus presented the spectacle of a city whose goal [334] was to live for the beautiful, and that had a consciousness of the seriousness of public life and of life overall and was active in practical occupation. This character one learns to recognize best from Pericles's funeral oration in the second book of Thucydides. Here he develops his consciousness about that which Athens is.

[61]In regard to the conduct of private persons, we see in the Athenian state the development of an urbanity in ethical custom, a freedom with delicatesse. This urbanity is a substantial courtesy, without it thereby assuming expressly the forms that we reckon in it. Everything that is for us form is, in Greek urbanity, substance; it contains the ongoing recognition of the rights of others, and testifies to this: that I in my opinionating respect the right of another's opinionating, and respect whether he wants to hear me, or not. If I speak without knowing whether he wants to hear, I deal against his right—and this goes also for what is said. [333] In all that I express there is a pushiness when I speak in the sense also of the hearer so that I demand of him a similar "Yes." This pushiness, over the freedom of others, must not come forth in this urbanity. In the Platonic dialogue is this urbanity developed to the heights.

[62]In Sparta, on the other hand, we witness rigid, abstract virtue—living for the state, but in such a way that the activity, the freedom, of individuality are put in the background. The state-construction of Sparta is based on institutions that are completely in the interest of the state, but whose goal is a *lifeless equality*, and have not the free activity for a goal.

[63][Griesheim: Sparta's origin is completely different from that of Athens. As Dorians they came into the Peloponnesus from Thessaly—as conquerors who made slaves, "Helots," of the native people whom they encountered, as they did later also of the Messenians.]

---

61. GW 27 [1] 332–33.
62. GW 27 [4] 1362 (~ 1840, 319).
63. GW 27 [1] 334 (~ GW 27 [2] 686; GW 27 [3] 1018; GW 27 [4] 1362–63; 1840, 319).

⁶⁴As in a slave ship the crew are constantly armed, and the greatest foresight is taken to prevent an insurrection, so were the Spartans constantly vigilant about the Helots, and always in a condition of war, as against enemies.

Property in land was divided, by Lycurgus, as Plutarch relates [in his biography of Lycurgus], into equal parts, of which nine thousand only belonged to the Spartans, that is, the inhabitants of the city, and thirty thousand to the Lacedaemonians or suburbanites. At the same time, it was appointed, in order to maintain this equality, that the portions of ground should not be sold. But how little such an institution succeeds is proved by the circumstance, that subsequently Lacedaemon fell especially on account of the inequality of possessions. As daughters could be heirs, many goods had come by marriage into the possession of a few families, and at last all the landed property was in the hands of a few—as if to show how foolish it is to want to institute an equality by force, which is little effective and also negates a most essential liberty: namely, the free disposition of property.

Another remarkable, essential phase of the legislation of Lycurgus is his forbidding all money except that made of iron—an enactment that necessitated a sublation of all foreign business and traffic. . . .

For the sake of similarity of ethical custom, and a more intimate acquaintance of the citizens with each other, it had to be especially arranged that the Spartans had meals in common—through which community, however, family life was suppressed; for eating and drinking is a private affair, and consequently belongs inside the house. . . .

[321] Now as to the political constitution of Sparta, its basis was surely democratic, but with major modifications that made it almost an aristocracy and oligarchy. At the head of the state stood two kings, at whose side stood a senate (Gerousia), that was chosen from the best, and that also performed the functions of a court of justice, deciding rather in accordance with ethical custom and just habits, than with written laws. . . . Lastly, one of the highest magistracies was that of the *ephors*. . . . Through Aristotle we become informed that even ordinary persons without nobility, without means, could attain this magistracy. The ephors had full power to convoke assemblies of the people, to put resolutions to the vote, to propose laws, almost as the *tribuni plebis* in Rome.

---

64. 1840, 320–21 (~ GW 27 [1] 335–37; GW 27 [2] 686–87; GW 27 [3] 1018–20; GW 27 [4] 1362–65).

⁶⁵Later we find ephors take the lead overall as the most significant persons, so that Sparta was only in name democracy, and really aristocracy or oligarchy. The dullness of spirit of the Spartan people had the consequence that control of the government fell into the hands of a few.

⁶⁶The ethical customs of the Lacedaemonians are especially famous. They consisted in the discipline, together with the duties to the fatherland: the state as end living in each, for each the highest thing; unqualified duty. This is in any case something great. . . . [1021] The Spartan democracy is in its substantial stability powerful. . . . This unity, in which the individuals were held fast, is why Plato and Aristotle turned yearning eyes in the direction of Lacedaemon. But in Athens there is the same spiritual unity, where the citizens, as individuals, stand in the one Athens, bound together with freedom of individuality and cultural development of genuine individuality. Insofar as in Athens the power, the activity, the maintenance of the spirit had a virtue that was not so based on this communitarianism, on virtue, Athens had, however, the need for virtuous individuals to come to the top: at the time of the Persian wars, Miltiades, Themistocles, Aristides—and then Pericles.

⁶⁷For where there are many, an individual must always put himself at the peak. . . . In a democracy, this peak is the personality as such, which must make itself count. And this freest, most virtuous individual is Pericles, in the highest perfection.

⁶⁸In that the Lacedaemonians so thoroughly directed their spirit to the state, it followed that cultural education of the spirit, in art and science, were not at home among them; the Spartans appeared to the rest of the Greeks as dull, clumsy, and awkward human beings, in that they couldn't carry out even a slightly complicated affair, or at least did so while conducting themselves ineptly; Thucydides says, when the Spartans came abroad they stood out by their hesitancy, weakness, inconsequence, and ineptness.

In their intercourse at home, the Spartans were, on the whole, just; but in their conduct toward other nations, they themselves candidly made clear that they held what they liked to be what was praiseworthy, and what was useful to be what was just. It is well known that in Sparta

---

65. GW 27 [1] 336.
66. GW 27 [3] 1020–21.
67. GW 27 [1] 338.
68. GW 27 [4] 1365 (~ GW 27 [1] 336; GW 27 [2] 687–88; 1840, 321).

itself theft was permitted—only, the thief must not allow himself to be discovered.

[69]So stand both states over and against one other: the ethical custom of the one is a strict directedness to the state; in the other such an ethically customary directedness to the state is also present, but with culturally educated consciousness and with endless activity in bringing forth the beautiful and then also the true. The most beautiful ethical custom is the midpoint of the Greek spirit; but in this beauty there is at the same time the defect: ... the spiritual exists thus only in the element of the external and not yet standing as known in its purity for itself; the spirit is in this configuration only the unity with the sensuous, it is not yet objective in pure essence. The self-consciousness, consciousness of one's own singularity, one's own will—this subjectivity had not yet liberated itself from being in bondage to the other element of reality overall; the element of subjectivity is the source of the further progress of the spirit, to true freedom and to consciousness of this freedom; the Greek spirit must necessarily progress to the principle of morality, of one's own reflection, of innerness overall; only for a short time can the spirit remain at this beautiful spiritual oneness: the most beautiful bloom of Greek life lasted only about sixty years—from the Median Wars, 492 BC, to the Peloponnesian War, 431 BC.

"The Principle of Morality Was the Principle of Corruption"

[70]The principle of morality, which entered, and necessarily had to enter, was the principle of corruption: the spirit having arrived at beautiful freedom must again go back into itself in order to become free. It indeed knew itself to be master of the natural and of the sensuous—and so it must be the same in relation to itself; but it had come to that intuition only in [1367] an element *external to itself*; it must come to know it in its own element.

The corruption showed itself in a different form in Athens from that in which it appeared in Sparta: the Athenians showed their corruption in a way not only lovely, but great, noble, and such as we must regret; in the Spartans, the element of subjectivity proceeded to a vulgar subjectivity and a vulgar corruption.

---

69. GW 27 [4] 1366 (~ 1840, 322–24).
70. GW 27 [4] 1366–67 (~ 1840, 323).

CHAPTER 6

[71]It is here also to be noted that many noble Athenians had a preference for Sparta. This can be compared with the way that in modern times Rousseau, for example, preferred the conditions in the wilds of North America to those in the cultivated European states. It is believed that the better lies backward from the developed cultural education. This better, however, lies forward. The Greek life overall—ethical custom, constitution—we look upon as loveable and beautiful and interesting in its configuration; but the spirit cannot find its highest satisfaction there, for it lacks a principal, essential phase of the objective absolute, of the truth—and of the right, of ethical custom, of the higher freedom in the subjective unity of self-consciousness. The higher principle is for the earlier world in the shape of corruption. The earlier has developed for itself its right, its ethical custom, into a present world and actuality. Against this, the higher principle appears as other, destroying this world, over and against which this world is not recognized, but negated. And this negation, which [338] constitutes the higher principle, will rob the state of its staying power, and individuals of their virtue; and consequently it appears as revolution and as corruption of ethical custom. This side we still have to consider, as the third period, and interesting here again is the distinction between Sparta and Athens.

[72]The principle of corruption revealed itself first in external political development, equally in the war of the Greek states against one another and in the struggle of factions within the state. The Greek ethical custom had rendered Greece incapable of constructing a single state; this separation of small states over and against one another, this concentration in cities—where the interest, the cultural education of the spirit, could be the same in the whole—was a necessary condition of the freedom.... A certain directedness to unity is not to be overlooked, but it was partly weak, partly offset by jealousy; and the struggle for the hegemony had brought the states into opposition: the general outbreak of enmity led eventually to the *Peloponnesian War*. Before that, and still at the start of the war, Pericles stood at the head of the Athenians, and a deep personality sustained him, as his standpoint surely proclaimed. Athens had had, since the Median War, the hegemony; a crowd of confederate particular islands and seaside cities had to deliver a contribution for carrying on the war against the Persians; instead of troops or ships, Athens made this contribution into one of money,

---

71. GW 27 [1] 337–38.
72. GW 27 [4] 1367–68 (~ GW 27 [1] 337; GW 27 [2] 689–90; GW 27 [3] 1023).

thereby concentrating all power in itself, as it undertook to defend its confederates; part of the contribution now came to be used for great works of architecture, in which [1368] the confederates also could have a communal enjoyment, since the highest enjoyment is in the work of the spirit.

[73]In the Peloponnesian War Athens was defeated by the enemy, the Lacedaemonians, who allied themselves with the Persians. The Spartans needed money, and this need led them to seek it from outside and to resort to the worst means to get the income.

Then for a second time Sparta betrayed Greece, in that they promised the Greek islands a liberation from Athens, but made them dependent on themselves, in all the cities transforming democracies into oligarchies.

A third betrayal was that, at the Peace of Antalcidas, the Lacedaemonians handed over the Greek cities in Asia Minor to the Persians.

Now the cities, with Thebes at the head, threw off the yoke of Sparta, and Sparta now sank down. We see the Messenians, and the Arcadians too, reestablished. Thebes, lifted up by Pelopidas and Epaminondas, [340] again assumed its earlier role. Greece found itself entangled now in mutual amity and hostility of every sort; and in such circumstances no state could endure—unless some kind of authority were to establish peace among all of them. This authority had to come from without.

This brought about the external political corruption of Greece. But also, each state was split inwardly into factions, so that always a portion of the citizenry was living in exile, then soon came back and exiled others, and so forth.

[74]The main shape in which change now came to the Greek people has its basis in the beginning of a self-comprehending thinking that is the freedom of the subjective self-consciousness. . . . [341] We now see this inwardness emerge in Greece in a twofold fashion. The idealism of thought threatens that beautiful religion, for the idealism of thought is something other than the idealism of beauty; and this same principle threatens the laws and the state constitution.

[75]As soon as reflection enters, each has his own opinion, and one inquires whether the law [309] cannot be improved. Instead of holding by the existing state of things, one discovers conviction in oneself; and

---

73. GW 27 [1] 339–40 (~ GW 27 [3] 1024–25; 1840, 324–26).
74. GW 27 [1] 340–41 (~ GW 27 [2] 688–90; 1840, 326–27).
75. 1840, 308–9.

CHAPTER 6

thus begins a subjective, independent freedom, in which the individual finds oneself in a position to bring everything to the test of one's conscience, against the existing constitution. Each one has his principles, and each has the conviction that what accords with one's own judgment is what is best, and what must be developed in actuality. Of this decay Thucydides indeed speaks, when he says each opines that things are going badly when he is not involved.

This condition, in which each presumes oneself to have judgment, is opposed to the trusting to great individuals. When the Athenians in earlier times commission Solon to legislate for them, when Lycurgus appears in Sparta as lawgiver and regulator, it is not implied therein that the people think that they know best what is just. Also later, it was great formative figures in whom the people fixed their trust: Cleisthenes, who made the constitution more democratic; Miltiades, Themistocles, Aristides, Cimon, who in the Median Wars stand at the head of Athenian affairs, and Pericles, the great shining point of Athens. But: as soon as any one of these great men had brought to a conclusion what was needed, envy intruded—that is, the recoil of the sentiment of equality against special talent—and he was either thrown into prison or exiled. Finally, there arose in the people the sycophants, who denigrated everything great in individuality along with the persons who stood at the top of affairs.

[76]The law is present, and the spirit is in it. But as soon as thought arises, it investigates the constitutions: it brings out what would be better and demands that what it thus recognizes take the place of what is present.

[77]And this idealism threatens the passions of individuals, the particular subjectivity. For on the one hand this inwardness is the universal, from which the true foundations originate; on the other hand, subjectivity is the particular, the willful, whatever is preferred.

[78]Parallel with the [327] advance in the cultural development of the religious art and of the political situation goes the strengthening of thought, their enemy and destroyer. . . .

[328] In beauty, as the principle of the Greek, there was bound up a concrete unity of spirit with reality, with fatherland and family, etc. In this unity no fixed point of view had as yet been established within the

---

76. 1840, 326.
77. GW 27 [1] 341 (~ 1840, 325).
78. 1840, 326–28.

spirit itself; and thought, which elevated itself over the unity, still had mere preference as what was decisive. But Anaxagoras had taught that thought itself was the absolute essence of the world.

[79]From Thales on we see the philosophers making these advances, and this could only happen in Greece. Initially, science emerges as reasoned understanding that applies to all objects. This activity and preoccupation in the realm of representation is widely praised. The scientific who pursued this were called sophists—such did the Greeks call the masters of thinking and [342] science. Inasmuch as thought strengthened so as to venture everything, it addressed all subjects: ethical custom, the legal, faith, trust—treating them exhaustively, resolving them, showing them in themselves to themselves. However, in the midst of this working over of all sorts of topics, the sophists did not yet comprehend themselves, did not yet discover their *own* central point.

[80]The cultivated sophists, neither erudite nor scientific men, but masters of subtle turns of thought, captivated the Greeks in astonishment. To all questions they had an answer; for all interests of a political or religious content they had general points of view; and their further development consisted in the ability to prove everything, to discover a justifiable side in everything. In democracy there is the special need to speak before the people, to make something vivid for them; and to this belongs the leading of their eyes to the point of view that makes the matter look essential. Here a cultural education of the spirit is necessary, and this gymnastic the Greeks acquired for themselves from their sophists. But this cultural education through thought then became the means of instilling one's own views and interests in the people: the expert sophist knew how to turn the subject of discussion this way or that way, and thus the doors were thrown wide open to passion and foolishness. A leading principle of the sophists held that "the human is the measure of all things"; in this, as in all [328] apothegms, lurks an ambiguity, however, since "human" may be spirit in its depth and truth, or also its mere preference and special interest. The sophists meant the human as simply subjective, and made it clear that mere preference was their principle of what is right, and that they held, as the ultimate, grounding determination, whatever might be useful to the subject. (This sophistic recurs again in all times, though in different

---

79. GW 27 [1] 341–42 (~ GW 27 [2] 690).
80. 1840, 327–28 (~ GW 27 [2] 690; GW 27 [3] 1027).

configurations; thus also in our times the subjective is held to be what is right—the feeling is held to be determining ground.)

[81]The objective truth is hereby denied. Thought makes everything vacillate before the preference of subjectivity. It is in Socrates that, finally, the independence of thought grasped itself, and the being-in-and-for-itself was recognized as the universal, as what counts: that the human being by oneself—but not by one's preferences; instead, by oneself as universal—had to recognize what is the right and the good, and that everything that ought to count has to justify itself before this inner tribunal of thought. In this way Socrates discovered with precision what is called morality. Ethical custom was already present and known in its entire objective content; but that the human being essentially has to determine this by oneself, by conviction, by [343] reasons, this is the standpoint at which Socrates arrived. He is no mere agitator, or cultural educator; rather, conversational dialogue is his distinguishing principle.

[82]In Socrates is the pure absolute innerness of the human being brought to conscious being, so that the decision as to what was right, good—what duty is—lies in one's own consciousness of oneself, the conscience. The ethically customary allowed for no conscience. One can therefore say, the Greek had no consciousness of being: for the conscience is the drawing back of the human being into one's innerness, where one makes the decision as to what right, good, and true may be. In Socrates is this innerness in its essentiality—though of course coming to consciousness only in its abstract [1028] essentiality. Thereby had been immediately discovered an antithesis to the previous way of the establishment of the ethically customary. In this time the question emerged, whether gods exist, and what they are. This innerness had put into doubt what was present at hand.

[83]Though Socrates himself continued to fulfill his duties as citizen, it was not this existing state and its religion, but the world of thought that was his true home. . . . The student of Socrates, Plato, banished from his state Homer and Hesiod, the originators of that mode of conceiving of religious objects of the Greeks; for he required a higher conception of what was to be reverenced as divine—one more in harmony with thought. Many citizens now seceded from practical life, from state

---

81. GW 27 [1] 342–43 (~ GW 27 [2] 690–91; 1840, 327–28).
82. GW 27 [3] 1027–28.
83. 1840, 329 (~ GW 27 [2] 690–91; GW 27 [3] 1028).

business, to live in the ideal world. The principle of Socrates manifests itself as revolutionary over and against the Athenian state; for the peculiarity of this state is that ethical custom is the form in which it exists, namely, in an inseparable connection of thought with actual life. When Socrates wishes to bring his friends to reflection, the dialogue is always negative—meaning, he brings them to the consciousness that they do not know what the right is.

[84]As Aristotle says, Socrates had grounded virtue on insight, had established virtue in insight. That is, as Aristotle said in criticizing the principle of Socrates overall, he had overlooked the other essential phase, habituation, that is, the heart, the feeling, the *hexis*—which we must not only have insight into, but this must also go over into the heart, and also be, as will, something fixed. For Socrates, justification had the form of appearing as *daimon* of Socrates. The Athenians condemned him for believing in other gods, in calling upon his *daimon*. This *daimon* was a decision of another kind from the previous as to what might be right, from what had before been the decision that was determining. The Athenians condemned him to death—and, if we can set aside what is thus suppressed according to our concept of the juridical, we must recognize that a principle according to which thought, insight, wants to be satisfied, and according to which what is true, good is to be recognized by this satisfaction, is the enemy, the destroyer of the Athenian way of life. This is the principle of the Christian world; but it is a revolutionary principle against the Athenian state. . . .

[1029] Furthermore, this manifestation is to be noted: that a politically actual individuality, a political individualism, came to the top in Greece—that what Socrates had expressed as inner also came to the fore externally, in actuality.

[85]With this, the break is expressed in which an inner world has found its firm ground, as an inner world that sets itself apart from what previously had been the sole objectivity. The previous actual world is now defined as exterior over and against this innerness. In that human beings thus found their tribunal in their innerness, from now on individuals could sustain themselves inwardly, could find satisfaction without taking part in the life of the state. It now began to be the case that thought wanted all that ought to count to be justified for it. This is when Plato bans the poets from his state: thought of the absolute is

---

84. GW 27 [3] 1028–29.
85. GW 27 [1] 343–46 (~ GW 27 [2] 690–91; GW 27 [3] 1026–29; 1840, 329–30).

required instead of sensible representation of it. This higher principle, of thought, of subjectivity, thus breaks in here.

The destiny of Socrates is that of highest tragedy.[86] He was condemned by the court—which can appear as the highest injustice. He had for himself the justification of thought; but the Athenian people must have had this deep consciousness: that such a principle of inner seeking for justice must bring with it the downfall of the fatherland. [Griesheim: His death can appear as the highest injustice, because he completely discharged his duties to his fatherland and opened up for his people an inner world. On the other side, the Athenian people also had complete right, in that it had the deep consciousness that through this innerness, the law of the state would be weakened in regard and the Athenian state destroyed.] The Athenian people thus had the entirely correct consciousness that the teaching of Socrates was revolutionary and had thereby condemned him to death. [Griesheim: So the teaching of Socrates appeared to the people, entirely rightly, as the highest revolution, and the death of Socrates as the highest justice.]

Peculiar to Greek life is this, that the form of the state is ethical custom, something that counts immediately—unity of the objective and the subjective. Our life of the state is organized otherwise, and can regard [344] the subjective disposition [Griesheim: this inner life—even when it opposes religion—] rather indifferently.[87] The inner moral is not a matter for the state. But the Athenian political life is still somewhat like that of the Asiatic, in that objectivity and subjectivity are inseparably united. Aristophanes understood in the most fundamental way what the Socratic principle involved. Also the remorse of the Athenian people over the condemnation of Socrates is necessary, inasmuch as what they had condemned was surely in their breast too; thus they had condemned what was in themselves too. Thus Socrates did not

---

86. See Hegel's 1825–26 *Lectures on the History of Philosophy* (GW 30 [3] 999): "In the genuinely tragic situation there must be a justified, ethically customary power on each side that comes into collision: such is the destiny of Socrates; it is the tragedy of Greece, and not merely his own tragedy, that comes to sight in him."

87. Cf. *Philosophy of Right* #270: "inasmuch as religion is for the state the deepest essential phase integrating the disposition, it ought to demand from all its members that they belong to a church community—but to any one in general, since the state cannot interfere in the content insofar as the latter involves the innerness of representational thought.... It is said that the individuals must have religion: if this means that ... the humans ought to have respect for the state—for this whole, of which they are branches—this of course comes about in the best way through philosophical insight into the essence of the state; but it can, when this is lacking, be brought about by the religious disposition. Thus the state can need religion and faith."

die an innocent man. [Griesheim: If he had, that would not be tragic but merely moving.] The great tragic figures are those who do not die innocently. In Socrates the higher principle appears in its purest free way, in the form of thought. Here is the break between actuality and thought. ... And one can say: the heart of the world must first break, and only then will reconciliation in the spirit come about. In Socrates the break with actuality is still abstract, and the reconciliation is still as abstract thought.

Art itself is now what destroys the beautiful religion. Art makes everything manifest. If the matter itself does not transcend the nature of art, and if art has wholly completed its journey, then everything sensuous is manifest, and the object itself is no longer of interest. Revelation can convey only this content: that the revealed at the same time remains secret, for the understanding and for sensuous experience. And such material is that [345] of speculative religion that does not lose itself in exteriority. It is also the case with the Athenian people that art itself reaches the point at which its principle itself ceases to have an interest in being the content of religion. It is ludicrous to say of Plato that he wanted to ban art and poetry. What Plato banned is not art and poetry in general, but what art represented as the highest, which it was said ought to be recognized as the absolute.

On the political side, the democracy is what overshoots itself. It requires peaks of individuality in order to carry out its decrees, and thus contradicts itself, in that here individuality is necessary to carry out the decision of the many. Thus when democracy is the constitution not of a rude people but of a beautifully developed one, it can only be of short duration. Individuality was sacrificed for Pericles: in the individuality of Pericles, universality realized itself in this one beautiful, plastic whole. But this can come only once, and later the state was sacrificed to individuality, even as previously individuality sacrificed itself to the state. We have said that interiority, subjectivity, can exist as universality, as thought, for example as in Socrates; but it can also exist as particular, as passion, as the greed of individuals, and this latter aspect is principally that of corruption. With the Athenians, however, this appears in a more genial and measured way. The dark aspects of this principle of particularity thus are more measured among the Athenian people than, for example, among the Spartans. With the latter, this appears as straight corruption, as the simple principle of the self-serving particularity [346] of the will, as the seeking for mastery and the seeking for possessions. But with the Athenians we see that they acknowledged their corruption, and made fun of their shortcomings and depravity, played them down. That the people laughed at and ridiculed themselves—this we find in no other people.

⁸⁸Individuality could only in Greece come to the fore. But such an individuality a Greek political constitution could not tolerate within itself. Plato's deeper sense grasped this very well. His picture of a constitution is simply this: to have grasped and depicted the actuality of Greek ethical custom, not as an ideal, but rather its expression as the actual nature of Greek ethical custom. But since he had the insight that the corruption of subjectivity here threatened this principle, he banished subjectivity and portrayed a condition in which only the substantial ethical custom ought to hold sway. In this subjectivity there lay, however, the principle of the higher that now ought to enter world-history.

⁸⁹Plato does not step outside his own time, as overall no individual can. Thus he has imagined nothing—though wanting to establish something beyond one-sided reflection—except the principle of the Greek ethically customary, and has excluded, in abstract consequence, subjective particularity, the being-for-self of the individual, the cultural development of innerness in itself, subjective freedom.⁹⁰

"The Decline of Greece"

⁹¹By a singular act of violence—namely, through desecrating and plundering the temple at Delphi—the Phocians attained momentary power. This deed completed the decline of Greece: the sanctuary was desecrated, the god was killed, so to speak; the last stopping point of unity was thereby annihilated; the reverence for that which in Greece had been, as it were, always the final will—what was the monarchical principle—was displaced from view, insulted, and trodden under foot.

---

88. GW 27 [1] 351.
89. GW 27 [3] 1034.
90. See also the fuller account of Plato and his dialogue *Republic* in Hegel's 1825-26 *Lectures on the History of Philosophy*, where we find (GW 30 [3] 1054): "when Plato says that philosophers should rule, he means the determination of the entire condition through universal principles. This is carried out far more in the modern states. Universal principles are the essential bases of the modern states—that is, not of every one, but of most. Some are already at this stage while others are struggling to reach it, but it is generally acknowledged that such principles ought to constitute the substantial element in the constitution, the government. What Plato demanded is thus in place."
91. 1840, 331 (~ GW 27 [1] 343; GW 27 [2] 692-94; GW 27 [3] 1029-30; GW 27 [4] 1375).

[92]The further advance is then the entirely naïve one, namely that there enters, *in the place* of the unseated *oracle*, another deciding will: an *actually* overpowering *kingship*. The Macedonian king Philip undertook on his own to avenge the violation of the oracle, and himself took its place, in that he made himself master of Greece. (After him emerged the youth Alexander, put himself at the peak of the Greeks, and brought about through his brilliant undertaking the conclusion.) Philip reduced under himself the Greek states, [1376] and brought them to the consciousness that it was all over with their independence, and they could no longer hold themselves to be independent. Pettiness, harshness, violence, political treachery—these hateful characteristics with which Philip has been reproached—no longer fell upon the Alexander, since he had no more necessity to let himself become guilty of similar things; he also had no need to form himself a military force, for he found one already in existence. . . .

By the deepest, and also in breadth the richest, thinker of antiquity—*Aristotle*—had *Alexander* been educated; this education was of such a kind, as Aristotle alone was worthy of. He initiated Alexander into the profoundest metaphysics (Alexander later wrote to him from Asia: Aristotle ought not to have made public what the two of them had worked upon—to which Aristotle replied, his book would be as unknown as it was known). Through this cultural education Alexander's great nature was thoroughly purified in itself from the usual bonds of opinion, crudity, and idle fancies and so on. Aristotle left this grand nature untrammeled, as it was; but impressed upon it a deep consciousness of what the true is.

As such did Alexander place himself at the head of the Greeks, in order to lead Greece against Asia. . . . He had as goal to avenge Greece for all that it had suffered for a long time from Asia, and to fight to the finish the old division and quarrel between East and West. [1377] While in this struggle he retaliated upon the oriental world all the bad, he did much more good; for he brought over to Asia the Greek supremacy of cultural education. . . .

[1378] Alexander had the luck to die at the proper time; one can call it luck, but it is much more a necessity: in order that he may stand for the world to come as a youth, an early death must take him away. Even as *Achilles* begins the Greek world, so *Alexander* concludes it: and these

---

92. GW 27 [4] 1375–78 (~ GW 27 [1] 344–46; GW 27 [2] 692–95; GW 27 [3] 1030–33; 1840, 332–34).

two youths give not only the most beautiful but at the same time a complete and perfect manifestation. Alexander made all of Near-Eastern Asia into a Greek world, and that is his great, immortal accomplishment; of course one may not measure him by a modern standard, the standard of virtue, of morality.

[93]One must therefore not repeat what is usually said, and what one historical writer has said: "although there is nothing here that counts but bloodshed, still, Alexander is great." One must be prepared for blood and unhappiness, when one turns to history, for they are the means by which the world-spirit drives itself forward. One must also not say that after Alexander's death this empire fell apart. His dynasty did not continue to hold sway; but the Greek lived on.... He could found a Greek world empire, but his individuality could not continue into a family mastery. For such a determination, the time had not yet arrived—that this is an essential phase of state lordship. Building an abstract unity no longer resided in the Greek principle, but in the Roman.

[94]In Alexander culminates this great individuality by which Greece held itself together. Earlier the greatest interest was in the destiny of the state itself. The individuals were herein great only as servants, through work and service for the fatherland. Here it is the individuality as such, which before was only an accompanying matter, that is essential. The life of the state has lost it interest. No matter is at hand that has affirmative interest. The individuality as such demands that to which interest is directed.

[95]We have come now to the third period of the Greek Empire: it embraces the protracted history of the misfortune of Greece, and interests us less. Those who had been Alexander's generals, now entering upon independent kingships, carried on long wars with each other, and experienced, almost all of them, the most adventurous revolutions of destiny.

[96]The situation in this interim period is sad: on the one side, the relationship between the states is diplomatic in such a way that only a wholly artificial web and play can preserve the states; and the other essential phase of this time is that there are special individualities on

---

93. GW 27 [1] 347.
94. GW 27 [2] 693 (~ GW 27 [1] 349).
95. GW 27 [4] 1380 (~ GW 27 [2] 695; GW 27 [3] 1034; 1840, 335).
96. GW 27 [1] 351-53 (~ GW 27 [2] 695-96; GW 27 [3] 1034-37; GW 27 [4] 1380-82; 1840, 335-38).

whom the destiny of states depends. These special interests and passions have torn asunder the states into factions, [352] which direct themselves to the outside in order to appeal to the favor of the king and to bring it to bear on the relations of the state. Athens still retained a measured position; the Aetolian Confederation was a band of robbers. The Peloponnese had maintained itself for a long time with fame and honor until it too fell under the baseness of its chiefs, who found support from the Romans. What can still interest us in this period are great individualities, great [Griesheim and Hagenbach: tragic] characters, who through their force and art, principally directed outward, temporarily still upheld their fatherlands, but were thereby unable to lead to any healthy condition, and in this struggle went under, without the just vindication of having provided fame and security to their fatherlands. For this period it is the biographical writings of Plutarch, and Polybius, that interest us. Polybius gives us the history of the states, but this is of less interest because then it was individuals who were great. Plutarch's biographical writings have the renown of being great cultural education. The biographies of ancients such as Theseus are partly mythological, and partly their lives are intertwined with the state. But the best accounts fall into the period that we are now considering. The friend of his fatherland had in this time to struggle against the parties within and on the outside, constantly, to find friends who were the enemies of their state. The Achaean Confederation furnishes beautifully such portraits, which one can contemplate in the history of Polybius—[353] how, in such circumstances, good, practical natures must either despair or seek a way to draw themselves back. And such circumstances, together with such strong individualities, make needed a force to which they themselves finally succumb. In such particularity, when all particularity in states and individualities rigidifies itself, a destiny emerges, blind and abstract, that can only negate the situation. And the Roman Empire plays the role of this fate.

Chapter 7

The Roman World

[1][Griesheim: The goal and the force of the state, as irresistible, must subject simple particularity; and this politics as power is now the deed of the Roman Empire, by which destiny, as the abstract universal, enters the world.] In the Pantheon of its world-mastery Rome imprisoned all gods,[2] and heaped up all unhappiness, all sorrow, breaking the heart of the world; and only out of the world's heartfelt unhappiness could free spirit raise itself up. In the Greek world we had individuality; in the Roman, abstract universality—whose concreteness is only the self-seeking of mastery. We thus here are not dealing with any inherently spiritual life; joy is envisaged theoretically, [354] and there is a vitality that has only practical understanding as its goal, making the inflexible universal what counts.

[3]The distinction between the Roman and the Persian principles is this: that the former stifles all vitality, while the latter allowed of its existence in the fullest measure. Through the aim of the state being

---

1. GW 27 [1] 353–54 (~ GW 27 [3] 1038–39; GW 27 [4] 1383–84).
2. See also the 1827 *Lectures on the Philosophy of Religion* (GW 29 [2] 165–66): "The Romans plundered the temples; all gods were dragged to Rome. Thus Rome became the collection of all religions—the Greek, Persian, Egyptian, Christian, Mithraism. It grabbed every religion, and made the common condition a confusion in which all kinds of worship interpenetrated."
3. 1840, 339–40 (~ GW 27 [4] 1383–84).

that the individuals, in their ethically customary life, should be sacrificed, the world is sunk in grief: its heart is broken, and it is *all over* with the naturalness of spirit, which has sunk into a feeling of unblessedness. Yet only from this feeling could the super-sensuous, the free spirit, come forward in Christianity. . . .

[340] For spirit must first develop itself to that form of abstract universality that exercised the severe discipline over humanity. Here in Rome we find now that free universality, that abstract freedom, which on the one hand sets the abstract state, the political and its force, over concrete individuality and thoroughly subordinates this; and on the other hand, creates over and against that universality the personhood— the freedom of the I in itself, which must certainly be distinguished from individuality. For personhood constitutes the fundamental condition of legal right: it enters into concrete existence chiefly as private property, but it is indifferent to the concrete characteristics of the living spirit, with which individuality has to do. These two elements that constitute Rome—the political universality for itself, and the abstract freedom of the individual in itself—are grasped, in the first instance, in the form of innerness itself. This innerness, this going back into one's self, which we observed as the corruption of the Greek spirit, becomes here the ground on which a new side of world-history arises.

[4]"In order that the principle of subjective innerness become actual, it must purify itself from particularity and must give to itself a second reality. So the determination is this: that the principle of subjective innerness is established as the principle of private property. . . .[5] And then, the private persons are held together by the state; but, as mutually repellent persons for one another, they are not capable of external holding together, and this latter can be brought about only by despotism. This is the process of history: the development, the sacred, realizing itself through personhood, private property. The transition from the innerness here is . . . a transition from sacredness into external

---

4. GW 27 [2] 708 (~ GW 27 [4] 1384; 1840, 343).

5. In his 1827 *Lectures on the Philosophy of Religion*, Hegel clarifies how he conceives the absence of the principle of private property in the Bible or the "Jewish religion" (GW 29 [2] 159): "the condition is on the whole patriarchal, the political constitution is imperfect. The people possesses a land; the particular family has its particular lot, share, family goods; this is an ironclad possession, which forever belongs to the family. In the Jubilee year [Leviticus 25], if it was sold or obligated for debts, it reverts to the family. This is not the presence of a rising above, an indifference to, worldly existence or property. [Boerner: Property in the legal sense is not yet present.]"

possession and the holding of this latter fast as private property.... The subjectivity winds up in the holding together of atomic units, that is, an external holding together—despotism.

⁶To the unfree, un-spiritual, and unfeeling understanding of the Roman world we owe the origin and the development of *positive* law. We saw earlier how in the Orient ethically customary and moralistic relationships [352] were made into legal commands; how among the Greeks, ethical custom was at the same time juristic right, and on that account the constitution and the stability was entirely dependent on ethical custom and on disposition, and had not yet the fixity within it against the mutability of innerness and particular subjectivity. The Romans now completed this great separation and discovered a principle of right that is external—that is, one that is without disposition and sentiment. While they have thus bestowed upon us a great gift, in point of *form*, we can use and enjoy it without becoming sacrificial victims to that barren understanding—without regarding it as the ultimate of wisdom and reason for itself. They became its sacrificial victims, who lived in it; but they thereby for others won the freedom of the spirit, namely the inner freedom that through this has become liberated from that sphere of the finite and the external. Spirit, heartfelt feeling, disposition, religion, have now no longer to fear that they will become involved in that abstract juristic understanding.

"Division in the History"

⁷The usual division is kingdom, republic, and Caesardom. This division expresses more the inner development of the people when it is taken for itself; but in the perspective of world-history the epochs are different. The first epoch is the beginning overall, and this is certainly to be considered. This beginning contains the still quiet unity that in its essence contains antithetical determinations. The unity is one in which the antithesis lies asleep; but then there is a period [709] until the strengthening of this antithesis, so that then a reconciliation is longed for, which the strength of the state embodies. Thus the unity is maintained, as being drilled in, and even thereby becoming strong. The Roman state turns itself essentially outward, and the encounter with the outside is such that the people enter the theater of the world-historical

---

6. 1840, 351–52 (~ GW 27 [1] 360–61; GW 27 [2] 699–700; GW 27 [3] 1043–44).
7. GW 27 [2] 708–9 (~ GW 27 [3] 1053; 1840, 343–44).

surroundings. This constitutes the second epoch: the Punic Wars, the most beautiful epoch. In this second period occurs, however, also the inner corruption, the antithesis, that develops itself until it is intolerable, whereby the whole is put in danger. This corruption ends itself through the introduction of despotism, and thereby brings about the third epoch: expansion of the mastery over the world and contact with the people that then brings death to it.

[8]In the third period occurs the contact with the north and the Germanic peoples, who now are to become world-historical.

"The Founding of the State"

[9]As regards the origin of the Roman people and land itself, one cannot speak properly of a land of origin, but of a distinctive emergence outside of any land: not in a defined area, not on a plane, but at a point, that has to work itself violently into a territory. Rome appears first in a corner where three territories of defined peoples meet—Latins, Sabines, and Etruscans—but outside of them. In this corner, the first state manifests itself, not as a patriarchal clan, not with the goal of a peaceful life, but as a gang of robbers. . . . [698] Livy makes them into moralistic robbers.

[10]This first society expanded itself to include castoffs, and thereby made itself into a free place for all peoples, into a city of everyone, an asylum for criminals and the homeless. . . . An equally fixed tradition is that these first Romans had no women, and therefore invited, to a religious festival, peoples with whom they had no relations of marriage, but with whom they wanted such. From the Sabines, who alone accepted the invitation, the Romans robbed for themselves their women. Here clearly expressed itself the chief character of the Roman religion: that its purpose was political. . . . [356] The Greeks, we saw, did not emerge from family relations; yet family love was present; the citizens united for a peaceful goal, having—in contrast to the robber Romans—the need to construct defenses against land and sea robbers. In contrast, Romulus and Remus were thrown out of the family, and so also the Romans acquired their women not lawfully but through violence and robbery.

---

8. 1840, 344.
9. GW 27 [2] 697–98 (~ GW 27 [3] 1038–40; GW 27 [4] 1388–89).
10. GW 27 [1] 355–58 (~ GW 27 [2] 697–700, 712–13; GW 27 [3] 1040–45; GW 27 [4] 1389–90, 1397–99; 1840, 344–45).

CHAPTER 7

Here the feeling for natural ethical custom was excluded, so that harshness against family feelings remained from this time forever.... [357] The ethically customary life we see wholly denaturalized, and a rigidity given to the husband over against the family. This active harshness correlated with the passive harshness under which the husband found himself in relation to the state; for an abstract commanding brings with it an abstract subjection. That the Roman thus found himself in a state-bonding that went with the sacrifice of all natural, ethical custom—this is the Roman greatness: this complete subordination approximates to how in our case things are in the military, although we still keep distinct the civilian life of someone in the military.... [358] If one wants to have a closer look at this relationship, one must consider the Romans in their relationship as warriors. It appears as something great, how the Romans had before their eyes, without wavering or weakness, the state and its commands. This appears from one side to be the Roman virtue. But one must consider how this character appeared not only in relation to the outside but also within Rome—how Rome owed its continuation to this character alone. In the dissensions that arose between the plebeians and the senate and that led to rebellion, in which the order of the state, the lawful connectedness, was broken, in such instances it very often happened that plebian reverence for order was brought back to order, putting a halt to their lawful and unlawful demands. Often, even though there was no war, a dictator was named, who then conscripted the citizens as soldiers and led them as soldiers from the city.... One does not grasp the history of this dissension unless one also sees this obedience to, this respect for, the dictates of the state.

[11]This founding of the state is what must be regarded by us as the essential basis of Rome's idiosyncrasy; for this idiosyncrasy flows from it: that origin carries with it the severest discipline, the sacrifice for the goal of the union; a state that had first to form itself by force, and which is based on force, must be held together by force (as we have seen in Sparta). It is not an ethically customary, more liberal union, but a compulsory condition of subordination, that leads itself forth from such an origin.

The Roman *virtus* is courage: not, however, simply the personal courage of the individual, but that which shows itself essentially connected with a union of associates, and is only for this union, where the work

---

11. GW 27 [4] 1390 (~ GW 27 [1] 358–59; GW 27 [2] 700–701; GW 27 [3] 1041; 1840, 346).

for the union counts as what is highest—and so, that virtue may be combined with violent force of all kinds.

"The Religion of the Romans"

[12]We go now over to the element of *religion*. In the preceding section, on the Greeks, the Greek religion was more closely considered; and now we find that the Roman doctrine of the gods was entirely the same, with the unessential change of the names of divinities—with a closer inspection, however, the great difference shows itself.

[13]We are accustomed to regard Greek and Roman religion as the same, and use the names Jupiter, Minerva, etc. as Roman deities, often without distinguishing them from those of Greeks. This applies insofar as the Greek divinities were more or less [353] introduced among the Romans; but, as little as the Egyptian religion therefore became the Greek, because Herodotus and the Greeks made the Egyptian divinities intelligible to themselves under the names "Latona," "Pallas," etc., so little is the Roman to be confounded with the Greek.

[14]It was said before that in the Greek religion the thrill of nature was fully developed into something spiritual, into a free intuition, and into a spiritual figure of fantasy—that the Greek spirit did not remain in the condition of inward fear, before an alien nature, but proceeded to make the relation to nature into a relation of freedom and cheerfulness.[15] The Romans, on the contrary, remained with a dull and dumb innerness, and thereby the external was only an object, an other, an irreconcilable—while among the Greeks the reconciliation of the spirit with the natural was present. But now the Roman spirit, which stayed with such innerness, came into a *relation of constraint*, of dependence,

---

12. GW 27 [4] 1393 (~ GW 27 [1] 362; GW 27 [2] 701; GW 27 [3] 1045; 1840, 352).
13. 1840, 352-53 (GW 27 [1] 362; GW 27 [3] 1045).
14. GW 27 [4] 1393-94 (~ GW 27 [2] 701; 1840, 352).
15. See also the 1827 *Lectures on the Philosophy of Religion* (GW 29 [2] 162-63): "In regard to the abstract feeling, the directedness of the spirit, what is primary is the *seriousness* of the Romans. . . . The cheerfulness of the Greek religion, what is foundational in regard to the feeling itself, has its ground in that while there is also a purpose, one that is revered and holy, there is present simultaneously freedom from purpose, immediately entailed in there being many Greek gods. Each Greek god had a more or less substantial, distinct attribute, an ethically customary essentiality; but precisely because there are many particularities, the consciousness, the spirit, stands simultaneously over this multiplicity, and outside of its particularity, letting go of what is essentially determined and what can even be considered as purpose: the consciousness is itself this ironizing. In contrast, where there is one principle, a highest principle, a highest purpose, this cheerfulness can find no place."

which is surely the origin of the word *religio* that has that meaning (Cicero himself gives it that meaning, from *religare*). . . . The Roman had always to do with something *secret*; in everything he believed in, and sought for, something *veiled*; in contrast, the Greek religion built a beautiful object—in it, everything is open, clear, present to sense and intuition, not a [1394] beyond, but something friendly, here and now. The Romans posit for themselves everything as *mysterious*, as *duplicate*: they saw in the object first itself, and then also in addition that which lies concealed in it; such duplicating intuition is prominent also in their history—the city of Rome had, other than its own name, Rome, another one that was secret, that only few knew; it was believed to be Valentia (the Latin translation of "Roma"; others said that this name was "Amor," with "Roma" readable in it).[16]

[17]Among the Romans the religious thrill remained undeveloped; it was shut up in subjective certainty of itself. Consciousness has therefore given itself no spiritual objectivity and has not elevated itself to the theoretical contemplation of the eternal divine nature, and to freedom in that; it has gained no religious substantiality for itself from spirit. The empty subjectivity of conscience lies in all that the Roman does and undertakes—in his covenants, relations to the state, duties, family relations, etc.; and all these relations receive thereby not merely the sanction of the laws, but a solemnity analogous to that of an oath. The infinite number of ceremonies at the comitia, on assuming offices, etc., are the expressions and declarations that concern this firm bond. . . .

[355] The Roman religion is in this way the entirely *prosaic* one of confinement, ends-means, utility. The divinities peculiar to them are entirely prosaic; they are conditions, sensations, useful arts, which their dry fantasy elevated to independent power and set above themselves; they are partly abstractions, which could only become shallow allegories, and partly conditions that appear as bringing advantage or injury, and that are left as objects of worship in their original, bare, and limited form. Only a few examples need be introduced. The Romans worshiped Pax, Tranquilitas, Vacuna (Repose), Angeronia (Care and Concern), as divinities; they consecrated altars to the Plague, to Hunger, to Mildew (Robigo), to Fever, and to the Dea Cloacina (Sewer Goddess). . . .

---

16. Cf. the 1831 *Lectures on the Philosophy of Religion* (GW 29 [2] 267): "The other side, however, is an abstract innerness, a shudder before an indeterminate inner, like an inner fate. To this belongs Rome's secret name: Amor, and Eros, or Valentia."

17. 1840, 354–56.

[356] The introduction of the gods and most of the Roman temples thus arose from need, from a vow, and an obligatory, not disinterested, gratitude. The Greeks, in contrast, erected and instituted their beautiful temples, and statues, and divine rites, out of love of beauty and of divinity as such.[18]

[19]Only one side of the Roman religion has something attractive, and it is indeed the ancient ethical customs and usages, which have their content from the earliest rural condition; it is a kind of recollection of the happy times of Saturn; there displays itself a natural feeling of the Romans, an influence from the natural delight in rural depictions, especially in autumn when there are the wine pressing, etc.—the occasions of such festivals as the Saturnalia and others. There emerges here in any case a linkage of the Roman religion with Greek conceptions (such as the Roman Vesta and the Greek Hestia). The mythology of the Roman poets is entirely taken from the Greek; but even with the poets of the Romans, the gods become like machinery; they are used in an external way, and everything that comes from them is miraculous.

To these general remarks about the Roman religion and its relation to the state there is one other thing to be brought in, about the *family piety* of the Romans: [1398] as the piety of the Romans carried with it overall the character of constraint and unfreedom, so the family relationship was not a free, beautiful one of love and feeling. In place of love, of trust, within the family, the Romans inserted the principle of hardness, of dependency, and of subordination. Marriage had exactly

---

18. For a helpful further explanation of how Hegel understands these prosaic divinities of individual self-interest to fit with the "Fortuna publica" divinity of Rome's "abstract universality" of "world-mastery," see the 1827 *Lectures on the Philosophy of Religion* (GW 29 [2] 164-66): "To hold sway is the goal of the citizen; but in this the individual is yet not eliminated; he has also his own particular goals. . . . It is the general particularity of humans in the many sides of their needs or connections with nature that here becomes prominent. . . . The human goals count as divine goals, thereby as divine powers. So we have these many special, extremely prosaic divinities. . . . [165] There is nothing more lacking in imagination than the sphere of such gods! . . . [166] The individual on the one side is submerged, in the holding sway, in Fortuna publica; on the other side, human goals count, the human subject has a substantial, essential value.—These extremes, and the contradiction itself, is that in which the Roman life tosses and turns.—The Roman virtue, the *virtus*, is this cold patriotism by which the individual serves the cause of the state, which is, to hold sway. This supression of the individual in general, this negativity, the Romans also made a spectacle; it is what is expressed as an essential feature of their *religious plays*. The interesting religious drama consists in nothing other than in the slaughter, extermination, of human beings, in buckets of streaming blood—no ethically customary interest, no tragic reversal and overturning that would be a content of ethically customary interest, tied to ethically customary determinations."

19. GW 27 [4] 1397-99 (~ GW 27 [3] 1047-48; 1840, 357-58).

the character of a slave relationship. . . . The relationship of the son was entirely similar. . . . [1399] The son was only free after the father had sold him three times. As regards inheritance, . . . among the Romans the willfulness of the testament was present in the highest degree. On every side we thus see the ethical custom denaturing feeling; in the family the Roman was a despot; outside it he was completely subordinate, given over, to the goals of the state; the rigid unity of the individuality with the state is the Roman virtus and the Roman greatness.

[20]We have spoken above about the *religious games* of the Greeks; as the Greeks built beautiful temples out of love for divinity as such, so were the games competitions of human talents and human skill; in the dramatic contests at the Bacchus festivals the poets participated, acting in their own dramas. The Romans, in contrast, did not themselves participate in their games (Nero did this later, but to the consternation of the entire Roman world); while the Greeks saw winning prizes in competitions as the highest, the Romans on the contrary entertained themselves with gladiators who were slaves, and who had an interest in victory only [1397] in order to save their own lives, since the loser was killed by the victor; so the games were a kind of human-hunting as well as beast-hunting.

[21]In place of human sufferings in the depths of feeling and spirit, brought about by the contradictions of life, and which find their resolution in destiny, the Romans instituted a cruel actuality of corporeal sufferings and blood in streams, the death rattle, and the expiring gasp of the soul, which were the scenes that interested them.

This cold negativity of simple murder depicts at the same time the inner murder of spiritually objective aim. I need only mention, in addition, the auguries, auspices, and Sibylline books, to remind of how fettered the Romans were by superstitions of all kinds, and how they pursued only their own aims in all such. . . . All this was in the hands of the patricians, who consciously made use of it as a mere outward means of constraint to further their own ends and against the people. . . .

Secular aims are left entirely free, not limited, by the religion—rather they are [359] justified by it. . . . The possession of mastery by the patricians is thereby made firmer, more sacred, without mediation or community: the political regime and the political right have the character of a sacred private property. There does not exist therefore a substantial

---

20. GW 27 [4] 1396-97 (~ GW 27 [1] 364; GW 27 [2] 705; GW 27 [3] 1048; 1840, 357-58).
21. 1840, 358-59 (~ GW 27 [1] 365; GW 27 [2] 706; GW 27 [3] 1048).

unity of the nationality—not that beautiful and ethically customary need for life together in the polis; but every *"gens"* is a fixed clan for itself, each having its own Penates and *sacra* for itself; each has its own political character, which it always preserves. . . . But even in that innerness of religion is, at the same time, the principle of willfulness given: and, against the willfulness of sacred possession pushes willfulness against the sacred. For the same content can, on the one side, be regarded as privileged by its religious form, and, on the other side, have the shape of being merely willed—existing by human willfulness. When the time had come that the sacred was degraded to the rank of form, so would it be as form also known and treated—and trodden under foot, represented as formalism.

The inequality, which enters into the domain of the sacred, forms the transition from religion to the actuality of the life of the state.

"No Democracy, Such as in Greece"

[22]So the religion is a religion of utility in which constraint is made absolute. This same sanctification of difference, of constraint, is also to be considered in regard to the state constitution. The entire principle entails that no democracy, such as in Greece, can find a place. The overwhelming mastery by one sector of the *gentes* is the foundational determination. Similarly, there is no possibility here of monarchy, which presupposes the spirit of the free evolving of particularity. And here the goal is still something constrained, within which, as the goal of the state, individuals are bound. The Roman constitution can thus only be aristocracy, and indeed one that is in itself constrained and internally hostile—that can never be the satisfied configuration for itself, but instead has opposition and struggle within it, and can be made good only momentarily, through unhappiness and necessity. The aristocracy is one that is in itself without unity and that can be unified only by great harshness.

[23]In the first space of time, several essential phases distinguish themselves from one another. The Roman state here undergoes its first building up under kings; then it has a republican constitution, at

---

22. GW 27 [1] 365 (~ GW 27 [2] 707-8; GW 27 [3] 1052-53; GW 27 [4] 1384-85, 1399-1400; 1840, 360).
23. 1840, 360, 363 (~ GW 27 [1] 366-67; GW 27 [2] 709-10; GW 27 [3] 1053-54; GW 27 [4] 1392-93, 1401-2).

whose head stand consuls. The struggle begins between patricians and plebeians; and, after this has been set at rest, by the satisfaction of the plebeian demands, there ensues a state of contentment in the internal affairs, and Rome acquires the strength to make itself victorious in the struggle with the previous world-historical people. . . .

[363] In the growth of the inner life of the state, the power of the patricians had been much reduced; and the kings often courted the support of the people. . . . The kings were expelled by the patricians, not by the plebeians.

[24]This transition from monarchic to republican is in fact of small significance. That previous condition was not monarchic, and the republic here is no beautiful democracy, but aristocracy. After the driving out of the kings nothing had really changed. The aristocrats took over the kingly force. . . . Before the kings had been hated by the patricians and had become favorable toward the populace and had raised it up, giving it a certain place in the legal, civil society. The kings were thus for the patricians an impediment to the subjugation of the plebeians. This impediment was now removed. And it is the constant relationship in every state that the populace has its friend in the higher kingly force, yet it allows itself to be deceived and aligns itself with the middle class that puts it down. . . .

[368] The plebs were later on allowed the use of the state lands, or were given them as full property. But all this was gained only through the gravest struggles. . . . In regard to lawful right, civil and political, the plebs gained these through the people's tribunes. . . . [369] Other than the people's tribunes and the weight of the people's decisions, a major point was that the plebs were at last allowed to serve in public office. . . . Four hundred years after the founding of the state this was brought about.

[25]Civil wars often have the consequence that a people wins for itself great strength and energy, and with this fresh life turns outward. To be sure, civil war can also lead to exhaustion and loss of the state—we see this in Poland; but the opposite in the French Revolution. The greater the civil wars are, the greater the energy toward the outside. This energy leads on to civil war when a truly fundamental principle is involved that unites the citizens where the people remains one. Then, through

---

24. GW 27 [1] 367–69 (~ GW 27 [2] 714–17; GW 27 [3] 1057–65; GW 27 [4] 1402–9; 1840, 364–65, 369–70).

25. GW 27 [3] 1065 (~ 1840, 370).

civil unrest, it happens that this principle sets aside impediments to its existence (when not all yet agree with it). When this is the case, thus the goal of the spirit of a people is reached, and it turns with desire for action to the outside.

After the plebs had come to enjoy rights of citizenship, as part of a lawful whole, and, in regard to politics, had achieved a far-reaching participation in action and community with the patricians, the Roman people advanced with great force nobly toward the outside.

[26]About the Roman constitution one can say that, as aristocracy, it is the worst [Griesheim: even though Aristotle wants to allow *hoi aristoi* to exercise mastery]. "The best ought to hold sway" is a beautiful tenet, although if the *aristoi* is simply a formula and they become bad, then this is the worst of constitutions. The Roman aristocracy also had its own internal opposition, and this produced practical results. So we see here an aristocracy but also its antithesis: two extremes that at first produced an equilibrium. [370] This, however, is the worst sort of relationship, because the equilibrium itself is what is essential; this must exist, not the two extremes that produce it. Beautiful indeed is the equilibrium of spirits and senses, but not in such a way that each side exists for itself, but rather so that the extreme is not independent for itself, but only this third, the equilibrium, exists. The equilibrium in the Roman state was therefore only temporary; and the breach broke out all the more frighteningly. The equilibrium, in which the antitheses positioned themselves, brought forth an outward orientation and acquired riches, fame, and advantage that contributed to holding together the weak inner bond; but at the same time it introduced need and lack of fortune—which, to be sure, again pulled together the abstract sides.

[27]Boring would it be, to pursue the wars of the Romans in Italy. . . . It is singular, in regard to these, that the Romans, who have the great justice of world-history on their side, should also claim for themselves the petty justice of manifestos, treaties with petty infringements for themselves, and should contend after the fashion of lawyers. But in political embroilments of this kind, either party may take to be evil the conduct of the other, when it wills to do so, when it regards it as expedient to take it as evil.[28]

---

26. GW 27 [1] 369–70.
27. 1840, 371.
28. See also GW 27 [1] 371: "Boring is Livy's tedious rhetoric and constant trotting out of positive right/law."

[29] The chief essential phase here is the steadfast solidarity, the obedience to the laws of the state, wherein is the seat of the Roman virtue—and that the Romans had in this virtue only a single content: what the state commands. This solidarity often saved Rome and distinguished Rome from other nations that did not have this abstract solidarity as their principle.

The art of war of the Romans is a second feature, dependent on the former. . . . [371] The great virtuous characters occur only in this first period. With this strengthening, Rome enters the second period, in which the Romans, through the assembling of smaller capital, became great capitalists, and now we can enter into a panorama of the world-theater.

"The Second Period"

[30] We have now finished the first epoch and are proceeding over to the following one. The Roman mastery was on the whole not yet very greatly extended: initially a few colonies had settled themselves on the other side of the Po, and in the south a great power confronted that of Rome. But the Romans soon entered upon the stage of the great world-theater, and in terrible collision with the most powerful states at hand; it is the second Punic War that constitutes this epoch or that gave it its impulse; through it, the Romans came into contact with Macedonia, Asia, Syria, and subsequently also with Egypt. For the great, far-stretching empire, the center remained Italy and Rome, but this center was not the less under compulsion and force. This great period of the contact of Rome with other states, and of the manifold consequent developments, one of the most beautiful periods, such as could make itself the subject of a writer of history, has been written about by Polybius, a noble Achaean.

[31] Polybius had to observe how his fatherland, through the disgrace of the passions of the Greeks and the baseness and inexorable consequence of the Romans, went to ground.

[32] In the First Punic War [264-241 BCE] the Romans had shown that they had become a match for mighty Carthage, which possessed

---

29. GW 27 [1] 370-71 (~ GW 27 [2] 717-18; GW 27 [3] 1065-66; GW 27 [4] 1409-10; 1840, 371-72).
30. GW 27 [4] 1411 (~ GW 27 [1] 371; GW 27 [3] 1066-67; 1840, 371-72).
31. 1840, 372.
32. GW 27 [4] 1411-13 (~ GW 27 [1] 371-72; GW 27 [2] 717-19; GW 27 [3] 1066-67; 1840, 372-74).

a great part of the coast of Africa and southern Spain, and had gained a firm footing in Sicily and Sardinia. The Second Punic War [218-201 BCE] threw down Carthage's power. . . . [1412] Through the same war the Romans came into hostile contact with the king of Macedonia; he was conquered five years later. Antiochus, the powerful king of Syria, opposed a tremendous power to the Romans, but was beaten at Thermopylae and Magnesia [190 BCE], and was compelled to surrender Asia Minor, as far as the Taurus, to the Romans. . . . Finally came the Third Punic War [149-146 BCE]; Carthage had once more raised itself and excited the jealousy of the Romans. After long resistance it was taken and laid in ashes. Nor could the Achaean league now maintain itself for long in the face of the Roman quest for mastery: the Romans sought war, destroyed Corinth in the same year as Carthage, and made Greece a province [146 BCE]. The fall of Carthage and the subjugation of Greece were the decisive moments from which the Romans extended their mastery. . . . The goal of war was no longer to maintain the city of Rome as a citizen city, for this had been achieved through the subjugation of all rival nations; it was rather *mastery* as such; and as soon as that is the goal of a nation, it builds itself essentially into a military power; and [1413] the individuals who distinguish themselves at the top of the army come to have greatest influence and power in the state. After Rome had achieved these great victories it had a standing army in the conquered provinces and on the borders of the empire. Proconsuls and propraetors were sent into the provinces as governors, . . . to whom the tolls and taxes were given as monopolies; thus soon there spread a net of monopolies over the entire Roman world.

Rome seemed now to have complete security; no external power confronted it; then entered the great drama of terrible unrest in Rome itself, with growing civil war at home.

[33]In the period of victory, it is the customarily ethical, great, and fortunate individuals, especially the Scipios, that attract our attention. They were fortunate in their customary ethics—although the greatest of the Scipios met with an end outwardly unfortunate—because they were active for their fatherland during a period when it enjoyed a sound and unified condition. But after the feeling for the fatherland—the dominant drive of Rome—had been satisfied, massive corruption immediately invaded the Roman state; the greatness of individuality became, on account of contrasting events, stronger in intensity

---

33. 1840, 374-76, 378-81 (~ GW 27 [1] 372-74; GW 27 [2] 719-24; GW 27 [3] 1067-70; GW 27 [4] 1413-19).

and means. We see the internal antithesis of Rome now beginning to manifest itself again in another form; and the epoch that concludes the second period is also the second mediation of the antithesis. We saw the antithesis earlier in the struggle of the patricians against the plebeians: now it assumes the form of particular interest against the patriotic disposition; and the sense for the state no longer holds these opposites in the necessary equilibrium. Rather, there appears now side by side with wars for conquest, for plunder, and for glory, the fearful spectacle of civil discords in Rome and intestine wars. There does not follow, as among the Greeks after the Median Wars, brilliant splendor in culture, art, and science, in which spirit enjoys, inwardly and ideally, that which it had previously achieved in practice. If inward satisfaction were to have followed the period of that external good fortune in war, the principle of Roman life would have had to be more concrete. But what was the concrete that could bring itself to consciousness, from inside, by imagination and thought? Their chief spectacles were the triumphs, the treasures gained as booty in victory, and captives from all nations, unsparingly subjected to the yoke [375] of abstract mastery. . . . The national individuality of peoples did not yet, as is the case today, demand respect from the Romans. The peoples did not yet count as legitimate; the states had not yet recognized each other as essentially existing. The equal right to existence entails a union of states, such as exists in modern Europe, or a condition like that of Greece, in which the states had an equal right under the Delphic god. The Romans do not enter into such a relation to the other peoples, for their god is only the *Jupiter Capitolinus*,[34] and they do not respect the sacra of the other peoples (any more than the plebeians those of the patricians); but as conquerors in the strict sense, they plunder the Palladia of the nations. . . . [376] Riches were acquired as spoils in war, and were not the fruit of industry and just activity—even as the navy had arisen, not from the necessities of commerce, but for the goal of war. The Roman

---

34. For the meaning of Jupiter Capitolinus, see Hegel's 1827 *Lectures on the Philosophy of Religion* (GW 29 [2] 163): "The character of the Roman feeling is this seriousness of the understanding that has a single goal. This goal is the goal of holding sway, and the god is the power to realize this goal—the superior, all-universal power to realize this mastery, . . . and this Roman mastery in the form of a mastering god is the Jupiter Capitolinus, a special Jupiter (for there are many Jupiters). This Jupiter Capitolinus is he who has the sense of mastery, who has his goal in the world, and the Roman people is that for which he brings to fulfillment this goal. Primary is this seriousness." See also GW 29 [2] 167: "It is entirely consequent that the Caesarian emperor, this power, become revered as god: he is after all this groundless power over the individuals and their condition."

state, drawing its means from robbery, came also thereby to divide itself by quarrels about distributing the spoil....

[378] We see the most frightful and dangerous powers arising against Rome; yet the military power of this state carries the victory over them all. Great individuals now appear, as during the times of the fall of Greece. The biographies of Plutarch are here again of the greatest interest. It was from the disruption of the state, which had no longer any hold or stability in itself, that these colossal individualities arose, with the need to restore that unity of the state that was no longer to be found in the dispositions. It was their misfortune that they could not maintain a pure customary ethics, for their course of action contravened things as they were, and was criminal. Even the noblest—the Gracchi— were not merely the victims of injustice and violence from others, but were themselves involved in the general corruption and injustice. But that which these individuals will and do has on its side the higher justification of the world-spirit, and must eventually carry the victory. Due to the total decay of the idea of an organization for the vast empire, the senate could not assert the authority of government. The mastery was made dependent on the people—which was now a mere mob.... So [379] we see in Pompey and Caesar the two foci of Rome's splendor coming into hostile opposition: on the one side, Pompey, with the senate, and therefore apparently the defender of the republic; on the other, Caesar with his legion, and the superiority of genius....

The Roman world-mastery became thus the property of a single possessor. This important change must not be regarded as something that came about by chance; rather, it was *necessary* and determined by the circumstances. The democratic constitution could no longer be really maintained in Rome, but only kept up in appearance.... Plato, whom Cicero wanted to take after, had the complete consciousness that the Athenian state, as it presented itself to him, could not stand, and so he developed a complete state constitution in accord with his views; Cicero, on the contrary, did not consider it impossible to preserve the Roman Republic longer, and always sought for it only some momentary assistance; about the nature of the state, and of the Roman state in particular, he had no consciousness. Cato, too, says of Caesar: "His virtues should be execrated, for they have corruptly destroyed my fatherland!" But it was not the accident of Caesar's existence that destroyed the republic—it was *necessity*. The Roman principle was completely established on mastery and military force; it had no spiritual center in itself as a goal for the occupation and satisfaction of the spirit....

CHAPTER 7

[380] Caesar—who may be adduced as a paragon of Roman adaptation of means to ends, who formed his resolves with correct understanding, and brought them to execution most actively and practically, without further passion—Caesar did what was right world-historically, in that he brought forth the mediation, and the manner and way of the connectedness, that was necessary. Caesar did two things: he calmed the internal antithesis, and [381] at the same time opened a new one outside. For the mastery of the world had been brought hitherto only to the circle of the Alps, but Caesar opened a new place of achievement: he founded the theater that now was to become the center of world-history.

[35]Caesar had brought together the conflicts outside, had opened what was beyond the Alps, had pressed into the Nordic world, and had thereby opened up a new world; and then he established himself at the apex of the Roman world, and not by a civil war in the Forum, but by subduing the entire Roman world. His struggle did not look like a private struggle, for instead he went against the republic, which remained only as an empty name. All the mediocre factions had sought refuge under this title; against these Caesar moved freely and openly; he subjugated for himself the power and the title of the republic, and set a willfulness of particularity in place of the many special interests and arbitrary wills. And over many must one be master. All affairs had become rife with factions; all was passion and special interest. In the place of these petty particularities Caesar set himself up, and thereby purified Rome. This mastery of a single willfulness was necessary.

[36]In spite of this we see that the noblest men of Rome held Caesar's rule to be a chance thing, and his mastery to be dependent on his individuality: so Cicero, so Brutus and Cassius; they believed that if this one individual were out of the way, the republic would be by itself restored. Through being captivated by this remarkable [1419] error, Brutus and Cassius, more active than Cicero, murdered the man whose virtues they treasured. But it became immediately manifest that only one could lead the Roman state, and now the Romans had to believe that. Overall, a state revolution will be held as sanctioned by people when it repeats itself (thus Napoleon was corralled, and the Bourbons expelled, *two times*). Augustus took Caesar's place.

---

35. GW 27 [1] 374 (~ GW 27 [2] 723).
36. GW 27 [4] 1418–19 (~ 1840, 381).

"The Third Period"

³⁷Rome's third period shapes itself in an entirely different antithesis. The first antithesis remained on the ground of the substantial unity. The second antithesis was abstract, soulless, without interest.³⁸ The third period contains the antithesis in which both parts are each total: the secular realm of the Caesars, and, on the other side, the spiritual realm, Christendom. . . . Roman history now proceeds by the higher principle of the actuality that stands over and against overcoming the Caesarian.

³⁹In this period we have *two* essential *sides* to consider: one is the *worldly* side, the other the *spiritual*. In the worldly side, we have again two chief essential phases to highlight—first, the essential phase of the masters, of the *mastery* over the individual; and then, the essential phase of the defining of the individual as such by way of *personhood*, the *world of right*.

"The Essential Phase of Mastery"

⁴⁰We have therefore first to grasp the essential phase of mastery. The Caesar-emperor now stood at the top of the Roman world: everything else was nothing; the force, which was essentially military force, was now in the hands of one individual. Augustus and Tiberius let stand the entire constitution, the entire formalism; there remained senate, consuls, tribunes, etc., but that was a form without substance, and to keep it that way the Caesar-emperor had the means, in that he had a barracks of several legions near Rome. The state business was brought before the senate and the Caesar-emperor appeared as only another [1420] member; but the senate must obey, and whoever spoke in opposition was punished with death and his property confiscated; that is why it came about that many, as soon as they foresaw their death, killed themselves, so that their families would at least have means.

⁴¹Here we see, then, in the emperor, particular subjectivity as self-impelled in an unlimited way. . . . The emperors express the complete

---

37. GW 27 [2] 724.
38. For the first two antitheses, see above, "Division in the History."
39. GW 27 [4] 1419 (~ 1840, 382).
40. GW 27 [4] 1419–20 (~ GW 27 [1] 381–82; GW 27 [2] 724–25; GW 27 [3] 1071–72; 1840, 383–84).
41. GW 27 [1] 375–76 (~ GW 27 [2] 726–27; GW 27 [3] 1076; GW 27 [4] 1421–22; 1840, 383–84).

coming-out-of-itself of the being of spirit, the complete knowing and willing finitude that is without constraint. . . . The concreteness of the emperor is of no interest. Even the noble ones in this configuration awaken no interest; they are a fortunate happenstance that leaves conditions just as they are, and they vanish without a trace. There is no opposition, no thought, nothing that [376] ought to be produced; it did not occur to the Antonines [138-92 CE] to establish any institutions—instead, they maintained particular will. The Roman world is, by this peak of pure particularity, secure and in order. No opposition is present anymore, whether from virtue or from vice: nothing counts—both are only matters of particularity.

[42]The particular subjectivity in its complete lack of bonds has no innerness, no look backward, no remorse, nor hope, nor fear—no thought; for all these involve fixed determinations and goals, while here every determination is completely contingent. It is desire, lust, passion, contingency—in short, willfulness completely unfettered. It finds so little limitation in the will of others that the relation of will to will is rather that of unlimited mastery and slavery. In the whole known world, no will is known by humans that lies outside the will of the emperor. But under the mastery of this one, everything is in *order*.

"The Individuals as Private Persons"

[43]Over and against this one we see the individuals as private persons, as a crowd of atoms without ethical customs. . . . Under a despotic regime all subjects are slaves, since no natural distinctions are at hand. Under the Caesarian emperors in Rome, slaves or freed slaves were more powerful and had more significance as Romans than the oldest families, nay, even more than the greatest statesmen—for they acquired the skill of insinuating themselves among the Caesarian emperors.

[44]Soon after the Social War [87 BCE], the inhabitants of the whole of Italy were given equal rights with Roman citizens; and under Caracalla [198-217 CE] all distinction between the subjects of the entire Roman Empire was sublated. The private right developed and completed this equality. The right of property had previously been limited by distinctions of various kinds, which were now done away with. We saw the

---

42. 1840, 384 (~ GW 27 [2] 727).
43. GW 27 [3] 1073 (~ GW 27 [2] 728).
44. 1840, 385-86 (~ GW 27 [2] 726-28, 730; GW 27 [3] 1073-76; GW 27 [4] 1422-23).

Romans proceed from the principle of abstract innerness—which now realizes itself, in private right, as personhood. The private right is, namely, this: that the person as such counts, in the reality that one gives to himself—in private property. The living body of the state, and the Roman disposition that lived in it as its soul, is now brought back to the isolation of a dead private right.... The state organism is lost in the atom of the private personhood. Such a condition is now the Roman life: on the one side, fate and the abstract universality of mastery; on the other, the individual abstraction, the person, which contains the determination that the individual is something in itself, no longer in accord with one's vitality, [386] with a full individuality, but as abstract individuum.

It is the pride of the units to count absolutely as private persons; for the I contains infinite claims of right; but their content and meaning is only an external matter, and the development of private right, which this high principle introduced, was tied to the decay of the political life....

So what stood before the consciousness of people was not the fatherland, or such an ethically customary unity; instead, the sole and only thing to which they were directed was to yield themselves to fate, and to strive for a perfect indifference in life—an indifference that they sought either in freedom of thought or in immediate sensuous enjoyment. So the human being was either in a break with concrete existence or entirely given over to sensual concrete existence. One either found one's determinateness in the toil of acquiring the means of enjoyment through the favor of the Caesarian emperor or through violence, testamentary frauds, and cunning; or else one sought one's tranquility in philosophy, which alone was still able to supply something firm and being-in-and-for-itself: for the systems of that time—Stoicism, Epicureanism, and skepticism—although in themselves opposed to each other, had the same general outcome, namely, rendering the spirit in itself indifferent to everything that actuality had to offer.

"The Philosophizing of That Time"

[45]These philosophies were widely extended among the cultivated: they produced an immobility in humanity itself through thinking—the

---

45. 1840, 387 (~ GW 27 [2] 728; GW 27 [3] 1077; GW 27 [4] 1423-24).

activity that brings forth the universal. But the inner reconciliation through philosophy was itself only an abstract one, in the pure principle of personhood; because the thinking, which, as pure, made itself into its own object, and reconciled itself, was completely without an object, and the immobility of skepticism made goal-lessness itself the goal of willing. This philosophy had known only the negativity of all content and became the counsel of despair for a world that no longer possessed anything stable. It could not satisfy the living spirit, which longed after a higher reconciliation.

[46]The Roman world became the fate that purged the heart of everything special, so that all that could be possessed by it became something accidental. Therewith originated the longing for something fixed. Since a universal skepticism was present in fact—an uncertainly about everything just—there raised itself up above this nullification of all ties of the present the negation of the particular, in the universal overall, the consciousness of the universal, this abstraction from all, this inner freedom. [1425] The spirit was thus set in the soil of the universal; this universal had as its object the principle of the philosophizing of that time: Stoicism stood forth as the true, as what is thought insofar as it is thought. Skepticism and Epicureanism had as content: that the subject as a thinking being restricting itself to the objective is something unshakeable, while the heart is bound to nothing fixed, so that, if the heart is something holy, then it can be wounded when it turns itself back to the universal, where there is nothing special to which it could become attached.

"Subjectivity Itself, as the Universal"

[47]In the spirit there is an opposition: it is a maintaining of the finite over and against the One, which is the infinite; this opposition that has come about is the sorrow of the subject; and the healing of this sorrow is nothing other than that the subjective individual achieves the consciousness of becoming taken up into the One, and [1079] receiving and holding the One in itself. This is the true reconciliation. Satisfaction is therein contained, when the One as the subjective, and the subject as the universal, come to appearance. In this way the subject

---

46. GW 27 [4] 1424-25 (~ GW 27 [3] 1077-79).
47. GW 27 [3] 1078-79.

possesses true worth, enjoyment, blessedness, objectivity. . . . What we have thus called the subject was the subjective human with God.

[48]From that unrest of the infinite sorrow, in which the two sides of the antithesis stand against each other, comes the unity of God with the reality that had been posited as negative, that is, as subjectivity that had been separated from him. . . . The identity of the subject and God comes into the world *"when the time was fulfilled"* [Galatians 4:4]: the consciousness of this identity is the recognition of God in his truth. . . . [394] For the spirit sets itself as its own other, over-and-against, and is the return from this difference into itself. The other, grasped in the pure Idea, is the Son of God, but this other, in its particularity, is the world, nature, and the finite spirit: the finite spirit is thereby itself established as an essential phase of God. The human is therefore contained in the concept of God, and this content may be thus expressed: that the unity of humanity with God is established in the Christian religion. This unity must not be superficially grasped, as if God were only human, and the human similarly were God; but the human is only God insofar as one sublates the naturalness and finitude of one's spirit and elevates oneself to God. That is to say, the human being who is a partaker of the truth, and knows oneself to be an essential phase of the divine Idea, is to fix the giving up of one's naturalness: for the natural is the unfree and unspiritual. . . . This unity as being-in-itself is at first only for the thinking, speculative consciousness; but it must also be for the sensuous, representing consciousness; it must become an object for the world—it must *appear*, and indeed in the sensuous shape of spirit, which is the human. *Christ has appeared*: a human, who is God, and God, who is the human; thereby has the world become peace and reconciliation. To be recalled here is what was said about the Greek anthropomorphism, that it did not go far enough. For the Greek natural cheerfulness had not yet advanced to the subjective freedom of the I itself. . . . To the appearance of the Christian God [395] belongs further its being *unique* in its kind; it can occur only once, for God is subject, and as appearing subjectivity is only exclusively one individual. The Lamas are ever chosen anew, because God is known in the East only as substance, which therefore is the infinite form only externalized in a multiplicity of particulars. But subjectivity as infinite relation to itself has its form in itself, and is, as appearing, only a one, excluding all others. Moreover,

---

48. 1840, 393–96 (~ GW 27 [3] 1079–80).

the spirit's sensuous concrete-existence is only a transitional essential phase. Christ has died; only as dead, is he sublated to heaven and sitting at the right hand of God; and only so is he spirit. He himself says: *"When I am no longer with thee, the Spirit will guide thee into all truth"* [John 16:13]. It was first at the Feast of Pentecost that the apostles became filled with the Holy Spirit. To the apostles, Christ as living was not that which he was to them subsequently as the Spirit of the community,[49] in which he first came to be for their true spiritual consciousness. Just as little is it the correct relationship, when we recall Christ only as a bygone historical person. . . . If Christ is to be looked upon only as an outstanding, even sinless individual, and is only this, then the conception of the speculative Idea, of the absolute truth is bleached away. But this latter is the point, and from this one must proceed. . . . [396] The only question is, what is the Idea, or the truth in and for itself? The believing in the divinity of Christ is, moreover, the testimony of one's own spirit, not the miracles; for only spirit recognizes spirit.

[50]Christ shielded the Jews when they demanded miracles. False prophets can work miracles; the church fathers conceded miracles to the oracle, but said, it is the Devil who thus appears.

[51]Christ himself said to the Pharisees: "You want to see miracles; but more will come working miracles, raising the dead, and them I will not recognize as belonging to me." The true believing is the spiritual.

"The Uniting of East and West"

[52]The essential phases in the concept of spirit we have to consider more closely. They are now the ruling categories of the world—and that they are, is what counts. . . . One category is the being-determined for itself of finitude, the category of being-for-self, of the believing that finitude

---

49. To appreciate the meaning of "the community" [Die Gemeinde] here and subsequently, it is relevant to refer to Hegel's statement in his 1827 *Lectures on the Philosophy of Religion* (GW 29 [2] 221): "the real community is that which we commonly call the church." In "the subsisting community of the church is overall the institution through which the subjects come to the truth, appropriate the truth, and thereby the Holy Spirit also becomes real in them, actually present, has its place in them—so that the truth is in them, and they are in the enjoyment, in the activity, of the truth of the Spirit, that they are the subjects of the activation of the Spirit."

50. GW 27 [2] 739.

51. GW 27 [3] 1083.

52. GW 27 [1] 380–85 (~ GW 27 [3] 1077–79; GW 27 [4] 1426–29, 1441–42).

is an absolute; and the other category is the belief in the infinity of the being-in-and-for-self.

When the two are separated we have in one instance finitude, the absolute separateness that we see in the Roman world: . . . the harsh servitude that becomes directed to sensuality and posits a constricted purpose, one upheld as a final validity. . . . The harshness of this servitude is in the Roman world, but: without this, there is no freedom; without fear there is no inwardness—without the sense of the negativity of the natural. It is first through the submission of the natural that freedom can come into being. . . .

[381] The other category is infinite freedom, is universality, the antithesis to the limited. This is the other side, and it is to be shown how it was a ground in the world.

It was in one way the ground for thought, as the philosophy of Stoicism, Epicureanism, and skepticism, which all took their point of departure from Socrates, [382] and all had the principle that human beings should not find their satisfaction in the world but instead should achieve it only in solitude with oneself, in *ataraxia*, the imperturbability that is brought about only through the complete indifference to all things, through holding nothing-to-be-true, to be right, to be valid. This is the closest form of this universality. The broader form is that which is as in the Orient, and the Roman world is the bringing together of the finitude of the West with the infinite breadth of the Orient. . . . This other essential phase, of the breadth, of the immeasurability, we find in the oriental intuition. . . . The breadth is therefore oriental, but in this representation it is not fixed as the ultimate, not as the nonsensual in the determination of the being-for-itself that is the ultimate, the true. This comes to the fore only in the Israelite representation, as the universal God that is for itself—not the Brahm, not the Light of Persia, but stripped away from this sensuousness. The God of Judah is this One, the universal, in such a way that only the universal is the ultimate. . . . [383] Here for the first time is the point reached at which this religion, this determination of God as the One, becomes world-historical.

These, now, are the two principles of the Idea: the One, and the intuition of the rigidity of singularity, of subjectivity. These are the two categories of the self-consciousness of this age. [Griesheim: The two principles of East and West come together here at first externally, through conquest, but also through inner working-through.] Separated, they are to be understood as one-sided, abstract. In their truth they are established as unified. This uniting of East and West, and the working-through of both principles, took place in the Roman world. The West longed for a deeper inwardness, for universality, and found it in the East; and such a uniting of its principle with the universal is such as disseminated itself in multiple ways and validated itself in obscure ways. This unification was the need of the times, of the spirit lost in a finite purposiveness, calling out for something infinite and finding it in the East. Thus arose the worship of Isis and the worship of Mithra. Thus arose the uniting of the concreteness of the West with the breadth of the East.

Especially Alexandria was the focal point where the two principles were worked out scientifically. Now is the Egyptian riddle grasped in thought and thereby solved. . . . Alexandria was thus the soil on which the unification emerged in manifold forms. We find there learned Jews who put together the Eastern representations with the thought of Plato, knowing how to unite with the logos.

[384] Studying the history of this era is a most interesting aspect of religious and philosophical conceptions, especially after Christian conceptions were initiated in Asia, in Syria. In all these sects is the same tendency, the same fermentation, that encounters the true, but with bizarre additions. . . . These manifold appearances are all depictions of the same drive. This Idea had not only, however, to be able to come to appearance in these incomplete ways, but had also to be revealed in its pure and complete shape. . . . That God revealed himself to humanity as human was what the world longed for: that humanity, which had grasped itself, was perceived as absolute, the human as finite elevated to being an essential phase of the divine essence, the human as [385] God, and conversely, God as human, come to appearance—this intuition is what constitutes the reconciliation of human beings with God and of God with human beings.

The essential determinations here are that the finite spirit finds itself in this unity with the divine essence not as it is naturally in the flesh; or, that the human in its simple naturalness is not good, but is unspiritual—and it is first by renouncing natural being, thus first through the negation of this naturalness, as for it what ought not to be, and so is evil, and not good, that the human first thereby comes to consciousness of the unity with God, comes to faith. The faith is this consciousness, that the divine spirit dwells within one, that one is in mystical unity with the divine.[53] It is first through working free from

---

53. On the final religion's "mystical unity, the self-feeling of God's immediate presence within the subject," see also Hegel's 1827 *Lectures on the Philosophy of Religion*, GW 29 [2] 224.

the natural that this faith can come about. But for the human who remains within it, thinking oneself good merely as one comes and goes, therein lies damnation. So the human has to sublate this natural mode in order to come to faith.

The intuition of this unity also had to be present in a natural appearing. So the immediate being, the *this one here*, belongs with the completion of this reconciliation. The unity, however, could appear in this way only one time. God is inherently only One, and so his appearing must also have the predicate of oneness, excluding multiplicity. The many human beings existing as they ought not to be are the ungodly. This appearing of the One emerges within the Jewish people; for this people prayed to God as the One, unmixed and nonsensuous. This religion remained still and unnoticed until it became world-historical, until the spirit had traversed the stations that characterized this essential phase, and had encountered the other essential phase, the absolutely bound, that required as its extreme the boundless onefold, a requirement through which this other essential phase emerged as world-historical.

[54]"This is now to be shown more precisely. We said of the Greeks that the law for their spirit was: "Human, know thyself!" The Greek spirit was a consciousness of spirit, but as limited, as having the natural element as essential ingredient. Spirit certainly held sway, but the unity, of the mastering and the mastered, was itself still natural; the spirit appeared as determined in a crowd [389] of individualities of spirits of peoples and of the gods, and was represented through art, in which the sensuous is elevated only to the middle ground of beautiful form and shape, but not to pure thought.

The essential phase of innerness that was lacking to the Greeks, we found among the Romans: but because it was formal and in itself indefinite, it took its content from passion and willfulness. . . . This element of innerness is then further realized as personhood of individuals. . . . Thereby individuals are posited as atoms; but they are at the same time subject to the severe mastery of the One, which as *monas monadum* is the power over the private persons. This private right is therefore a lack of concrete existence, a nonrecognition of the person, and this condition of right is completely without right. This contradiction is the misery of the Roman world. . . . The misery of this contradiction is, however, the *disciplining of the world*. . . . But primarily this appears only to us as disciplining, and this is [390] to those who are drawn along by it a blind destiny, to which they submit in dumb suffering; there is still

---

54. 1840, 388–93 (~ GW 27 [2] 729–35).

lacking the higher defining.... What has been reflection only on our part must arise in the subject of this discipline in the form of a consciousness that, in oneself, one is miserable and nothing. The external unhappiness must, as already said, become a sorrow of the human in oneself: one must feel oneself as the negative of oneself; one must have the insight that one's unhappiness is the unhappiness of one's nature, that one is in oneself the divided and discordant.

This defining of the disciplining in oneself, ... with the yearning to transcend this condition of the inner, is to be sought elsewhere than in the strictly Roman world; it gives to the *Jewish people* its world-historical meaning and importance, for out of it arose the higher, which brought the spirit to absolute self-consciousness.... At its purest and most beautiful we find this defining of the Jewish people expressed in the Psalms of David and in the Prophets, where the content expressed is the thirst of the soul after God, its profound sorrow for its transgressions, and the longing for righteousness and piety. Of this spirit the mythical depiction is found right at the beginning of the Jewish books, in the account of the *Fall into sin*.... Sin consists here only in knowledge.... This is a deep truth, that evil lies in consciousness, for the beasts are [391] neither evil nor good—even so the simply natural human being. Consciousness first gives the separation of the I, in its infinite freedom as willfulness, from the pure content of the will, the good. Knowledge as the sublation of the natural unity is the Fall into sin, which is not contingent, but the eternal history of the spirit.... This being-for-oneself, this consciousness, is, however, at the same time the separation from the universal divine spirit. Holding myself in my abstract freedom, against the good, this is the standpoint of evil. The Fall into sin is therefore the eternal myth of humanity, through which it even becomes human. The remaining at this standpoint is thus the evil, and the experience of this sorrow over oneself, and the longing, we find in David, when he sings: "Lord, create in me a pure heart, a new conscientious spirit" [Psalm 51:10]. This experience we find present even in the Fall into sin, where, however, there is expressed not the reconciliation but the persistence in unhappiness.... The satisfaction of the reconciliation is for the human not yet at hand.... [392] The satisfaction that the human finds at first consists in the finite satisfaction in the family, and in the possession of the land of Canaan. There is not satisfaction in God.... This external satisfaction, in the family and possession, was taken away from the Jewish people, however, in the disciplining inflicted by the Roman Empire.... The Temple of Zion is destroyed; the God-serving nation is scattered. So here every satisfaction is taken away, and the people is driven back to the standpoint of that original myth—to the standpoint of the sorrow of human nature in itself.... Previously what counted as concrete for the Jews was the land of Canaan and themselves, as the people of God. This content is now, however, lost; and from this loss originates the feeling of unhappiness and of the despairing about God, to whom was essentially tied every reality. The misery here is therefore not passivity under a blind fate, but infinite energy of longing. Stoicism taught only: the negative is not, and there is no sorrow; but the Jewish experience persists much more in the reality, and longs for reconciliation therein; for it rests on the oriental unity of nature—that is, of reality, of the subjectivity and the substance of the One. Through the loss of mere outward reality, the spirit is driven back within itself.... The oriental antithesis [393] of light and darkness is here transferred into the spirit, and the darkness is here sin.

[55]The universal nature of humanity is contained in the story of the creation of humans and the Fall into sin—that the human being has been created in the image of God, and through sin the knowledge of good and evil has come about with the forfeiture of Paradise, as the natural happiness.... In the knowledge of good and of evil the human becomes like God. This is put into the mouth of the serpent, but God ratifies it, saying: "Adam has become like one of us" [Gen. 3:22]. Thus in this story the higher concept of human nature is represented—in an insight whose higher meaning is that humanity is to be considered not according to its naturalness but according to its concept, in its being formed in the image of God, so that the nature of humanity in itself is unified with that of God. This representation we find neither in oriental representations nor in Greek myths.... But in the Jewish intuition, this account stands isolated, as myth; and in the Old Testament there is found [388] neither looking back to this concept of the human, nor a recollection of this concept. It is first in the harsh servitude to [Roman] fate that the conditions are such that what was given to the Greeks— "Human being, know thyself!"—progresses not simply to beauty, but completes itself, comes to universal consciousness through the representation, that God has become human being, and thus the reconciliation, the liberation, has come about.... So, as the divine idea has within

---

55. GW 27 [1] 387–89 (~ GW 27 [2] 735–37; GW 27 [3] 1080–84).

itself this crossover to human being, the human being knows itself as infinity in itself, knows itself as, in this determination, being eternity in its very self.

One thus possesses one's true existence in an infinite inwardness, in opposition to one's natural, concrete existence and willing; and this citizenship in eternity one wins only through one's labor in breaking out of the natural. This break is the sorrow of nature; evil enters here as a process of the divine essence itself, while previously it was something incomprehensible, simply in existence. The unhappiness is now called the lack of blessed happiness; the negative is only a one-sided negative, overturning itself conceptually, and, as negating itself, the affirmative, positive! [389] This overturning to the positive is not the natural, not the goodness of the human being from nature, but instead the engendering of itself from the negativity—spirit, an innerness that is self-conscious about itself, that works itself out, and only so succeeds.

These are the determinations of the religious consciousness.

"The Christian Religion of Reason"

[56]This religion in its beginning is something past, but it is even so living, present spirit that progressively grounds itself, that has been brought to a deeper consciousness. [Hagenbach: So it doesn't matter that it is not expressly stated in the Bible that God is three-in-one—that's literalism.] The spirit of the community, of the church, of the spirit as concretely existing, is actual spirit: Christ will be in his community and teach it. "The spirit will lead to all truth" [John 16:13]. This means that one is not to refer to literalism: the spirit of the church, of the community, has stopped this consciousness. The latter is the foundational teaching of the Christian religion of reason and of the speculative Idea.

[57]The Holy Spirit is the spirit of actuality, in that God, this Father that is in and for himself, [1084] as Spirit relates to an Other—and yet in this Other remains only with himself, and relates to himself: that is the Trinity. God is the excluding of himself from himself: he manifests himself, relates to an Other; this is therefore to be differentiated as distinct from his original unity. The Other is, however, just as much God; he therefore relates to himself in it, is in the Other the same as himself, and thus is the Spirit. In this fundamental determination of God lies

---

56. GW 27 [1] 379.
57. GW 27 [3] 1083-84 (~ GW 27 [2] 740).

the indicated relationship of humans to God. The community in which the Spirit of God is present, the community that thus has hallowed itself through the consciousness that the human being is the image of God (this spiritual community is in existence) must thus be organized, in itself; what the spirit is, must be expressed: *that is the teaching.*

[58]The entrance of the Christian principle into the world had the distinctive property of abstraction, of distancing from what was present.... With an infinite frankness of speech Christ encountered the Jewish people.... [1438] "Thou shalt be perfect, as your Father in heaven is perfect" [Matt. 5:48]—we have here an entirely characteristic expression of Christ, a demand. The infinite elevation of the spirit in simple purity is set forth as the peak of the foundation.... "Seek first the empire of God and his justice, so all else will fall to you" [Matt. 6:33]; ... in relation to property and business is it said: "Care not for your living, what you will eat and drink, also not for your body, how it shall be clothed ..." [Matt. 6:25-26]. Working for one's subsistence is thus condemned. "If you want to be perfect, go and sell what you have and give it to the poor, so that you shall have a treasure in heaven; and come, and follow after me" [Matt. 19:21]. Were this to be followed without mediation, a revolution would result, the poor would become the rich. So high does the teaching of Christ stand that all duties and ethically customary limits are in comparison indifferent.... [1439] Herein lies an abstraction from everything that belongs to actuality, even from ethically cultural bonds; in this first pure form is the principle expressed.... [1440] The Christian religion must thoroughly avoid being simply led back to the express statements of Christ himself; in the apostles the law first establishes itself, developing truth there: the consciousness of the absolute truth is the consciousness of the nature of the Spirit. This content developed itself in the Christian community; the community thus found itself in a *double relationship*—in relation to the Roman world, then also to the truth itself, whose development was its goal....

[1441] It is especially important to note that the *dogma*, the theoretical, became built up under the Roman world—in contrast, the building up, from this principle, of the state, comes much later. The church fathers and councils put forth the dogma, and a chief essential phase of this cultural development was the previous cultural development

---

58. GW 27 [4] 1437–44 (~ GW 27 [2] 740–44; GW 27 [3] 1081–84; 1840, 396–403).

of philosophy. The philosophy had achieved its development in Alexandria—there where the East and West coalesced. . . . The deep thinker in Alexandria had grasped the unity of Platonic and Aristotelian philosophy; the [1442] speculative thought arrived at the abstract concepts that are the foundational content of the Christian religion; this philosophical cultural development now crossed over to being the cultural development of the teaching of the Christian religion.[59] . . . [1443] In the revealed religion the spirit must be able to find the satisfaction that it requires; therefore it builds up the dogma. Great strife and parties emerged. . . . In the Nicene Council (325 AD) there was finally established a fixed recognition of the faith, to which we still now hold. This recognition had no speculative shape; but the deep speculation at its core is interwoven with the appearance of Christ himself: certainly in John ("in the beginning was the logos, and the logos was related to God, and God was the logos") we see the beginning of a deeper grasp. [1444] The deepest thought is unified with the figure of Christ, with the historical and external—and that is the greatness of the Christian religion, that with all this depth it is yet easy for the consciousness to grasp it in its external look, which also leads to deeper levels; it is so for every level of cultural education, and yet satisfies the highest demands.

"The Church"

[60]The community found itself *in the Roman world*; the spread of the Christian religion occurred in the Roman world. The community first kept itself removed from all activity in the state, constituted for itself a separate society, and did not react against the decrees, views, and transactions of the state; but as it was separated from the state, and even did not hold the Caesar-emperor to be its unlimited overmaster, it was the object of persecution and hate. Then showed itself that infinite, inner freedom in the great steadfastness with which the Christians willed to bear all sufferings and sorrows [1441] patiently for the sake of the highest truth. It was less the miracles of the apostles that gave

---

59. See also 1840, 402: "But that it was by philosophy that the dogmas came into the Christian religion should not lead one to assert that they were foreign to Christianity and had nothing to do with it. . . . Many believe that by pronouncing something to be Neoplatonic, they have banished it from Christianity. Whether a Christian doctrine stands exactly thus or thus in the Bible—to which all the exegetical scholars of modern times look—is not the only question. The Letter kills, the Spirit makes alive: this they say themselves."

60. GW 27 [4] 1440–41 (~ GW 27 [2] 744; 1840, 399–400).

to Christianity its outward extension and inward strength, than the content, the truth of the doctrine itself.

[61]Having spoken about the relation of the community to the Roman world, on the one side, and about the truth contained in its dogma, on the other side, we come now to the third, in which both doctrine and external world are concerned, namely to the *church*.

The community is the empire of Christ, whose actually present spirit is Christ: for this empire has an actual present, no merely future one. . . . Into this empire of God an organization must now be introduced.

In the first place, all individuals know themselves filled with the spirit; the whole community recognizes the truth and gives expression to it; yet together with this communitarianism arises the necessity of a presiding body of guidance and teaching that is different from the crowd of the community. Those are chosen to preside who distinguish themselves by talents, character, energy of piety, a holy life, learning, and cultural education overall. . . . [404] Through this differentiation there originates, within the empire of God, a *spiritual empire*. This is essentially necessary, but the existence of a ruling authority for the spiritual has its ground primarily in the fact that human subjectivity as such has not yet developed itself. In the heart, indeed, the evil will is surrendered; but the will, as human, is not yet thoroughly cultivated by the deity, and the human will is emancipated only abstractly, not in its concrete actuality; for the entire subsequent history is primarily the realization of this concrete freedom. . . .

Besides this inner organization, the community takes on also a definite externality and possesses its own worldly *property*. As property of the spiritual world, it stands under special protection. . . . [405] Connected with this, the church has its own governance in regard to its wherewithal and its individuals. Thus there emerges in the church this contrasting spectacle: on the worldly side stand only private persons and the power of the Caesar-emperor; on the other side proceeds the complete democracy of the community, which chooses its own presiding officers.

This democracy soon gives way, however, through the consecration of priests, to an aristocracy—though the further development of the church does not have its place here, but belongs to the later world.

---

61. 1840, 403–5 (~ GW 27 [2] 744).

"Wider Worldly Consequences"

[62]So, through the Christian religion the absolute Idea of God in its truth came to consciousness—whereby humanity also discovered itself given, according to its true nature, in the definite intuition of the Son. The human being, as finite when regarded for itself, is at the same time also the image of God and in itself source of the infinite; it is end in itself, it has in itself infinite worth, and the directedness to eternity. It has thereby its true home in a supersensible world, in an infinite innerness, which it wins only through the break with natural concrete existence and volition, and through one's labor to break this within one. This is the religious self-consciousness. But in order to enter the sphere and the activity of the religious life, human nature must become capable of it. This capability is the *dunamis* for that *energeia*. What we therefore now have to consider are the determinations that give themselves inasmuch as humanity is absolute self-consciousness overall—insofar as humanity's spiritual nature is the starting point and presupposition. These determinations are themselves not yet of a concrete sort, but are only the first *abstract principles*, which are won, through the Christian religion, for the *secular empire*.

[63]The first consequence in regard to actuality is that slavery is banished in Christianity, since the human being as Christ is established as in itself an absolute value—is taken up into the divine nature. Inasmuch as the human being is viewed as in God, all particularity vanishes: one counts, not as Greek, as Roman, as Brahman, but has infinite worth in oneself as a human being, is directed to freedom and for oneself. Christianity, insofar as it is actual, can have no slavery. One must not, however, will to embrace external history, saying that slavery was not abolished by councils, and the like; the abolition is worldly, but the true truth is Christianity, for the external manner of the appearance is not the truth.

The second consequence is that the forms of ethically customary life become altered. The beautiful customary ethics of the Greeks cannot be present in Christianity; the ethically customary must indeed also become custom and habit, but must come forth from what is inner—for subjectivity has now become free and justified, as has also particularity. The true manner of [390] subjectivity is the inner, the spiritual.

---

62. 1840, 405 (~ GW 27 [1] 389; GW 27 [2] 744–45).
63. GW 27 [1] 389–92 (~ GW 27 [2] 745–46; 1840, 405–8).

But with Christianity, particularity, which previously appears only as corruption, also becomes liberated.[64] Particularity itself has, however, in innerness its restraint: the external of action therefore loses its value; the worth of external concrete existence as simply external becomes insignificant and takes on the form of something merely external. This has the implication that everything is mediated by free will, partly through the sentiments overall, partly through the particular will. Particularity in limited purpose should count for its own sake, and true inwardness demands even more highly its own right.[65]

Through this there originates, in the third place, two worlds: one supersensible, spiritual, through the truthfulness of subjectivity—but this, as belonging to subjective consciousness, is at the same time temporal, having a concrete existence, entering into concrete existence, making itself count, as the church; and, on the other side, worldliness as such. So, a duality of states: one that is eternal within time, and another that embodies worldly purposes.

A fourth consequence is the question: What is now the Idea of the actuality of the state, that is, what constitution is its goal?

This constitution can be no oriental despotism. Ethical custom and right cannot be present as external command, any more than as the oriental being-bound to nature. The human being is in itself free, and this freedom is to be maintained and worked out.

Nor can there be present a Greek democracy, [391] with its unselfconscious unity of ethical custom, such that my subjectivity is unified

---

64. See also the formulation in 1840, 407: "The piety of the heart does not yet include in itself the submission of the subjective will, in its external relations, to this piety, but we still see all passions increasingly rampant in actuality, because they are determined to be lawless and worthless, from the height of the intelligible world. The task is therefore that of making the Idea of spirit instilled in the world of the spiritually unmediated present."

65. See also the formulation in 1840, 406: "The other, second principle is the innerness of humans in relation to the fortuitous.... The place where the divine spirit should be dwelling and present, this ground is the spiritual innerness, and becomes the place of decision for all the fortuitous. From this it follows that what we earlier considered among the Greeks in the form of ethical custom can no longer have its standpoint in the same determination, since that ethical custom is unreflective habituation, while the Christian principle is innerness standing for itself—the ground on which grows the true. An unreflective ethical custom can no longer find a standpoint against the principle of subjective freedom. The Greek freedom was that of luck and genius; it was still conditioned through *slaves* and *oracle*; but ... the human being is now no longer in a relation of dependence, but of love, in the consciousness that one belongs to the divine essence. In regard to particular aims, the human being now forms one's own determinations and knows oneself as universal power over all that is finite.... Thereby collapses all superstition of oracles and bird flights: the human being is recognized as the infinite power of decision."

with the objectivity of the state. Rather, my own subjective will is now in an inner ownership for itself.

Nor can there be present Roman aristocracy, being-bound to service for a finite goal. The inner singularity now has an infinite goal. The secular authority has, to an extent, its place in what is external, quite apart from the church; but within its own domain it can no longer exercise control over morality and ethical custom and family relationships, can no longer sacrifice and oppress as in the Roman world. The obedience to the secular mastery must now be mediated, so that the private interest of individuals, the particular, inner will, like the higher spiritual will, has *one's own* advantage, one's own liberation, in the secular mastery.

The law, the state, must thus be inherently justified in its goal, independent of private interest and particular opinion. It lets itself be made a means for particularity, but even therein, the state must be strong for itself, must be able to endure this misappropriation of itself by private interests, but in such a way that at the same time the private interests satisfy themselves within it. Therefore the state must be a system that does not stand directly in need of what is moral—a self-sufficient, secure nature, as is the external nature over against self-consciousness, that abides on its own account even though the heart does not understand it, and to which the subject must subordinate itself. In thus developing itself as this bulwark, the state must be rational in itself, even when it is not recognized by private interests. Therefore rationality, the concept, must now be realized in the state. From these [392] essential phases it follows that, in the state as this in-itself-and-for-itself necessary world, all the essential phases of the Idea, in their independence, emerge and are fully developed. And this totality of organization is the monarchy of modern times. In the latter all the determinations of the Idea are worked out in such a way that each essential phase is an independent force and at the same time an organ of the whole organism.

The kind and the manner of the historical coming into being of such a state is another question. This is necessarily romantic, that is, it takes place in such a way that what occurs toward this end occurs as though unconsciously, appearing to constitute itself as something accidental. For this origin takes on the shape of external necessity. None of the modern states has had the honor of framing a constitution for itself as in ancient states through Solon and Lycurgus. Instead, all appear to have made themselves by chance. Special interests, passions of class and of cities, have been determining, along with the arrogation of power of sectors over and against one another. The whole that came about in this way, the goal that spirit has, assembles itself out of such single components, in part amicably, in part violently.

[66]Here there are also some general remarks to bring to the fore. There has been a will to maintain that there is an opposition between *reason* and *religion*; [1430] considered more closely, there is only a distinction. Reason is the essential of the nature of the spirit, and thus the essential of the divine; we distinguish only inasmuch as religion as such is in the feelings, in the heart, a concern of the individual in oneself; reason has the same content, in this sense: that the truth now is known, in actual life, in the human spirit, in the consciousness that has become engaged in worldly concrete existence. The connection is, that in religion, the heart is the temple of freedom in God, while according to reason, the world, the state, is a temple of freedom, enabling a content that itself is divine, so that the freedom in the state is guaranteed and activated through the religion, in that the ethically customary right in the state is only the carrying out of what the foundational principle of religion constitutes. The broader achievement of history is now that religion appears as reason, that the religious principle dwells in the heart and the feelings of humans, and becomes brought forward as worldly freedom. The history that follows shall sublate this division between the inner of the heart and concrete existence, making the reconciliation actualized, by which the Christian religion may be reality. Now we have further to recollect which essential phases in the state are to be considered.

First: in the state *laws* are necessary; the just and the ethically customary must become known as a positive law; and it is not enough that it be in the will, in the disposition of humans, but rather the humans will to be treated in accord with something lawful, in accord with a positive law. It is entirely false [1431] to praise a condition in which people experience lawful claims and action in accord with their insight and experience: to freedom belongs the knowing of the law. But what is the *content of the law*? Nothing other than freedom, which expresses the absolute principle of Christianity; this principle is, for the existing spirit, explained—and the explanation is given by a system of determinations of freedom; and that is, the laws. . . . What follows immediately from the Christian principle is that the subject as propertied

---

66. GW 27 [4] 1429–37 (~ 1840, 407–8).

is capable, that the individual now has an infinite worth, is spirit, is directed to reconciliation. . . . Through the laws, the individual now is given the material and the opportunity for the development of one's forces and inclinations; the means of subsistence are given to the individual, so that through industry and work one can stand on one's own, can achieve respect in lawfulness. The individual is thus constrained in external complications, on account of which a universal providence by law is necessary.

The system of law is thus one side; the other is the *execution* of the same: the law does not complete itself; it becomes known, but its actualization must also be in the subject; the subject is what the law completes and must handle; the law must be the subject's will; for with infinite freedom, in which the subject [1432] partakes, the deepest evil is also possible—the highest peak of abstraction, to which the subject, against the true and rational will, can attain. This most external abstraction is possible only in the infinite freedom. Against the evil, the law must now become externally wielded; against this violence that is against the laws, contrary violence must be established. What is essential is that the disposition not be evil; the law is only form, and the formal, against the *disposition*; law has its actualization only in the spirit, in the will; it must therefore be ethical custom, disposition; the disposition without the law is the previously mentioned patriarchal; the law without the disposition is something formal. The importance of both essential phases is thus to be noted because of the tremendous error of our age—as if an organization of laws is sufficient, as if this alone is determining: one considers the law as a yardstick that one needs only bring to lay down in order to show the straight line; the subjective cultural education, experience, knowledge, insight become contemned as nothing; but these subjective sides must essentially correspond to the law so that the law first through these becomes actual. . . .

[1433] In order that the disposition can be true, the truth must lie at its foundation, must be actual in the state. The worldly and religious conscience are not separate, when what is present is grounded on the truth. The continuing education in history consists in the cultural education of the individual in just disposition; this is the task of history— to actualize the Christian principle, so that the true legislation will be constructed more and more. . . .

[1434] The *life of the state* is the general business of the people's spirit, which must bring this about; . . . every individual stands within this work and takes a share in it; that it *be something*, the framework for the thinking, in this work, is the *constitution*, and this depends on the *intelligence*, of which the foundation is the religion: the Christian religion rests on the *truth*; the development of the spirit, the intelligence of a people, arises from making the constitution accord with this principle of religion. So every people has the constitution that is proportionate to the level of its intelligence and of which it is worthy. . . . [1435] The ultimate of the disposition is the conscience; the ultimate of the conscience is the religion; the disposition can be true when it has the principle of the true religion and when the constitution proceeds from this principle. The details of the legislation can be so or otherwise, but the essential foundation is the consciousness of the eternal, absolute truth. The obedience can therefore be true disposition, insofar as it knows that its state has this foundation. . . . [1436] Thus originates the universal *trust* that is thoroughly necessary: in the life of the state there is much that must become believed and acted upon out of trust.

The state must, in regard to its external relations, be considered as an individual that is in many ways dependent on the temporal conditions, the neighbors, and other relationships: its policy is the affair of shrewdness, not of reason; thus it has many affairs of shrewdness and understanding. The rational makes itself count by itself, while the development of the constitution makes itself from itself through the history of the people. The state must have an ultimate, stable, decisive force: . . . and this comes only from a single individual, whose will is the ultimate. Where the highest peak is not this singularity, and the individual who embodies this is not determined through nature (i.e., birth), there this decisive unity is not present; . . . struggle is what decides, and civil wars are the [1437] necessary consequence.

[67]These, then, are the [393] worldly consequences of the Christian religion. The development of these consequences is the history up to the present time, and we ourselves stand in this development. So we now have to proceed to the appearing of this development.

"The Decline"

[68]The decline has three determinations. The first is that the empire through its own corruption in itself destroys itself, through the loss of spirit of private persons, in that subjectivity continues to stay with

---

67. GW 27 [1] 392–93 (~ GW 27 [2] 746–47; 1840, 407).
68. GW 27 [1] 393–94 (~ 1840, 407–8).

private pleasure and private interest, and isolates all persons, so that the whole is a spiritless corpse in which there is a lot of movement, but only by worms. Avarice, all sorts of depravity, are the powers of private willfulness, and are unleashed by the formula of private rights.

The second is that the spirit [394] withdraws into itself, into the higher—on the one side in the philosophies of Stoicism and so on, and on the other side in Christianity. Both are revolutionary against the Roman world, but not simply the negative of corruption; instead, the Christian religion is the positive, from which the new world comes forth.

The third is the decline as it comes upon the Roman world externally, through the onrush of foreign peoples (the migration of peoples), and since these northern and eastern barbarians were called "Germans" (Germanen) the world-historical people becomes now the "Germanic" (Germanische).

[69]The business of history is only that religion appear as human reason, that the religious principle that dwells in the heart of humans become also brought forward as worldly freedom. Thus the discord [408] between the inner of the heart and the concrete existence is sublated. For this actualization, however, another people, or other peoples, are called—namely, the *Germanic*. Inside ancient Rome itself Christianity cannot find its actual ground on which to found an empire.

[70]The eastern Caesarian empire long survived, while in the western a new people formed itself, of Christians from the invading barbarian hordes. So we see [1447] two Christian states in contrast with one another. . . . We now see the Christian religion in two forms: on the one side barbarian nations, which in regard to all cultural education have to start from scratch; on the other side culturally educated peoples, in possession of all Greek science and the refined oriental cultural education. The civil legislation among them was complete, since the great Roman legal scholars had built it to completion, so that the collection, which the Caesarian emperor Justinian had instituted, still today excites the admiration of the world. . . .

These two empires present a most noteworthy contrast. . . . In this great antithesis of the universal we have before our eyes the tremendous example of the necessity that a people must have its cultural education brought about in the sense of the Christian religion. The history of the

---

69. 1840, 407–8 (~ GW 27 [2] 746–47; GW 27 [3] 1084–85).
70. GW [4] 1446–51 (~ GW 27 [2] 748–51; GW 27 [3] 1086–87; 1840, 410–14).

highly cultured Eastern Roman Empire—where, as one might believe, the spirit of Christianity could be taken up in its truth and [1448] purity—exhibits to us a thousand-year sequence (for it led a feeble life from 395 to 1453) of continuous crimes, weaknesses, basenesses, and want of character: a most repulsive and in this way a most uninteresting picture. This shows how the Christian religion can be abstract, and, as such, is weak, even on account of its being so pure and in itself spiritual.... It is a habitual conception and saying ... that if the Christian love were universal, the private life as well as the political would be perfect, and the condition perfectly lawful and ethically customary. This seems to be a pious wish, but it does not contain the truth; for the religion is an inner principle, it belongs essentially to knowing, but on the side of the real there belongs also all passions, appetites, etc., and in order that the heart, will, intelligence, may become true, they must be *thoroughly educated culturally* through the real side; the law must become ethical custom, habit; practical activity must be elevated to a rational temple; [1449] the state must be rationally organized, and this organization makes the will of individuals actually lawful. The Byzantine Empire is a grand example of how the Christian religion remains abstract among a culturally educated people, if the whole organization of the state, of the laws, is not reconstructed according to its principle. Christianity was in Byzantium in the hands of the offscourings: the popular wildness on the one side and then the courtly baseness on the other side legitimized themselves in the religion, and degraded the latter to something disgusting. Therein lay the gross corruption of the Eastern Roman Empire; in regard to the religious side, two interests prevailed: first, the determination of the doctrinal concepts, and then, the appointment to ecclesiastical offices.... The principle of the Christian religion is: freedom, subjective insight. As a consequence, these interests were matters of contention in the hands of the masses; violent civil wars arose, and everywhere one witnessed scenes of murder, conflagration, and pillage, perpetrated in the cause of Christian dogmas.... The appointment to the office of the patriarchate at Constantinople was a basic cause of such raging civil wars, as was the jealousy of the patriarchs in Constantinople, Antioch, and Rome. [1450] Notorious is also the strife over icons; for it often happened that the Caesarian emperor declared for the icon party and the patriarch against, or conversely.... The gladiatorial contests spawned an opposition between the blue and green colors, between which the people divided themselves in parties....

The Christians of the Byzantine Empire remained sunk in the dream of superstition to the end, persisting in blind obedience to the patriarchs and the priesthood....

[1451] The Byzantine Caesarian Empire was thus torn by passions of all kinds within, and pressed by the barbarians outside, to whom the Caesarian emperors could offer but feeble resistance. The empire found itself in a continuing condition of uncertainty and insecurity. Rebellion on the part of field commanders, depositions of the Caesarian emperor by their means or through the intrigues of the courtiers, murder or poisoning of the Caesarian emperors by their own wives and sons, women surrendering themselves to lusts and shamefulness of all kinds and no longer respected in the world—such are the images that the history presents to us: till at last, about the middle of the fifteenth century (1453), this rotten edifice was destroyed by the strong Turks.

CHAPTER 8

The Germanic World

[1]With the Byzantine Caesarian Empire disappeared the last remnant of the Roman world: its sinking has filled us with disgust. Now we turn ourselves to a more cheering picture, to the beginning of the fourth world-historical people, the *Germanic*. It builds for itself a Germanic Caesarian empire, [1452] to which all of western Christianity belongs: this constitutes a unity that recognizes its worldly peak in the German Caesar (Kaiser). The principle of this empire was to be commensurate with the Christian religion; the defining of these peoples was to be, the bearers of the Christian principle. The principle of spiritual freedom, as much in secular as in religious regard—the principle of the reconciliation—was introduced into the still unrestrained, culturally uneducated hearts of those peoples, and to these there was given, to have as substance, in the service of the world-spirit, the concept of true freedom and, through it, to shape themselves so that the true concept would be actualized in them.

[2]When we proceed now to the division of the Germanic world into its periods, it is to be remarked that it cannot be done as for the Greeks and Romans, through the double relation to the outside—backward,

---
1. GW 27 [4] 1451–52 (~ GW 27 [2] 747–48; 1840, 415).
2. 1840, 415–16 (~ GW [2] 747–49).

to the earlier world-historical people, and forward to the later.... The Greeks and Romans were mature within when they turned themselves outward. The Germans, on the contrary, began with self-diffusion, [416] deluging the world, and subjugating to themselves the inwardly rotten and hollowed-out states of the cultured peoples. Then their development first began, kindled by a foreign culture, foreign religion, state-construction, and legislation. They culturally educated themselves through the taking up in themselves and dominating of the foreign, and their history is much more a going within themselves and a developing out of themselves....

The relation to the external is thus something entirely different from that of the Greeks and Romans. For the Christian world is the world of completion; the principle is fulfilled and thereby the end of days is fully come: the Idea can in Christianity see nothing more that is unsatisfied.... Thus the Christian world no longer has any absolute outside, but only a relative one, which is in itself overcome, and in respect to this the only thing left to do is to make it apparent that it has been overcome.

[3]We have here, in the history, first, the Idea as such, then the particularity from which the fulfillment of the absolute, final end shall emerge. There cannot be unification of these two sides in the beginning: rather, the two are essentially separate, and yet mediated by one another.... At first the particular will does not recognize the absolute end, and is in a struggle; it wills this end, but misunderstands this drive, flailing about in particular ends, and is thus in struggle with itself. In this struggle it brings about the absolute, by struggling with it.... [395] This comes to the fore in European history—that it only arrives at its final end by rejecting the truth.... In this history it is plain to see that the Idea as Providence, as a veiled inner, has held sway, such that what it brings about is often the opposite of what the peoples will. With the Greeks and Romans there is not such a separation, inasmuch as they had the true consciousness of what they willed and ought to do....

[396] The first aspect is that the states strive for sovereignty, for independence from one another, and have in this their honor. This tenaciousness Europe has in common with the Greek world....

The second aspect to this independence is the orientation of the states to their unity.... [397] The orientation of the states toward

---

3. GW 27 [1] 394–98 (~ GW 27 [4] 1455–56).

general unity corresponds to what was hegemony with the Greeks. In Europe, however, there is the hegemony of the spirit, which seeks its own kind of unity, such as was seen under Charlemagne and in the Crusades, and in more modern times as the Holy Alliance. . . .

The third aspect of these two factors is that once again all the states of Europe have a relation to the outside world as a single unity. . . . For the Christian world, this relationship to the outside is currently the Mohammaden world; the Mohammaden today exists as only an inessential phase. The Christian [398] world has circumnavigated the world, dominates the world, and what is not dominated is not worth dominating, or will soon submit.

"Again Three Periods"

[4]We distinguish here again *three periods*. The *first* begins with the entrance of the Germanic nations into the Roman Empire; the first development of these nations, who have now established themselves as Christian peoples in possession of the lands of the West, attracts no great interest on account of their wildness and lack of constraint. . . . This epoch extends to *Charlemagne*.

With this begins the *second* period; now begins the building of the state in itself, and so the cultural building of the Germanic principle from itself. Charlemagne joined himself with the Roman church against the old errors of the sects; thus there came about a union between the spiritual and the secular power, and it ought now to be that "after the reconciliation was fulfilled a heavenly empire on earth"; but precisely in this time there appears to us, instead of the spiritual empire of heaven, [1453] the innerness of the Christian principle utterly directed outward and coming out of itself; Christian freedom is perverted into its opposite, as much in a religious as in a secular respect—on the one side to the severest bondage of the spirit, on the other side to the most unethically customary excess and to crudeness of all passions. For cultural education, it is necessary to go through this point of division: the spirit must know itself as other, that is outside itself—as was emphatically said earlier. In this period two points of view are especially to be highlighted: one is the cultural formation of the states, which ordered themselves in a hierarchy of obedience such that all became a firmly fixed, particular

---

4. GW 27 [4] 1452–54 (~ GW 27 [2] 755–56; GW 27 [3] 1093–94; 1840, 418–19).

right, without the sense of the universal: this hierarchy of obedience appears in the *feudal system* in the Middle Ages. The second viewpoint is the antithesis between church and state: this antithesis is present only because the church, to whose management the holy was committed, had itself sunk down into every kind of worldliness; this worldliness appears only the more detestable, in that all passions give themselves the legitimation of the religion.

The time of the reign of *Charles the Fifth*, the end of the fifteenth and the beginning of the sixteenth century, makes the end of the second, and simultaneously the beginning of the *third* period. Secularity appears now as in itself coming to consciousness, that it too has a right in the customary ethics, lawfulness, administration of justice, and activity of humanity; there entered the consciousness of its own legitimacy, through the restoration of Christian freedom. The Christian principle has now passed through the frightful discipline of cultural education; through the *Reformation* its truth and actuality is given to it. [1454] This third period extends from the Reformation to the most modern times: the principle of the free spirit is here made the banner of the world, and from this principle develop the universal axioms of reason. Formal thinking, the understanding, had been already culturally developed; but thinking received its true content first through the Reformation, through the reviving, concrete consciousness of the free spirit. Thinking began to gain its own cultural education: axioms were established from it according to which the constitution of the state must be reconstructed: the life of the state ought now to be erected in accord with the consciousness of reason; ethical custom, tradition, no longer counted; the various claims of right must legitimate themselves on the basis of rational axioms. Thus the freedom of the spirit comes for the first time to reality.[5]

---

5. Contrast the rather different characterization of the second period in GW 27 [1] 402-4: "the beginning is characterized as the migration of peoples. After this are three epochs: (1) Charlemagne, holding sway over the Franks, the universal royal empire over the Germans, which was thereby the Roman Caesarian Empire. . . . [403] The second epoch is the second form of unity, which, in contrast to the first, real, unity, is to be designated as an ideal. It is the age of the great Spanish monarchy of Charles V, and still more of the age before him, when the real unity no longer existed, but the various states and classes in themselves, in their special situations, became established. Since the real unity had disintegrated, the outer relationship was one of only external politics. The relationship was thus diplomatic; no state could exist without the others. The notion arises of the balance of power. . . . Here too is when occurs the discovery of America and so forth. In the arts, religion clarifies and transfigures itself, in the clarity of the sensible element. But it also does so in the innermost spirit, in the Reformation. This age is to be compared with the age of Pericles. Luther corresponds to the being-in-self

"Freedom" and "Fidelity"

[6]Germany overall has from way back had free individuals, and the Romans understood the Germans to contrast with themselves in this respect. Freedom has been from way back the banner of the Germans.... [407] As this element of freedom of the individuals progresses into the social, this progress can only build itself into peoples' assemblies, whose members are all free, and who confer about each and every matter.... That the people's assembly validated the individual as particular is a fundamental trait that Tacitus described [*Germania* #11-15], and it was still evident in the March Days of the Franks and later at the German Reichstag....

The other essential phase of this validation of the particularity of the individual is the formation of enduring, specific focal points in the kings. The formation of such a focal point, [408] even if it also had the external enablement through birth, also came from a voluntary following by the individuals. It is a common bond of fidelity, for fidelity is the second banner of the Germans. They freely attach themselves to a subject and to his service, and in this have their honor, and make this relationship something unbreakable. This relationship did not exist among either the Romans or the Greeks.... The principle of fidelity is thus a principle of the modern world. The self, this innermost personhood, is what individuals ought to be drawn together by. The relationship is, then, one of subjectivity; that is, one subject must be placed on top of the other....

Two ways of relating manifest themselves here: the one according to which the individual belongs to his association, and the other where it is the top individual [409] who is the commander....

The third is the unification of both relationships, and out of their combination comes the formation of the state.... The state should remain the soul, the master; from it should proceed the determination and legal justification....

---

of Socrates. To be sure, this world manifested no Pericles. Charles the Fifth had the awesome possibility, through external means, but he had not [404] that which made Pericles into a master: the inner spirit, the absolute means of mastery failed him. ... The third period is that of the most modern time, which we could compare with the Roman world, for in it the universal is at hand: not the abstract universality, but rather the hegemony of self-conscious thought that wills and brings to completion the universal. It is now the understood end that governments achieve."

6. GW 27 [1] 406-10 (~ GW 27 [2] 756-61; GW 27 [3] 1098-99; GW 27 [4] 1457, 1499; 1840, 427-30).

In the initial stage there is a collision between both sides, and what is most salient in the Germanic states is the particular subjectivity, which constitutes the first form in which all rights and duties are comprehended. The rights thus do not contain the character of universal legal determinations, but all laws of the state institution sink into the form of private rights. . . . From this condition, full of struggle, there is worked out only late something universal, understandable, [410] essentially put together out of private relationships, that looks like something that lacks organic unity in itself. . . . The older history of Germany is therefore a painful finitude of determinations, and one has to go through a tedious course of these singularities, whereas in other histories there is always present the image of a whole. . . . There is here absolute singularization and distancing from all sense for the state. To this singularization, this particularity of relationships, there comes the particularity of the heart and of the passions, resulting in the greatest atrocity. The religion does work against this, but the church living in this time acquires, like the others, disparate rights.

[7]Since the secular rule had at the same time spiritual legitimacy, property became secured, and led to the formation of forms of mastery so independent that they did not allow themselves to be brought into unification. No unity could come about here by coercion, nor by the dying of the master, nor by a division, nor by inheritance. This fragmentation, built on such firm ground, is what has been called German freedom right up to the present day: an independence of particular mastery, a fragmentation, that has always counted as the dignity and honor of Germany, but that has brought disgrace and misfortune. Germany thus inwardly fragmented persists in innerness, in its principle that possession does not come about by conquest. This simple innerness of this principle endures. But this principle seeks to be and ought to be in itself concrete, ought to unite itself, from being alienated. The German principle must therefore have the drive to make itself concrete through unification with something initially other than it, as was indeed the case with others at their first origin. Germany thus must have the drive to unite itself with something other. This [427] determines the situation of Germany. It is a willing and an incapacity, an ought and a not-possible, and the result is impotence of supposed power.

---

7. GW 27 [1] 426–27.

"The Revolution of the East" (Islam)

[8]While the West began to enclose itself in chance, entanglement, and particularity, so must the opposite direction make its appearance in the world, for the integration of the whole; and this happened in the *Revolution of the East*, which destroyed all particularity and dependence, and completely cleared up and purified the heart, in that it made only the abstract One into the absolute object, and accordingly made the pure subjective consciousness, the knowledge only of this One, the sole aim of actuality—the Unconditioned as condition of existence.

We have certainly earlier become familiar with the nature of the oriental principle, and [432] have seen that its highest is only negative, and that the affirmative means a falling away into naturalness and the real enslavement of the spirit. Only among the Jews have we observed that the principle of single unity has elevated itself to thinking; for only among them was the One, which is for thinking, worshiped. This Oneness now remained, in the purification to abstract spirit; but it was freed from the particularity by which the worship of Jehovah had been hampered. Jehovah was only the god of this single people, the god of Abraham, Isaac, and Jacob: only with the Jews had this god made a pact, only to this people had he revealed himself. That particularity of the relationship is done away with in Muhammadanism. In this spiritual universality, in this purity without limit and without definiteness, the subject has no other aim than the realization of this universality and purity. *Allah* no longer has the affirmative, limited aim of the Judaic God. The veneration of the One is the single ultimate aim of Muhammadanism, and subjectivity has only this veneration as content of its activity, combined with the design to subjugate secularity to the One. This One is now indeed determined as spirit; yet because subjectivity allows itself to be absorbed in the object, this One lacks every concrete determination, so that neither does subjectivity become for itself spiritually free, nor is its object itself concrete. But Muhammadanism is not the Indian, not the monkish, immersion in the Absolute; rather, subjectivity is here living and infinite, an activity that enters into secular life only negatively, and works and mediates only in such a way as shall promote the existence of the pure veneration of the One. The object of

---

8. 1840, 431-34 (~ GW 27 [1] 411-12; GW 27 [2] 751-52; GW 27 [3] 1089-90; GW 27 [4] 1461-63).

Muhammadanism is purely intellectual; no image, no representation of Allah is tolerated: Muhammad is a prophet but human, and not elevated above human weaknesses. [433] The foundations of Muhammadanism involve this, that in actuality nothing can become fixed, but that everything is active, proceeding alive in the infinite amplitude of the world, so that the veneration of the One remains the only bond by which all is bound together. In this amplitude, in this power, all limits, all national and caste distinctions vanish; no race, no political right of birth and of possession has any worth, but the human only as believer. To adore the One, to believe in him, to fast, to do away with the vital feeling of specialness, to give alms (that is, to get rid of particular possessions): these are the simple commandments; the highest service, however, is to die for the faith, and he who does so for it in battle is sure of Paradise....

[434] Abstraction held sway over the Muhammadans: their aim was to make count the abstract worship, and for that they strove with the greatest spiritual enthusiasm. This spiritual enthusiasm was *fanaticism*, that is, a spiritual enthusiasm for something abstract, for an abstract thought that sustains a negative relationship to the way things are. Fanaticism essentially exists only through maintaining for itself a desolating, destructive relation to the concrete.

[9]It is Muhammadanism, then, that in its splendor, in its freedom, in its breadth and untroubled clarity, stands opposed to the plunge of the Christian world into the particular.

[10]Real life is after all concrete, however, and introduces particular aims; conquest leads to mastery and wealth, to the rights of the mastering family, to a union of individuals. But all this is only accidental and built on sand; it is today, and tomorrow it is nothing; the Muhammadan is, with all his passion, indifferent, and engages himself in wild changes of fortune. By its spread, Muhammadanism founded many empires and dynasties. This boundless sea becomes ever wider; nothing is set; whatever curls up into a configuration remains transparent, and as such glides away. Those dynasties were without the bond of an organic firmness: the empires, therefore, only degenerated; the individuals in them simply vanished. Where, however, a noble soul makes itself prominent—like a billow in the surging [435] sea—there it manifests

---

9. GW 27 [1] 412 (~ GW 27 [4] 1464).
10. 1840, 434-37 (~ GW 27 [1] 412-15; GW 27 [2] 752-53; GW 27 [3] 1091-92; GW 27 [4] 1463-66).

itself in a freedom, such that there was never produced anything more noble, more magnanimous, more courageous, more resigned. The special, determinate object that the individual embraces is grasped by him entirely. While the Europeans are involved in a crowd of convoluted relationships, in Muhammadanism the individual is only *this*, and indeed in the superlative: cruel, cunning, courageous, magnanimous, in the highest degree. Where the sentiment of love exists, there is an equal abandonment—and love from the heart. . . . This reckless innerness shows itself also in the glow of the Arabic and Saracen poetry. This glow is the perfect freedom of fancy, from all, so that it is entirely nothing but the life of its object and the experience of this, so that it has no selfishness and egotism for itself. Never has *spiritual enthusiasm*, as such, brought forth greater deeds. . . .

As rapidly as the Arabs had made their conquests, so rapidly did the arts and sciences attain among them their highest bloom. At first we see the conquerors destroying everything connected with art and science. . . . But soon afterward the Arabs allowed themselves to promote the arts and sciences and to spread them everywhere. [436] Their empire reached its highest bloom under the caliphs Al-Mansur and Harun al-Raschid. Great cities originated in all parts of the empire, where commerce and business flourished, splendid palaces were built, and schools instituted. The learned of the empire found themselves together at the caliph's court, and the court was brilliant not only through the outward pomp of the costliest jewels, furniture, and palaces, but above all with the bloom of the art of poetry and all the sciences. . . .

The great empire of the caliphs did not last long: for on the basis of universality nothing is firm. The great Arabian Empire fell about the same time as that of the Franks: thrones were demolished by slaves and by fresh invading peoples, the Seljuks and Mongols, and new empires founded, new dynasties raised to the throne. The Ottomans at last succeeded in establishing a firm mastery, and indeed through forming for themselves a firm center in the Janissaries. After the fanaticism had ebbed away, no customary ethical principle remained in the hearts. In the struggle with the Saracens, European courage had idealized itself to a beautiful, noble chivalry. Science and knowledge, especially that of philosophy, came from the Arabs into the West. A noble poetry and free imagination were kindled by the Germans in the Orient—and so Goethe also turned himself to the Orient and in his *Divan* composed a string of lyric pearls whose innerness and felicity [437] of fantasy cannot be surpassed.

The Orient itself, however, when by degrees spiritual enthusiasm had vanished, sank into the grossest vice. . . . At present, driven back into its Asia and Africa, and tolerated only in one corner of Europe through the jealousy of the Christian powers, Islam has long vanished from the ground of world-history, and has retreated into oriental ease and repose.

[11]The western part of Europe is the natural site from which the West originated, but the Orient is its higher, more spiritual father. The Romans received Christianity from the Orient—the element of freedom, of universality, over against the Nordic resting on singular subjectivity. The courage of the Europeans flowered into beautiful chivalry in Spain through the Arabs, who also disseminated the sciences. Similarly, free fantasy is grounded in the Orient. . . .

This then is the general character of the Orient and the relationship to the West. In respect to the practical, never has spiritual enthusiasm completed greater acts than this oriental spiritual enthusiasm. This spiritual enthusiasm had no specific goal; rather it is purely abstract, all encompassing, needing nothing.

"The Continuation of the Old Roman Empire"

[12]One could be inclined to regard the picture of the beautiful, rational constitution of the Frankish monarchy under Charlemagne—which exhibited itself as strong, great, and full of order, internally and externally—as an empty dream. Yet it stood, although the entire state structure was held together only through the strength, the greatness, and the noble sense of this individual, and was not grounded in the spirit of the people, not having become living in it. . . . What much more constitutes the actuality of a constitution is that it exists as objective freedom, the substantial manner of volition—as duty and obligation in the subjects. But for the German spirit, which at first existed only as heart and subjective willfulness, there was as yet no duty at hand, as yet no innerness [448] of unity, but only an innerness of indifferent, superficial selfishness overall.

[13]Thus was the Frankish Empire created, this first self-consolidation of Christianity into a state construction, that came out of it after the Roman Empire had been swallowed by Christianity. The constitution

---

11. GW 27 [1] 414.
12. 1840, 447–48 (~ GW 27 [2] 757–58, 761–62; GW 27 [3] 1102–3; GW 27 [4] 1469–71).
13. 1840, 443.

as described looks outstanding; it provided a firm war organization and provided for lawfulness within; and nonetheless, it proved itself, after Charlemagne's death, utterly powerless: as much externally defenseless against the onslaught of the Normans, Hungarians, Arabs, as it was internally weak against lawlessness, pillage, and oppression of every kind.

"The Feudal System"

[14]The brilliant state force of Charlemagne had vanished without leaving a trace, and the immediate consequence of that was the general defenselessness of individuals.... [449] The individuals therefore had to themselves take refuge with individuals, and were established under the power of certain persons having force, who out of the authority that formerly belonged to the universality constructed a private possession and personal mastery.... As in earlier times the king or other high person gave fiefs to their vassals by way of rewards, now, conversely, the weaker and poorer gave their possessions to the powerful, for the sake of gaining a severe protection; they gave over their goods to a master, a convent, an abbot, a bishop (*feudom oblatum*), and received them back, encumbered with a list of duties to these masters. From free they became feudal vassals, and their property became a loan. This is the relationship of the feudal system. *Feudum* is related to *fides*; the *fidelity* is here a bond through injustice, a relationship that aims at something just but whose content even so is very unjust; for the *fidelity* of the vassal is not a duty in relation to the universal, but a private duty, which is therefore rooted in chance, willfulness, and force. Universal injustice, universal lawlessness, was brought into a system of private dependence and private obligation.... [450] Only in a few cities, where communities of free men were strong enough to guarantee for themselves defense and security even without the king's help, did relics of the old free constitution remain....

The force of the kaiser was on the whole presented as something very great and high; the kaiser counted as the secular authority of collective Christendom; but the greater these representations were, the less did the power of the kaiser count in actuality. The Frankish regime derived extraordinary advantage through entirely distancing itself from this

---

14. 1840, 448–50, 453–54 (~ GW 27 [1] 425–30; GW 27 [2] 760–65; GW 27 [3] 1110–12, 1115–17, 1125–27; GW 27 [4] 1477–87).

hollow assumption, while in Germany the advance of cultural education was hindered by that pretense. . . .

[453] So all right vanished before particular might; for equality of right, rationality of law, was not present. . . . There ran through the world something like a feeling of the *nothingness* of its condition. In that condition of complete individual isolation, where nothing counted except the force of the power holders, humanity could come to its rest, and something like an evil conscience pervaded Christianity. In the eleventh century, the fear of the approaching last judgment and the belief in the imminent going-under of the world spread through all Europe. . . . [454] Every virtue was foreign to this time, and so *virtus* had lost its very meaning: it designated in usage nothing other than force, violence, sometimes even rape. The priesthood found itself in the same corruption.

[15]The hardness of self-seeking, out of the heart's standing alone—this knotty oak of the Germanic heart—was broken and mellowed by the terrible discipline of the Middle Ages. The two iron rods of this discipline were the church and serfdom.

The church brought the heart out of itself, led the spirit through the hardest bondage, so that the soul was no longer its own; but it did not bring it down to Indian dumbness, for Christianity is [492] in itself spiritual principle and has as such a boundless elasticity.

Similarly, serfdom, which made the body not belong to a human, but to another, dragged humanity through all the savagery of slavery and unbridled desire—and thus smashed itself on itself. It was not so much *from* slavery as *through* slavery that humanity was liberated. For savagery, lust, injustice, are what is evil: the human, as imprisoned in oneself, is unfit for customary ethics and religiousness; and it is from this violent volition that the discipline liberated the human.[16]

The church fought the struggle against the wildness of the savage ethical customs in a manner that was equally wild and terroristic: by the strength of the horrors of hell, it prostrated the core and held it in lasting subjection, in order to bring the wild spirit to stupefaction and to tame it into repose. It was declared in the dogma that every human

---

15. 1840, 491-93 (~ GW 27 [1] 419; GW 27 [4] 1526-28).

16. Discussing the master-slave dialectical relationship in the *Encyclopedia* (sec. 435, Zusatz), Hegel says: "Without having experienced this discipline, breaking self-will, no one becomes free, rational, capable of command. In order to become free, in order to acquire the capacity for self-rule, all peoples, therefore, must undergo the severe discipline of subordination under a master."

must necessarily pass through this struggle, since one is by nature evil, and only by passing through inner laceration does one come to the certainty of reconciliation.

While we concede this on one side, it must on the other side be said that the form of the struggle is very much altered when the foundation is a different one, and the reconciliation is brought fully into actuality. The path of agony has then fallen away (it does indeed make its appearance again later, but in an entirely different configuration), for then, as the consciousness awakens, the human being finds oneself in the element of a customarily ethical condition. The essential phase of negation is of course a necessary one in humans, but it has now assumed the tranquil form of upbringing, and thereby all the terrible characteristics of that inward struggle vanish.

Humanity has today attained the feeling of actual reconciliation of the spirit in itself, and a good conscience in its actuality, in secularity. The human spirit has come to stand on its own feet. In this achieved self-feeling of [493] humanity lies no revolt against the divine, but a manifestation therein of the better subjectivity, which experiences the divine in itself: which is imbued with respect, and whose activity is directed to universal goals of rationality and of the beautiful.

"The Independence of the Church"

[17]*Gregory VII* [1020–85], already famous as Cardinal Hildebrand, now sought to secure the independence of the church in these terrible circumstances—especially through two regulations. First he made fixed the *celibacy of the priesthood*.... [1489] Gregory VII established the regulation by excommunicating all the married clergy as well as the laity who should hear Mass by these. In this way the spiritual was excluded from the customary ethics of the state. The second measure was directed against *simony*, namely, against the sale of, or willful appointment to, bishoprics—even to the papal see itself.

"The Deepening of Religion in the Hearts"

[18]Spirit is deepening itself in itself, entering into the depth of the truth of the Christian religion. In this regard now there is a threefold

---

17. GW 27 [4] 1488–89 (~ GW 27 [1] 419; GW 27 [2] 766–67; GW 27 [3] 1117–18; 1840, 455).
18. GW 27 [1] 418–20.

development: first, the way in which the scientific enters the religion—how thinking had seized the religion. Thought is the innermost of spirit in its abstract freedom. Earlier the teaching of the church was firmly established through the councils and church fathers, and thereby already made ready. What is now at hand is the rebuilding of this subject through the theologians of the West, who were essentially philosophers. And every theology must be philosophical, since the simple historical reflection does not reach the content as truth. In the Middle Ages it now happened that the objective in the teaching [419] of Christendom is thought through, and indeed in the Scholastic philosophy.[19]

... A second deepening is that of feeling. With the spread of Christianity was tied the spread of convents and monastic orders. In this monastic existence there is a turning of the hearts of individuals, and calling here is the conversion, the suffusion, of the hearts of individuals with ideals. Here German life was pierced by the figure of the ideal. It is the tremendous force that breaks the rigid barbarian self-will and throws the natural strength to the ground, buckles the inner in women and men, strips away the innocence and beautiful love, buries this vitality, and grants it to find calm and peace only in the form of yearning, a heavenly yearning. Monks and nuns had to take the oath of chastity, of obedience, and of poverty—thus against the love and the customary ethic of marriage, against obedience to higher-ups, and with renunciation of private possession. . . . This killing of the natural will also happens in part simply because of the cloistered existence; in part, however, the killing is the result only of a long struggle that is tied up with manifold events—and interesting here are the stories of individuals [420] who with all their courage could not find satisfaction in the world, and distressed themselves through the demand of something higher, and in this cleavage went to ground or else found peace in the bosom of the church through renunciation of all interests and passions.

---

19. See also GW 27 [2] 772 (~ GW 27 [3] 1128-30; GW 27 [4] 1513-15): "Scholastic thinking sublated the beyond of the objectivity, and this is the devotion of the Scholastic: to make valid in religious content the thinking form of what was at first only external, sensuous, singular intuition—which Scholasticism took on the one hand from tradition, and which on the other hand it reconstructed, and elevated the movement of the spirit to a universal cultural education. Scholastic thinking had in it the greatness that philosophy was not yet separated from theology, that the absolute truth ought to be thought—as was said, proven by reasoning, established as product of thinking, while thinking and I is one and the same thing, a tautology. This spirit of freedom is thus here not only not to be misunderstood, but appears in infinite elasticity."

The two sides of this inbuilding of the ideal—one through thought as the universal, then through the heart—became formalized through a third: that law overall, especially private law, became transformed in the eyes of the church. . . . What was merely a private offense became now established as a public crime, and especially the law of marriage attained a new place.

[20]From the eleventh to the thirteenth centuries there emerged a drive that expressed itself in manifold ways. The communities began to build tremendous houses of God, cathedrals, erected to contain the community. (Architecture is always the first fine art, forming the inorganic essential phase, the domiciling of the god; only after that does art attempt to exhibit to the community the god itself, the objective.) From the cities on Italian, Spanish, and Flanders coasts a vigorous sea traffic was undertaken, which reaped for them great riches of crafts. The sciences began in some degree to revive: Scholasticism was in its high tide; schools of law were founded at Bologna and other places, as also for the study of medicine. All these creations are grounded largely in the *origin* and growing *importance* of the *cities*. . . . For this emergence of the city a great need was present. Like the church, namely, the cities established themselves as reactions against the violence of the feudal essence—as the earliest in-itself lawful power. . . .

[466] The ancient Germans had known only free private property, but this principle had perverted itself into complete unfreedom, and now for the first time we glimpse a few feeble beginnings of a reawakening of a sense of freedom. Individuals, who through the soil that they cultivated had been brought closer to one another, constructed among themselves a kind of union, confederation, or conjuration. They agreed to be and to perform on their own behalf that which they had previously performed in the service of their feudal lord alone. . . . The determination of the union was, in this way, to construct a kind of militia. The further progress was a government. . . . Trenches and walls were built as common defenses. . . . In such community, crafts that distinguish themselves from agriculture are at home. The artisans must soon have won a necessary superiority to the tillers of the ground, for the latter were forcibly [467] driven to work; but the former had as their own their activity, diligence, and interest in their craft. . . . By degrees the towns secured their own legal jurisdiction and likewise freed themselves from

---

20. 1840, 465–69 (~ GW 27 [2] 767–78; GW 27 [3] 1119, 1129–30; GW 27 [4] 1497–1503).

all taxes, tolls, and rents.... The artisans divided themselves later into *guilds*, to each of which were attached special rights and obligations.... By degrees cities grew to be free republics: especially in Italy, then in the Netherlands, in Germany, and France.... [468] The history of the cities is a continual change of constitutions, according as this part among the citizens or the other, this faction or that, got the upper hand.... As we contemplate these restless and changing drives in the heart of the cities—the continual struggles of factions—we are astonished when we see on the other side the industry, the commerce by land and water, in the highest degree flourishing. It is the same principle of [469] vitality that, nourished by this very internal excitement, brings to the fore this phenomenon.

"The Church Sought Mastery"

[21]The church sought, as divine power, mastery over the secular, proceeding on the abstract principle that the divine stands higher than the secular....

[1490] Soon the church attained the greatest influence in secular affairs: it arrogated to itself the decision as to the crowns of princes, and assumed the part of mediator between the powers, in war and peace.... The peoples and those holding sway recognized [1491] clearly that the church by this mixing had worldly goals in view; step by step there came to be contempt for the higher itself.... Thus as the papacy gained in land and goods and direct mastery, it lost regard and respect.

[22]While the rest of the Roman Empire on the whole now lived at peace with the church, and had only secular conflicts, Germany was in a struggle of an entirely different sort: the kaiser against the pope—a tragedy, in which the family of the kaiser and the power of the German state went under. The church was victorious, just as it had prevailed peaceably in other states.... [430] The struggle of Germany with the church, as large a place as it takes up in the Middle Ages, was on the whole a partial affair and of little interest to the rest of Europe,... and the result was that the religion and church elevated itself to power over all the private and state interests, was master of scientific scholarship, made itself tutor to every kaiser, and the essential, hourly, daily life was

---

21. GW 27 [4] 1489–91 (~ GW 27 [3] 1117–18; 1840, 455–57).
22. GW 27 [1] 429–30 (~ GW 27 [2] 767–69; GW 27 [3] 1126–28; GW 27 [4] 1504–5; 1840, 469–72).

only life in the church. The mastery by this ideal empire, in place of the real, is thus the next point that we reach.

"What Was This Church Missing?"

[23]The question is now: What was this church lacking? One can accuse it of transgression, misuse, corruption, but these are merely individual failings, and the content of the doctrine is that of the highest truth—and the actualization of this doctrine is the dispensing of all the treasure of the Spirit.... There showed itself a need of Christianity to give itself a finality. This need grounded itself on something missing, and in order to discover it we must determine the shape that the Christian religion had given to itself....

The absolute content of Christianity was worked out long before, through the ancient church fathers. In this the philosophy of the Middle Ages had changed nothing, and besides, philosophy can only transpose the content into the form of the concept. This doctrine has now the dimension that the divine essence is nothing beyond the human, but the foundational determination is unity of the human and divine nature—that God appears to humanity and is utterly present to it. The infinite form deals here with this dimension. The divine nature thus has the determination of the this-here-in-itself. Christ has appeared, and this Presence, this unity of the human and the divine, this is what [431] the world has eternally been striving for; this Presence it is, whose specification overall is being dealt with: ... the peak point is that the determination of the this-here, that the miracle of the Presence that in the Spirit is present, is to be activated. This Presence could be in no way external, not in an unmediated way: the God-man Jesus Christ is, as a human being, as without mediation, departed; and the Presence necessary for the spirit could not be, for the spirit, as in a Dalai Lama, where the god is present to the human: the pope, the height in Christianity, cannot be for this a Dalai Lama. And about this, one has to give an explanation. The why is to be clarified. What has gone is nothing, and the *this-here* ought still to be. But *this human being here* is something natural, external, immediately natural; and this naturalness is, in the Christian religion, what is sublated.... In the Indian [religion], God is only substance that exists in singulars in contingent ways, which are

---

23. GW 27 [1] 430–32 (~ 1840, 470–72).

only modes, accidents of substance. In the Christian religion, however, the singularity is an absolute essential phase, and the single human being is therefore no mere mode but rather infinite for itself, excluding any other this-here. . . . [432] Christ cannot as a singular appear again in another. His natural singularity is gone; but this divine singularity should be present. . . . The main shape in which Christ is, as *this one*, known and present in the church is: this-here, as he is in the Mass and the Last Supper. In the Mass is the life, suffering, and death of the actual Christ daily at hand; it did not just occur once, but eternally; for it is the life, suffering, and death of God, and in relation to time must be the in-and-for-itself-being for every time. The sacrifice thus happens daily and always, and as actual Presence. It is shallow and irreligious to take the life, suffering, and death of Christ as merely historical, for it is divine history. God is appearing; the actual God; and this must take place always in the community. And the community is the participant; Christ sacrifices himself inside the human being and rises again in the human being. And this is not at all a simple represented Christ, as the reformed churches have it.

[24]Once it is established that God also lets himself be established as external, the external sensuous Presence becomes an endless multiplicity, and the need for it manifests itself in manifold ways. Christ as appearing here is also so defined that he gives himself to be recognized in many ways—so that his divine mother also shows herself as present, as well as other saints and blessed ones. These appearances, these effects of the divine in something present, the images of Mary—all these are hosts, present in an active, actual way.

A third and different manner of miracle, the relics, all these are connected with this Presence, and are maintained by those who belong to heaven. Miracles are then also appearances of the universal in special ways. All these are connected with the need for the presence of divinity.

In such ages the church becomes a world of miracles, and the pious community has no satisfaction in the world as such; instead, satisfaction is found in singularity perverted into a special appearing of the divine, as a portrayal of the divine as a this-here, in this place, in this time. . . .

[434] Christ himself, however, as Son of God, is only *one*; as the Host, this divinity is only substance, although conveyed into sensuous presence of singularity; but this singularity is at the same time a universal

---

24. GW 27 [1] 433–34 (~ GW 27 [2] 769–70; GW 27 [4] 1493–94; 1840, 473–74).

singularity that is in all communities, thus itself only a reflected-universal, not the *one* ultimate in a *space*, but instead the one under many, not the utterly one singular. This utterly one this-here-below Christendom must seek. The ultimate singularity into which the Presence gathers itself is that which is in a space, in a locality. Even if in time the singularity of the person has passed away, the singularity of the space maintains itself. And this singularity Christendom seeks. This ultimate peak of the sensuous singularity, this singularity of space, Christendom had to find and to make its own. Access to it is blocked by unbelievers. This is their lack of worth. To wipe away this disgrace united Christendom.

The Crusades

[25]In this feeling Christendom became one; it was on account of this that the *Crusades* were undertaken, and they therefore had not this or that but a single goal—to conquer the *Holy Land*.

[26]We saw of course a time when, under Alexander, the West went against the East, headed thus by an actual [435] individual. Christendom did not have this at its head, but went out after the *this-here*, wanting to win it and to enjoy it. . . . And they achieved their goal, winning Jordan, Jerusalem, Gethsemane, the Holy Sepulcher, Golgotha. This was their goal: to win what was their highest as Presence; to see it before oneself, to feel it, to savor this Presence. On the one side, the Christians were serious; on the other side, they founded here kingdoms, they conquered Constantinople, the Greek Caesardom. . . . Yet the westerners conducted their journey so ineptly that hundreds of thousands of them fell. They exhibited the same lack of understanding in founding their empire in the East.

[27]The Crusades began immediately in the West itself: many thousands of Jews were massacred and plundered; after this terrible beginning, the Christian populace set off. The monk *Peter the Hermit* from Amiens led the way with a tremendous mass of rabble: the mass passed in the greatest disorder through Hungary, robbing and plundering everywhere; but the mass itself dwindled away, and only a few reached Constantinople. Without having any rational grounds to give, the crowd believed that God would miraculously lead and protect them. That the inspiration of the peoples almost drove them to insanity is shown most by the fact

---

25. 1840, 474 (~ GW 27 [2] 770).
26. GW 27 [1] 434–35 (~ GW 27 [2] 769–70; GW 27 [3] 1119–20).
27. GW 27 [4] 1507–8 (~ 1840, 474–75).

that at a later time troops of children, most of whom ran away from their parents, went to Marseilles, to take ship for themselves for the promised land. Most lost their way, and the few who reached Marseilles were sold by the merchants to the Saracens as slaves.

At last, with much trouble and [1508] tremendous loss, more orderly armies attained their goal. . . . In the whole expedition, in all the dealings of the Christians, appeared that monstrous contrast that was present overall: the transition on the part of the Christian host from the grossest excesses and violence to the highest contrition and humbling. Still dripping with the blood of the murdered inhabitants of Jerusalem, the Christians fell down on their faces at the tomb of the Redeemer and directed fervent supplications to him.

[28]Here, in this grave, must rot the Christian opinion holding that in the sensuous could be found Christianity's ultimate meaning; for the response sounded a second time: "Why do you seek the resurrected among the dead?" [Luke 24:5-6]. In this resurrection there lies, for the understanding, the certain impossibility of being able to have relics. If this understanding had been sufficient, the church would have certainly been over and done with the matter. [436] Christ is risen, the sensuous Presence is removed; and that speaks for itself; after his sensuous presence, the Holy Spirit would "come to lead humanity into all truth" [John 16:13]. The peak of subjectivity is to be sought not among the dead but among the spiritually living: this is the result of the Crusades. The tomb disillusioned them about the meaning of the this-here.

[29]Thus the world won the consciousness that the human being must look for the *this-here*, which is of a divine kind, in oneself: thereby subjectivity becomes absolutely justified, and has in its very self the determination of the relationship to the divine. This, however, was the absolute result of the Crusades, and from here begins the age of self-reliance, of self-activity. The West had at the Holy Sepulcher bid its eternal goodbye to the East, and grasped its own principle of [477] subjective, infinite freedom. Christianity never again set forth as one whole. . . .

[478] From now on we see movements in which the spirit, transcending its gruesome and irrational existence, either turns within itself, and seeks to create out of itself satisfaction, or else gives itself to the actuality of universal and just goals, which are even therewith goals

---

28. GW 27 [1] 435-36 (~ GW 27 [3] 1120-21; GW 27 [4] 1508).
29. 1840, 476-78 (~ GW 27 [2] 770-71; GW 27 [4] 1508-9).

of freedom. The efforts that thus originate are now to be presented: they are the preparations for spirit's grasping the goal of its freedom in higher purity and justification.

"The Human Being Turns to the World"

[30]The principle of the *this-here*, which drove the world to the Crusades, instead developed itself in worldliness for itself.... The church, however, stayed with and held on to the principle; but also in it, it transpired that the principle did not remain in its externality without mediation, but became illuminated through *fine art*. Fine art spiritualizes, gives feeling to this external, to the simply sensuous, with form that expresses soul, sentiment, spirit.... It is something else entirely, when the spirit has before it a mere thing, such as the Host as such, or some stone, wood, a wretched image, as opposed to a painting full of spirit, a beautiful work of sculpture, in which soul relates itself to soul and spirit to spirit. In the former case, spirit is outside itself, bound down to something utterly other to it, which is the sensuous, unspiritual. In the latter, the sensuous is something beautiful, and the spiritual form has in itself soulfulness and a truth in itself. But on the one side, this truth, as *appearing*, is only in the mode of something sensuous, [494] not in its form commensurate with itself; and on the other side, ... this kind of religion does not find its satisfaction in a relationship with the beautiful, but instead, the totally coarse, ugly, shallow picturing has even as such a *suitability to the purpose*, or perhaps a greater such suitability. So as is said, the true works of fine art—for example, Raphael's Madonnas— do not enjoy veneration, or elicit a crowd of offerings, anywhere nearly as much as do coarse paintings that become sought out and treated as objects of the greatest devotion and liberality; piety passes by the former for this very reason, that piety would be summoned and called to inner feeling—but such stimulus is of an alien kind, where all that is to be enacted is the feeling of selfless obedience and dependent stupor. So, fine art is surely beyond the principle of the church. But as fine art has only sensuous depictions, it counts at first as something not dangerous. The church, therefore, continued to follow it; but separated from it as soon as the free spirit, from which art originated, as itself elevated itself to thought and to science.

---

30. 1840, 493-95 (~ GW 27 [2] 771-73; GW 27 [4] 1511-14 and 1527-30).

Then in the second place, fine art was supported and elevated through the *study of antiquity* (the name *humaniora* is very expressive, for in those works of antiquity honor is done to the human and to the cultural education of humanity): through this the West became acquainted with what is true and eternal in human activity. Externally, this revival of science was a by-product of the fall of the Byzantine Caesarian Empire. A crowd of Greeks fled for refuge to the West and brought in the Greek literature; . . . [495] there appeared totally different forms, a different virtue, from that previously known; a totally different standard for what was to be honored, commended, and imitated. The Greeks in their works exhibited totally different moral commands from those that the West knew; in the place of Scholastic formalism entered a totally different content: Plato became known in the West, and in him a new human world presented itself. These novel ideas met with a principal organ of diffusion in the newly discovered *art of book printing*. . . . Insofar as in the study of the ancients the love of human deeds and virtues manifested itself, the church did not have anger against it, and did not observe that in those alien works a totally alien principle confronted it.

[31]Inasmuch as human beings grasped their subjectivity as justified, they found joy in their work. A symptom of this is the awakening to classical literature. The early church fathers called the virtues of the heathens only brilliant vices. Now one began to honor them as human overall. Reformation is affirmative significance given to the subjective activity of humanity—a joy in the human; but, this content is only limited, heathen content. The absolute content is the spirit in its concept.

[32]This is the situation that now discloses itself in world-history: the this-here as sensuous is now what is external to spirit. . . . This external is nature, is separated from spirit, as its other, that it, however, at the same time wants, and with which spirit feels justified in occupying itself—but only when it is outside the church. What results is that the human being turns oneself to the world, freely lets it be as a *this-here*, is confident over and against it, deals practically with it. The spirit is, in the church, freed from the sensuous this-here. Herewith thus begins an entire proceeding of spirit, and this is the third[33] determination of [437] this period. The first was the mastery by the church, the second, that it wants the this-here and finds it outside itself. The third is the satisfied

---

31. GW 27 [2] 776.
32. GW 27 [1] 436-40 (~ GW 27 [2] 772-74; GW 27 [3] 1126-31; GW 27 [4] 1529-30).
33. Correcting the text here, which reads "second."

relationship to this externality, making it one's own, constructing it inwardly, outside the church. . . . This character now enters the world and assumes many forms of appearance.

The first of these configurations is that all kinds of industry and trade come alive, especially on the coast of Italy. . . . Here belongs the flowering of business. . . .

Falling within this period are a crowd of inventions. . . . Outstanding are gunpowder and the book printing press. . . . Gunpowder's invention altered the art of warfare, and important were the following points: the weakening of the defense of cities, for good and bad goals, and of the overall defense of the body by sturdy defensive weaponry; the difference between the weapons of masters [438] and those of serfs was now diminished (there is much complaint that courage could now be vanquished by the weak; but that was also the case earlier, and gunpowder has essentially brought about a higher determination of spiritual bravery, since in the present-day art of war, leadership is the main factor . . .); through the use of gunpowder it has also come about that the relationship to the individual as enemy has been removed, and the fighting is against an abstract enemy, and so wars are now less bloody because the understanding grasps more the whole in its violence since it can be seen more at a distance. One must therefore view the invention of gunpowder as a means that is essentially linked with the modern understanding.

The printing press is the means for the easy spread of opinions and thoughts, which have inundated Germany like an epidemic after its invention. . . .

Directly related were the heroic sea voyages of discovery by the Portuguese, the circumnavigation of the Cape of Good Hope, and the discovery of America launched from Spain—whose knighthood sought for itself a new field of action, seeming limited in the first place to pleasure, but displaying its courage in this element.

With this first industriousness is linked, secondly, inseparably, and in part, the origin of freedom in the cities. For by the human being looking to one's own hands and seeing their accomplishments, the self-consciousness setting itself to work in nature, one is in this legitimated, and, shaping oneself in this legitimation, sees oneself required to conduct oneself according to the nature of things [439] in order to satisfy needs. The human being puts oneself in the service of one's occupation, has to repress oneself and overcome one's willfulness and coarseness. One culturally educates oneself—that is, one must comport oneself in a not merely particular, but universal fashion. There originates thus in the first place associations for industry, but in addition the human being knows oneself to be justified in this business, and the association becomes in another dimension an association of rights and of civic freedom through which there arises in the European world a new world, that differs on one side from the church, which, as we saw, shut out the externality, thus setting it free. This externality is opposed to the system of dependent bondsmen that previously counted. . . .

[440] Three essential classes emerge: peasants, bourgeois class, and class of the masters, near which stands the class of the clergy. These are the classes that we saw in India as castes, and that are conditioned by the essential physical and spiritual requirements. These are therefore the classes that must emerge on the whole, overall. . . . They are essentially defined and established legally; . . . thus these essential estates are established partly naturally and partly legally. It is important to note further that these classes, while on one side indeed classes of civil society, are on the other side also determinations under the force of the state, which likewise is divided into these estates and is tied to them. These classes, which also initially are ways of living, are at the same time political. This is a very important distinction. One customarily does not understand as classes also distinctions of particular ways of making a living, so that they are conceived as simply political and not as rooted in their needs that the differing ways of life bring with them.

"The Advance from Feudalism to Monarchy"

[34]At this point we have to consider more closely the practical changes in the state. . . . This is the advance *from feudalism to monarchy*. . . . The monarchical principle is the opposite; it is the domination over such as possess no independent power for their individual willfulness; the domination of monarchy is essentially a force of the state; it has essentially in itself [1516] a substantial, lawful goal. Feudal mastery is overall a polyarchy: it is unqualified lords and serfs; in monarchy, there is one lord and no serf; through it, serfdom is broken, and in it what counts are right and rightful law; from it proceeds real freedom. Freedom is a word with many meanings: German freedom has, in relation to feudal lordship, been called especially the justified maintenance of willful

---

34. GW 27 [4] 1515–17 (~ GW 27 [2] 773–74; GW 27 [3] 1123–24; 1840, 482–83).

force. The resistance to kingly domination invokes freedom, when it is only opposition to the one possessing power as such and the force of a willfulness as such; and when the subordinate aims only thereby at his own mastery this is not freedom but the opposite. In monarchy the willfulness of individuals is suppressed and a collective essence of lordship is established; this makes universal dispositions necessary.... Monarchy succeeds feudalism and has characteristic consequences: the individuals who are closest to the chief are nonetheless powerful through their collectivity. This collectiveness is that from which the classes and the corporate bodies originate. The vassals transition into a class, and each person now counts only as a member of a class; the corporate bodies of the vassals, of the barons, etc., [1517] the cities, have power in communal essence; thus the power of the one holding sway cannot be simply willful, but needs the consent of the corporate bodies: he must will the just and equitable if he is to reckon of their support. We now see a beginning of the building of a state, while feudal mastery knows no state.

[35]In Italy the same spectacle repeats itself; ... a countless number of dynasties and chief condottieri had made themselves independent; gradually they were subjected as a collectivity to the one mastery of the pope. How, in such subjugation, there was present a justice, in the ethically customary sense, one learns from the history of the Italian cities—best seen from Machiavelli's famous writing *The Prince*; one has often thrown aside this book [1521] in disgust, as filled with the maxims of the cruelest tyranny; but Machiavelli has set forth the foundation of the necessity of a state-building according to which in those circumstances states ought to be founded: the single masters and mastery ought to be entirely subdued; the means that Machiavelli offers are certainly not to be reconciled with our concept of freedom; but they are the means that we recognize as the only ones, and at the same time as perfectly justified, in those circumstances: to them belong the most reckless violence, all kinds of deception, murder, and so forth. But the dynasties that had to be thereby thrown down were assailable only so, since an indomitable lack of conscience, and a complete depravity, thoroughly belonged to them.

[36]We are now arrived at the *third period* of the Germanic Empire; we enter upon the period of the spirit that knows itself to be free, inasmuch as it knows and wills the true, eternal, what is in and for itself universal.

---

35. GW 27 [4] 1520–21 (~ 1840, 487).
36. GW 27 [4] 1531 (~ GW 27 [3] 1136–37; 1840, 497).

In this third period there are again *three subdivisions* to make: first, we have to consider the Reformation as such; then the unfolding of the state of things after the Reformation; and lastly the modern times from the middle of the last century on.

"The Corruption of the Church"

[37]As for the corruption of the church, it has been noted what it was that the church lacked, and how it integrated this deficiency. Its corruption should not be seen as accidental [Griesheim: rather, the corruption was necessary]. One can say, "it arose from a misuse of power." One then presupposes that the matter itself had become free of deficiency, and that only the accidental will of some human beings corrupted this goodness, as a means to the goals of passion. . . . The corruption of the church, however, was produced by the church itself in itself, and consists in its having failed to truly expel the this-here as sensuous. Fine art was not enough to transfigure this sensuosity, for fine art itself has the form of the sensuous, which form cannot satisfy the spirit in its ultimate needs. . . . The world-spirit had already excluded the sensuous and thereby stood above the church, which took no part in this excluding division, but instead retained the sensuous within itself. [Griesheim: The church henceforth lags behind the world-spirit.] The world-spirit has now accepted external as external, and we [444] have a subjectivity that is justified in subordinating the external to itself. The sensuous has thus remained within the church, and this relationship now develops within itself to the point of corruption. . . . Thus the corruption can be understood as in the piety itself, as superstition, that is bound to a sensuous this-here, and it is supposed to be venerated as absolute. Bound in this way the spirit is unfree. The belief in miracles of the most absurd kind is an example of this lack of freedom.

The divine becomes expressed in the most peculiar shapes as concrete existence. Everything passionate now comes to the fore, becomes free—in its own, that is, crude and wild, way. The virtue of the church is, in contrast, now only abstract negativity against the sensuous; it is not ethical custom in itself, but is only the fleeing from worldliness, its renunciation. This is the contrast within the church that now comes to prominence: crude appetite, and depravity; and, on the other side, all

---

37. GW 27 [1] 443–45 (~ GW 27 [4] 1531–32; 1840, 497–99).

elevation of renunciation [Griesheim: of religious souls, who sacrifice everything]. This contrast becomes still stronger through the antithesis over and against the energy of the understanding in its worldly essence, in which humanity has now won for itself an absolute justification.

The ultimate corruption of the church is that it ought to save the souls from corruption, and itself corrupts this salvation itself by making it into a merely external means: this is, the indulgences for the sins. Subjectivity seeks the highest satisfaction in the certainty of the oneness with God. Because the church grants this satisfaction externally and carelessly, and because this occurs for the sake of an external goal, [445] outraged indignation necessarily arises against such activity. Yet the purpose for this service was not opulent living, but also the building of the church of St. Peter; ... which Michelangelo adorned with the painting of the Last Judgment—a last judgment on the church itself in its corruption.

[38]The piece of bread, consecrated through the priest, is the present [458] God, who comes to intuition and is eternally sacrificed. In this it is correctly recognized that the sacrifice of Christ is an actual and eternal happening, insofar as Christ is not simply sensuous and single, but is a completely universal, that is, divine, individuum; but the perversion is that the sensuous essential phase becomes isolated for itself and the revering of the Host remains, even insofar as it is not being partaken of, and so the presence of Christ is not posited essentially in the representation and the spirit. With right therefore did the Lutheran Reformation go especially against this dogma. Luther proclaimed the great doctrine that the Host was something, and Christ was received only by the *faith* in him; otherwise, the Host was a mere external thing that had no greater value than any other thing. But the Catholic falls down before the Host; and thus the outward is made into something holy. The holy as a thing has the character of externality, and thus it is capable of being taken possession of by another over and against me. . . . Here enters accordingly a separation between such who possess this, and such who have to receive it from another—between the *clergy* and the *laity*. The laity are alien to the divine. This is the absolute schism in which the church in the Middle Ages was trapped: it arose from the holy being known as something external. . . .

---

38. 1840, 457–62; see also 473–74 (~ GW 27 [2] 769, 774–76; GW 27 [3] 1107–9, 1113–15; GW 27 [4] 1491–96).

[459] The layman also cannot without mediation apply oneself to the divine being in one's prayers, but only through middlemen—through human conciliators, the dead, the perfect—*the saints*. Thus originated the adoration of the saints, and with it that mass of fables and lies that attend the saints and their biographies. In the East, the worship of images had early become predominant, and after a lengthened struggle prevailed: the *image*, the painting, belongs still to representation; but the coarser nature of the West desired something more immediate for intuition, and thus arose the worship of relics. . . . The chief object of adoration among the saints was the *Mother Mary*. She is in any case the beautiful image of pure love—of mother's love; but spirit and thought are still higher; and in the worship of this image that of God in the Spirit was lost, and Christ himself was set aside. The mediation between God and human was thus grasped, and held, as something external: thus through the perversion of the principle of freedom, absolute unfreedom became the law. The wider determinations and relations are a consequence of this principle. . . . [460] The individual has to confess—is bound to expose all the particularity of his conduct to the view of the confessor-father—and then is informed how he is to comport himself. Thus the church took the place of the *conscience*: it put the individuals in leading strings like children. . . . Thus there is a complete derangement of all that was recognized as good and ethically customary in the Christian church: only external demands were made on humans, and these were complied with in an external way. . . .

[461] With this perversion is connected the absolute separation of the spiritual from the secular principle overall. . . . The piety is outside of the history, and without history, for history is much more the empire of the spirit becoming present in its subjective freedom, as customary ethics of the state. Now in the Middle Ages there is not that actualizing of the divine; the antithesis was not resolved. Ethical custom became established as a nothing, and indeed, in its *three* truest highpoints.

One ethical custom is that of *love*, the emotional experience in the *marriage relationship*. . . . Now marriage was indeed reckoned by the church among the sacraments, but in spite of this standpoint it was degraded, inasmuch as the unmarried state counted as the more holy. *Another* ethical custom lies in *activity*—in the work of the human for one's subsistence. Therein lies one's dignity. . . . In direct contravention of this, *poverty*, indolence and inactivity, was established as higher: and what is contrary to ethical custom thus was consecrated. A *third* essential phase of the ethically customary is that *obedience* be rendered to the ethically customary and rational, as an obedience to laws that [462] I know as the just—not, however, the blind and unconditional, that does not know. . . . But it was exactly this latter kind of obedience that counted for the most pleasing to God.

"The Lutheran Principle"

[39]The old authenticated innerness of the German people is what led to this fall of the old way; and from it the true unity was again established, and this also had to work out the principle of freedom. All other peoples went forth to India and America, to achieve worldly mastery for themselves. Against this it was a simple monk, in whom was the consciousness that the this-here is to be found in the deep sepulcher of the heart, in the absolute Ideality of the inner, who arose. In him his deepest heart was distressed by the distortion of the truth. Luther's simple teaching is that the consciousness of the this-here in the present is nothing sensuous but is something actual, something spiritual, of an actual Presence, not in the sensuous, but in faith and enjoyment. This is no consciousness of a God that is supposed to be existing sensuously as a thing, nor also is it that this Presence is merely mental representation; rather, it is actually present—but not sensuously; and therefore Luther in the teaching on the Last Supper could make no concessions.

[40]He also could make no concession to the reformed church—that Christ is a mere commemoration, a recollection; rather, in this he agreed much more with the Catholic Church, that Christ is a Presence—but in faith, in the spirit. The Spirit of Christ actually fills the human heart; Christ therefore is not to be taken as a mere historical person, but the human being has to him an *immediate relationship* in the spirit.

[41]Connected to this renunciation of the sensuousness of the this-here, many other teachings are included as central, such as for example the nullity of works, as action that comes not from faith but brought forward from some external ground. Concerning faith, it is to be firmly grasped that the Lutheran faith is no certainty regarding what is merely finite; it is therefore not a certainty that depends on the merely finite subject as such. [446] . . . Christ disparaged the Jews for having wanted

---

39. GW 27 [1] 445 (~ GW 27 [3] 1133-34; GW 27 [4] 1532-33; 1840, 499-500).
40. 1840, 501 (~ GW 27 [4] 1532).
41. GW 27 [1] 445-48 (~ GW 27 [2] 777-78; GW 27 [3] 1134-35; GW 27 [4] 1532-33; 1840, 501-2).

signs and miracles in order to have faith [Mark 8:11-13 and Matt. 16:1-4]—that is, to allow oneself to seek certainty about the divine in an external, isolated occurrence. The certainty or truth about God is something entirely different from such externalities. Faith is certainty about the eternal, about the truth that is in and for and by itself. This certainty, the Reformation says, is given only by the Holy Spirit, which comes to the individual not according to one's particularity, but according to one's essence. The Lutheran doctrine is pure Catholic, only pruned of what that teaching has brought in from external relations. The Lutheran doctrine is therefore not opposed to the Catholic insofar as the latter does not assert this externality.

One aspect still needs to be emphasized here: the distinction between the priesthood and the laity. . . . In the Lutheran principle this distinction has fallen away, and the heart, the feeling spirituality, ought to come into possession of the truth, with the stipulation that the individual subject as particular identifies itself with this truth.

Hereby freedom has come into the church—the innerness of soul that belongs to religion. . . . The subjectivity of the individuals is now only true, only in faith, as having been itself born again in the knowledge of the Spirit, of the truth. The subjectivity is not the natural, but the substantial, made true—making the objective content its own. [447] . . . The subjective certainty, that is, the subject's knowledge of the true, which should be for it an objective truth, subsisting in and for itself, becomes authentic when, in relation to this content, the particular subjectivity is relinquished—which happens only by making the objective truth one's own. That which the subject makes one's own is the truth, the Spirit, the Trinity. This Spirit is the absolute essence, the essence of the subjective spirit—by relating to which, the subjective spirit becomes free in that the subject in its essence itself relates to itself, negating its own particularity. In this negativity toward oneself one comes to oneself. This is how Christian freedom is actualized. If subjectivity is based on feeling alone without this content, one remains standing at mere naturalness—for humanity is only human when going through the process of consciousness, and is only spirit when participating in the true, the objective content, and appropriating it within itself.

This is the ultimate banner around which the peoples gather themselves, the flag of freedom, of the true spirit. This is the spirit of the modern era, and the time prior to us had no other work, but to build this principle into actuality, thereby winning for this principle the form of freedom, of universality.

Thus there are three configurations that are now in the world: the empire of the old church, which had a true content, but burdened with externality and therefore not elevated to subjective freedom. Beyond that, we have the external world in which all external relationships fall—mastery, civil society; and then third, there is the modern church, the freedom of spirit [448] in the shape of subjective innerness.

What must happen now is that this reconciliation of actuality, which has happened in itself, becomes culturally constructed, in that it becomes itself objective by its form—that it take on the form of thought. This form belongs to cultural education, for this is the activity of the universal, of thinking overall. As regards the spheres of the finite will—law, state, administration—they must come to be determined in a universal mode in accord with the concept. It is in this way, then, that the truth appears to spirit in the external, natural, subjective will. . . .

The religion thus constitutes the basis of the state—not in the sense that the state makes use of religion as a means, but that states are only the appearance of the true content of religion.[42]

[43]But Luther's onslaught, which at first concerned only limited points, soon extended itself to the dogmas, and attacked not individuals, but interrelated institutions: cloister life, the secular lordships of the bishops, etc.—not only single expressions of the pope and the councils, but the entire manner and way of such expressions: the *authority of the church*. Luther repudiated that authority, and set up in its stead the *Bible* and the testimony of the human spirit. That the Bible itself has become the foundation of the Christian church is of tremendous importance: each ought now to learn from it for oneself; each can determine his conscience from it. This is a tremendous change in the principle: the entire authority of the church, the entire split is thereby overturned. [1534] The translation that Luther made of the Bible has been of incalculable value to the German people; this has supplied a *people's book*, such as no other nation in the Catholic world possesses as a people's book. . . .

---

42. See also the 1831 *Lectures on the Philosophy of Religion* (GW 29 [2] 438): "It is in the organization of the state that the divine breaks into actuality, permeating it; and the worldly is now justified in and for itself, since its foundation is the divine will, the law of right and freedom. The true reconciliation, whereby the divine realizes itself in the field of actuality, consists in the ethically customary and rightful life of the state: this is the true discipline of worldliness."

43. GW 27 [4] 1533–35 (~ 1840, 503–8).

Through the denial of the authority of the church, separation became necessitated. The Council of Trent made fast the foundation of the Catholic Church, and after this council there can be no more talk of a unification. The churches became parties against each other, for even in respect to the secular order a striking difference emerged. In the non-Catholic lands the cloisters and bishoprics were sublated, and the very rights of ownership unrecognized; the upbringing of children [1535] was organized differently; the fasts, the holy days, etc., were abolished. Thus there was also a secular reform in regard to external conditions, and in this way the Reformation could not work without the secular princes: there was also rebellion against the secular mastery in many places. . . .

The Reformation also had an essential influence on the Catholic Church: it had the reins of discipline drawn tighter, and had that which was most justly shameful disposed of, done away with; much that lay outside its rule, but with which it had previously maintained unconstrained relations, it now repudiated: it severed itself from the flourishing science, from the philosophy and the humanistic literature. . . . The Catholic world thus remained behind in cultural education, and sank into gross stupidity.

"Why Did the Reformation Limit Its Spread?"

[44]A major question, which now is to be answered, is: *Why did the Reformation in its spread limit itself to certain nations*? Why did it not permeate the whole Catholic world? —The Reformation originated in Germany and was accepted only by the pure Germanic peoples; outside of Germany it permeated also Scandinavia and England; the Romanic and Slavic nations kept themselves far away from it; even South Germany has adopted only a mixed Reformation. . . . [1536] In Austria, in Bavaria, in Bohemia, the Reformation had already made great progress; and though it is said that when the truth has once penetrated the hearts, it cannot be rooted out from them again, it was here indisputably driven out again, by force of arms, cunning, and persuasion.

The *Slavic* nations have not grasped the truth; . . . they, so far as we know, were *agricultural nations*; this brings with it, however, the relation of lord and serf; in agriculture the drives of nature are predominant; human industry, understanding, and subjective activity play on the

---

44. GW 27 [4] 1535–38 (~ GW 27 [1] 448–50; GW 27 [3] 1136–41; 1840, 505–8).

whole less of a role in this work; the Slavs did not arrive at that agility of the soul in itself, at the fundamental feeling of the subjective self, nor at the consciousness of universality—not at that which we designated earlier as state power; they therefore also could not take part in the arising freedom.

But also the *Romanic nations*: Italy, Spain, Portugal, and in part even France, were not permeated with the Reformation. In large part external force explains this, but one cannot invoke this alone, for when the spirit of a nation craves anything, no force can thus stop it; nor can it be said, as in the case of the Slavs, that these nations were deficient in cultural education; [1537] on the contrary, they were well in advance of the Germans in this respect. It *lies much more in the fundamental character of these nations* that they did not accept the Reformation. But what is the peculiarity of their characters, which became a hindrance to the freedom of the spirit? The pure innerness of the Germanic nation was the proper soil for the liberation of the spirit; but the Romanic nations have maintained the *fundamental character of the split*: they came of the mixture of the Roman and the Germanic world, and retained this heterogeneity always still in themselves. . . . In those nations the secular interest is split from the spiritual interest: they pursue their sensuous needs on the one side and on the other [1538] they practice their religious duties. The self-will is thus apart from the religion, and the religious is separate from the self of humans: this is the split.

"The Torture of the Uncertainty"

[45]The reconciliation of God and the world was at first *still in abstract form*, not yet developed into this system of customary ethical worldliness. About the appearance of this abstract form there is still something to say.

The reconciliation should first take place in the subject as such: the subject should gain the assurance that the divine Spirit dwells in him, that divine grace has thoroughly entered. The human is not what he ought to be from nature; he arrives at truth first through the process of cultural education. . . . The dogmatics wanted the human being to know that he is evil; . . . and then again that the good spirit dwells in him.

[1541] In that the reconciliation had thus assumed this abstract form, the human being caught in this torture came to know oneself as

---

45. GW 27 [4] 1540–43 (~ GW 27 [3] 1142–43; 1840, 510–14).

evil: the simplest hearts and most innocent natures were accustomed, in brooding, to follow the most secret workings of their hearts, for an exact examination of them; with this duty was also conjoined that of the opposite, however; namely that the human should also know that the good spirit dwells in him, that divine grace has made a breakthrough into him. The great distinction was not understood. . . . The torture of uncertainty entered, as to whether the good spirit dwelled in a human; it was even made into a duty, that one ought not to believe it. The whole process of reeducation had to be known in the subject oneself. An echo of this torture we have in much spiritual poetry from that time; the Psalms of David that have a similar character were then introduced into the hymns of churches. This angst, this brooding essence we see lasting for a long time as the fundamental character of Protestant religiosity. . . .

With this was connected another, wider, phenomenon. The human being was driven into the inner, abstract; and the spiritual became held to be divorced from the worldly: [1542] this divorce came now to the fore manifesting itself as the belief in a power of inner evil, as the inner power of the secular; this belief was common to the Protestant Church along with the Catholic. . . . This belief in the *evil* and the power of the evil brought in an infinite crowd of *trials for witchcraft* both in Catholic and Protestant countries. . . . [1543] Like an epidemic this delusion raged widely over Italy, Spain, France, Germany.

"The Relation of the New Church to Secularity"

[46]We spoke above of the relation *of the new church to secularity*: now we have only to consider it more closely. The spirit has to bring the reconciliation in itself to completion; its very self must go into itself; into this reconciliation and religiosity there now enters also the ethically customary. The divine ceases to have a fixed place in the beyond: it became recognized that it is the ethically customary and the legal that is the divine and the commandment of God—that as regards content, there is nothing higher, holier.

From this it followed that marriage has nothing higher above it— as before was celibacy. . . . There now also essentially disappeared the external relationship of the laity and clergy. The human being entered

---

46. GW 27 [4] 1538–40 (~ 1840, 508–10).

into the community, into the ethically customary relationships of society....

Unemployment is now no longer counted as sanctity, but what became seen as higher is for a person to rise from a state of dependence by activity and understanding and industry, [1539] making oneself independent.... Activity, being employed, is now much more the customarily ethical; industriousness is made into a principle of customary ethics. Trade, and the diligence of trade, is what is proper, and the obstacles from the side of the church have now vanished: for the church had pronounced it a sin to lend money at interest: but the necessity of the matter itself demanded it....

The third essential phase of sanctity in the Catholic Church, blind obedience, is now likewise sublated. Now, obedience to the laws of the state, as the rational element in volition and action, comes to be made the principle.... In this obedience, the human being is free, the particular yields to the universal; the human being has a conscience for oneself and obeys freely.... The reality of freedom experiences no contradiction from the side of the conscience: it can quietly develop with absolute justification....

[1540] The laws of freedom have still first to be built up into a system from that which is in and for itself right.... The spirit does not enter into this completeness immediately after the Reformation, for it must develop step by step.

[47]But what is especially important, following in the train of the Reformation, is the *struggle of the Protestant Church* for a political existence.... Without war the existence of the Protestants could not be secured, for the question was not the conscience as such, but political and private ownership, which had been taken possession of in contravention of the rights of the church, and whose restitution the church demanded. A relationship of absolute mistrust entered; absolute, because mistrust [522] bound up with the religious conscience was its basis.... The cause must be fought through from the ground up. This took place in the *Thirty Years' War*.... The struggle ends without an idea, without having won a foundational principle of thought, with the exhaustion of all, total desolation, where all the contending forces have been wrecked—it ends in letting parties simply take their course and maintain their

---

47. 1840, 521–22, 524–26 (~ GW 27 [1] 452–54, 458–60; GW 27 [4] 1551–52, 1554).

existence on the basis of external power. The issue is only of a *political* nature....

[524] Through the *Peace of Westphalia* the Protestant Church had been acknowledged as independent—to the terrible dismay and humiliation of the Catholic. This peace has often passed for the palladium of Germany, because it established the political constitution of Germany. But this constitution was in fact a confirmation of the private rights of the countries into which Germany had been broken up. As regards the purpose of a state, it involves no thought and no conception....

[525] But more broadly and later the Protestant Church completed its political guarantee, in that one of the states that belonged to it raised itself to the position of an independent European power. This power had to start a new life with Protestantism: it is *Prussia*, which, emerging at the end of the seventeenth century, owed, if not its origination, yet certainly its stability and secure individual establishment, to Frederick the Great; and in the Seven Years' War was found the struggle for this stabilizing and secure establishment.... [526] But Frederick the Great not only led Prussia to be one of the great state powers of Europe as a Protestant power, but he also became a philosopher-king, an altogether peculiar and unique phenomenon in the modern age. The English kings had been subtle theologians, contending for the principle of absolutism: Frederick on the contrary seized the Protestant principle in its secular side, and while he held off from religious controversies, and did not decide for one opinion or the other, he had the consciousness of the universal, which is the ultimate depth of the spirit, and is the self-conscious force of thinking.

[48]Frederick is a world-historical person, he is a known philosopher-king, because he grasped the universal thought of the state and was distinguished as the first ruler who first brought this principle into execution. It was he who held to the state's purpose and made it what counts, ceasing to bow to special interest insofar as it opposed the maintenance of the state. The actual foreign policy, the wars, of this period we can here call constitutional, in contrast with the previous, which were religious or else simply externally political.

[49]As regards first the *building of the state*, we observe the monarchy now consolidating itself, and the monarch becoming invested with the

---

48. GW 27 [1] 459 (~ GW 27 [2] 783; GW 27 [3] 1145-46; GW 27 [4] 1554; 1840, 529).
49. GW 27 [4] 1544-47, 1549 (~ 1840, 514-19).

state power.... [1545] With the rooting of the state force was also connected that what had been private property, now became state property: the rights of dynasties and barons became annulled, in that they must content themselves with state offices. This transformation of the rights of vassals into state duties took place in the several governments in various ways.... The concept of monarchy carries the implication that if it is to be self-sufficient, it must have an independent power; [1546] this latter it found in the *standing armies*; they were of the highest importance for the security of the center against the rebellion of individual subjects....

[1547] There came about now essentially an *interrelationship of the states over and against one another*. They involved themselves in many wars.... [1549] Common interests did arise, and the goal of the commonality was this: the maintenance of the particular states with their independence—or the *political balance of power*.... The maintenance of the balance of power thus became the more common goal, and this goal had thus now taken the place of the earlier common aim—that there should be one Christendom, whose center was the papal authority.

"The Enlightenment"

[50]The next matter to be discussed at this point is the form of culture that is constituted by the now emerging sciences. The church has not placed itself at the head of religious freedom, and similarly not at the head of the sciences—neither in the sciences of the experiences of thinking nor in those of external nature. It is especially in France and England that they first emerge.

[51]In the Protestant Church the principle of innerness, and the satisfaction in oneself [Wichern: freedom—but also, the belief in the innerness as the evil] had emerged; the same preoccupation with the innerness of the spirit had also found an inlet into the Catholic Church: here, however, through the Jesuits, a dialectic had come about through which everything particular was made to waver [Wichern: and through the Jesuits, the evil was perverted into good], so that [1555] at last for the consciousness there remained nothing left but the form of the universal....

---

50. GW 27 [1] 456 (~ GW 27 [2] 782; GW 27 [3] 1142).
51. GW 27 [4] 1554–57 (~ GW 27 [3] 1142–44; 1840, 526–30).

So: the ultimate peak of innerness is thinking; it is in itself free, in that it has as content the universal, which relates itself only to itself. The human being is not free insofar as he is not thinking, because then he relates himself to what is other, and is with that other.... The thinking is now the matter, to which the spirit has access; the spirit now recognizes that nature, that the world, must also have a reason in it, for God created it rationally: there is now a general interest in learning to know [1556] and in contemplating the objective world, and in discovering the laws of nature and their system. The universal in nature is the kinds, the species, the forces, the gravity, reduced to their appearances, and so forth. Thus the *empirical* became the science of the world: the empirical is on one side the perception, then also the law—in that is the interest in the universal.

The consciousness of the universal emerged in Descartes. In the pure Germanic nation the consciousness of the spirit emerged; in a Romanic nation the universal, the abstract, was first grasped; thereby emerged a new standpoint, a new interest; it was for the human beings as if God had but just created the sun, the moon, the stars, plants, animals, etc.—as if mass, its laws, were now first defined: for now did they first have an interest in them. With the laws of nature one was able to contend against the terrible superstition of the time, against all representations of alien, mighty powers over which one could be powerful only through magic. [Wichern: The human beings thus became free from nature through the acquaintance with the laws of nature.] Thinking then directed itself also to the spiritual side: one considered justice and customary ethics as grounded on the examined soil of the will of humans, whereas formerly it was viewed as the distant command of God: one now had an entirely different ground; in the first place, one had observations based on empirical experience (as in Grotius)—thus have [1557] the nations behaved; then one saw, as the source of what is present, the drives of humans that nature has planted in their hearts: sociality was supposed to be driving humans to sociability. Similarly, the law of the state was grasped, in accord with universal determinations.... The laws and the rights of nature one called reason: that these laws are what counts one called *Enlightenment*. From France it came over into Germany. A new world of conceptions proceeded therefrom.

[52]The spirit as thinker sets itself in relation with nature, in that it takes it as external, that it sets itself free from it, allows it validity,

---

52. GW 27 [1] 456–58 (~ GW 27 [2] 782–83; GW 27 [3] 1142–43).

does not fear for itself before it, knows how to reconcile itself with the external and how to find itself therein. To these sciences belong the knowledge of empirical, concrete existence, and moreover, the universal laws in nature. The universal seeks the spirit, which is here nearer to the understanding. These sciences of the understanding now maintain their validity, and it is said of them that they do honor to humanity. That they also do honor to God, this the church did not want to concede, and forced Galileo to recant, because his system [457] appeared a contradiction of what the Bible expresses. . . . The church in its old shape entered here as hostile toward the sciences.

On the other side, however, the church also had a rightful claim against the sciences, in saying that they lead to materialism and atheism. For nature itself and its laws were here asserted to be something ultimate, as a universal for itself, and one can add that God has created this nature, and these laws, but in these sciences the demand is for the insight into what has been discovered, and the transition to God is not demonstrated; the connection of these laws with God is not expressed, and this directly contradicts the principle of these sciences, to accept only what has been looked into. Thus a contradiction discovers itself here. This law, this cognition, has in the first place experience, sensible being, as its ground; and then this: the way in which this manifold of perception is grasped together in a universal, as law and species. In this universal the spirit is by itself; the sensuous material gives the matter, the point of departure; it is in the universal that the understanding recognizes itself, has made itself proportionate to the previously found, has elevated the manifold into a universal. Here the understanding has for itself this identity, that it itself is. So this is the activity of the understanding on the side of the sciences. . . .

This initially theoretical, this knowledge, turns itself to the practical, so that [458] this foundation, this law, is applied, as standard, as fixed perspective and presupposition. . . . The understanding with its knowledge has the dimension that it turns itself against the spiritually concrete, the religious. . . . The laws of nature are for it the true, and its method is that of efficient-cause-and-effect (der Consequenz). To its pregivens belong also the spiritual singularities, the drives, the naturalness of spirit. In that the understanding operates in its way, it is Enlightenment, against which religion cannot stand fast, in that the understanding stays with its presuppositions; for the principle of religion is that the natural is precisely the negative that is to be sublated, and further, that religion is speculative, and thereby opposes the abstract efficient-cause-and-effect of the understanding. [Griesheim: The religion has a speculative content, it is rational and, over and against the understanding, is not efficient-cause-and-effect, for reason is even that which grasps the separated as unity, as concrete; the understanding in contrast stops short; it says, "the finite is not infinite." Everything mysterious, that is, the speculative of religion, is for it a nothing.]

"The State, as an Aggregate of Many Singulars"

[53]The abstractly cultivated, understanding consciousness can let religion lie off on the side; but religion is the universal form in which the truth exists for the nonabstract consciousness. . . . That formal, individual will is now made the foundation; right in society is that which the law wills, and the will is as *singular*; thus the state, as aggregate of many singulars, is not an in and for itself substantial unity, not the truth of right in and for itself, to which [534] the will of the singulars must be conformed in order to be truer, in order to be freer will; instead, it emerges from the willing atoms, and each will is represented as immediately absolute. . . . One must therefore not speak in opposition when it is said that the Revolution received its first impulse from philosophy. But this philosophy is in the first instance only abstract thought, not the concrete comprehension of the absolute truth—and this is an immeasurable difference.

[54]With this principle of freedom we proceed to the last stage of world-history, [1558] to the form of our day.

---

53. 1840, 533–34 (~ GW 27 [4] 1560–61).
54. GW 27 [4] 1557–58 (~ GW 27 [2] 782).

CHAPTER 9

The Last Stage of World-History

[1]Experiences, sensuousness, drives, present only something transient; what ought to be just and customarily ethical must also be grounded in the *will*; but in the will as universal in itself; one must know what the will in itself is; the drives also belong to the will—they are a determinate willing, and can as such come into conflict with one another; they are themselves principles, but subordinate principles: the question is, what is the ultimate principle that is not subordinate, and not specific. The nonspecific is the will in itself; and the will in itself, in that it is one that is not specific, wills only itself. The will that is only for the sake of the will is the *pure free will*. This principle is now grasped in thinking. The will that wills itself, the free will, is known as the most inner ultimate, as the substantial ground of all justice. The will wills to produce an existent; in its purity, however, it is the same universal as thinking. This principle was established in France through Rousseau [Wichern: Rousseau established this, and later this will was also established in Germany—this is the Kantian philosophy as the theoretical reasoning where the I is the simple oneness of the self-consciousness of the *pure* will, is the reasoning of the will to the extent

---

1. GW 27 [4] 1558–60 (~ 1840, 530–33).

that it is not specific but wills only itself, only for the sake of duty and the just]: the human being is will, and one is free only insofar as one wills what one's will is. In Germany, theoretical reason then made itself count: the real will is the reasoning of the will; the human being shall will only one's freedom; one shall will to do [1559] one's duty, the right only for the sake of duty and right; thinking is absolute, and even so is the will. In my will is nothing alien; nothing can for me be established against it as authority; in my will I am to the purest extent brought back to myself. To this peak has consciousness come. The principle of willing and thinking is formal (especially as constructed by Kant): therein does not yet lie the content, what duty and right are; it is only form, no content. In any case categories full of content are also being dealt with: thus, for example, the question is asked—which are the needs of the society? The goal of the society is: maintaining the natural rights of human beings, as freedom of the will, equality (there is much that is similar, but there is one thing identical, for all humans are wills and their essence is to be as free wills).

One can ask: Why is freedom first grasped thus, in this abstract form?—In that reason is grasping itself, its first grasping is the unmediated form, which is the form of abstraction: the human being, having come to the independence of reason, takes it up at first in this simplicity.

There arises here moreover the question: Why is it the French who transitioned from theoretical to practical, whereas the Germans remained with the theoretical? One can say: . . . this formal principle stands over and against the concrete actuality; the Germans kept themselves tranquilly with it because they were reconciled in actuality: in this regard it is certainly to be remarked that only the Protestants could become tranquil with the legal and ethically customary actuality—among them, reconciliation was already present. In Germany the Enlightenment was on the side of theology; in France it directed itself against the church. In Germany, [1560] with regard to the secular, everything had through the Reformation already become better; those perverted institutions of celibacy, poverty, and laziness had already been done away with; there was no longer present that unspeakable injustice, nor that demand for blind servitude of the spirit; the kingship was not to be something abstractly divine, as in France through the anointment of the kings; instead it was legitimate, inasmuch as the choice of the land itself demanded it. Thus was the principle of thinking already so widely reconciled. Moreover, the Protestant world had in it the consciousness that for a further building up of justice the source was at hand in the principle of reconciliation, which already had its absolute authorization as principle of the religion.

"The French Revolution"

[2]The change was necessarily violent, because the reconfiguration was not undertaken by the government. It was not undertaken by the government because the court, the clergy, the nobility, the parliaments themselves, were unwilling to surrender the privileges they possessed, either for the sake of need or for the sake of right in and for itself; moreover, because the government, as the concrete central point of the state power, could not adopt as principle the abstract singular wills, and reconstruct the state on this basis; and finally, because it was Catholic, and therefore the concept of freedom, reason embodied in law, did not count as the ultimate absolute obligation, since they are separate from the holy and the religious conscience.

[3]Therefore, now a constitution was instituted on thought about right; on this ground all was to be based. As long as the sun had stood in the firmament, and the planets revolved around it, this had not been seen—that [1562] the human being on his own head, that is, on thinking, establishes oneself and builds up actuality in accord with thought. Anaxagoras had first said that *nous* governs the world; but now for the first time humanity had come to know that thought ought to govern spiritual actuality. This was accordingly a mastering dawn. A sublime emotion held sway in that time; an enthusiasm of the spirit thrilled the world, as if the divine now first came to actual reconciliation with the world.

"The Three Elements and Powers of the Living State"

[4]The three elements and powers of the living state are to be considered, though the details we leave to the lectures on the Philosophy of Right.

   a. The *laws* of rationality, of right in itself, the objective or the real freedom: here belong freedom of property and freedom of the

---

2. 1840, 535 (~ GW 27 [4] 1561).
3. GW 27 [4] 1561–62 (~ 1840, 535–36).
4. 1840, 536–38 (~ GW 27 [4] 1562–64).

person. All feudal unfreedom is hereby swept away.... To real freedom belongs further the freedom of commerce—that the human being is allowed to use one's force as one wills and has free admission to all state offices. These are the essential phases of real freedom, which do not rest on feeling—for feeling allows even for owning the body and slavery to remain—but on the thinking and the being-self-conscious of humans by their spiritual essence.

b. The actual activity of the law, however, is overall the *government*. The government is primarily formal carrying out of the law and maintaining the legitimacy of the same; in external relations it follows the aim of the state, which is the independence of the nation as an individuality over and against others; lastly, it has to provide domestically for the well-being of the state and all its classes [537]—and that is administration: for it is not enough that the citizen can pursue a trade, one must also make a profit from it.... So in the state there is a universality and an application of the same.... The making of the laws, the discovery and positive enactment of these determinations, is an application.

Further, then, is the decision and execution. Here now the question enters: Which shall be the will that decides? It is to the monarch that the ultimate decision comes: but in the state grounded on freedom, the many wills of the individuals also will to have a share in the decisions. The *many*, however, are *all*; and it appears empty propaganda, and a monstrous inconsistency, to allow only *few* to take part in those decisions, since each wills that he take part with his will in determining what ought to be law for him. The few ought to *represent* the many, but often only *despoil* them. Nor is the sway of the majority over the minority a less gross inconsistency.

c. This collision of the subjective wills leads then on to a third essential phase, to the essential phase of *disposition*, which is the inner willing of the laws—not only ethical custom, but the disposition that is the fixing of the laws and the constitution overall, and this is the highest duty of individuals, supporting these with their particular wills. There can be many opinions and views about laws, constitution, and government, but there must be a disposition to subordinate all these opinions to, and to give them up for, the substantiality of the state; moreover, nothing must be considered higher and more holy over and against this disposition toward the state; or, if religion is higher and more holy, there must be contained in it nothing differing from the state constitution or contrary to it. It does, indeed, [538] count as a foundational maxim of wisdom to keep the state laws and constitution entirely separate from the religion, since one fears bigotry and hypocrisy from a state religion; but while religion and state are also different in what they contain, they are still in their root one; and the laws have their highest verification in the religion.

Here it must be stated absolutely that with the Catholic religion no rational constitution is possible; for government and people must reciprocally possess that final guarantee of the disposition, and can have it only in a religion that is not opposed to the rational state constitution.

Plato in his *Republic* makes everything depend upon the government, and makes disposition into the principle, on account of which he lays the chief stress on the upbringing. Totally opposite is the modern theory, which refers everything to the individual will. In this, however, there is no guarantee that this will also has the just disposition by which the state can be maintained.

"The Remodeling of the State"

[5]In accord with these leading determinations we now have to trace the course of the *French Revolution* and the remodeling of the state by the concept of right.... The first constitution in France was the constituting of *kingship*: the monarch ought to stand at the head of the state, and on him in conjunction with his ministers ought to devolve the execution; the legislative body on the other hand ought to make the laws. But this constitution was thereby an internal contradiction; for the whole power of the administration was given to the legislative force: the budget, war and peace, the levying of the armed forces, were in the hands of the legislative chamber. Everything was set under law. The budget, however, is by its concept not at all law, for it renews itself [539] annually, and the force that it has to exert is ruling force. With this, moreover, is connected the indirect nomination of the ministry and officers of state, etc. The ruling was thus transferred to the legislative chamber, as in England in its Parliament.

---

5. 1840, 538–40 (~ GW 27 [4] 1564–67).

This constitution was further vitiated by absolute mistrust; the dynasty lay under suspicion, because it had lost its previous power, and the priests refused the oath. Ruling and constitution could not be maintained thus, and were ruined.

But ruling is always present. The question is therefore, whence did it emanate? In theory, it came from the people; in fact, still from the National Convention and its committees. Holding sway now are the abstract principles: *freedom*, and, as it exists in the subjective will—*virtue*. This virtue has now to rule in opposition to the many, who on account of their corruption and with their old attachments, or also on account of excess of freedom and passion, are unfaithful to virtue. Virtue is here a one-dimensional principle and makes a division only between those who have the disposition and those who do not. But disposition can only be recognized and judged of by disposition. *Suspicion* therefore holds sway; but virtue, as soon as it becomes suspected, is already condemned. Suspicion attained a terrible force and brought to the scaffold the monarch, whose subjective will was in fact the Catholic religious conscience. By Robespierre the principle of virtue was set up as the highest, and one can say that for this man virtue was a serious matter. What held sway then was *virtue* and *terror*; for subjective virtue, whose ruling is based simply on disposition, brings with it the most frightful tyranny. It exercises its power without legal forms, and its punishment is accordingly only simple: *death*. This tyranny had to go to ground; for all inclinations, all interests, rationality itself, was against this frightfully [540] logical freedom, which in its concentration emerged so fanatically.

There came in again an organized rule, like the one earlier, except that the chief and monarch is now a changeable Directory of Five, which may indeed form a moral, but not an individual, unity. Suspicion again held sway under them, the ruling was in the hands of the legislative assemblies; this therefore had the same fate, of downfall, for it had proved for itself the absolute need for a ruling *force*.

Napoleon directed it as military force, and then established himself as an individual will again at the head of the state: he knew how to hold sway, and soon settled the internal affairs. What was left of the lawyers, ideologues, and men of principle, he scattered—and what held sway was no more mistrust, but instead respect and fear. With the terrible power of his character he then turned himself to external affairs, subjected all Europe, and spread his liberal institutions everywhere. No greater victories were ever gained, no policy fuller of genius was ever pursued; but also never did the powerlessness of victory appear in a clearer light than then. The disposition of the peoples, that is, their religious and that of their nationality, ultimately brought down this colossus, and in France again a constitutional monarchy, with the "Charte" [*Charte constitutionnelle du 4 juin 1814*] as its foundation, was erected.

Here again, however, appeared the antithesis between the disposition and the mistrust. . . . A fifteen years' farce was played. For although the "Charte" was the universal banner, and both parties had sworn to it, yet the disposition on the one side was a Catholic one, which made it as a matter of conscience to do away with the existing institutions. So again a breach took place, and the government was destroyed.

"Liberalism as the Atomizing Principle"

[6]Finally, after forty years of war and immeasurable [541] confusion, an old heart might congratulate itself on seeing an end to it, and satisfaction making an entrance. But, although one chief point is balanced, there remains on the one side always that breach on the side of the Catholic principle, and on the other side that breach from the subjective will. In regard to the latter, there is maintained still the one-sidedness according to which the universal will ought to be also the *empirical* universal, that is, that the individuals as such should rule, or should take part in the regime. Not satisfied that what counts is rational rights, freedom of the person and of property, that there is an organization of the state, and that civil-bourgeois life is in its sphere and conducts business by itself, and in which those with understanding hold sway, having influence on the people and their trust, *liberalism* sets up in opposition to all this the atomizing principle of the singular will: everything should emanate from its express power, and express singular willing. With this formalism of freedom, with this abstraction, they allow no fixity of organization to emerge. Freedom thereby opposes the ministering of the government by particulars, for they are particular will, and so willfulness. The will of the many expels the ministry, and the previous opposition now moves in; but the latter, inasmuch as it now is the government, has in its turn the many against it. Thus agitation and unrest are perpetuated. This collision, this knot, this problem, is that point at which history now stands, and that it has to solve in the future times.

---

6. 1840, 540–41 (~ GW 27 [4] 1566–67).

"The French Revolution Is World-historical"

⁷According to its content the French Revolution is world-historical; the struggle of the formalism must certainly be distinguished from it. As regards the outward spread, all modern states were conquered, and thereby became open to the French principle, to the atomistic principle, to the so-called liberalism; but everywhere this liberalism was forced into bankruptcy. First, the firm from France was made bankrupt in Spain, then in Italy, then Germany, etc. —Yes! in Spain, in Italy, the liberalism was shattered yet a second time, when it wanted to validate itself through its inner condition; liberalism ran through the whole Romanic world; but this latter, already split by Catholicism, has sunk back into its old condition.

⁸For it is a false principle that the chains on right and freedom can be broken without the freeing of the conscience—that there can be a Revolution without Reformation.

⁹The revolutions and the wars of modern times have brought about changes of state constitutions, and these changes have come from below. These revolutions have their origin in thought. For it is the cultural education by thought that now makes itself firmer, establishes universal conceptions as ultimate, and compares them to what has been. The highest determination that thought can find in this regard is that of the freedom of will. Other fundamental principles, of blessed happiness, etc., are more and more indeterminate. Freedom of the will [460] alone is determinate in and for itself. And thought has now grasped the determination of freedom of the will as what is highest in actuality. . . . Freedom of the will is freedom of the spirit in affairs, in directing itself to what is actual. Freedom of the will emerges from the principle of the Evangelical Church. However, this freedom of the will, of which the state is the actualization, is to be distinguished from the will as particular. Freedom of will is here the same as that which is the freedom of the spirit overall in accord with its essence. . . .

In the Romance lands the overthrow of the throne has so far again come to naught. With these revolutions it must be emphasized that here political revolutions without change in religion were made. But without a change in religion, no true political change can take place.

---

7. GW 27 [4] 1567 (~ 1840, 541–42).
8. 1840, 542.
9. GW 27 [1] 459–61 (~ GW 27 [3] 1145–46).

The freedom of spirit, the principles of freedom, which in these lands [461] were made principles of the constitution, are themselves quite abstract, in that they emerged in opposition to a positive state of affairs, and not from the freedom of spirit as it is in the religion. [Griesheim: Hence this is not the freedom of spirit that is in religion, and that is the divine and authentic freedom.] The lands of the Evangelical Church have thus already made their revolution, for in them what is present, what ought to happen, has taken place, through general cultural education, peacefully. There is here no absolute opposition to the thought of the concrete goal of the state; but in the Romanic lands, what opposes the goal of the state is so legitimated that it is capable of mounting an absolute resistance to it.... The constitutions of the evangelical states are diverse, but in all of them the essential principle is present—that what ought to count proceeds from the universal goal of the state, and is thereby justified. This is, abstractly, the necessary determination.

"What Englishmen Call Their Liberty"

[10]*England*, with great exertions, has maintained itself on its old foundations; the English *constitution* maintained itself amid the general convulsion, though this lay so much nearer, even within itself, through the public Parliament, through that habit shared by all classes of assembling in public meeting, through the free press: there was an easy possibility of bringing about an introduction of the French principles of liberty and equality among all classes of the people.... Was the English constitution already so entirely a constitution of freedom—was that foundation already so completely realized in it, that the French principles could no longer excite opposition or even interest? The English nation approved of the emancipation of France; but knew with pride its own constitution and its own freedom, and instead of taking on what was foreign, maintained its accustomed hostility, and was soon involved in a popular war with France.

England's constitution is a complex of mere *particular rights* and special privileges: the ruling is essentially administrative, that is, guaranteeing the interests of all particular orders and classes; and these particular churches, communities, counties, societies, take care of themselves, so that the government, strictly speaking, has nowhere less to do than in

---

10. 1840, 543–45 (~ GW 27 [3] 1140–41; GW 27 [4] 1568–69).

England. This is the leading feature of what Englishmen call their freedom, and is the antithesis of a centralization of administration as exists in France, where down to the smallest village the mayor is named by the ministry or their agents. Nowhere can people less tolerate free action on the part of others than in France: [544] the ministry combines in itself all administrative force, to which, on the other hand, the Chamber of Deputies lays claim. In England, on the contrary, every community, every subordinate sphere and association has its part to perform. The universal interest is in this way concrete, and the particular is therein known and willed. These institutions of the particular interests leave no place for a universal system. Therefore also abstract and universal principles do not speak to the English and are addressed to inattentive ears. These particular interests have their positive rights, which date from the antique times of feudal law, and have preserved themselves in England more than in any other land. With the highest inconsistency, there is at the same time the highest injustice; and of institutions of real freedom there are nowhere fewer than precisely in England. In private right, in freedom of property, they are incredibly backward: one thinks of primogeniture, involving the purchasing or otherwise providing military or ecclesiastical appointments for the younger sons.

The Parliament rules, although the English are unwilling to allow that such is the case. Now it is worthy of remark that what has been always regarded as the period of the corruption of a republican people is here the case; namely, the choice of parliament is by means of bribery. But this also is called freedom by them—that one sells one's vote, and that one can purchase for oneself a seat in Parliament.

But this utterly complete inconsistency and corrupt state of things has nevertheless the advantage that it grounds the possibility of ruling, that is, a majority of men in Parliament who are statesmen, who from their youth have devoted themselves to state business and have worked and lived in it. And the nation has the correct sense and understanding to recognize that there must be ruling, and is therefore willing to give its confidence to a unified body of men who [545] have had experience in ruling; and then the sense for particularity recognizes also the universal particularity of knowledge, of experience, of the facility, which the aristocracy who devote themselves to such interests possess. This is quite opposed to the sense of principles and abstraction that everyone can acquire, and which is in all constitutions and charters.

It is a question to what extent the reform in Parliament now afoot, if consistently carried out, will still leave the possibility of a government.

England's material existence is based on commerce and industry, and the English have undertaken the great determination of being the missionaries of *civilization* to the entire world; for their commercial spirit drives them to traverse every sea and every land, to form connections with barbarous peoples, to awaken in them wants and industry, and above all to establish among them the conditions necessary to commerce, namely the relinquishment of a life of violent force, the respect for property, and hospitality to strangers.

"Germany's Law of Rights"

[11]In Germany, a high essential phase is the law of rights, which was partly in any case allowed in by the French conquest, in that the defects of the earlier institution came especially to light. The feudal obligations have become sublated, although not through plunder as in France; the principles of freedom of property, of the person, etc. have been made into fundamental principles. Every citizen has access to offices of state, though skill and knowledge are necessary conditions. As regards the ruling force and the offices, the personal decision of the monarch stands at the peak; a subjective will, though it can be called willful, must exist; also there remains for him on the whole little that is complicated to decide, since the entire organization is determined through the laws; in regard to what is substantial, what is left to the sole decision of the monarch is not much to be concerned about. . . . It is by the officers, as has already been said, that the determinations are made, on the basis of knowledge, practice, and experience: [1570] those whom the Greeks called *hoi aristoi*—those whose cultural education is scientific and who have the moral will. Finally, as regards disposition: as has been already said, through the Protestant Church there has been brought about the reconciliation of the religion with the law of the state; there is nothing holy, no religious conscience, that would be at odds with or would oppose the secular justice.

Conclusion

[12]This is the point to which consciousness has come. These are the chief essential phases of the form in which the principle of freedom

---

11. GW 27 [4] 1569–70 (~ 1840, 545–47).
12. GW 27 [4] 1570 (~ 1840, 546–47).

has actualized itself; world-history is the development of the concept of freedom; but objective freedom demands the subjugation of the contingent will; the side of the subjective will is only formal—the insight: when the law is in itself rational, then the insight can correspond to it, and then the essential phase of subjective freedom is also at hand. . . .

The development of the principle of the spirit [Wichern: of world-history] is the true theodicy; the concept has completed itself in history, and this is the honor of God, for God has in it actualized and revealed himself.

[13]The consciousness of our day no longer consists in a simple devotion; religion has given humanity liberation and self-actualization. This consists in the ethical custom in the life of the state. The philosophy of history can in this way be called the justification of God: the spirit sought itself in the entire course of history; it came finally to itself; [1147] it knows itself, and gives actuality to this high consciousness. How highly this self-consciousness is to be treasured can be easily seen from the great efforts of the spirit that it gave to itself in order to know and to find itself. The world-spirit must possess time in order to work through itself, and must expend, give up, entire peoples, in order to be able to have the truth, and its own determination, and its very self. The spirit is only that into which it makes itself; as spirit being in itself, it is only unmediated. But it has the seed of its progress in itself; to develop this is its determination; and the necessary path of steps of that, we have sought to show in general in the course of these lectures.

---

13. GW 27 [3] 1146–47 (~ GW 27 [2] 785).

Glossary

English to German

activation Bethätigung

actuality; actual; to actualize; actualization (*see also* reality) Wirklichkeit; wirklich; verwirklichen; Verwirklichung

administration Verwaltung

ambition Ehrgeiz

antithesis (*see* opposition or antithesis)

appearance as semblance Schein

appetite, desire Begierde

bad (*see also* evil) übel

baseness Niederträchtigkeit

bourgeois (*see also* citizen; civil) Bürger, bürgerlich

boyhood Knabenalter

caprice Beleiben

cause (*see also* efficient cause) Ursache

chance or contingency Zufall

character Beschaffenheit

charity Mildthätigkeit

charming anmutig

cheerfulness Heiterkeit

childhood Kindesalter

citizen, citizenship (*see also* bourgeois) Bürger, Bürgerschaft

civil (*see also* bourgeois) bürgerlich

class, standing Ständ

collectivity Gesammtheit

commandment Gebot

commerce or business Handel or Gewerbe

communitarianism Gemeinsamkeit

community Gemeinschaft, Gemeinde

concept Begriff

conception (*see also* representation [mental], idea, depiction) Gedanke

concrete existence (*see also* existence) Dasein or Daseyn

configuration (*see* shape)
conflict Zwiespalt
conscience Gewissen
consciousness Bewusstsein
constitution Verfassung
contentment (*see also* happiness) Beruhrigung
contradiction Widerspruch
conviction überzeugung
corporate bodies Korporationen
corruption; to corrupt Verderbung or Verbildung; verderben
courage; courageous Tapferkeit; tapfer
creative; to create schöpferisch; erschaffen
crime Verbrechen
cultural education; to educate culturally Bildung; bilden
culture Cultur or Kultur
cunning List
decline or fall; to decline or fall Untergang; untergehen
deserving Verdienstes
destiny Schicksal
determination or determinacy or directedness; determinate or determined; to determine Bestimmung; bestimmt; bestimmen
development Entwicklung
discipline (*see also* upbringing, educating, disciplining) Zucht
disposition Gesinnung
drive (noun), impulse Drang or Trieb
duty Pflicht
education (*see* cultural education; upbringing, educating, disciplining)
efficient cause (*see also* cause) Consequenz
empire Reich
empirical (noun) Erfahrung
end, goal, purpose Ende or Zweck
end-goal Endzweck
end-in-itself Selbstzweck
enthusiasm Begeisterung
essence Wesen
essential phase Moment
eternal; eternity ewige; Ewigkeit
ethical custom or customary ethics; ethically customary (*see also* morality) Sittlichkeit or Sitte; sittlich
evangelical or Protestant evangelisch

GLOSSARY 273

evil (*see also* bad) Böse
existence (*see also* concrete existence) Existenz
faith Glaube
feeling (*see* sentiment)
fidelity Treue
figure (*see* shape)
force (*see also* power) Gewalt
genius Genie
German Deutsch
Germanic Germanisch
goal (*see* end)
government (*see* rule)
guilt (*see* responsibility)
habituation, habitual routine Gewohnheit
happiness (*see also* contentment) Glück, Glückseligkeit
history Geschichte or Historie
holding sway (*see* mastery)
humane (noun) Humane
humility; humiliation or humbling Demuth; Demüthigung
idealism or ideality Idealität
inclination Neigung
individuality (*see also* single) Individualität
infinite; finite unendlich; endlich
innocence (*see* responsibility)
interest Interesse
intimation; to intimate Vermutung; vermuten
ironizing Ironisierin
justice or right or law; lawful justice; rightful or just (*see also* law) Recht; Gerechtigkeit; rechtlich
kingship (*see also* monarchy) Königtum
law (*see also* justice) Gesetz
mastery, holding sway; to hold sway over Herrlichkeit or Herrschaft; herrschen or beherrschen
matter Stoffe or Stuffe, or Materie
mature age Mannesalter
member (organic) Glied
mission Beruf
modesty Bescheidenheit
monarchy (*see also* kingship) Monarchie
morality (*see also* ethical custom) Moralität

GLOSSARY

need Bedürfnis
obscure trübe
occupation Geschäft
offscourings Abschaum
old age Greisenalter
opposition or antithesis Gegensatz or Entgegensetzung
oppressor; to oppress Unterdrücker; unterdrucken
ought to; the ought sollen; Sollen
overall überhaupt
particularity; particular or special Besonderheit, Particularität; besonder
passion Leidenschaft
peasant Knecht
a people Völk
perception Wahrnehmung
perfectibility Perfectibilität
personhood Persönlichkeit
to pervert verkehren
pious; piety fromme; Fromheit
polyarchy Polyarchie
potency Vermögen
power (*see also* force) Macht
priesthood, clergy Geistlichkeit
problem or task Aufgabe
Protestant (*see* evangelical)
to prove erweisen
providence; providential care Vorsehung; Vorsorge
purpose (*see* end)
reality; real; to realize (*see also* actuality) Realität; real or reel; realisieren
reason Vernunft
recognition; to recognize Anerkennung; anerkennen
reconciliation Versöhnung
remorse Zerknirschung
representation (mental), idea, depiction Vorstellung
representation (political); to represent Vertretung; vertreten
responsibility or guilt; innocence Schuld; Unschuld
revaluation Umwälzung
revelation; revealed Offenbarung; offenbar
right (*see* justice)
ritual worship Cultus
rule or government; to rule or to govern Regierung; regieren
satisfaction Befriedigung

GLOSSARY

secularity or worldliness; secular or worldly Weltlichkeit; weltlich
sentiment or feeling or temperament or heart; heartfelt Gemüt or Empfindung, Herz; gemüthlich
separation, division, differentiation Trennung
serfdom Leibeigenschaft
seriousness Ernsthaftigkeit
service; servitude Dienste; Dienstbarkeit
shape or figure or configuration Gestalt
shrewdness Klugheit
sin Sünde
single, singular, individual (*see also* individuality) einzeln
sociability Geselligkeit
sociality Socialität
sorcerer; sorcery Zauberer; Zauberei
sorrow Schmerz
soundness Gediegenheit
species Gattung
spirit Geist
state of innocence Stand der Unschuld
state of nature Naturzustand
strength Kraft
sublation; to sublate Aufhebung; aufheben
sublimity Erhabenheit
subsistence; to subsist or to consist Bestehen; bestehen
substance Substanz
thought; to think Danke; denken
understanding Verstand
universality; universal Allgemeinheit; allgemein
upbringing, educating, disciplining; to bring up or educate or discipline (*see also* cultural education; discipline) Erziehung; erziehen
valid; validity; to count as valid gültig; Gültiges or Geltung; gelten
virtue Tugend
volitional willenvollen
will Wille
willfulness Willkür or Willkühr
wisdom Weisheit
world-history Weltgeschichte
world-spirit Weltgeist
worldview Weltanschauung
yearning Sehnsucht
youth (age of) Jünglingsalter

GLOSSARY

German to English

Abschaum offscourings
Allgemeinheit; allgemein universality; universal
Anerkennung; anerkennen recognition; to recognize
anmutig charming
Aufgabe problem or task
Aufhebung; aufheben sublation; to sublate
Bedürfnis need
Befriedigung satisfaction
Begeisterung enthusiasm
Begierde appetite, desire
Begriff concept
Beleiben caprice
Beruf mission
Beruhrigung (*see also* Glück) contentment
Beschaffenheit character
Bescheidenheit modesty
Besonderheit; besonder (*see also* Particularität) particularity; particular or special
Bestehen; bestehen subsistence; to subsist or to consist
Bestimmung; bestimmt; bestimmen determination or determinacy or directedness; determinate or determined; to determine
Bethätigung activation
Bewusstsein consciousness
Bildung; bilden (*see also* Cultur or Kultur) cultural education; to educate culturally
Böse (*see also* übel) evil
Bürger, Bürgerschaft; bürgerlich a citizen or a bourgeois; civil or bourgeois
Consequenz (*see also* Ursache) efficient cause
Cultur or Kultur culture
Cultus ritual worship
Danke; denken thought; to think
Dasein or Daseyn (*see also* Existenz) concrete existence (literally, there-to-be)
Demuth; Demüthigung humility; humiliation or humbling
Deutsch (*see also* Germanisch) German
Dienste; Dienstbarkeit service; servitude
Drang (*see also* Trieb) drive (noun)
Ehrgeiz ambition
einzeln (*see also* Individualität) single, singular, individual
Empfindung (*see also* Gemüt) feeling or sentiment

Ende (*see also* Zweck) end
Endzweck end-goal
Entwicklung development
Erfahrung empirical (noun)
Erhabenheit sublimity
Ernsthaftigkeit seriousness
erweisen to prove
Erziehung; erziehen (*see also* Zucht) upbringing or educating or disciplining; to bring up or educate or discipline
evangelisch evangelical or Protestant
ewige; Ewigkeit eternal; eternity
Existenz (*see also* Dasein or Daseyn) existence
fromme; Fromheit pious; piety
Gattung species
Gebot commandment
Gedanke (*see also* Vorstellung) conception
Gediegenheit soundness
Gegensatz or Entgegensetzung opposition or antithesis
Geist spirit
Geistlichkeit priesthood, clergy
Gemeinsamkeit communitarianism
Gemeinschaft or Gemeinde community
Gemüt; gemüthlich (*see also* Empfindung) feeling or heartfelt feeling; heartfelt
Genie genius
Germanisch (*see also* Deutsch) Germanic
Gesammtheit collectivity
Geschäft occupation
Geschichte (*see also* Historie) history
Geselligkeit sociability
Gesetz (*see also* Recht) law
Gesinnung disposition
Gestalt shape or figure or configuration
Gewalt (*see also* Macht) force
Gewerbe (*see also* Handel) commerce
Gewissen conscience
Gewohnheit habituation or habitual routine
Glaube faith
Glied member (organic)
Glück or Glückseligkeit happiness
Greisenalter old age

gültig; Gültiges; gelten valid; validity; to count as valid
Handel (*see also* Gewerbe) commerce or business
Heiterkeit cheerfulness
Herrlichkeit or Herrschaft; herrschen or beherrschen mastery or holding sway; to master or hold sway over
Historie (*see also* Geschichte) historical record and scholarship
Humane humane (noun)
Idealität idealism or ideality
Individualität (*see also* einzeln) individuality
Interesse interest
Ironisierin ironizing
Jünglingsalter age of youth
Kindesalter childhood
Klugheit shrewdness
Knabenalter boyhood
Knecht peasant
Königtum (*see also* Monarchie) kingship
Korporationen corporate bodies
Kraft strength
Kultur (*see* Cultur or Kultur)
Kultus (*see* Cultus)
Leibeigenschaft serfdom
Leidenschaft passion
List cunning
Macht (*see also* Gewalt) power
Mannesalter mature age
Materie (*see also* Stoffe or Stuffe) matter
Mildthätigkeit charity
Moment essential phase
Monarchie (*see also* Königtum) monarchy
Moralität (*see also* Sittlichkeit or Sitte; Sollen) morality
Naturzustand state of nature
Neigung inclination
Niederträchtigkeit baseness
Offenbarung; offenbar revelation; revealed
Particularität (*see also* Besonderheit) particularity
Perfectibilität perfectibility
Persönlichkeit personhood
Pflicht duty
Polyarchie polyarchy

GLOSSARY

Realität; real or reel; realisieren (*see also* Wirklichkeit) reality; real; to realize
Recht; Gerechtigkeit; rechtlich (*see also* Gesetz) right, justice, law; lawful justice; rightful, just
Regierung; regieren rule or government; to rule or to govern
Reich empire
Schein appearance as semblance
Schicksal destiny
Schmerz sorrow
schöpferisch; erschaffen creative; to create
Schuld; Unschuld responsibility or guilt; innocence
Sehnsucht yearning
Selbstzweck end-in-itself
Sittlichkeit or Sitte; sittlich (*see also* Moralität; Sollen) ethical custom or customary ethics (mores); ethically customary
Socialität sociality
sollen; Sollen (*see also* Moralität; Sittlichkeit or Sitte) ought to; the ought
Ständ class, standing
Stand der Unschuld state of innocence
Stoffe or Stuffe (*see also* Materie) matter
Substanz substance
Sünde sin
Tapferkeit; tapfer courage; courageous
Trennung separation, division, differentiation
Treue fidelity
Trieb (*see also* Drang) impulse, drive
trübe obscure
Tugend virtue
übel (*see also* Böse) bad
überhaupt overall
überzeugung conviction
Umwälzung revaluation
unendlich; endlich infinite; finite
Unterdrücker; unterdrucken oppressor; to oppress
Untergang; untergehen decline or fall; to decline or fall
Ursache (*see also* Consequenz) cause
Verbildung (*see also* Verderbung; verderben) corruption
Verbrechen crime
Verderbung; verderben (*see also* Verbildung) corruption; to corrupt
Verdienstes deserving
Verfassung constitution

verkehren to pervert
Vermögen potency
Vermutung; vermuten intimation; to intimate
Vernunft reason
Versöhnung reconciliation
Verstand understanding
Vertretung; vertreten representation (political); to represent
Verwaltung administration
Völk a people
Vorsehung; Vorsorge providence; providential care
Vorstellung representation (mental), idea, depiction
Wahrnehmung perception
Weisheit wisdom
Weltanschauung worldview
Weltgeist world-spirit
Weltgeschichte world-history
Weltlichkeit; weltlich secularity or worldliness; secular or worldly
Wesen essence
Widerspruch contradiction
Wille will
willenvollen volitional
Willkür or Willkühr willfulness
Wirklichkeit; wirklich; verwirklichen; Verwirklichung (*see also* Realität) actuality; actual; to actualize; actualization
Zauberer; Zauberei sorcerer; sorcery
Zerknirschung remorse
Zucht (*see also* Erziehung) discipline
Zufall chance or contingency
Zweck goal, end, purpose
Zwiespalt conflict

Index

"Africa proper" (sub-Saharan), 42–46, 115
aristocracy. *See* constitutionalism
art, fine art (in general), 6, 29, 123, 172–73, 239
Asia. *See* East

Bible, 4–8, 57, 78n, 93, 105, 107, 204, 206, 208, 249; 1 Corinthians, 4–5; Book of Wisdom, 105, 106; Deuteronomy, 109; Galatians, 112, 199; Genesis, 1–2, 6–8, 204–5; John, 4–5, 153, 200, 206; Leviticus, 179n; Luke, 238; Mark, 248; Matthew, 207, 248; Prophets, 204; Proverbs, 62; Psalms, 204, 252

China: art, 62–63, 84; ethical customs, centered on respect for elders, 28–29, 56–59, 60–62, 65–67, 74, 79, 88, 93, 99, 180; geography, 46, 47, 91–92; nonstate religions of Buddha and Lamas, 66–68; sciences, 28, 62, 64n18, 67; state, lawful, homogeneous patriarchy, 54, 56–58, 60–61, 70, 93, 97–98, 130; state religion, patriarchal with sorcery and many spirits, 63–67, 98, 117, 128
Christianity, 6–7, 108n, 112; Christ, 5n, 88, 200, 202n, 206, 236–37, 245, 247; dogma, 201–2, 207–8, 235; emergence under Roman despotism, 112, 195, 199–206, 208; and ethical custom, 210–12; foundation of rational citizen's heart, 214–15, 249, 263; human as image of God, 199, 202–3, 210, 235; Protestantism superior to Catholicism, 39–40, 243–47, 249–50, 253, 261, 263, 266–67, 269
classes, economic and social, 10, 18, 24, 41, 54, 60–61, 72–78, 81, 84–86, 98–99, 115–16, 135, 137, 158, 188, 212, 222n, 226, 242–43, 262, 267; absent in orient, 53, 61, 71, 74
conscience, 7, 246; feudal rulers, 243; goes with morality, 10; Greece, 136, 151, 155, 170; meaning of, 27, 48, 151, 170; in rational state freed, and foundation of citizenship, 33, 214–15, 231, 266; refounded by Luther, 249, 253, 269; replaced by confessor in late Catholicism, 246; makes hereditary monarchy necessary, 152, 168, 212, 215; untouched by clamor of world-history, 27. *See also* morality
constitutionalism, 34; aristocracy, 34–35, 48, 54, 60, 151–54, 187–88, 212; Catholicism makes rational constitution impossible, 263, 266–67; democracy, 34, 48, 150–54, 187; monarchy, 35, 41, 60, 135–36, 152, 212, 222n, 262, 265, 269; republic, 23, 35, 110n
cultural education, 13, 15, 18, 30–31, 33, 36, 46, 62; deficient among Catholics and Slavs, 250–51; defined, 249; evolves through bondage of spirit, 221–22, 230; today establishes universal conceptions as ultimate, 214, 266–67

democracy. *See* constitutionalism
duty, 8n, 10, 14, 24; and Christ, 153, 207; essential to good will as moral will, 153; to fatherland, 8, 24, 16; highest is knowing and loving God, 4, 7; to humanity, 84; in rational state, integrates ethical custom with morality and universality, 8n, 28, 53; religious, 251; to state, 255; as universal justice, world history's ultimate goal, 159n, 260. *See also* conscience; morality

281

INDEX

East, Asia: "childhood" of history, dawning of self-consciousness, 46–47; contrast with West or Europe, 115, 151, 156–57; no consciousness of individual freedom, 16, 48, 53, 131, 147; state patriarchal-theocratic, 49, 53, 151–52, 156, 180; unifies unfree spirit with nonhuman nature in "natural spirituality," 53, 107–8, 211, 225

Egypt: ethical customs, 115–17, 126–27; mediates transition from Persia to Greece, which solves riddle, 56, 114–15, 122, 128–32, 142–43; religion, 117–21, 125–26; spirit of, as riddle, 114–15, 118, 122–23, 126–31, 142–43, 147

end-goal of world history, 2, 4–5, 8, 10, 15–23, 52, 201–2, 220–21, 248

England, the English: commercial and industrial spirit makes them missionaries of civilization, 269; constitution a complex of particular rights and privileges with no universal principles, in contrast to French, 267–68; parliament corrupted by bribery but thereby enabling lifelong statesmen, 60, 268; today, 12; tremendous wealth and horrible poverty, 41, 60

ethical custom (in general), 5n, 9–10, 12, 14, 24–26, 36, 39–40, 47, 50, 165, 207; as disposition like a force of nature, 28, 30, 50, 52–53, 262–65; dissolution of, 14, 25–27, 33, 167–74; guaranteed in hearts by Protestantism, 19, 212, 270; opposed to nature of spirit, whose drive is to change, 117, 171–72; in rational state integrated with morality as a matter of positive law, 8n, 28, 212, 217, 262–63

Europe: contrasted with America, 39–42; contrasted with Asia and East, 84, 115; has enslaved Africans, 43; has dominated India, 75; manifold geography with each type offset by others, 47–48; Mediterranean Sea leads all together—without it, world history would not exist, 47–48; nations have arisen from ethnic intermingling, 134; soil frees humans more from forces of nature, 47

family: contrasted with true state, 30–31, 36–37, 59; earliest form of ethically customary life, 36; family piety essential to rational state, 37; love for, 19; patriarchy characteristic of East, 46, 49, 136; patriarchy defined, 37; a whole like state, but unified by love, 30, 37

freedom (in general): arose among Greeks, but only as freedom for some, 17; consciousness of, defined, 28; expresses proper nature of humans, 17, 155; lacking in East, 16–17; positively realized in obedience to rational laws, 29–31; promoted by commerce, 47; rational versus natural, 35; religious, 39; as subjective inwardness, incompatible with democracy, 153, 155; realization is end-goal of history, 52; substantial versus subjective, 48; its unity with necessity, 24

geography, an essential cause of history, with climate, but higher cause is spirit, 37–38, 45–46

Germanic peoples: corruption of Church, leading to Reformation, 244–49, 251–55, 259, 266; Crusades, 235–38; Enlightenment, 255–57, 259; feudal system, 221–22, 229–32; French Revolution, 258, 263–64; history's old age, not as weakness but as maturity, with three major periods, 51, 219–21, 228–29; Renaissance and emergence of modern state, 239–44

God: death of God essential, 106, 114–15, 150, 200; in East, God in our sense, as essence of thought beyond nature, is not present, 49, 54, 117; as end-goal of history, 16; fully known today, as unity of divine and human nature, 4–5, 7–8, 199, 235; as providence, 3–4, 7, 10, 16, 145–46; as rational creator, 256; true theodicy is philosophy of world-history, 270

Greece: "adolescence" of spirit, needing repression by Roman "maturity," 49, 131–32; Athens superior as more individualistic, 8n, 22, 31, 62, 127–28, 138n, 150, 153, 155, 158–62, 164–65, 167–68, 173, 177, 193, 212; citizenship without duty, 147, 151–52, 161n; compared with Christianity, 117, 135,

149, 199; democracy, defined, 151; democracy requires single person or council, thus contradicts itself, can only be of short duration, 158-59, 164, 168, 173; emergence of free self-consciousness provoked doubt of laws, ethical customs, religion, led by philosophers, 169-71; ethical custom of beautiful individuality, 56, 88, 114-15, 127-31, 139-40, 147-49, 158, 160-61, 164-65, 172; Fate, 221-22; geography, 48, 133-34, 140; greatest opposition was between Athenian and Spartan versions, 156-67; has been, and can only be, in small states of Greece, 15, 116, 132-33, 150-51, 187; heroic royal dynasties, 135-37, 158-59; lacking conscience, 151, 155, 170; lacking infinite subjectivity, 147, 161n, 166, 170, 172-73; lacking morality, 152-53, 155, 165, 170; Montesquieu's "virtue" as foundation, 155; oratory crucial, 154-55, 169; poet finds divine meaningfulness in nature, 141-42, 146-47, 183-84; religion compared with biblical, 111, 138, 141-46, 183-84; religion honored both for itself and as human art, 6, 148-49; slavery pervasive, 17, 48; Sparta as powerfully stable but inferior to Athens, 16, 24, 138, 155-56, 162-64, 167-68, 182, 212; still rooted in natural, as habit, thus lacking self-determining spirituality, 147-49, 151-53, 155, 161n, 165, 166, 170, 172-73; superstition of oracles, 143-45, 211n

happiness, 28, 43, 109, 205-6; not, as Greeks supposed, the highest goal, 8-9, 34, 159n, 266; today, more and more indeterminate, 266; unhappiness the means by which world-spirit drives itself forward, 20, 26, 133, 176
Hegel, G. W. F., other works of: *Encyclopedia of the Philosophical Sciences*, 6n, 159n; *Lectures on the History of Philosophy*, 87-88, 101n, 137-38n, 159n, 161n, 172n, 174n, *Lectures on the Philosophy of Religion*, 5n, 6n, 44n, 64n18, 67-68, 78n18, 123n, 124-25nn,144n, 179n, 183n, 184n, 192n, 200n, 249n, *Philosophy of Right*, 8n, 172n, *Science of Logic*, 2n, 23n

Idea, 79, 125n, 158, 220; as combining two principles—the One, and subjectivity, 201-2; completes end-goal of history through crimes and passions, 10, 25-26; as "cunning of reason," 23-24; first opposed to, later reconciled with, nonhuman nature as Idea's externalization, 109; as having essential phases, 55, 202, 212; knowledge of Idea as power in history is goal of philosophy of history, 17-18; makes all of world-history eternally present, 16; meaning of term, 2n; rational state is Idea wholly present, 18-19, 30, 73, 212; relation to religion, 2n, 5-6; as "the ought," 42-43; through Christ human knows oneself to be an essential phase of divine Idea, 199-200, 210; world-historical individuals are true connection of passion and Idea, 25-26
India: aims at annihilation of consciousness, 29, 78, 84; Brahmins are gods, 81, 84; civil legislation, of Manu, has not a shadow of justice and personal rights, 75-78, 84; ethical custom lacking in freedom, 8, 28-29, 71-74, 76, 78-79, 83-84, 87-88, 98; geography, 46-47, 56, 70, 91-92; higher antithesis beyond Chinese unity, through occupational classes—a universal need, 71-73; no moral or religious respect for human life, 84-85; only duties of caste, 84, 98; religion of single absolute substance, everything only its modification, with belief in transmigration of souls to and from animals, without self-consciousness, 78-82, 83, 87-88, 97-98, 108, 117, 201, 235-36; rigid caste system under despotism of theocratic aristocracy, 54, 72-78, 81, 84-86, 93, 98-99, 115, 135, 226, 242; ritual worship expressed in constant vacillation among 1) imaginative, wild sensuality 2) prescribed external rites 3) withdrawal from life in self-sacrifice, 79, 82-85, 102, 105; very different and more humane is Buddhism linked to Lamaism and Sikhs, 85-87, 106-7n

INDEX

Islam: as antithesis to Germanic, 225–26; ebbing of fanaticism left no customary ethics, and Islam has long ceased to ground world-history, 227–28

Jewish people: becomes world-historical through synthesis with Roman and Greek, 201; entails exclusivity, only for Jewish people, 105, 108, 110, 225; ethical customs, family is central, 110, 112, 204–5; God sublime and holy in relation to world, 111–12; here the break occurs between East and West, 108; nature reduced to what is created, 108–9; offshoot of religion of Persians, with difference that Light loses physical aspect, becomes subject purified from nature, 107, 201; one among many petty Syrian peoples, 107; opposes Asiatic unity of unfree spirit with nature, 107–8; purity of heart, repentance, devotion, but not as free individual, hence no belief in immortality, 110; religion of separation, 6; religion of Moses is what is important, 107; ritual worship unspiritual, limited to ceremonial law, 109–10; ruler only expresses will of God, 60; state, alien to legislation of Moses, 110; true morality and righteousness here emerge, 109, 111

justice, right(s), righteousness, law, rectitude, 5, 8–10, 13, 19–27, 29–32, 35, 36, 44, 48; along with duty, ultimate goal of world history, 28, 74, 159n, 259–60; and conscience, 48; in family, 37; free will as ground, 36, 259–60; gives absolute right, even of criminality, to world-historical individuals, 24–26; "great justice" of world history and "higher justification of world-spirit" versus "petty justice" of treaties, etc., 189, 193; inner disposition, 40, 112, 136, 177; "natural" rights in "state of nature" dubious, 36; natural will lacks justice, 29; rests on abstract personhood as private property, 53, 180, 261–62; subject's infinite right, 20, 24, 26, 27, 145, 261–63; true, equal laws and rights of nature identified with reason ruling nature, the goal of rational state, 256, 260

love: Christian love inadequate for sound state, ethical custom, or religion, 217; defined, 37; for family, fatherland, and friends, 19; for God, 4; for humanity, 11; intensity among Muslims and in their poetry, 227; for rectitude and virtues, 19

monarchy. *See* constitutionalism
Montesquieu, 10, 11n, 42n, 56n, 155
morality, 10, 11, 19; as absolute end, 9; closely connected with consciousness of freedom, but can be pure while deficient in such consciousness, 28, 73; distinction from ethical custom, 8n; "eternal and divine" in individuals, 26; moral freedom, 62; moral sorrow, 20; in rational society integrated with ethical custom, but not a matter for state regulation, 8n, 172; as standard for judging peoples, 157. *See also* conscience; ethical custom

nature (nonhuman): externalization of reason, 109; humans have always sensed that they must overcome it, 43–44; organization brought forth out of reason as cause, 3

"New World": in contrast to Europe, a splitting of religious opinions, 40; danger of civil war between south and north, 40–41; ethical custom is lawfulness, without inner disposition of justice, 40; example of republic but arises from aggregation of individuals as atoms, with state merely external, 39–41; indigenous peoples, 39; North America the land of the future, 38, 42; not yet, but coming, a distinction of classes of wealth and poverty, 41; the private person aimed only at business and gain, 40; South America (including Mexico) contrasted with North, 39–40; of yearning, hope, immigration, 38–39

passions, 9, 36; arm by which Idea actualizes itself, 18–26; natural side of human being, 23, 147; world-historical humans exhibit true connection of passion and Idea, 25
peoples (in general) 4, 9, 18, 20; art forms, 29, 33; deaths, 12–15, 19; distinct in individual spirits or

souls, having reciprocal relation with geography, 11–14, 32–33, 38, 93, 250–51; ethical customs, 12, 14; happiness, 20, 133; individual as part of people, 29–30; peoples with obscure consciousness or history not relevant, 17; personhoods, 17; philosophies, 6, 28, 33, 65–66, 87–88; principles, 13, 14, 47; religions, 6, 28, 32–33, 65–66, 87–88; virtues, 14; world-historical must have ethnic diversity, 134

Persia: allows all humans equal access to becoming hallowed, 99; civil laws show simplicity, 103; defeated by superior Greek cultural education, discipline, and organization, 131–32; distinctive rituals, 101–2; ethical customs aim at making oneself and others pure, independent, courageous, but lack of cultural education allows corruption by luxury, 95, 100; first outwardly directed, and so first to move world-history, 91–92; first real empire as mastery holding together heterogeneous subjects, 92–93, 130; first that has passed away, thus, first historical people, 97; lawful theocratic monarchy of holy elite mastering subject peoples left to their own ethical customs, 55–56, 92–94, 131, 178; nearer to idea of state than what preceded, 93; no idols, and Persians despise Greek anthropomorphic idols, 96, 97, 99, 156; religion, founded by Hom and revived by Zoroaster, 100, 102; sacred scriptures teach universal spirit as visible Light versus nature as nonspiritual Darkness, 56, 96–99, 117, 201

personhood: contrasted with individuality, 51, 179, 195; a cornerstone of modern rational right and law, 180, 195; meaning of term, 28; originated and developed by Rome, 50–51, 53, 179–80, 193–94, 196–97; private property as abstract personhood, 50–51, 53, 179, 193–94, 196–97

philosophy, 1–4, 6, 7, 17, 22, 24; attacks everything sacred then reestablishes, 33, 167–74; depends on religion, 6; distinguished from religion, 87; has to do with eternally present, 16; of history, as true theodicy, 108, 270; how grasps state, 29–30; in life of state as cultural education, 33; prophecy excluded, 42; religion of Romans, Greeks, and Christians not as close to philosophy as religion of East, which has philosophy as abstract, 6, 28, 65–66, 87–88; truly concrete only among Greeks and Christians, 6. *See also* Greece; Rome; Socrates

religion (in general): as absolute end, 9; and the absolute Idea, 2n; corruption and loss of, 27; versus doctrines, 13; as fine art's source, 6; a "laxity of our times" to hold that all are good, 108–9; making religion human reason is the only business of history, 213–16; ritual worship, 5, 44, 63–66, 79, 82–85; striving of all religion is for self-knowledge, 128; true idea of religion, 5; truth and divine are present in all religion, however erroneous, 108–9; two types—of separation, and of unity, of finite and infinite, 6

Rome, 10, 22; antithesis emerges of Christendom versus Caesarian, spiritual versus worldly, 195; aristocracy of patricians over plebians with no unity except by harshness, 187–88; became unified by conquest of Italy, in accord with "great justice" of world-history, 189; could not satisfy, induced longing for divine universality found in Christ as pure Idea in the flesh, 51, 198–202; crushing individuality and subjectivity under universality as self-seeking mastery, 50, 131, 178; decline and fall in East (Byzantium), 216–17, 223; downfall in West, 215–16; ethical custom, created personhood as opposed to individuality, 51, 179, 195; familial piety slavishly despotic, 182, 185–86; history's "adulthood," of hard work and duty serving universal laws, 50, 132; human spirit reacts either by escape into sensuous enjoyment or by withdrawal to philosophic tranquility in despair—Stoicism, Epicureanism, Skepticism, 51, 179, 197–98, 201, 203–4; imprisoning all gods, breaking

286   INDEX

Rome (*continued*)
heart of world—only out of this could free spirit raise itself in Christianity, 178-79; individuals violently subordinated to gang, soon replaced by state: "this is Roman greatness" and "virtue" and "idiosyncrasy," 182, 186, 190; needed despot to hold together personhoods as mutually repellent crowd of enslaved atoms, 50-51, 179, 193-94, 196-97, 203-4; originally a landless gang of robbers, and remained a criminal operation, 181, 192-93; religion, took gods from Greeks but radically changed, 183-84, 186-87; second period, unified by Punic Wars, Rome reaches its peak—which spawns competition among great criminal individuals, having higher justification of world-spirit, 180-81, 190-95; state, first period, republic after overthrow of kingdom, 23, 163, 180, 187-88; third period, Caesarian despotism within and over world, willfulness completely unchained, and then involvement with people who become Rome's destroyers and successors, 22-23, 49, 51, 181, 194-96

sacrifice: of Christ in Mass, 5n, 236, 245; by religious souls, 245; truest sacrifice is for a human's willfulness and subjective particularity to be overcome through universal, 83; for universality, of peoples and their happiness, of states, of virtues, of individuals, 20, 26, 50, 270; by world-historical humans, 26

slavery (and serfdom): all peoples must undergo master-slave dialectical relationship, 159n; essential disciplining stage in advance to higher ethical custom and cultural education, 31, 43; gradual abolition more measured and just than sudden, 43; but historically this "ought not" has lacked ethical custom of fully rational state, 42; unjust and ought not to be, 17, 60-61, 154-55, 196, 210, 230, 262

Socrates, 3-4, 62, 67, 157, 161, 201, 222-23n; against sophists who turned cultural education in relativistic, private-interested direction, 169; thus discovered morality, duty, and conscience, but as abstract, 170; first made independent thinking understand itself by seeing that everything must be justified by one's own thought as universal, 170; overlooked habit, feeling, heart, 171; his principle destructive of Athenian state, ethical custom, and religion, so Athens condemned him to death—this the highest tragedy: both Socrates and Athenian people were in the right, the tragedy of Greece, and not merely of Socrates, 170-72

state, 9-10, 22, 192-93, 212; an abstraction, which only has reality in individual volition and activity as citizen, rooted in religion and conscience, 34, 214-15, 228; can only be great in connection with sea, 47; falsely conceived as a collection of human beings in which freedom of all is limited, 29; falsely premised that human being by nature is free, that in society and state, natural freedom must be restricted, 35; goes with false notion of pre-political "state-of-nature," in which individuals have "natural rights," and thus freedom, 36; limited as a particular people's spirit, 31; manifests true content of religion, 212, 249; organic whole, where everything is end and means simultaneously, of coordinated, competing individuals in occupational classes, 30-32, 73; positively realizes freedom, 29-30; as rational, 8n, 21, 29-37, 212, 261-63; requires hereditary monarchy, 152, 212, 215; rests on religion, comes out from religion, 33; three forms through which all states run, 32; in truth, pre-political, so-called "state-of-nature" is a condition of injustice, violence, uncontrolled natural drives, subhuman deeds and emotions, 36-37, 43; virtue of, 21; wisdom of, 20

subjectivity: corrupts peoples' spirits prior to liberation by Christianity, 14, 21; and the good will that is the moral will of inner rationality and duty, 153;

infinite subjectivity is awareness that ego is soil for all that ought to count, 147, 170; the principle of modern, constructed age, 161n; requires subject be developed to condition of free ownership, 29; to which the conscience belongs, 151, 170; unity of subjective with universal is end-goal of history, 52, 98, 201–2

Syria (within Persian empire): festival of death of god Adonis expresses essential aspect of true God, 105–6, 114–15; here human feeling comes on the stage of world-history, with sorrow given respect due to it, as sensing of subjectivity in its universal negativity and at the same time its infinite affirmation, 106, 115, 119; Phoenician maritime commerce an "entirely new principle" because pursued for its own sake, not as part of a larger whole, and employs seafaring to make humans masters of nature, 104–5, 131; religion, of nature as universal, but in antithesis to Persian, immersed in sensuous, 105, 114–15, 140–41

virtue(s): of antiquity, 240; civic virtues as sacrifices to state, 20; destined to be sacrificed to world-history, 8, 19–20, 193; foreign to feudalism, 230, 240, 244; as forms of love, 19; misunderstood in French Revolution, 264; moral versus civic virtue, 151, 157, 162, 164, 166, 240, 264; moral virtue as conceived by Socrates versus Aristotle, 171; moral virtues, 10; only in actualization by singular individuals is reason actualized, 19; of peoples, 12, 14; as private, 11; Roman virtue a perversion of civic, 182–83, 185n, 190, 196; of states, 21

will: as basis of justice and customary ethics, 256; Christianity makes everything mediated by free will, 211–12; contingent, 270; drives also belong to, 262–63, 265; free will distinguished from will as particular, 266; free will emerges from principle of Evangelical Church, 266–67; of God, 60, 109, 249n; God's will not different from Himself as Idea, 2n; good, 153; Idea's own, 10; individual's, 7, 8n, 10, 18, 20–21, 24, 25, 28, 29, 31–32, 34, 36, 45, 53–56, 58, 64, 68, 74, 93, 98, 100–101, 104, 109n, 116, 136, 151–53, 155, 171, 173, 196, 212, 213, 214, 217, 220, 249, 256, 258, 259–60; meaning of will as free and as ultimate principle, 259–60; monarchic, 60, 135, 174–75, 215, 262; moral, 269; objective, 74, 152–53, 155; a people's, 12, 18, 126, 220; rational versus natural (in which justice and law are not yet present), 29, 48, 211n; spirit's, 132; subjective, 74, 145, 153, 165, 211n, 212, 214, 249, 264–65, 269–70; subjective versus substantial, this opposition the principle of all world-historical change, 48, 56; true, 30, 214, 217, 232, 249; universal, 58, 74, 265; versus willfulness (as opposite of freedom), 16, 24, 28, 29, 34, 36, 45, 50–51, 59, 61, 75, 187, 196, 204, 209, 210, 211, 215–16, 228, 230n, 232, 242–43, 251

world-historical individuals, 11, 22–23, 25–26, 94–95, 193–94, 254; Cyrus, 93–94, 102, 137–38; Julius Caesar the leading example, 22–23, 193–94

world-spirit, 3n, 22, 270; gives "higher justification" to massive criminality, 193

www.ingramcontent.com/pod-product-compliance
Lightning Source LLC
Chambersburg PA
CBHW030119240426
43673CB00041B/1333